Major General Adam Stephen
and the Cause of
American Liberty

MAJOR GENERAL

Adam Stephen

AND THE CAUSE OF

AMERICAN LIBERTY

Harry M. Ward

University Press of Virginia
Charlottesville

THE UNIVERSITY PRESS OF VIRGINIA
Copyright © 1989 by the Rector and Visitors
of the University of Virginia

First published 1989

Library of Congress Cataloging-in-Publication Data

Ward, Harry M.
  Major General Adam Stephen and the cause of the American liberty /
Harry M. Ward.
    p. cm.
  Bibliography: p.
  Includes index.
  ISBN 0-8139-1227-X
  1. Stephen, Adam. 2. United States—History—Revolution,
1775–1783—Biography. 3. Virginia—History—Revolution, 1775–1783—
Biography. 4. Generals—United States—Biography. 5. United
States. Continental Army—Biography. 6. Virginia—History—French
and Indian War, 1755–1763—Biography. 7. United States—History—
French and Indian War, 1755–1763—Biography. I. Title.
E207.S798W37   1989
973.3′092′4—dc19   89-30959
                                                              CIP

Printed in the United States of America

Contents

Illustrations

Maps

Preface

Washington's general officers were an unusual breed. Most were well established in civilian life: tavern keepers, farmers, large planters, businessmen, politicians, and professionals—lawyers, physicians, and even, rarely, clergymen. Most of the generals of the American Revolution had engaged in military duty before the commencement of the war, whether holding militia commissions or having actually served in military campaigns. Characteristically, the French and Indian War was the testing ground of the mettle of those who rose to the top ranks in the Continental army. The generals were by and large rough-hewn leaders. Many of them were colorful in expression, and they took a keen interest in the course of events, which many were involved in and helped to shape. Above all, they quickly became imbued with a sense of military professionalism and regarded themselves as a fraternity set apart as watchdogs of American safety and liberty. Adam Stephen, an émigré from Scotland, fitted this mold, but in a highly individualized way.

Few Americans of the Revolutionary War era had careers as varied as that of Adam Stephen: wealthy planter, industrialist, town proprietor, physician-surgeon, politician and public servant, commander of Virginia troops in the French and Indian War, and major general in the Revolution. Uncommon also were Stephen's staying power, extreme self-confidence, and broad intellect, even tinged as they were with adventurism and outspokenness.

Adam Stephen was always getting into trouble by doing things his own way, whether from antagonizing prominent men or skirting the edge of insubordination as a field and general officer. He had a self-inflated estimation of his own abilities, which sometimes, especially in military service, led to gullibility and exaggeration. Occasionally he bridged propriety with conflict of interest. While possessed of a superb education and a penetrating mind, Stephen still had a common touch, which appealed to constituency and soldiers alike.

The life of Adam Stephen affords insight into the qualities of a "gentleman of distinction" and also into the times. A biography of Stephen, to some degree, fleshes out George Washington. Stephen's and Washington's paths paralleled and crossed. During the long, tedious years of wilderness campaigning of the French and Indian War, Stephen was Washington's second in command, and Stephen himself at that conflict's end was in charge of Virginia's military forces. During the early part of the Revolution, Stephen was for a time Washington's ninth ranking general (though, of course, Congress, not the commander in chief, was responsible for Stephen's promotions). The two were always having a falling out, though disagreements were usually patched up in order for both men to save face. Stephen ran against his commander in chief in a bitter contest for election as a burgess. Washington distrusted Stephen's abilities during the Revolutionary War. Stephen criticized his commander in chief's tactics and strategy. After the failures at Brandywine and Germantown, army frustrations ran high, and many officers were held to account for conduct unbecoming an officer. Stephen was one. He was dismissed from service, and his division was taken over by Washington's protégé, the marquis de Lafayette. Remarkably, Stephen did not suffer any real opprobrium from Virginians because of his dismissal from the army. He again entered politics and had an important role at the Virginia Convention for the ratification of the Constitution.

Certainly the major factor that has deterred the writing of a biography of Adam Stephen has been the lack of family papers. On the personal side there is a small Adam Stephen collection at the Library of Congress, which, however, relates mostly to superficial aspects of business and plantation management. Yet there have been important finds, a scattering of Stephen letters and accounts in various depositories. It seems there was a large body of Stephen family papers, which, however, has been lost, or at least has not resurfaced. Among this collection was even the court-martial record, which was not allowed to be made public at the time of the event but must have been retained by Stephen in order to make a planned protest. The Stephen family papers were last known to be in the possession of the Reverend Blackburn Hughes, who married Sally Dandridge, a direct descendant of Adam Stephen, and their son, Alexander Hughes. The Hughes family moved to South Carolina in the nineteenth century, where this line of Adam Stephen's descendants died out, and the collection has disappeared (see Bedinger-Dandridge Family Papers, Duke University Library).

I am most grateful to Herbert J. York, curator of the General Adam Stephen Memorial Association, Inc. in Martinsburg, West Virginia, for his assistance, especially in answering queries and clarifying points relating to the local history. Francis Silver V, president of the association, offered encouragement. John W. Small, Jr., County Clerk of Berkeley County, and Helen L. Vickers, Chief Deputy Clerk, graciously expedited a particular request. I am indebted to the staffs of the Virginia State Library and Archives and the Virginia Historical Society for their aid in probing the substantial collections relating to virtually every aspect of early Virginia history. Kay McCall and Melissa Loggans at the Virginia State Library and Sue Ratchford at the Boatwright Library of the University of Richmond secured the many interlibrary loans. Credit is also deserved by the librarians and curators of many depositories for providing photocopies of Stephen material. A research grant from the Virginia Society of the Cincinnati facilitated work on the biography.

Major General Adam Stephen
and the Cause of
American Liberty

ONE

From Scotland to Great Meadows

The young Scottish physician arriving in Virginia in 1748 could hardly envision that one day he would be a major general in the army of a new nation. Yet Adam Stephen anticipated untold opportunity in America. He had only a few kinsmen in the New World, for large-scale Scottish immigration did not commence until after mid-eighteenth century. Stephen did encounter occasionally Scotsmen who were merchants and professionals (physicians, tutors, schoolmasters, and clergymen). Perhaps there was a rare acquaintance among the several hundred refugees and transported prisoners, Highlanders who had fought for the Pretender in the Jacobite uprisings of 1715 and 1745. Stephen's native Aberdeenshire, which contained both Highland and Lowland country, was divided in loyalties during the insurrections. Stephen's immediate family probably did not side with the Scottish rebels, although some of his kin were counted among their numbers. For Adam Stephen, however, nonpolitical factors impelled him to strike out in the world on his own.

Adam Stephen was born about 1721 in the parish of Rhynie, Aberdeenshire. His home region offered scant opportunity for economic advancement. The barren hills and marshy bottoms were not very conducive for agriculture. So forbidding was the area that two centuries later the population of the parish was only 793. Stephen's father may have been a skilled artisan or a shopkeeper in one of the two tiny villages, but most likely his main livelihood came from rearing cattle on the grass-patched slopes at the Highland-Lowland line. Cattle were a major export commodity of the port of Aberdeen. Stephen himself in America was a stockman.[1] Adam Stephen's siblings made the same decision as he to break away from the home moorings; brothers Alexander, Robert, and John joined him in America, and two sisters resided in London.[2]

Whatever the economic and social status of his family, Adam Stephen received a fine education. He probably attended the parish school between ages seven and ten; then came grammar school, most likely the one in Aberdeen. In 1736 Stephen matriculated at King's College of the University of Aberdeen. For four years he attended the five-month sessions (November 1–April 1), and he received a Master of Arts degree on March 27, 1740.[3] Because the average age of most students entering Scottish universities at the time was fourteen to fifteen, it may be conjectured that Stephen was perhaps about fifteen years old when he began his college education. Stephen studied the classics and honed his Greek and Latin. One of his professors was the renowned Homer scholar Thomas Blackwell. Scottish university students at the time were also amply exposed to the natural rights school of political philosophy. The class on moral philosophy, required of all seniors, emphasized a rigorous rational analysis of motives and consequences of social behavior and no doubt contributed to Stephen's proneness to question the actions of others. He seems to have been a diligent student at Aberdeen. He noted in a brief autobiography prepared for Benjamin Rush in 1775 that he and Donald Munroe (who later taught Rush) "bore away the palm in all the Classes, of philosophy, Mathematic & physic."[4]

Upon graduation from Aberdeen, Stephen entered the three-year medical program at the University of Edinburgh. He probably received a medical degree, which was conferred upon completion of the prescribed curriculum and the submission and defense of a thesis. During the course of medical study, Stephen took classes in anatomy, physiology, chemistry, practice of physic, and midwifery, among others; he also availed himself of the clinical teaching at the Royal Infirmary, which opened in 1741.[5] Although medical student records at the university have not survived for the period before 1760, Stephen's name appears on a 1743 list of students attending the classes of Alexander Monro, professor of anatomy and surgery. Certainly Stephen gained skills in surgery.[6] But all apparently was not drudgery and work for a young aspiring physician at Edinburgh, as a comment of Arthur Lee (of the class of 1764 and one of 106 Virginians who studied medicine at the university from 1750 to 1800) reveals; to Lee, "more licentious youths are hardly to be found anywhere" than among the native Scotsmen at the university.[7]

When Stephen left Edinburgh, England and France were at war, and for a footloose young man eager to obtain medical experience as well as see the world, military service was appealing. In 1745 Stephen went to London where he passed an examination to become a naval surgeon. He refused the first ship assignment offered him because the officers and crew were a "parcel of Bears." Stephen did agree, however, to a surgeon's post on the *Neptune*, an army hospital ship. In August–September 1746 Stephen found himself part of a military expedition consisting of 3,000 soldiers and sailors commanded by Gen. James Murray and Adm. Richard Lestock. The destination was Port l'Orient, a city in northwest France on the Bay of Biscay, where the French East India Company had a large depot. With only 10-pounders for artillery and not enough ammunition, the siege of the port town bogged down, and the British force withdrew, unaware that the French defenders had decided to capitulate. On the return to England, the *Neptune*, at least in Stephen's recollection, was attacked in the Channel by a French privateer. Stephen boasted that "by his coolness & presence of Mind," he saved the ship from capture. The vessel's commander had become so confused that he "gave Order upon Order so Quickly that none were Executed and the Enemy within a hundred yards on the Lee Quarter ready to Board." Stephen then "waited on the Captain in a respectful manner & requested the Command of the Guns in the Cabin, four 9 pounders, with the Cabin Boy & a young lad brought up in the Coal Trade to Assist." The ship's captain agreed to Stephen's request. The "Enemy crowded on the forecastle & Boltsprit ready to Board; were greatly hurt by the fire of the first two guns brought to bear upon them. After three Cheers They gave the Ship a yaw, brought the other two guns to bear & compleated the destruction of the Enemy."

Stephen's brief combat service left him "a little habituated to danger," as he said, and when word spread of his alleged shipboard feat, he was "courted" by London merchants. The British East India Company offered him a position as surgeon on one of its ships, "but the Sea disagreed with him so much that he could not be preval'd on to undertake so long a Voyage." So "after Wandering for a Certain period; Natural to the Young & Curious," Adam Stephen decided to go to America and practice medicine.[8]

Debarking in Maryland in 1748, Stephen made his way to Virginia and settled at Falmouth, across from Fredericksburg on the upper Rappahannock River. He felt at home with his countrymen who represented Scottish mercantile firms at the port. Perhaps he was not too glad, however, to be competing in medical practice with Scotsmen William Lynn at Fredericksburg and Michael Wallace at Falmouth and other physicians in the area.[9] Presumably Stephen made a fair living as a physician-surgeon during the next five years.[10] For a Mrs. Mercer, suffering from a hepatic abscess, he made an incision into the liver, "cleansing, & healing the Ulcers there, Contrary to the Opinion of all the faculty employ'd to cure the Lady." He also ligated an aneurysm in Abraham Hill's arm, restoring the limb to use.[11]

With a surfeit of doctors in Virginia's communities, Stephen could expect only a modest income if he continued solely in medical practice. At Falmouth-Fredericksburg, he met many of the colony's first gentlemen. He realized that if he became the proprietor of a large plantation, he, too, could achieve status among the social and political elite. Lands were plenty for the offering in the northwestern part of the Fairfax proprietary grant, at the northern (lower) end of the Great Valley. Probably Adam's brother Alexander, a rent collector for the Fairfax family and also then engaged in the Ohio Valley fur trade, influenced him to acquire a plantation. By 1753 Adam Stephen had taken up some 2,000 acres along Opequon Creek in Frederick County. The cost was minimal, only the payment of an annual quitrent of 1s. per 50 acres.[12] Stephen's readiness to turn to farming suggests that he expected to draw upon agricultural experience he probably had as a youth in Scotland. Land speculation also interested him. He could secure more grants from the Fairfax proprietary and sell them for a profit; he might also participate in schemes to appropriate lands along the frontier. Stephen was among those who served as witnesses to the signatures of the Ohio Company's Articles of Agreement.[13]

In late 1753 Stephen moved to his new plantation, which he called Adam's Bower (and later simply the Bower). The house, on a slope overlooking Opequon Creek, was a two-story log hut, with timbers in an upright position, not contrasting much with the slave quarters adjoining it on both sides. Stephen engaged in subsistence farming, though with an eye for marketing possibilities, as did his German, Scotch-Irish, and Scottish neighbors. He raised Indian corn and grains and probably attempted growing a staple crop, such as flax, hemp, or tobacco, though the latter proved not very suited to the rich Valley soils. He started raising cattle, a pursuit he followed the rest of his life. In August 1753 Stephen bought forty steers from William Williams, "the Choice of his Stock all Above three year old," for £130 in Virginia currency.[14]

Had not war intervened, Stephen might have found himself a wife. He undoubtedly cut a good physical appearance, although all that is known is that he was of medium stature and had a thirty-six inch chest span.[15] Stephen was splendidly educated, debonair, a natural leader, shrewd in business, and ambitious. Perhaps, though, he was too much a hell-raiser and too fond of strong drink for the daughters of his stern pioneer neighbors. On occasion, during his early military career, Stephen was accompanied by a woman companion, and during the Revolution he was known to be overly friendly with female camp followers. Eventually Stephen took an interest in his brother's housekeeper, Phoebe Seaman, who after Alexander's death came to live with Adam and was presumably the mother of his daughter. Perhaps there had been an old flame in Scotland. Adam Stephen wrote Ann Miller of Edinburgh in 1753, telling her of his increasing fortune. Ann, who had married, replied "that your Situation and Circumstance gives me the utmost pleasure. I never made any doubt of your Returning a good Character. May you long enjoy it, and Every other quality that is Amiable." As

for Stephen being a bachelor, "you need not doubt I Should be glad
you Continue So, till you think my Jeany is fitt for matrimony."[16]

Any thoughts of immediate domesticity were soon far from Adam
Stephen's mind. He would answer a call to arms. A duel over the
possession of the Ohio Valley country—and for a continent—was
impending between Great Britain and France. By the Treaty of
Logstown in 1752, which confirmed the Lancaster treaty of 1744,
Iroquois and Delaware chiefs ceded lands east and south of the Ohio
River and agreed to permit the English to construct two trading
posts on the river. In spring 1753 the French began erecting forts
from Lake Erie to the forks of the Ohio, garrisoned by 1,500 troops.
George Washington, sent on a mission to the French forts by Governor Robert Dinwiddie late in the year, returned with a brusque
reply that no Englishmen would be allowed to trade on the Ohio
and anyone attempting to do so would be made a prisoner.[17]

In defiance of the French warning, William Trent and 100 Virginians built a trading post–fort at the junction of the Monongahela and Ohio rivers. It was obvious that in order to protect this
venture from any French attack, Trent's men would have to be reinforced. The Virginia assembly voted £10,000 for this purpose
and authorized the raising of a 300-man regiment. Joshua Fry, formerly a professor of mathematics at the College of William and
Mary, was appointed colonel and commander; George Washington, lieutenant colonel; George Muse, senior captain and soon promoted to major; and Adam Stephen, one of several captains. That
Stephen gained a commission over applicants from prominent Virginia families was owing primarily to the recommendation of Col.
William Fairfax, who was impressed with Stephen's telling of his
shipboard experience during the last war.[18] Few Virginians had any
wartime service. Muse was selected largely because he had been
with the ill-fated Cartagena expedition in 1741. Of course, Governor Dinwiddie was a Scotsman. Five of the fifteen commissions
issued by the governor went to Scottish immigrants. Interestingly,
Stephen did not seek a medical appointment; James Craik, a Scottish physician, was named surgeon to the regiment.[19]

Stephen was motivated in part, as were others, to sign on in the colony's little army because of the opportunity to receive land grants in addition to pay as a reward for military service. Governor Dinwiddie on February 19, 1754, issued a proclamation which ordered setting aside 200,000 acres of land east of the Ohio River for all persons who immediately joined the Virginia Regiment; there would be no costs to recipients, and quitrents would be deferred for fifteen years.[20]

The Virginia governor insisted that the new troops march as quickly as possible to relieve Trent and his men on the Ohio. While Colonel Fry stayed behind to gather the last recruits, Washington and Peter Hog's and Jacob Van Braam's companies left Alexandria on April 2. At Winchester they met Adam Stephen and 39 recruits whom he had recruited in Frederick County. The little regiment of 159 men crossed the Potomoc to the mouth of Wills Creek, where there was an Ohio Company post (soon to be called Fort Cumberland). Here they learned that a large French force had compelled Trent and his men to abandon their position. In a council of war on April 23 the officers voted to advance slowly while cutting a road across the mountains. The first goal was to reach an Ohio Company storehouse at the junction of Redstone Creek and the Monongahela River. At the Forks of the Ohio, thirty-seven miles to the northward, the French were constructing Fort Duquesne.[21]

From an encampment at the Little Meadows (straddling the Pennsylvania-Maryland line), Washington dispatched Stephen and Ens. William La Péronie to the vicinity of Christopher Gist's plantation in the Monongahela Valley in order to determine if there were indications of French troops in the field. Stephen was also to decide upon a site to build a fort at the mouth of Redstone Creek. When their four days of provisions were exhausted, Stephen's men had to live on game they hunted. Arriving at the Monongahela near Redstone Creek, Stephen learned from several Indian traders that because of the rainy weather a large French detachment had retired from the field back to Fort Duquesne. Unwilling to return without any positive information, Stephen sent a spy, actually an Indian "double agent," to Fort Duquesne. After five days Stephen had a detailed report on the physical features of the fort and its manpower. He awarded the spy £5. Memorizing the intelligence, Stephen returned with his detachment to Washington's camp, now at the Great Crossing on the Youghiogheny River.[22]

Captain Stephen found the officers seething over news that a legislative committee which had authority for setting the compensation for the Virginia troops had limited to £1 6s. an officer's allowance for recruiting each soldier; it refused to raise the pay of the officers and gave them only the same rations as a common soldier. Knowledge that three independent companies of the king's regulars would soon be joining the Virginians at a higher rate of pay also annoyed the officers. They formed a committee, making Stephen chairman, and sent a formal protest to Governor Dinwiddie, stating that "nothing prevents their throwing down their commissions . . . but the approaching danger." Washington wrote the governor that he thought the officers' complaints were justified, though he himself was determined to stay in service. Governor Dinwiddie sternly discounted the "ill timed" grievances. Any objections about pay should have been made before joining the service; the recruiting allowance was good enough as it was; and British officers had the same ration allotment as common soldiers and had to meet their own out-of-pocket expenses. Hardships were to be expected; besides, the troops remaining with Colonel Fry had voiced no concerns.[23] Whether Washington felt any personal slight by the officers' protest is not known, but he made a mental note that Adam Stephen was at the forefront of the dissent.

Meanwhile the officers did their duty, as there was little time to wrangle over grievances. Their mettle would soon be tested. On May 27, at Great Meadows, Washington learned that a small French detachment had come within five miles of the Virginia camp. Taking forty men with him and joining up with about the same number of Ohio Indians under the Seneca chief, the Half-King, Washington that night went in search of the enemy party. After pushing their way in the darkness through the rain-drenched woods, at sunrise the Virginians spotted the intruders, getting ready to prepare breakfast in a grassy section between two slopes of Laurel Hill (Ridge), sixty miles southeast of Fort Duquesne. It was decided to ambush the enemy. Washington and some of the troops fell on the Frenchmen from the left, and Stephen did the same on the right, with the Indians coming up through the mouth of the ravine. It was not known who fired first, but the Virginians had the advantage of surprise and made use of bayonets. Fearing further savagery from the Indians, who already were scalping the dead bodies, the Frenchmen surrendered. During the fray, the Half-King "split the head" of the French commander, Joseph Coulon de Villiers, sieur de Jumonville, and "then took out his Brains, and washed his hands with them, And then Scalped him." About ten of the enemy were killed, and two or three wounded; twenty-one prisoners were sent to Alexandria.[24] Thus the struggle began which would expand into a world war. The French would use the death of Jumonville as propaganda, claiming that he was killed while trying to parley.

Being apprised that the French could put at least 500 men in the field, Washington set some of his men to erecting a post at Great Meadows. The installation—simply a stockade, fifty feet in diameter, around a log cabin—was named Fort Necessity, because of the "great difficulty of procuring necessaries for subsistence."[25] Meanwhile, some of the troops cleared a thirteen-mile road to Gist's plantation, on Chestnut Ridge, where entrenchments were put in place. On June 9 Major Muse with three companies (Robert Stobo's, Andrew Lewis's, and George Mercer's) arrived, making the total number of men with Washington now 293. News also came of Colonel Fry's death after he fell off his horse. Washington, finding a blank commission "amongst Colonel Fry's Papers," gave a major's commission to Stephen. On June 12 Capt. James Mackay brought in a British independent company of regulars from South Carolina. With 400 men and the expectation of soon being joined by two New York independent companies (word had come that they had already reached Virginia), Washington would have a force to contend with the French on fairly even terms.

Most of Washington's troops were at Gist's plantation when intelligence came that a large French party was on its way to attack. Stephen wrote a report of the subsequent developments, printed in the Pennsylvania, Maryland, and Virginia newspapers. A council of war decided to make a hasty retreat back to Fort Necessity. "As we had but two very indifferent Teams, and few Horses," commented

Stephen, "the Officers loaded their own Horses with Ammunition, and left part of their Baggage behind; Col. Washington setting them an Example, by ordering his Horse to be loaded first, and giving four Pistoles to some Soldiers to carry his necessary Baggage." There were only nine swivels for the cannon, which were drawn by the Virginia soldiers over "the roughest and most hilly Road of any on the Alleghany Mountains." Stephen complained that "the independents refused to lend a Hand to draw the Guns, which had an unhappy Effect on our Men, who no sooner learned that it was not the proper Duty of Soldiers to perform these Services, than they became as backward as the Independents."[26]

At the Great Meadows fort on July 1, the men worked "clearing the Woods nearest to us, and carrying in the Logs, to raise a Breastwork, and enlarge the Fort." Midmorning on the third, the enemy, some 500 Canadians and 400 Indians, appeared. Washington and Mackay had their troops drawn up outside the fort ready to do battle. However, the French commander, Capt. Louis Coulon de Villiers, did not bring on his men directly but put them along the nearby hill crests overlooking the fort. The deadly fusillade from the enemy on the higher ground forced Washington and Mackay to collect their men within the tiny stockade. They kept up irregular fire until evening, conserving ammunition because they expected the French to storm the fort. Stephen had sections of the stockade torn apart so that the fieldpieces could be fired from ground level. Because of the defensive position of the French, however, the American cannon firing had little effect. Stephen went from man to man, examining their arms, and "supplying them with Ammunition," which "made his hands as black as Negroe's, & guarding his face against the Trusts[?] made his face as Black as his hands." When firing ceased at nightfall, 30 of the American force had been killed, and 70 wounded; the French had lost 2, with 15 Frenchmen and 2 Indians wounded. The French commander called for a parley; Washington refused at first, fearing a trick, and then sent Captain Van Braam to receive the proposals. Van Braam, the only person at the fort who could understand French, returned with the message that the enemy was eager to negotiate. "This was no disagreeable News to us," Stephen noted, because further reinforcements had not arrived and within the fort there were "only a Couple Bags of Flour and a little Bacon. . . . We had intended to have killed the Milch Cows which were our greatest Dependence before the Engagement, but had no salt to preserve them." A persistent downpour had flooded the trenches and made most of the firearms inoperable; there were "only a Couple of Screws in the whole Regiment" to clean the weapons. "What was still worse, it was no sooner dark, than one-half of our Men got drunk."[27]

Van Braam again met with the French commander and returned with terms of surrender. Not only could no one else among the American troops read French, conditions were such that Van Braam could not effectively convey the actual language of the document. Stephen commented that "we were obliged to take the Sense of them by word of Mouth; It rained so heavily that he could not give us a written Translation of them; we could scarcely keep the Candle light to read them; they were wrote in a bad Hand, on wet and blotted Paper." Unfortunately the document included a phrase stating that Jumonville had been "assassinated" by Washington at the Little Meadows engagement. Stephen insisted that in presenting the articles of capitulation to the Virginia officers, Van Braam only spoke of the "Death of Jumonville." If assassination had been mentioned, Stephen contended, it could have been easily "altered," as the French "seemed very condescending, and willing to bring Things to a Conclusion." Under the terms of the surrender, each side was to retire without molestation—the French to Fort Duquesne and the American troops to Wills Creek. The Americans could march away with all the honors of war, keeping their baggage and stores; muskets, however, would be forfeited, and the French promised to destroy the cannon left behind. Captains Van Braam and Stobo were to remain as hostages until the French captives of the previous engagement were returned (which condition Governor Dinwiddie would repudiate). Stephen accused Van Braam of not mentioning the retention of hostages. Stephen also thought the former Dutch fencing master had been misleading in not correctly translating an article having the English agree not only to refrain from further settlement west of the mountains but also to give implicit recognition of the French right to claim the Ohio Valley. Thus, as Stephen wrote in late August, "by the evil Intention or Negligence of Van Braam, our Conduct is blamed by a busy World." Let any "brave Gentlemen, who fight so many successful Engagements over a Bottle, imagine himself at the Head of 300 Men, and laboring under all the Disadvantages abovementioned, and would not accept of worse Terms than Col. Washington agreed to?" All that the Virginia commander had done was to consent to "all the Honours of War, without the mention of 'Assassination' or any other Expression objected to in the abovementioned Articles."[28]

At dawn, July 4, Washington and Mackay officially surrendered. As Stephen recalled, the weather "was Showery, the ditches half full of Water," and the fort was "half Leg deep of Mud." Stephen himself "was Wet; Muddy half thigh up; without Stockings, face & hands besmear'd with powder, & in this pickle form'd the Men to march out of the Fort early in the Morning of the 4th according to the Capitulation."

While Stephen was getting his men into formation, an incident occurred which he reported with braggadocio. Stephen's servant "cry'd out Major a Frenchman has Carried off your Cloaths." Stephen looked around and "observ'd the Corner of his port Mantua on a Frenchman's Shoulder." He rushed over to the offender and "Seiz'd the protmantua, kicked the fellows back side & Returned." Two French officers went over to Stephen and told him that if "he Struck the Men & behaved So, they could not be answerable for the Capitulation." Stephen "damned the Capitulation, & Swore they had Broke it already." The Frenchmen, "Observing such pertness in a dirty, half naked fellow," then asked Stephen "if he were an Officer—Upon Which Stephen, made his Servant Open his portmantua, & put on a flaming suit of laced Regimentals." The French officers upon seeing "the flaming Regimentals, on Such a dirty fellow without Stockings, were extremely Complaisant" and "told us, as we had given hostages, we ought to get hostages of them; that they were very desirous of going to Virginia, as they understood there were a great many Belles Madommoiselle there."[29]

Leaving the surrender ground, the dejected Virginians trekked slowly along the mountain road to Wills Creek. The wounded were carried on stretchers at the rear of the line. One hundred hostile

Indians who had just arrived to reinforce the French snatched whatever they could from the baggage, even destroying Dr. Craik's medicine chest, thereby making it more difficult to treat the wounded.
Much of the remaining transportable equipment had to be destroyed to keep it from falling into the hands of the Indians.[30]

At Wills Creek, the veterans of the campaign began construction
of Fort Cumberland. They were soon joined by Col. James Innes
and his North Carolina Regiment and the two New York independent companies. Although Governor Dinwiddie intended to send
this combined force immediately on another western offensive, ade-
quate transport was lacking, and the Virginia House of Burgesses,
in session during the summer, refused for the time being to allocate
funds needed for another expedition.[31]

Washington and Mackay went to Williamsburg, leaving the garrison in charge of Innes and Stephen. The Virginia commander
found a grateful governor and assembly. Washington received a
colonel's commission, and all other officers were raised in rank, except Van Braam and Muse, who had been accused of cowardice.
Muse resigned, and Stephen took his place as lieutenant colonel.
The legislature awarded each soldier a bounty of one pistole each.
Dinwiddie saw to it that £600 was delivered to the troops, not quite
in time, however, to prevent desertions and "disorder and mutinous
Behaviour" in the Virginia Regiment.[32] The Virginia governor ordered Innes, whom he appointed commander in chief of the next
Ohio expedition, to make preparations for another invasion. In addition to the 300 men of the Virginia Regiment, the governor encouraged Stephen to enlist some of the backcountry settlers to go as
volunteers.[33]

While Stephen lamented the ill success of the late foray into the
wilderness, he took heart that the campaign aroused patriotism and
renewed determination to oust the French from the western country. It even seemed that intercolonial cooperation was stirring. At
Great Meadows both the Virginia Regiment and the independent
company from South Carolina had engaged in the fighting. Although the New York independent companies and the North Carolina regiment did not arrive in time for the battle, they were ready
to participate in another expedition. Pennsylvania and Maryland

voted money for defense. Benjamin Franklin caught the new mood during summer 1754 when he published his famous snake cartoon, "Unite or Die!"[34]

In October 1754 Governor Arthur Dobbs of North Carolina returned from England with royal instructions for a new offensive. The colonies were to recruit a force of 700 men, to be under the general command of Governor Horatio Sharpe of Maryland. The little intercolonial army would consist of the Virginia and North Carolina provincials, Captain Mackay's South Carolina independents, and the New York regulars. James Innes, as "Camp Master General," was to take charge of the soldiers at Fort Cumberland. According to the king's orders, all regular officers outranked those with provincial commissions. Washington, frustrated in attempting to recruit and train soldiers at Alexandria and offended that regular officers of less rank would have precedence over him, resigned his commission in November 1754.[35]

At Fort Cumberland during the fall, Stephen did what he could to keep the Virginia troops in proper condition. Governor Dinwiddie commended him for preventing the loss of cattle.[36] When Colonel Innes left for North Carolina to attend private business, he gave the garrison command to Stephen. Governor Dinwiddie notified Stephen that he was to take charge of the Virginia troops until further orders. Particular attention was to be given to recruiting, and the governor directed Stephen to send several officers to Winchester to enlist men from the backcountry. Stephen got some money from Governor Sharpe for recruiting.[37] He also did duty as the paymaster of the Virginia Regiment, serving in this capacity until spring 1755. Dr. Thomas Walker, one of the two newly appointed commissaries, was made adjutant for the frontier counties and assisted in recruiting.[38] During December and January, Stephen had some success in gathering new enlistees and was congratulated by the governor, though there were problems of discipline and desertion.[39] Stephen spent most of January in Alexandria, probably assuming some of the recruiting duties there that Washington had performed until he resigned. Dinwiddie had to prod him to go to Winchester, which he finally did in early February, in order to collect troops there and pay them.[40]

While at Alexandria, Stephen secured for Washington six black walnut chairs and some blacksmith tools. Apparently at the time, however, there was an unevenness in the relationship between the two men, and perhaps some rivalry. The Scottish doctor-farmer from Frederick County in effect had replaced Washington as commander of the Virginia troops, while Washington now was a civilian. In a note to Washington, Stephen said that it was "with Greatest Chearfulness" that he complied "with your Desire in letting the Soldiers enjoy your Gratuity mention'd to Capt. Perouny: Believe me, Sir, we will always Set a high value upon every Mark of your Esteem"; but "for my own part it gives me the Greatest uneasiness to have Reason to believe that I do not Enjoy the same Share of your Confidence and friendship that I once was happy in: Depend on it, Sir, my Constant Endeavours Shall be to deserve it."[41]

Meanwhile, Governor Dinwiddie had applied to the British government for a further commitment in manpower. The ministry responded by ordering troops to America and appointing Maj. Gen. Edward Braddock to command an expeditionary force against the French in the Ohio Valley. Because provincial officers would be outranked by their British counterparts, Washington refused a commission. Stephen faced the same decision as his former commander, but rather than forgo any participation in the next campaign, he accepted a captaincy; at least he would be a company commander.

In February 1755 Braddock and the 44th and 48th British regiments arrived in Virginia. The British commander met with the governors of Virginia, Maryland, Pennsylvania, New York, and Massachusetts and Col. William Johnson, the northern Indian superintendent, at a conference in Alexandria during April to plan military strategy. Braddock would lead an expedition against Fort Duquesne and then attack the other forts on the western Pennsylvania frontier; Governor William Shirley of Massachusetts, the second in command, would strike at Niagara, and Johnson would assault Crown Point. In all, the military force under Braddock was to consist of the two British regiments, the three independent companies, artillerymen, eleven companies of provincials (nine from Virginia and one each from Maryland and North Carolina), and assorted frontiersmen from Pennsylvania.[42]

Until joining Braddock's force at Alexandria, Stephen still commanded the Virginia troops at Fort Cumberland. Recruiting for
the Virginia contingent in the new army did not meet expectations; of 2,000 originally sought, only 800 had enlisted by the end of
February 1755. In late spring £20,000 royal coin and credit was
made available for the army. Though from the beginning there
were difficulties with army contractors and supply deliveries, it was
expected that there would be enough rations for 3,000 men for
eight months.[43]

Washington finally consented to serve as a volunteer aide-de-
camp to General Braddock. Stephen himself was not especially unhappy at serving at a lesser rank on the upcoming expedition. He
was the senior captain among the provincials in the king's service; a
few months before he had been merely a captain in the Virginia
Regiment. Stephen joined Braddock's army at the Alexandria camp
in March, and his "Company of Rangers" (fifty men) and the other
Virginia troops were brigaded with Sir Peter Halkett's 44th Regiment. Braddock at last marched the army from Alexandria and on
May 10, 1755, arrived at Fort Cumberland. Stephen's company was
now placed in the second brigade, along with the 48th Regiment of
Col. Thomas Dunbar, Capt. Paul Demeré's South Carolina Independent Company (Demeré having succeeded Mackay), Capt.
Edward Brice Dobbs's North Carolina company, and the other Virginia companies under Captains George Mercer, Peter Hog, and
Thomas Cocke.[44] The grand offensive was one that a young, ambitious officer could not afford to miss. Adam Stephen anticipated
that the new army of royal and provincial troops, supposedly superior to any force that the French could field, would certainly gain
victory and glory.

TWO

Defeat at the Monongahela

Excitement ran high at Fort Cumberland as the grand army prepared to march into the western country. Braddock's force mustered at 1,736 men, including the provincial companies.[1] Although the British general planned to use Indian auxiliaries, this aid came to naught. Indian trader George Croghan did bring into the Fort Cumberland camp a band of Delawares and Mingoes, with their families. But the Indians were disaffected, largely because of what they considered Braddock's contemptuous attitude, and soon departed. All the Indian assistance Braddock would have during the campaign were a half dozen Indian scouts.[2]

On May 30, 1755, the expeditionary force started its 144-mile march to Fort Duquesne. Laden with supplies and hampered by insufficient transportation despite the 200 wagons and 500 packhorses, the troops made only two miles a day. At Little Meadows, Braddock divided his army. He marched forward with 1,300 men, leaving the rest under Col. Thomas Dunbar to form a convoy escort to bring up supplies. Stephen and his company of rangers stayed with Dunbar. The army as a whole traveled with little encumbrance, with the officers and sergeants discarding spontoons and halbreds, replacing them with lightweight muskets; only two women were assigned a company, unlike the six per unit back at Fort Cumberland. On June 24 Braddock's advanced troops reached the Great Crossing of the Youghiogheny River. Hostile Indians killed several persons beyond the sentry line. Not having either an accompanying Indian party or enough frontiersmen-soldiers knowledgeable of the western terrain, Braddock had great difficulty in obtaining information on the area through which the army marched. As a commissary officer noted, the troops passed through "a desolate country, uninhabited by anything but wild Indians, bears, and rattle snakes."[3]

Meanwhile, Dunbar's convoy fell farther behind. Many of the escort troops suffered from the flux. Washington was so ill that he remained with Dunbar's detachment. Capt. Roger Morris wrote Washington, suggesting he "follow the Advice" of the surgeon attached to Dunbar's troops, "to whom I know you are recommended as a proper Man, by Dr Stephen."[4]

With Braddock's forward troops needing more supplies, Adam Stephen with 100 men set out from Dunbar's camp with a train of 100 flour-loaded packhorses and 100 head of beef-oxen. Stephen claimed that he was "dogged night & day" by the savages and that the only reason he was not attacked by the French and Indians was because they wanted to lure Braddock's army farther into the wilderness; as Douglas Southall Freeman states, however, there is no evidence in French documents to substantiate Stephen's assertion that the enemy was constantly nearby. Stephen and his supply train made it to Braddock's camp on July 5; Washington, who had wanted to accompany Stephen but was too sick, came on a few days later.[5]

The army was now about ten miles from the French fort. Although following a thoroughly European military procedure of advancing by a heavy column, Braddock took precautions against surprise attack, employing scouts and also a screening party flanking the army;[6] but inexplicably later, on the day of battle, the army was not on a full alert. Braddock's plans called for a siege of Fort Duquesne. As for the French, with a much inferior force, the only chance of beating Braddock's army was to cause a surprise encounter outside the fort on favorable ground. It was necessary for the French to attack quickly before their 800 Indians absconded. The sieur de Contrecoeur, the commandant of the fort, sent out the man who had come to replace him, Daniel Lienard de Beaujeu, with a detachment of nearly 900 troops—108 French regulars, 146 Canadians, and 637 Indians.[7]

Early July 9 the British army crossed to the south side of the Monongahela. A detachment under Lt. Col. Thomas Gage struck out ahead, followed by a road-making party under Lt. Col. John St. Clair. One hundred Virginians provided a rear guard. Midafternoon, the French and Indians began firing on the advanced troops. Braddock ordered Col. Ralph Burton with the 48th Regiment and Virginians led by Washington and Col. Andrew Lewis to assist Gage's detachment. Stephen and his company of rangers remained initially with other Virginians at the rear. The French and Indians fired from high ground on both sides of the British troops. Gage's men and those of St. Clair fell back to the twelve-foot-wide road. Virginians and others moved forward, and the thoroughfare became jammed. The beleaguered British regulars and provincials fired aimlessly against the concealed enemy; even smoke from the opposing musketry could scarcely be detected because of the thick brush. Parties of soldiers, many of them Virginians, charged up the slopes of the hills; they suffered heavy casualties, and when their officers were picked off, they fled. The sight of mutilated and scalped bodies heightened the terror.[8] During the three hours of fighting, the enemy continued to hold both flanks, and Indians hidden in the ravines exacted a substantial toll. Washington repeatedly tried to re-form Virginia troops to rush the enemy, but the men, who had seen so many of their comrades already fallen, refused to make further assaults. It was now feared that the French and Indians would complete an encirclement, sealing off the rear, and all caught in the vise would be slaughtered and scalped. Braddock gave the order to withdraw.[9]

Stephen's rangers, probably remaining in the rear guard, may have engaged the enemy at the edge of the battle site, perhaps creeping up a hill themselves in Indian style. Stephen and his men certainly did some fighting in covering the retreat of the army. Stephen himself had two superficial wounds. His brother Alexander, serving as a volunteer with Braddock, was severely injured. The casualties of the battle were staggering. Of the 1,459 troops of Braddock's army in the action, 914 men and 63 officers were killed or wounded. Braddock lay dying. Six of the Virginia company commanders were killed.[10]

Of the eyewitness accounts submitted after the battle, Stephen's was most critical of the British troops. He had been in a position to view the full scope of the fighting in front of him. As Stephen reported to John Hunter, "the private men of the Two Regiments were entirely at a Loss in the Woods." The French and Indians "kept on their Bellies in the Bushes & behind the Trees, & took particular Aim at Our Men, & Officers especially." The British troops "were thunderstruck to feel the Effects of a heavy fire, & see no Enemy. They threw away their Fire in the most indiscreet manner." Braddock "strove most incessantly to rally Them, & make the proper Dispositions, but all was in vain: They kept in a meer huddle in spite of the most ardent Endeavours of many brave Officers." Stephen thought Braddock should have relied more on the Virginians and independents instead of the British regulars. The army should have fought by the same mode as the enemy. The British commander "found to his woeful Experience, what had been frequently told him, that formal Attacks & platoon firing never would Answer against the Savages & Canadians." It should "be laid down as a Maxim to attack Them first, to fight Them in their own way, & go against Them light & naked, as They come against us, creeping near & hunting us, as They would do a Herd of Buffaloes or Deer." One "might as well send a Cow in pursuit of a hare, as an English Soldier loaded in their way, with a Coat, Jacket &c &c &c after Canadians in their Shirts, who can shoot & run well, or naked Indians accustomed to the Woods." Stephen believed that the British officers had been lulled into "a fatal security" and were too confident that the French would avoid battle and abandon Fort Duquesne. Stephen insisted after the battle that he had "always declared openly, & at that time was not the better thought of for it, that They would be attacked before They arrived at the Fort," because the French were afraid of losing the Indians. Stephen claimed that he had "the honor to receive the General's Thanks for my Services in the field, & if he had lived a Week, I should have been provided for."[11]

Though he may never have learned of it, Stephen did gain recognition from British authorities in London. His report on the battle to John Hunter, July 18, 1755, was forwarded by Hunter to Sir Thomas Robinson of the Board of Trade and came into the hands of the duke of Newcastle, the British prime minister. Newcastle in turn sent it to the earl of Holderness, commenting that it was written by Captain Stephen, "who seems to have behaved very well It gives as clear an account of the most Surprizing, and unfortunate Event as any other letter."[12]

After the battle, retreat became a rout. The soldiers fled to Dunbar's camp at Laurel Hill. On July 20 the ragtag fugitives along with Dunbar's detachment reached Fort Cumberland.[13] Dr. Alexander Hamilton of Annapolis, Maryland, was visiting the fort when the refugees arrived and reported that many of the wounded "lay dead upon the road" and others "died that had no wounds thro faintness, weariness and hunger, the Men having eat little or nothing for 48 hours before the day of Battle and drank only water under an excessive hot sun." Those who had "reached Colls Dunbars Camp appeared liker Spirits than men and their wounds alive with Maggots."[14]

Colonel Dunbar, who succeeded Braddock in command, was not in the mood to resume the offensive. If he had done so immediately, there would probably have been success. Yet the troops were demoralized, and equipment and supplies had to be replaced. On August 2 Dunbar and the British regulars headed for New York. Their departure left 200 Virginians, 30 Marylanders, and a few North Carolina troops at Fort Cumberland, under Col. James Innes, whom Braddock had appointed governor of the fort. Innes soon left for North Carolina, and Adam Stephen assumed command of the garrison.[15]

Despite the terrible defeat on the Monongahela, Stephen and his fellow Virginians felt pride in their conduct during the battle. Washington wrote Governor Dinwiddie praising the behavior of the colony's troops. The British press lauded the Americans and heavily criticized Braddock and the British regulars. The ineffectiveness and confusion of the battle, commented a Boston letter writer in the *Public Advertiser*, "is, and always will be the Consequence of Old England Officers and Soldiers being sent to America; they have neither Skill nor Courage for this Method of Fighting, for the Indians will kill them as fast as Pigeons, and they stand no Chance, either offensive or defensive." The colonial soldiers acquired prestige, as the same newspaper observed in November

1755: "Our American Countrymen have shewn us" what could be "very reasonably expected" from militia. "They had Property to lose, and that gave them Spirit to defend it. They were not dragged from Home to be exposed to the Fire of Foreign Invaders for a precarious, and . . . a very scanty Subsistence;" they "voluntarily took up Arms, and went to seek that Enemy, who threatened their Neighbours and themselves with Destruction."[16] Braddock's defeat was finely etched in the memories of the Virginia participants. For Adam Stephen, Washington, and others, July 9 would always be a day for hallowed reflection. Even during the thick of the Revolution, Stephen and other veterans paused to contemplate this blood sacrifice for American liberty.

With the departure of Colonel Dunbar and the British regulars from Fort Cumberland, the protection of the Virginia frontier devolved entirely upon the colony itself. Adam Stephen stayed on at the fort in charge of the remnant Virginia troops. Governor Dinwiddie advised him that until the new assembly could "regulate our Forces by new Commissions," the soldiers at the fort should "remain easy." Stephen and the captains should keep better pay records; the governor informed Stephen that the legislative committee in charge of military affairs had already found "much Fault with Yr Accts & as to the Arrears due to the Men."[17]

A new military arrangement was soon forthcoming. The General Assembly, called into special session by the governor, voted to raise 1,200 troops and appropriated £40,000 for their maintenance. Washington was named colonel and commander in chief; Stephen, lieutenant colonel, and Andrew Lewis, major. The new levies were to rendezvous at Fredericksburg, Alexandria, and Winchester. While Stephen looked after the troops tantamount to two companies at Fort Cumberland, Washington in early September made an inspection tour of frontier stations from Fort Cumberland to 120 miles southward at Fort Dinwiddie. Eventually Washington superintended recruiting in Alexandria, and Stephen generally had the responsibility of gathering troops at the other two rendezvous points. Governor Dinwiddie kept pestering him over insufficient accounting for moneys received for paying the soldiers.[18]

During the lull in activity there was a morale booster for Stephen.

He could now wear a better set of regimentals. As ordered by Washington in September 1755, each officer was to secure a uniform from London tailors, to include a blue cloth suit, with the coat faced and cuffed with scarlet, and a scarlet waistcoat trimmed with silver lace. For garrison or camp duty, the officers were to wear a silver-laced hat.[19]

Alarms on the frontier forced Washington to keep Stephen at Fort Cumberland, away from recruiting duties.[20] Indian depredations in the lower Valley persisted, and by October about 100 persons had been killed or taken prisoner. Fort Cumberland was vulnerable. Although perched on elevated ground overlooking the Potomac on the Maryland shore, it was an easy mark for enemy fire from two hills nearby. The 4-pounders and smaller fieldpieces at the four bastions of the quadrangular fort had limited range capabilities. In September, Capt. John Dagworthy brought in 30 Marylanders, raising the total number of defenders to 137. Dagworthy, who formerly held a royal commission and had retired on half pay (which he subsequently sold), would soon claim the right of command at the fort. Initially, however, it seems that he and Stephen avoided any disputes over precedence of rank.[21] Washington ordered Stephen to finish building a stockade around the magazine and also to send three sergeants to the rendezvous points to pick up new recruits.[22]

Lurking Indians in the western Potomac country kept Adam Stephen and his little force constantly on their toes. There were kidnappings and occasionally a raid on a pioneer settlement. Every day Stephen sent out a small party several miles from the fort. Lt. Robert Stewart's light horse and volunteers under Capt. John Savage infrequently sought to catch up with marauding Indians, who, however, always seemed to disappear. Stephen could not afford protection to any distant settlements. He complained that "it Sits heavy upon me, to be oblig'd to let the Enemy pass under our Noses without ever putting them in bodily fear. This increases their Insolence, and adds to the Contemptible Opinion the Indians have of Us." Actually the French and Indians who came close to the fort were more interested in intelligence than scalps.[23] Because shoetracks revealed to the Indians the whereabouts of the reconnoitering and pursuit parties, Stephen recommended to Washington that his men be equipped with shoepacks (tanned leather without a separate sole) or moccasins.[24]

With the troops mostly inactive at the fort, Stephen had more than the usual discipline problems. He ordered one young Irishman whipped with 600 lashes "for Uttering Treasonable Expressions." Several Virginia soldiers even deserted the French, arousing the fear that the enemy learned of the weakness of the post. Stephen, nevertheless, did not expect a French attack. He had intelligence that there were only 200 French soldiers at Fort Duquesne, and Fort Cumberland was strong enough to resist an assault by that number, provided that the French did not bring up any cannon.[25] Stephen was still a little careless in his administrative duties. Governor Dinwiddie, who now discontinued signing letters to him with "Your Friend," again took Stephen to task for negligence in keeping records for pay purposes; "it's a monstrous Error," chided the governor in early October, "that You have not sent me a proper Roll of the Men with You."[26]

At Fort Cumberland, Stephen engaged in his first controversy with Sir John St. Clair, the deputy quartermaster general of His Majesty's forces in North America. St. Clair visited Fort Cumberland and promptly put his nose into the various affairs of the Virginia Regiment. He complained to the Virginia governor of several instances of impropriety on the part of Stephen, all of which charges never became quite clear. Over the next year, with Governor Dinwiddie taking an interest, Stephen was still trying to extricate himself from the accusations. The first inkling of the dispute is revealed in Stephen's letter to St. Clair of September 3, 1755. Stephen expressed disbelief that St. Clair had "represented" him to the governor "as a person Guilty of Malpractices." Stephen asked St. Clair to "be so good as to let me into this whole Affair; in order that I may see matters in their proper light, depend on it, I will leave no Stone unturnd to do myself, and nothing but what is worthy of a Gentleman and a Soldier is to be expected from."[27]

St. Clair, a Scottish baronet who undoubtedly considered Stephen something of a boor, only replied evasively. "At my first Arrival in this Country I had heard of several Things you had done which might very properly be called mal practices," he said. "I had Complaints of some myself, and Sir Peter Halket had Complaints of some more." At Fort Cumberland there had been criticisms of Stephen and other officers, but these "were hushed up for reasons that need not be mentioned." Thus Stephen's character "was not only in Question, but very Publickly so Consequently that, I cou'd not be singular in aspersing you." St. Clair acknowledged that he had mentioned one complaint to several people, namely "Your taking a Mare for a Man's discharge, whom I had ordered before to be discharg'd for being a Roman Catholick." St. Clair said that he had "overlooked" and "stifled" other complaints he had against Stephen. Indeed, if Stephen wanted to leave no stone unturned "to Convince the World that you acted like an Officer and a Gentleman in these Affairs," he should seek vindication by applying to Gen. William Shirley, the newly appointed commander in chief in America, for a general court-martial to try the charges of the alleged misconduct against him.[28] Stephen did not follow St. Clair's suggestion, and the dispute abated. But ill feeling between the two men persisted.

By early October the Indians stepped up depredations in the outlying area of Fort Cumberland. Stephen informed Washington that communications with the settlers were cut off and as many as 150 warriors had been seen near the fort. The Indians "go about their Outrages at all hours of the day and nothing is to be seen or heard of, but Desolation and murders heightened with all Barbarous Circumstances and unheard of Instances of Cruelty." Young women were carried away "to gratify the Brutal passions of Lawless Savages. The Smouk of the Burning Plantations darken the day, and hide the neighbouring mountains from our Sight."

Stephen himself was in an Indian fight. When he was on his way to Winchester to check on recruiting and to confer with Washington, Indians concealed along the road fired on him and his party, and he had to retreat back to Fort Cumberland. One of Stephen's men was killed. Stephen sent Lt. John Bacon and his Maryland company of twenty-five men to pursue the hostiles, but after a brief skirmish in which two soldiers were lost, they, too, came back to the fort. Stephen complained to Washington that "We are intirly acquainted with the Routes and Courses of these Bodies of Indians, but have not Men to Spare to Intercept them."[29]

Stephen could offer the settlers little assistance. Although some persons sought refuge at Fort Cumberland, the German and Scotch-Irish pioneers were so clannish that they refused to leave their homes, nor did they do much in organizing defense. Most of the farmers, Stephen noted, "refused to stir," preferring "to die with their wives and families." Stephen issued a call for militia from nearby counties which was endorsed by Washington. He himself went to Williamsburg to pick up £1,000 in pay for the troops and also lead back recruits. In early November, Stephen mustered some 250 enlistees at Winchester and then led them to Fort Cumberland. Later in the month he went to a trading post on Conococheague Creek to purchase cattle, only to find that they were too weak to be driven.[30]

Washington appealed to Governor Dinwiddie and the legislature for a new militia law that would insure stronger discipline. Stephen, Washington pointed out, "can give some late proofs" of the troops' "disobedience, and inconsistent behaviour."[31] The General Assembly complied and in November enacted a statute which provided for an "articles of war." Courts-martial could mete out the death sentence for mutiny, desertion, and disobedience. Washington urged Stephen to follow closely the stipulations of the new act so that "strict Order is observed among our Soldiers." There is no indication, however, that any military panels convened under Stephen's authority passed any sentences of death. Washington reminded Stephen that the government had provided rewards for apprehending deserters and "severe punishment" for anyone who sheltered them. The Virginia commander in chief also informed Stephen of the declaration of war by Great Britain and underscored the importance of the role of the Virginia troops. "Gentlemen from England say," Washington noted, "that the behaviour of the Virginia Troops is greatly extold, and meets with public praises in all the Coffee Houses in London." Stephen heeded Washington's advice in trying to exact sterner discipline at Fort Cumberland, and he frequently read the articles of war to his men.[32]

At Fort Cumberland, Stephen now had 330 troops (including 50 from North Carolina and Maryland) fit for duty. He also stationed 17 men at Watkin's Ferry (Maidstone), on the Virginia side of the Potomac; 18 at Enoch's fort, on the south bank of the Cacapon River, ten miles from the Potomac; and 57 at Fort Dinwiddie, in Augusta County, and kept 30 new recruits at Winchester. There were 60 Maryland militiamen at Thomas Cresap's fortified trading post, at the mouth of the South Branch of the Potomac. When Indians again murdered settlers in the vicinity of Fort Cumberland, Stephen sent out Capt. Henry Woodward and 100 volunteers, who pursued a warrior band as far as Raystown (Bedford), Pennsylvania.[33] Terror engulfed the Pennsylvania frontier, and inhabitants blamed Stephen for driving the Indians their way. Stephen thought the Pennsylvanians were not doing enough to defend themselves. Part of the problem, as he saw it, was owing to the antimilitary stance of the pacificists in that colony.[34]

Stephen asked the Pennsylvania government to establish a chain of posts on the colony's western frontier. His letter of November 9 was published eleven days later in the *Pennsylvania Gazette*. Stephen recommended that a post be erected at Raystown, "another in the Fork of the North and south Branch of Juniata, some others up Sasquehanna, at the proper Passes. Unless this is done the pacifick Gentlemen of your Colony will either from Necessity change their Principles, or have their Throats cut." By spring 1756 Pennsylvania had several western forts garrisoned by paid troops.[35]

Recruiting was still a headache. Washington complained of the inattention to duty among some of the recruiting officers, who, while "spend'g their time in all the gaiety of pleasurable mirth with their relations and Friends," had not obtained a single enlistee.[36] There were other problems as well. Stephen considered that he was too much involved in apprehending deserters. As he told Washington in a letter of November 29, he had caught four "out of a gang of 20 Banditti, all with Arms and ammunition. . . . We are in hot pursuit of the rest through Augusta." Of another group of fourteen who had absconded, six were soon captured. Stephen prosecuted one person for aiding and abetting a deserter. He offered a reward of two pistoles for any deserter "taken dead, or alive." Stephen expected to execute several deserters as examples,[37] but there is no indication he did; inflicting the extreme penalty would normally call for a review by Washington, who left no record of consenting to capital punishment in the instances that Stephen mentioned. On December 8 Stephen could report 333 Virginia soldiers (43 sick and 22 away) at Fort Cumberland; also at the post were Edward Brice Dobbs's North Carolina company of 18 men and Capt. John Dagworthy's Maryland company of 47 militiamen.[38]

Stephen occasionally was able to get away from the routine administrative and command functions at Fort Cumberland by visiting Winchester to receive instructions from Washington and to check on recruiting there. Washington had his headquarters in the town. Stephen also hoped to take on a special assignment which would be a further respite from garrison duty. For a possible offensive campaign in the spring, it was planned to enlist Catawba and Cherokee warriors to join with the Virginia force. Commissioners, with substantial presents, would be sent to the Indian tribes to drum up military assistance. Stephen asked Washington to secure for him an appointment as one of the Indian commissioners. But Washington replied that he had "no more right to give leave for as long as absence, than I have to commission you with proper authorities for such an undertaking: both must proceed from the Governour. If he approves, I have no objection." Washington, however, thought the governor would not appoint Stephen because Colonels William Byrd and Peter Randolph had already been designated the Indian emissaries.[39] The idea of being an agent to the Indians continued to interest Stephen, however, and he later sought similar appointments. Serving as an Indian commissioner would afford him opportunities for personal profit through trade and land speculation.

Probably one reason that Washington preferred to have his headquarters at Winchester and leave Stephen in charge of Fort Cumberland was a rivalry with Capt. John Dagworthy, commander of the little Maryland contingent at the fort. Dagworthy was now insisting that he had total charge of the men at the post, including Virginians. Previously Innes had exercised the general command before he returned to North Carolina. Although Dagworthy based his claim on having held a king's commission, the Virginia government's position was that the Maryland officer was serving only in the provincial line of his colony. Stephen had warned Washington that Dagworthy might attempt to assume the overall command. Although Stephen did not accede to Dagworthy's pretension, Governor Dinwiddie thought he did; in January 1756 the Virginia governor wrote Washington: "How Colo. Stephens came to give the Com'd to C'T Dagworthy, I know not."[40] In order to assure the priority of Virginia command at Fort Cumberland, Governor Dinwiddie requested Governor William Shirley of Massachusetts, the commander in chief of His Majesty's forces in America, to grant brevet commissions of colonel to Washington and lieutenant colonel to Stephen. Shirley, in turn, asked Governor Sharpe of Maryland to settle the dispute. Sharpe, hoping for a compromise, ordered Dagworthy to have command of the fort but not over the barracks or the Virginia troops. Dagworthy said nothing of Sharpe's orders to the Virginians, and the controversy persisted well into the next year.[41]

Meanwhile, as the year closed, Adam Stephen found himself concerned with the political fortunes of George Washington. For burgess from Fairfax County, Washington enthusiastically supported the candidacy of his friend George William Fairfax versus John West and William Ellzey; only two of the three could win. Washington had a heated argument with William Payne, who rapped Washington with a cane and felled him. While the whole town of Alexandria was astir at this affront upon the colony's highest and most respected military official, Washington constrained his temper, and a duel was avoided when the next day he met with Payne and apologized to him for being in the wrong. Fairfax and West won the election, held on December 11. To Washington's surprise, however, he himself was presented as a candidate for burgess in Frederick County only a day before the election. The poll in that county gave a victory to Hugh West and Thomas Swearingen with 271 and 270 votes respectively; Washington had a tally of 40.[42]

Stephen and the Virginians at Fort Cumberland were incensed to learn that their commander in chief had been assaulted during the election contest. Writing to Washington two days before Christmas, Stephen said that "Such a Spirit of Revenge and Indignation prevaild here, upon hearing you were insulted at the Fairfax Election, that we all were ready and violent to run and tear Your Enemies to pieces." Stephen suggested that Washington should have informed him that he was standing for election in Frederick County. "I imagine my self interested in all that Concerns you," Stephen declared. "I cannot forbear telling you that it would have been far better to have acquainted me with your Intention of Standing Candidate for Frederick, my acquaintance there is very general." Stephen said he "would have touchd on the tender part, So gently that with a Weeks Notice, I am perfectly Sure you would have gone Unanimously, in the mean time I think your Poll was not despicable, as the people were a Stranger [to] your purpose, Untill the Election began."[43]

As Christmas time approached, some of Stephen's men went home without leave to be with their families during the holiday. Stephen considered them deserters, and he advertised in the *Virginia Gazette* the names of ten persons who had left the fort with their regimentals and arms. Two pistoles were offered for the delivery of each deserter to Fort Cumberland. Stephen's notice also pointed out that according to the militia act, anyone harboring a deserter faced a six-month prison term and would have to serve in the culprit's place if he was not apprehended.[44]

Despite this concern, Stephen and the Virginia Regiment at Fort Cumberland had a merry Christmas. There were festivities on both the twenty-fourth and twenty-fifth, when the officers joined Stephen in dinner, drinking, singing, and dancing. On Christmas night, after "an extremely good dinner" and a round of toasts, as Stephen wrote Washington, the officers "amus'd" themselves "with acting part of a Play, and spending the Night in mirth, Jollity and Dancing, we parted very affectionately at 12 O'Clock, remembering all Absent Friends."[45]

Indeed the theatrical fare presented by the officer-thespians was most appropriate, conveying the warmth of family and love and also of patriotism. It was an excerpt from *Tamerlane* (first produced in London about 1702), by Nicholas Rowe, which was popular in America during the French and Indian War and in the pre-Revolutionary

War period. The play was an allegory of English-French relations at the turn of the century. Tamerlane, king of the Parthians, is a thinly disguised William III, and the antagonist-tyrant, Bajazet, emperor of the Turks, is really Louis XIV. Capt. Henry Woodward, in a letter to the absent Captain Dagworthy, named the cast: besides himself there were Capt. William Peachey; Lt. John Hall; Ens. Edward Hubbard; John Lawson (a volunteer, later an ensign); David Kennedy, the assistant commissary; Ens. Nathaniel Thompson; Lt. Austin Brockenbrough; John Defever, conductor of the king's stores at the fort; and several slaves belonging to the officers. Woodward, Defever, and one or two slaves had female roles. Seventeen-year-old Brockenbrough was so affected by his participation "that he will never never Act Again."[46]

There is no mention of Adam Stephen joining in the performance, though the part of Tamerlane (acted by Peachey) or that of a rival older general, Omar (played by "Mr. Peachys Man"), would have suited him. Stephen probably preferred to be one of the small audience, thus retaining his dignity as the commander of the fort. He nevertheless very much believed in bolstering morale among his troops by promoting camaraderie and healthy entertainment, all the more welcomed at the godforsaken frontier post. The joyous celebrations at year's end contrasted with the scenes of horror six months before.

For a year and a half Adam Stephen had undergone induction into military life. He had gained a breadth of experience—commanding Virginia troops both in the field and in garrison duty, witnessing the routine activities of a professional army, learning the ways of the Indians and of frontier survival, and, not the least, fighting in wilderness battles. Stephen did not take too well, however, to administrative responsibilities. It was the broader aspect of command, war itself, that most interested the young physician and farmer. Yet military service, for the most part, did not lure Stephen far from home. Fort Cumberland was only fifty miles from his Bower farm, and Winchester was but half that distance. Stephen found that he could keep an eye on his agricultural pursuits much of the time he was soldiering. He expected further service in the colony's regiment would provide opportunity for supplying army posts with his commodities at a good price. Already holding high rank, Stephen realized also that his army position afforded public visibility, upon which he could draw to advance socially and politically in the colony. He would not allow military life to exclude him totally from civilian objectives. As did other officers, including George Washington, Stephen in effect had enlisted in his country's service for the duration of the necessity of contending with aggression from a foreign enemy. With war prolonged, however, he would become even more the soldier, albeit expectant of personal gain.

THREE

Fort Cumberland and Charleston

T he New Year found Lt. Col. Adam Stephen in Winchester, where he conferred with Washington about the command at Fort Cumberland and protection for the frontier inhabitants. Stephen presided over several courts-martial at the James Lemen house. One conviction of cheating at cards led to Ens. Lehaynsius De Keyser's dismissal from service. Stephen wrote the lengthy decision. Washington was greatly disturbed by De Keyser's conduct and presented an "Address" to Stephen to be read to the officers at Fort Cumberland. The De Keyser case should serve as a "timely warning of the Effects of misbehaviour" and "be instrumental in animating the younger Officers to a laudable Emulation in the Service of their Country," Washington said. De Keyser had been guilty not only of a crime but also of conduct unbecoming an officer and a gentleman. "Remember, that it is the actions, and not the commission, that make the Officer—and that there is more expected from him than the *Title*."[1] This admonition Stephen himself would take to heart; in time he would have an even greater awareness of the responsibility of older officers in setting examples of good conduct for the younger ones.

In January 1756 the Virginia Regiment was rearranged into sixteen companies.[2] Washington gave Stephen detailed orders for supervising the organization of the troops at Fort Cumberland and for straightening out pay and quartermaster accounts. Stephen also was to decide on a location for a major fort on the Virginia side of the Potomac and to erect small posts for the protection of settlers.[3] Stephen surveyed a fort site, while also chartering a wagon road; there was no action taken, however, to erect a fort at the location he selected on Patterson Creek a mile above Ashby's Fort.

Back at Fort Cumberland, Stephen was bothered by the poor performances of his officers. He informed Washington that "factions have rose to a great height amongst us: You will See by the proceedings of a Certain Court inclosd which I am ashamed of, how much your Officers know what they are about, and how much they Can discern." Desertion was still prevalent, and Washington recommended that Stephen "stoutly" whip any runaways; the death penalty should be avoided because Washington now thought the militia act needed further clarification. In January and February, Indians caused havoc in the western Potomac country. Periodically Stephen sent out parties, sometimes numbering as many as 100 men, "to Scour the mountains," but the hostiles were as evasive as before. A few soldiers were lost to the Indians.[4]

Meanwhile, the Dagworthy-Washington controversy had not been settled. Washington decided to take the question of the jurisdictional command at Fort Cumberland to General Shirley in Boston. While he was away, Stephen served as acting commander of the Virginia Regiment.[5] In Boston, though Washington was unable to obtain brevet commissions for his Virginia officers as regular troops, he did receive recognition that all soldiers at Fort Cumberland were under his full command.[6] Stephen, however, still found the situation rather complicated. Shirley had also appointed Governor Sharpe of Maryland as commander of the forces of the southern colonies "for the protection of the Frontiers." Stephen complained to Washington that Dagworthy "declares openly that He has the greatest Influence over Governor Sharpe" and "will insist upon our being reduced to Independent Companies again." Dagworthy threatened to have James Livingston, a Maryland officer who was the fort major and acting adjutant for the Virginia troops, "Broke—because he insists upon doing his duty, and I suppose will bring about Several other great Changes worthy of the Gun Room [a naval term]. Unheard of Insolence!" Stephen told

Washington that "I shall look upon my Interest to be Inseparable from Yours, will Steer for the same Port." He would "never Submit to any Regulations but what You approve; nor will I ever Serve in the provincialls below the Rank I bear, If the Duke of Cumberland were to C[ome?] in, besides a Braddock." Stephen complained that Dagworthy "declared himself Counsellor & Aid de Camp to Govr Sharpe—He is big with hopes and Expectations, Exults for Joy at the Change, Struts like a Bull Frog."[7]

In spring 1756 there was not much Adam Stephen and the troops at Fort Cumberland and outlying posts could do to protect settlers from the attacks of marauding Shawnees. These Indians ranged from the Potomac to the North Carolina border, even at times wreaking destruction only a few miles from Stephen's plantation in Frederick County. Governor Dinwiddie proposed sending a volunteer force against the Shawnee villages in the Ohio country and asked Washington to appoint either Andrew Lewis or Stephen to be the commander. Washington selected Lewis, who lived in Augusta County, which had been particularly susceptible to Indian depredations. Lewis assembled 340 men at Fort Frederick on the New River. Leaving that post on February 18, 1756, the Sandy Creek expedition, as it was to be called, encountered an acute shortage of provisions, unfordable rivers, and desertions. After several weeks, Lewis had to abandon the mission. The General Assembly then voted £20,000 to erect a string of little forts, fifteen to eighteen miles apart, from the Mayo River (in present-day Patrick County) to the Potomac. Eighteen of the proposed installations were built, but when the governor ordered out militia from ten counties, only half of the quota of men needed for the garrisons was obtained.[8]

Neither Stephen nor Washington had much faith in the usefulness of a chain of forts along the long Virginia frontier. It seemed to make more sense to have a strong post at the gateway to the Great Valley in Virginia. Such a facility not only would better protect against foreign and Indian invasion but also could be a base to launch another western expedition. Stephen thought it "preposterous to build in so many different places when we cannot keep the Communication open, nor maintain to advantage the Works already raisd." The governor and the legislature agreed upon the necessity of a principal fort in northwestern Virginia, and by May 1756 construction had begun on Fort Loudoun, just outside Winchester.[9] Despite the intention to remove Virginia troops from Fort Cumberland, a large detachment was kept there, still commanded by Stephen. At the end of May, Virginians at Fort Cumberland numbered 41 officers and noncommissioned officers and 321 rank and file. The whole Virginia Regiment consisted of about 1,000 effectives, including drafted militia, scouts, and two ranger companies of 50 men each.[10] Stephen thought there were too many officers at Fort Cumberland. "We stand in need of a purgation," he told Washington, "and after you have reduced our numbers to men of spirit & honour—proper things may be Expected from Us; and we Can better answer the Expectations of Our Country."[11]

After eight months' leave in North Carolina, Col. James Innes returned to Fort Cumberland briefly and reassumed his role as governor of the fort, but left to Stephen the actual command. "The Old Gentleman [Innes] meddles with nothing," commented Stephen, "not even the Parole." He "desird that we Would look on him as a mere passenger—a transient person willing to give advice if necessary."[12]

The local militia, which were the mainstay of the strung-out Virginia frontier posts, proved unreliable. Stephen complained in mid-summer that militia attached to Lt. Thomas Rutherford's company of rangers at Ashby's Fort "absolutely refusd to Escort the Express" to Fort Cumberland "and am afraid never will get over the pannick which Seiz'd them." Stephen urged Washington to request more troops for the regiment in order to assist manning the posts as "the Militia will add to our disgrace but nothing to our Strength." Furthermore, "Forts without a Sufficient number of men to defend them & Scour the Country about, are a useless Burthen to the province." At Fort Cumberland there was need for a physician and medical supplies. Stephen asked Washington to "Send us Little Crocus [slang for a British army or navy surgeon]." Stephen also reported that at last he had found an effective punishment. "We catchd two in the very Act of desertion," he told Washington, "and have wheal'd them 'till they pissd themselves and the Spectators Shed tears for them." In order to build character, Stephen was having his troops attend divine worship on Sundays. Capt. Henry Woodward conducted the services and presumably read the sermons, which, however, were becoming a little shopworn. Stephen therefore asked Washington "if you can come across a Cargo of Second hand Sermons please to forward them by the first Waggons."[13]

Another worry for Stephen was that officers and men were taking up stray horses and selling them. Local inhabitants protested to Washington, who himself was miffed that a soldier had disposed of a horse that he had arranged to purchase. He advised Stephen not to consider any horses as strays; rather, such animals should be appraised by several officers and given a registered mark, and every effort should be made to find the owners.[14]

As if there were not already enough disharmony at Fort Cumberland, an external slander enraged Stephen and the officers. Rumors circulated at Williamsburg impugning the good character of officers of the Virginia Regiment. As early as April 1756 John Robinson, Speaker of the House of Burgesses, wrote Washington of complaints he had heard of the behavior at the fort. Governor Dinwiddie noted that the House of Burgesses was "greatly inflamed, being told that the greatest Immoralities & Drunkenness have been much countenanced and proper Discipline neglected."[15] The accusations spread, and even the Reverend Samuel Davies preached against the "spirit of security, sloth, and cowardice" that prevailed in the regiment. A series of articles under the title of "the Virginia Centinel" in the *Virginia Gazette* criticized the colony's war effort and especially the misbehavior and incompetence of officers at Fort Cumberland. Because Stephen commanded the garrison, the charges reflected on him and in part probably were aimed at his own personal conduct. Perhaps the Christmas 1755 festivities had invited scorn. The anonymous "Centinel X" (number 10, published on September 3) was so vicious that Washington was ready to resign if he discovered that the piece truly represented the views of the colony's leaders. Stephen and his fellow officers were extremely riled, and they, too, were on the verge of returning their commissions.

"Centinel X" did not spare any vitriol in its condemnation. The officers at Fort Cumberland were "raw Novices and Rakes, Spendthrifts and Bankrupts, who have never been used to command, or who have been found insufficient for the Management of their own private affairs." They had been advanced in rank not for merit but because of seniority and "the Interests and influence of Friends." The common soldiers had been abused. Furthermore, the officers "give their Men an Example of all Manner of Debauchery, Vice and Idleness . . . they lie sculking in Forts, and there dissolving in Pleasure, till alarmed by the Approach of the Enemy. . . . Men of Virtue and true Courage can have no Heart to enlist, and mingle in such a Crowd."[16]

The officers at Fort Cumberland first had in their hands a copy of "Centinel X" on October 5, and the next day they addressed a memorial to Stephen declaring their "no small Astonishment"; the newspaper article was "so Scandalous and altogether so Unjust" that only the "Strictest" protest was in order. The officers expressed their "great and just Regard for Collo: Washington and Yourself," but they would not submit to ridicule before their countrymen in Virginia and in "the Neighbouring Colonies." If there was no apology from the Virginia governor and the assembly by November 20, they would all resign.[17] Washington persuaded the officers to postpone their intention of leaving until he could make a full investigation. The officers also sent an address to the House of Burgesses asking for "public testimony, that in your esteem we have not deserved the obloquy complained of."[18] Although the protestors received no real satisfaction from the governor or the assembly, tensions eventually subsided. An unpublished article (attributed to Richard Bland, a prominent burgess), which found distribution though not published in the *Gazette* for which it was probably intended, helped to diffuse the ire of the officers. It rehearsed events of Virginia's struggle with the French and charged that much of the ineffectiveness of frontier defense was owing to negligence of the legislature rather than that of the officers.[19]

Throughout summer and fall 1756 the Indians continued to plague settlers along the Virginia and Maryland frontiers. In May, Col. Thomas Cresap, a Maryland trader and land speculator, and his volunteers, known as "Red Caps" because they usually wore Indian attire, left Fort Cumberland in pursuit of Frenchmen and Indians who had been raiding the Conococheague settlement. The Indians had murdered Cresap's son and also Capt. John Fenton Mercer. Cresap and his men encountered briefly the offending Indians and killed several of them. Nathaniel Gist with eighteen men of the regiment and seven Nottoway Indians skirmished with hostile warriors "on the Top of the mountains," as Stephen reported, and killed six of them, while losing four Virginians.[20]

At one time a large party of Indians spent an entire day firing on Fort Cumberland from a nearby hill. At dusk Stephen sent seventy-five men to dislodge the enemy. Lying quietly on their weapons all night, at dawn they completely surprised the Indians, of whom only a few escaped being captured or killed. On another occasion, Kill-buck, a Shawnee chief, professed friendship and asked that he and some of his warriors be admitted into the fort for a consultation. Upon gaining entry, with the garrison off guard and the gates opened, the wily chief planned that other Indians would then slip inside the stockade. But Stephen had arranged a surprise. Kill-buck and his companions were admitted, but were immediately disarmed and forced into petticoats, a supreme humiliation, and then let out of the fort.[21] In August, Charles Langdale, a French trader, and a group of Indians approached the fort on a reconnaissance mission, and some firing ensued.[22]

Stephen considered intelligence gathering an important part of his duties. From time to time he sent the Pennsylvania government information he received relating to that province's frontier. Stephen requested the authorities of that colony to send an agent to the Susquehannas and other western Pennsylvania Indians in order to persuade them not to engage in hostilities; if accomplished, this would "have a good Effect upon the Confederate tribes of the Twightwees [Ohio country Indians], none of whom have yet taken up Arms against Us."[23] In October 1756 some 200 Frenchmen and Indians hovered around Fort Cumberland. About the same time two spies were captured. One, an "Irish papist," Stephen had hanged from a tree outside the fort. The other, William Johnson (actually twenty-eight-year-old William Marshall), an itinerant farm worker who professed to have been captured by the Indians, was spared and sent on to Governor Sharpe in Annapolis on condition he give information about the enemy.[24]

Piecing together the latter's story and other intelligence, Stephen concluded that an offensive should be mounted immediately against the French forts. He informed Governor Dinwiddie that 300 Virginia, Maryland, and Pennsylvania infantry and 400 Indians, without artillery, would be sufficient "to reduce the Ohio from the Lower Shawnese Town to Presque'Isle." Stephen said that he "would chearfully venture Honor & Life on Success of the Enterprize, provided the Design is imediately put in execution, for on Secrecy & Dispatch depends the Success." Various factors would contribute to victory. "The Waters are now low, there is yet plenty of Food for the Carriage Horses, & they are strong & in good Order at this Season of the Year." Stephen knew "the Situation of all the Indian Towns, their Strength & present Temper," and he was "certain no great Body can be assembled against us before Spring." He asked Dinwiddie's pardon "for expressing myself with so much Assurance, but it proceeds from the perfect Knowledge I have of Matters on the other Side the Mountains. I long to chastise their Insolence—And by the Assistance of that God whom they dispise I would roast them." An expedition would vindicate the honor of the soldiers and the colony. Stephen added that the Delawares "have roasted ten English Prisoners alive since Spring last, amongst them was a Woman. . . . About 30 French Men sent up from Fort Du Quesne had a principal hand in burning, & tormenting this poor Woman, who behaved like an Ancient Martyr, in the most exemplary Christian Manner." Some women captives "have been lately compelld on pain of Death to marry Indian Husbands—The French buy & sell the Prisoners of War to one another for five & some seven Years."[25]

Dinwiddie, however, vetoed Stephen's proposed offensive. Even though Stephen's letter contained "so much Spirit and good Sense," his plan was "impracticable" because no men could be expected from Maryland, the Pennsylvania troops were needed to protect their own frontier, and anticipated aid from the Cherokees had not materialized. Stephen in the meantime should remain on the alert

and obtain intelligence.[26] Dinwiddie forwarded Stephen's information and proposal to the new commander in chief, Lord Loudoun.[27]
It seems that Stephen also prepared a detailed plan of offensive operations for Washington, stressing logistical aspects along Braddock's
road; the document later found its way into the papers of British
colonel Henry Bouquet. Several historians have mulled over the
true authorship of the plan but finally assigned it to Stephen. Dis-
crepancies in handwriting and style of expression from Stephen's
habitual mode raise questions, yet it is probable that Stephen did
submit such a plan.[28]

Given the precariousness of Fort Cumberland, Governor Dinwiddie ordered Washington to convene a council of war of officers
at the fort and nearby posts to determine the feasibility of retaining
Virginia troops at it. Stephen and fifteen officers reviewed the short-
comings, which included inadequate construction, vulnerability
from cannon fire from the surrounding hills, the protective cover
afforded an enemy along the banks of the Potomac River and Wills
Creek, the sole dependence on the two streams for water, and the
great distance from pioneer settlements. The council of officers
nevertheless agreed that a strong post in the area was needed and
that Fort Cumberland, provided it was strengthened and reinforced
by Maryland and Pennsylvania troops, should be maintained for the
time being. Washington concurred, though the final decision rested
with Lord Loudoun.[29] Stephen, awaiting Loudoun's determination,
had the responsibility of making improvements at Fort Cumberland, despite a lack of tools. At the north side of the fort he erected
a ravelin facing a hill on one side and the creek on the other. The
V-shaped outwork contained a rampart twenty feet in depth and at
a level with the hill and a parapet of the same thickness and six feet
high. Within the angle of the ravelin Stephen built a magazine
which could withstand small artillery fire and a tunnel which led to
the creek.[30] Intermittently Stephen had the assistance of some 120
Catawba and 30 Tuscarora Indians, who were an effective covering
body for Fort Cumberland. On one occasion 100 soldiers and the
Catawbas pursued a band of hostiles and returned with a number of
scalps.[31]

From January to March 1757 Washington made his headquarters

at Fort Cumberland, instead of Winchester or Fort Loudoun, which eased Stephen's responsibilities. But at last it was decided that Fort Cumberland would be turned over to Maryland troops. General Loudoun met with the Pennsylvania and southern governors in March 1757 in Philadelphia, with Washington attending, and the group concluded that Fort Cumberland would be garrisoned by a 300-man Maryland force. The Virginians would now be stationed at Fort Loudoun.

The Philadelphia conference also determined that 2,000 provincials (including 400 Virginians) would be sent to aid in the defense of South Carolina and Georgia. South Carolina's governor had appealed for military assistance in anticipation of a French invasion "by Sea from Hispaniola & by Land from Mississippi." Dinwiddie decided that only half of the colony's quota would be sent because of manpower needs on Virginia's frontier. Stephen was named commander of the colony's expeditionary detachment.[32] Dinwiddie on April 5, 1757, ordered the immediate evacuation of Fort Cumberland by Virginia troops. Stephen was to form two companies of 100 men each at Fredericksburg and be prepared to debark for South Carolina; Dinwiddie would send a vessel to pick them up. Reception of the governor's evacuation order was delayed, however, and a council of war at Fort Cumberland resolved that the Virginia troops would not leave the fort until Captain Dagworthy arrived with the replacement troops.[33] The Maryland commander and 150 men came into Fort Cumberland about May 1.[34]

Stephen's handling of the transition at Fort Cumberland drew substantial criticism. According to Dagworthy, the beef left by the Virginians was unfit for consumption, and the Marylanders had to subsist on fish until they could get a fresh supply of provisions. It irked Washington that Stephen had not made the replacement troops pay for the fish that the Virginians had left at the fort.[35] Washington fumed at Stephen's giving so many of the regimental stores to the Catawba Indians, including 122 blankets, thus depleting those available for the soldiers. Washington informed Dinwiddie that he had strictly ordered Capt. George Mercer and the quartermaster not to relinquish any of the regimental stores. Stephen, in Washington's view, had acted contrary to these instructions. Washington said that had he met with Stephen at Fort Loudoun, "I shou'd most assuredly have made him answer for his conduct."[36] To Speaker John Robinson, Washington wrote at the end of May that "we receive fresh proofs of the bad direction of our Indian affairs. It is not easy to tell what expences have arisen on account of these Indians."[37] Governor Dinwiddie concurred with Washington that Stephen was highly blamable for giving military equipment to the Indians.[38]

The perceived dereliction of duty at Fort Cumberland made Washington distrustful of Stephen. Stephen depended too much on his own on-the-spot judgment, which Washington seemed to encourage. Moreover, there was obviously a communication gap. Washington himself acknowledged that his orders about the military stores went directly to a subordinate and a staff officer at fort, and apparently not simultaneously to Stephen. Washington perhaps should have kept a closer inspection at Fort Cumberland. There were other actions of Stephen that did not set well with the Virginia commander in chief. In writing to Robert McKenzie on July 29, Washington declared that Stephen "has given so many strange orders" that were "so inconsistent with my Instructions and incompatible with his own—that it will be with great difficulty, if it is even possible, to extricate the Officers and myself from the dilemma and trouble *they* have occasioned." Furthermore, Stephen had no right "to order any repairs to your fort, without giving me previous notice of his design . . . why you shou'd apply to him for those orders (when I was nearly as convenient, and alone had the right to direct) is matter of surprize to me."[39]

Stephen also displeased Governor Dinwiddie in being so dilatory in bringing the Carolina detachment down the James. The governor had expected him in Williamsburg on May 20. Stephen finally arrived at the capital on May 26 with the two companies and was handed orders from the governor to sail to Hampton, where two schooners would transport the Virginians to Charleston. Stephen was informed that he would serve under Lt. Col. Henry Bouquet, "who is Commander of the Forces in the Southern Colonies on this Continent." The governor instructed Stephen to keep his men under "proper Discipline and good Order, inculcating into them

Morality and Fear of God, the Director and Disposer of all Victorys. Take Care to prevent Gaming and Swearing." At Charleston, Stephen was to deliver a letter to Benjamin Stead, who would pay the Virginia troops.[40] Dinwiddie complained that twelve of Stephen's men had deserted, which "I've reason to think was by Carelessness." The governor also suspected that Stephen brought with him more than the six women alloted per company.[41] Washington added his own grievance to that of Dinwiddie's. "I imagine your Honor must have been much surprized," he told the governor, "to find so few of the Officers whom you had ordered for Carolina with the Detachment." It was a "matter of astonishment" when he learned that Stephen "had taken the liberty to dispense with your Orders on this point—However, this is not the only instance in which he has used such liberties."[42]

It was true that Stephen had ordered several officers not to accompany him to South Carolina, even though they had been directed to do so by both Dinwiddie and Washington. At a court of inquiry at Fort Loudoun on June 9, 1757, to determine why Lt. John Campbell did not go with Stephen as ordered, Campbell testified that he had joined Stephen at Fredericksburg, but Stephen ordered him to return to his former company, on grounds that he had failed to bring a horse. From other testimony it seems that Stephen did not find Campbell congenial and preferred instead the company of Ens. Edward Hubbard, whom Stephen took with him in place of Campbell. Washington sent Dinwiddie a transcript of the proceedings of the court of inquiry, noting that Stephen also had substituted another officer in the place of Lt. Peter Steenbergen; moreover, there were "many other cases extraordinary in their nature" which "were transacted by Colo. Stevens, while I was at Williamsburg."[43]

Unquestionably Stephen's violation of his instructions was insubordination. But from his point of view, he considered the directives as only guidelines, and he felt he had the discretionary authority to arrange his detachment as he saw fit. In Stephen's mind the troops were essentially volunteers because they were leaving the colony, and perhaps selection had been on this basis. In such instances the commander of an expedition had a voice in selecting the officers. In any event, Stephen and his detachment were out of the colony before the controversy had gained momentum. At Hampton on May 31 the two Virginia companies, accompanied by Henry Bouquet and 500 troops of the 60th Royal American Regiment, set sail for Charleston, with HMS *Garland* convoying the transports.[44]

Although Stephen and his men did not fancy a long hot summer in the Carolinas, a bit of sea air and at least a stay in Charleston offered respite from the tedious garrison duty on the frontier. The troops reached Charleston on June 15. Stephen expected to be stationed only briefly at the southern port before venturing out to fight the French and their Indian allies. But the visit to Charleston extended to ten months. In September 1,000 Highlanders arrived. The rumored French and Indian offensive, however, never materialized. The Creeks remained neutral, largely because the Cherokees "made the Path to the French bloody." One of Stephen's companies was sent by sea to Savannah; this detachment was led by Lt. William Stewart of the Royal Americans, substituting for the ailing Capt. George Mercer. For the Virginians who stayed in Charleston it was an uncomfortable time. Smallpox was rampant, and the climate unbearably stifling and rainy. Pay was often delayed. The Virginians had to make do with an "old Brick Barracks" without furniture, and some of the men had to take to "open Quarters, Some laying upon the Ground in a Church half build." Stephen and the other officers were crammed together in an old house.[45]

Stephen soon heard from Governor Dinwiddie, who complained that a return of the Virginians showed only 177 troops instead of the full complement of 200. "I can't tell how to reconcile this," Dinwiddie wrote Stephen on July 22, "unless contrary to Orders You carr'd more Women than I directed." If Stephen had violated his orders on this point, he would have to bear the extra expense himself.[46] Stephen in December reported that he had only 173 troops—87 in his own and 86 in Mercer's company.[47]

The Charlestonians did not exactly warm to the Virginians presence. "What adds to make this Place at present disagreeable," Mercer informed Washington in August, "is that most of the Gent. of Note are out at their Indigo Plantations, so that we have nothing left but a Set of trading ones, who esteem you for Nothing but your

Money." The women of the city "are very far inferior to the Beauties of our own Country. . . . A great Imperfection here too is the
bad Shape of the Ladies, many of Them are crooked & have a very
bad Air & not those enticing heaving throbbing alluring Letch ex-
citing plump Breasts common with our Northern Belles." Stephen
also lightheartedly told Washington that the "mighty Conqueror
Love has made havock in the Corps"; but "the Fair in this place
must give way in Beauty easy Behaviour, & other female Accom-
plishments to the Daughters of the more northe[r]n Climes."

Stephen expressed pride that his Carolina detachment had mas-
tered both European and American tactical skills—an objective
that Washington himself had sought to impress upon his troops.
Stephen reported that his men were "well disciplin'd" and knew
"the parade as well as prussians, and the fighting in a Close Country
as well as Tartars." Whatever the degree of proficiency of Stephen's
troops, he was acquiring a sense of military professionalism. Even
the British officers were amazed that Stephen's men "made a good
& Soldier like Appearance and performed in every Particular as
well as coud be expected from any Troops with Officers whom they
found to be Gent.," at least Mercer so noted. The British officers
also were astonished that their American counterparts were attired
with "a Sash & Gorget," a "genteel Uniform, a Sword properly
hung, a Hat cocked," and "a White Shirt, with any other than a
black Leather Stock." Stephen had definitely improved his own image. "Youl scarce believe," Mercer told Washington, "that the Colonel never appears here but in full dressed laced Suits."[48]

In the fall General Loudoun ordered the two Virginia companies
to return home, but getting Stewart's detachment back from Savannah caused a delay.[49] By early November, Stephen's men were
3-½ months without pay, and he sent "an Express" to Governor
Dinwiddie saying that it would be impossible to keep the men in
service of the colony without compensation. It would be unfortunate, Captain Mercer seconded, to "lose so many good Men after
becoming serviceable; and I dont much doubt but they may with
one Consent refuse to serve Us, & inlist with the Regulars; some of
Them have attempted it already, & been Severely punished." What

greatly promoted "Uneasiness & Discontent in Them, is that they see every Soldier here except Themselves paid Weekly."[50]

Stephen was anxious to return to Virginia, even if this meant immediately resuming duty on the frontier. At last, on March 26, 1758, British war vessels appeared in Charleston harbor to take the Virginians and the Royal Americans aboard. While the regulars went to New York, Stephen and his men arrived in Virginia on April 10. There was no time for a leave, as preparations were underway for a new offensive against the French in western Pennsylvania. By April 22 Stephen and his two companies were in Fredericksburg, where they stayed briefly to receive new recruits.[51] Stephen then led his men to Fort Loudoun in Virginia. For the time being he served as acting commander of the 1st Virginia Regiment, while Washington met with the colony's authorities in Williamsburg to work out arrangements for the ensuing campaign. The Virginia assembly voted to put two 1,000-men regiments in the field. In addition to Washington's 1st Regiment, a second was to be raised under the command of William Byrd.[52]

In response to Col. Bouquet's request for 600 Virginians, Stephen on June 1 marched with five companies of the 1st Regiment and a company of artificers from the 2d Regiment to another Fort Loudoun in south central Pennsylvania. This post (near present Chambersburg) was to be the starting point for building a new road to Fort Duquesne. Twenty-five Catawba Indians and a few Cherokees accompanied Stephen's detachment. The going was tough. Cattle had to be watched over, the Potomac was high, and the roads were muddy. On June 6 Stephen and his men arrived at the Pennsylvania fort, where they were joined several weeks later by 200 more Virginians under Maj. Andrew Lewis.[53] If the garrison duty of the past year on the frontier and the service in far-off Charleston had not been what he had expected, Stephen was hardly excited about facing his new assignment—helping to establish a thoroughfare and advanced posts in the rugged western Pennsylvania country. The experience in road and fort building and the related logistics management, however, would be important to the further development of his capabilities as a military commander.

"Col. Stephens *Upon the Road*"

Adam Stephen predicted that before the end of summer the British and American troops would have a complete victory over the French western posts. Braddock's expedition had gone too slow for him. He soon discovered, however, that the new expeditionary commander was meticulous in making preparations and determined to move at slow but deliberate speed. The grand strategy of 1758 called for a three-prong campaign: Brig. Gen. John Forbes to lead provincials and regulars against Fort Duquesne; Maj. Gen. Jeffery Amherst's army, with support from a fleet under Adm. Edward Boscawen, to assault Louisbourg and Cape Breton Island; and Maj. Gen. James Abercromby, largely with northern militia and regulars, to attack Crown Point and Ticonderoga and then to join Amherst's force for a campaign along the St. Lawrence River.

When Adam Stephen arrived at Fort Loudoun in Pennsylvania, he expected that the army would be collected and then be moved to Fort Cumberland, and from there would ascend the old Braddock's road to Fort Duquesne. Washington and the Virginia government favored this route. Pennsylvania authorities, however, contended for a new road through their colony. Such a route would allow easy access to provisions; at stake, of course, were military contracts and handsome war profiteering. In June, Forbes decided that Raystown (Bedford) would be the forward army base instead of Fort Cumberland, and in early July he declared that the troops would move westward through Pennsylvania. The British general wanted several strong posts built along the way in order to secure supplies and communications and, if the unexpected happened, to have bastions the army could fall back on. The proposed Pennsylvania road had a topographical advantage over Braddock's route in that there was little underbrush and river and creek crossings were shallow.[1]

Stephen's first task was to take a detachment of Pennsylvania and Virginia troops to clear a thoroughfare from Fort Loudoun to Raystown. The way was "hilly & stony," Stephen reported. The work party opened the road some twenty miles to the Juniata River, where they erected a small stockade, and by June 24, 1758, they had covered the next eighteen miles to Raystown.[2] Stephen complained of hardships to Colonel Bouquet. He had no surgeon or medical supplies, nor did he have any wine, rice, barley, oatmeal, or butter; many of the Pennsylvania soldiers had "sore Legs." At least the artificers were hard workers; they "are young men accustomd to Live on Strong food Such as Hominy & bread made of Indian meal."[3] Adam Hoops, a subcontractor for the Pennsylvania troops, complained that Stephen unjustly put a soldier in the guardhouse. Hoops also questioned Stephen's management of supplies, and he informed Bouquet "that Method which Collo. Stephen had Introduced I am Resolved not to put up with."[4] Actually Hoops, who was scarcely literate, himself had a reputation for careless bookkeeping. At Raystown, Stephen's work detachment erected a fort and storehouses capable of holding three months' supplies for 6,000 men.[5]

Washington had stayed at Fort Cumberland with the remainder of the 1st and 2d regiments. For several months, even after the decision was made, Washington wrangled with British officers on his insistence that the Braddock road be used. For a while, some Virginians, under orders from the British command, did some work on Braddock's road, primarily to deceive the enemy as to the actual route. Washington, in July, also had politics on his mind and entered the burgess election in Frederick County. He wrote Stephen at Raystown to use his influence to have Bouquet allow Washington a brief furlough from Fort Cumberland at election time to go to Winchester. Stephen replied that Bouquet was concerned that if Washington was absent from Fort Cumberland, the responsibility for that post would be on Bouquet's shoulders. Hence Washington did not take leave. Stephen himself went down to Winchester from Raystown, chiefly to muster new recruits but also to pursue a lawsuit against John Harrow. No doubt he put in a good word for Washington among his neighbors. Washington easily won the election.[6]

On returning to Raystown, Stephen brought with him 50 new enlistees. Smallpox had broken out among his soldiers in Pennsylvania during his absence. Road cutting westward nevertheless began immediately. Stephen took charge of 550 Virginians to clear a way over and through Allegheny Mountain. Bouquet sent 600 Pennsylvanians to assist Stephen's work force. No time could be lost if Fort Duquesne was to be captured before winter. It was also urgent to traverse Laurel Hill to a settlement on Loyalhanna Creek which would be the last staging area for the attack.[7]

On August 7 Stephen and his detachment reached Edmund's Swamp Creek, twenty-five miles from Raystown, where they set up an "entrenched camp" and "temporary depot."[8] Stephen reported to Bouquet that his men were at work "bridging the Swamp" and that he and a party were setting out "to reconnoitre the Shades of Death [so named because the density of the forest would not allow sunlight to penetrate], a dismal Place! and wants only a Cerebus to represent Virgils gloomy description of Æneas's entering the Infernal Regions." Stephen promised that he would make "as Easy a passage through them as possible but it will be an Herculian Labour." If Bouquet would send him 400 more men, Stephen said, "I will then Answer your Expectation—Hurl Mountains out of their Seat—Shortly have a Waggon Road to the Top of Lawrel-Hill, & keep Scouting parties Constantly beyond the Loyal Hannin."[9]

To avenge the killing of settlers by Indians about twenty-five miles from Fort Duquesne, Stephen sent out a small party of the Pennsylvania troops led by Maj. George Armstrong. The Indians discovered Armstrong's detachment "by their fires, reconnoitred their camp, & no doubt would have Cut them to pieces, had they not found them too strong." Stephen considered keeping 150 of his men beyond Laurel Hill as cover against the Indians, but Sir John St. Clair had arrived in Stephen's camp and dissuaded him from doing it; Stephen instead reinforced a post at Kickenpauling's, a settlement at the crossing of Quemahoning Creek.[10]

On August 10 Stephen informed Bouquet that he and his work force had made it through the Shades of Death. "I attempted them on horse back, but found Admittance so difficult that I was Obliged to part with horse, Sword & Coat, and make my way good with the Tomahawk," he said. "Near thirty of Us Spread, & wandered through those Shades, perplexd with Lawrels, Logs & Rocks; coverd with weeds, or Brambles interwoven with Young Locust; and were so lucky in our researches, that had it not been for this days Rain, before night a Coach & Six might have easily past through the Place."[11] The greatest difficulty that Stephen found in getting over Laurel Hill was the stony terrain, as he told Bouquet two days later: "There is nothing would have a greater Effect upon these Rocks, than the Essence of Fat Beef gradually mixt with a Puncheon of Rum. This would add weight to every stroke given them." Stephen asked Bouquet to send "three or four Cross Cut saws to Seperate the numberless, damn'd, petryfyd old Logs hard as Iron, & Breaks our Axes to pieces." This letter was endorsed by Bouquet: "Col. Stephens *Upon the Road.*"[12]

On the fourteenth Stephen and his men made it to the top of the ridge, and four days later he could report that the way was cleared for wagon travel twelve to twenty miles westward. "My men are in good spirits and we are willing, and Capable to do anything," he boasted.[13] Stephen's efforts led Bouquet to commend him to General Forbes along with Ens. Charles Rohr, who also had reported on the road work. "These gentlemen," Bouquet noted, "deserve much praise for having surmounted all these obstacles in so short a time; and what gives me much satisfaction—they have kept their troops in a good humor. Every one is contented, and believes himself immortalized by having worked to open this route."[14]

Though Stephen favorably impressed Colonel Bouquet, his relationship with Sir John St. Clair, the quartermaster general, went from bad to worse. St. Clair, irascible and crafty, had an inflated estimation of his own importance. Strictly a staff officer, he nevertheless considered that he had a right to command in the field and especially thought he could give orders to Stephen and other mere provincials. Stephen's own troops were already edgy over having received less rations than the regulars and St. Clair's having held back their rum.[15]

Stephen reported that on August 18 he received "Orders in a very Odd manner" from St. Clair "about erecting Shades for Provisions at Edmunds Swamp." Stephen, who now made his camp at Quemahoning Creek, about nine miles in advance of the camp at Edmund's, had the work done as he had been told. On the twenty-first he went back to the Edmund's Swamp Creek camp to confer with St. Clair. A series of confrontations over the next several days culminated with St. Clair, on August 24, placing Stephen under arrest for mutinous behavior. What the dispute came down to was St. Clair's insistence on superseding Stephen in command of the work force. From Stephen's point of view, however, St. Clair interfered with the road building, "Ordering troops or Work in an arbitary manner" without "regard to Detail." More offensive was a single occurrence one evening, when St. Clair issued the parole and "necessary Orders for the Guard," encroaching upon Stephen's authority as the commander of the troops. Stephen quite properly insisted that a staff officer could not usurp a command in the field. Stephen defied St. Clair and gave out his own parole, whereupon the British staff officer demanded that he rescind it. Stephen refused and, supported by most of his officers, sent a note to St. Clair telling him that he had no right to exercise any command of the troops. St. Clair, upon receiving the protest, "bellow'd out Mutiny; & appearing to be in the greatest dilemma! roard out what shall I do; shall I fire upon them!" One thing he did do was to order Stephen's arrest.[16]

Though supposedly confined to camp, Stephen actually had freedom of movement to go anywhere he wanted to, and he did, but Maj. Andrew Lewis temporarily assumed his command "upon the Road."[17] St. Clair justified his action to Bouquet. Stephen's "behaviour is the most extraordinary, I ever saw or hear'd of," he said. "I have confined him for Mutiny in the Camp, so that the Virginians are now under Major Lewis, if it had not been for that Officer I had Reason to suspect that there wou'd have been a genl mutiny amongst both Officers and Men of the Virginians." St. Clair also said that he attempted to send Stephen to Raystown, but Stephen "refused after he was arrested to come down with his Major." Because St. Clair did not have "sufficient Strength to take him by the neck from amongst his own Men," he was "obliged to let him have his own way" so that there would be no "Occasion of Blood Shed." The reason St. Clair gave specifically for Stephen's arrest was "that he told me" that he "had given out his Parole and that rather than receive any Orders from me he woud brake his Sword in pieces."[18]

Bouquet certainly disapproved of Stephen's arrest, and he reminded St. Clair of the proper role of a staff officer. "I am afraid," Bouquet informed St. Clair, "that there has been Some heat in this affair, and that you will have a good deal to do to justify the necessity of Such a violent measure against an officer of his Ranck, Commanding a Corps." St. Clair did not have a field command; he was serving only as the quartermaster general. St. Clair could give out the parole, "the Ensign of Command," only as a "Compliment" bestowed by the commanding officer. Bouquet asked St. Clair to "make up matters" with Stephen; meanwhile he would make no report to General Forbes until he heard further from St. Clair. Bouquet advised St. Clair to contact the British commander in chief of the expedition if he still wanted to complain, but Bouquet warned that Forbes's "intentions and repeated orders" to him had been "to establish and preserve a good harmony wth the Provincial Troops, and you may be Sure that he will find this measure & you both precipitate and unseasonable."[19]

The Stephen–St. Clair fracas elicited comment from various officers. Col. James Burd of the Pennsylvanians, also at the camp at Quemahoning, noted: "We shall use all means to Reconcile Coll: Stephens & the Knight but I'm afraid it has gone too far."[20] William Ramsay wrote Washington that "Lt. Col. Stephens has been under an arrest for some time by Sr. John Wildair, Stephens says he is right & will not be released without a publick justification."[21] Stephen himself informed Washington of the matter, mentioning St. Clair's "daring to Call us Mutineers."[22]

St. Clair did take his complaint in person to Forbes, who himself had a low esteem for the provincial forces. Forbes had written Secretary of State for the Southern Department William Pitt, who was now co-prime minister, on September 6 that among the Virginia and Pennsylvania troops, except for a "few of their principle Officers . . . all the rest are an extream bad Collection of broken

Innkeepers, Horse Jockeys, & Indian traders, and that the Men under them, are a direct copy of their Officers, nor can it well be otherwise, as they are a gathering from the scum of the worst of people."[23] Forbes decided to stay clear of the Stephen–St. Clair controversy but made a suggestion to Bouquet: "Sir John St. Clair says that if I say he was in the wrong to Colonel Stevens, he will readily acknowledge it. I do not choose meddling, but I think Colonel Stevens might act, and trust to Sir John's acknowledgement."[24] Because the terminally ill Forbes refused to intervene, Bouquet saw to it that the dispute was ended. Stephen wrote Washington on September 14 that because of General Forbes's "Indisposition," Bouquet "has therefore ordered me to take upon Me the Command of the Detachmt again." Stephen had been unquestionably correct in his position. The British army held fast to the distinction between the duties of staff and line officers. Thus also would be the situation with the American forces during the Revolution, when the Stephen–St. Clair affair was cited by one American general as an important precedent.[25]

Stephen had quickly put his quarrel with St. Clair behind him and apparently even during his "arrest" had resumed his supervision of road building to Loyalhanna Creek and the erecting of a fort there. Briefly he had "a severe spell of sickness a thing very uncommon to me," as he wrote Col. James Wood at Winchester.[26] By early September the road was finished to the Loyalhanna,[27] forty-five miles southeast of Fort Duquesne. Pennsylvanians and Virginians soon had the fort completed (called Loyalhanna, but soon to be renamed Fort Ligonier). A large detachment from Forbes's army, 800 troops consisting of Highlanders, Royal Americans, and provincials (including 200 Virginians), had "taken post" ten miles west of Stephen's detachment.[28] This force, commanded by Maj. James Grant, had been sent out by Bouquet to reconnoiter the country all the way to Fort Duquesne. On September 14 Grant's detachment approached to within a quarter mile of the French fort. Thinking that there were only 200 French and Indians, Grant had Capt. William McDonald's company of 100 Highlanders march up to the fort with drums beating. Suddenly a much larger number of French and Indians rushed out of the fort and fell on McDonald's men, most of whom were killed or captured. The provincials, taking cover behind trees and brush, conducted an effective fire for awhile but were overpowered and had to retreat. Some soldiers jumped into the Ohio River and drowned; Grant and Maj. Andrew Lewis both were captured. The fleeing troops halted at the baggage station, about two miles from the fort, where Capt. Thomas Bullitt rallied them and made a heroic stand which at least stopped the advance of the enemy.[29]

At the time of the disaster, Stephen was at Dagworthy's camp (three miles north of present Greensburg), helping to erect the Three Redoubts, which were intended to be the main fortification between Loyalhanna and Fort Duquesne. Bouquet immediately ordered him and 300 men to cover the retreat. Stephen and his detachment moved fifteen miles westward and gave "Assistance to the Stragglers" and "succord the distressed." Stephen attributed the defeat to the enemy's familiarity with the ground and stated that "the Gentlemen were beat by detail."[30] Of the 200 Virginians who had been with Grant, 62 were killed or missing, including 5 officers dead.[31] Despite the defeat, the expedition had demonstrated that Fort Duquesne was easily accessible. Moreover, it showed the advantages of depots and strong points to secure a retreat.[32]

Although the facility in reaching Fort Duquesne over the last thirty miles may have changed Stephen's estimate of the worth of Forbes's road, a few days before the Grant debacle he had written Washington: "You have no reason to alter your opinion of the route of the army."[33] Washington arrived at Raystown on the sixteenth and argued with General Forbes that the old Braddock road should still be used. But Forbes once and for all squelched any criticism of using the new road and sent Washington back to Fort Cumberland to bring up the rest of the Virginia troops, including those of Byrd's regiment.[34]

The French and Indians soon repaid "Grant's visit." On October 12, 440 French soldiers and 150 Indians approached Fort Loyalhanna. Stephen and his Virginians undoubtedly had returned to this post. Col. James Burd, who commanded at the fort, sent 500 troops to resist the enemy. The British-Americans, facing a hot fire, had to retreat to the earthwork of the garrison. The French and In-

dians, outnumbered and up against heavy artillery, made no direct
assault on the post; after several hours they withdrew, although
returning for another round of fire briefly in the evening. The
British-American casualties numbered 12 killed, 18 wounded, and
31 missing; of the 1st Virginia Regiment, 4 were killed, 6 wounded,
and none missing. Forbes, still at Raystown, upon learning of the
battle, thought it should have been followed by a counterattack.
The battle of Fort Loyalhanna, nevertheless, was the significant victory of the campaign; it adversely affected French and Indian morale, and it demonstrated that the Loyalhanna post could withstand
attack.[35]

Washington and the rest of the Virginia troops arrived at Fort
Loyalhanna from Raystown on October 19, followed two weeks
later by General Forbes. A formidable British-American force had
now collected at the fort, nearly 6,500 troops and 1,000 wagons.[36] It
seemed that the campaign could be quickly and successfully concluded by immediately going the remaining distance, along a sloping terrain, to attack the French fort. But the weather turned cold,
and there was some snow. It was believed that the French had a sizable force at Fort Duquesne. Rations were short. A council of war
on November 11 voted to delay the campaign until spring. The following day, however, it was learned that the Indians had deserted
the French. About the same time an Indian raiding party came up to
Fort Loyalhanna. Forbes sent out two detachments, both consisting
entirely of Virginians. Attired in brown buckskin, the two groups,
at dusk, mistook the other for Indians and fired on each other. Despite this accident, two Indians and a British deserter who had gone
over to the French were captured. The white man, in fear of being
put to death, revealed that the actual strength of the French fort
was only several hundred troops. On the basis of this intelligence,
Forbes ordered the march on Fort Duquesne.[37]

Three brigades consisting of 2,500 picked men formed the expedition. Washington commanded the right wing—the 1st Virginia Regiment, two companies of artificers, North Carolinians,
Marylanders, and Delaware troops; at the center Col. Archibald
Montgomery led the Highlanders and the 2d Virginia Regiment;
and, on the left, Bouquet conducted the first battalion of Royal

Americans and the Pennsylvania troops. The advance began November 15. The new road along the south side of Loyalhanna Creek, on which so much work had been done, had to be abandoned because of the soggy ground from the fall rains, and the expeditionary force instead went over Chestnut Ridge. Washington and his regiment moved on ahead on the twenty-first to open a road connecting with the Old Path (Trader's Path). On the night of the twenty-fourth the army lay on its arms on the hills overlooking Turkey Creek, near Braddock's field. Scouts returned, reporting that they had seen smoke over Fort Duquesne and that it had been evacuated. At midnight a loud boom resounded through the forest. The French had blown up their fortifications and had fired the barracks and storehouse. On November 25 the army marched the few miles to the French fort in battle formation, with troops on the flank to avoid surprise. At nightfall the British-American army entered the smoldering ruins. Greeting the soldiers just outside the gates were grisly trophies from Grant's defeat: perched on stakes were the heads and kilts of captured Highlanders who had been tortured and killed. The next day, Sunday, was proclaimed a day of Thanksgiving, and the troops were ordered to attend religious services. Then the soldiers who had fallen during Grant's attack were buried, along with the scattered bones remaining from Braddock's defeat. Forbes proudly reported to Pitt on the mission accomplished, in a letter dated "Pittsburgh," November 27, 1758, saying that he had taken the liberty to rename the French post Fort Pitt and also "two other Forts that I built . . . the one Fort Ligonier [formerly Loyalhanna] & the other Bedford [formerly Raystown]."[38]

Except for 250 Virginians and Pennsylvanians, Forbes immediately sent home the colonial troops, "as their provinces will pay them no longer."[39] Washington, planning to marry in January and to assume his seat in the House of Burgesses, resigned his commission. With Forbes leaving for Philadelphia on December 3, there was need for a commandant of Fort Pitt (Pittsburgh). Stephen, who decided to remain on the frontier, and Lt. Col. Hugh Mercer of the Pennsylvania troops both applied to their fellow Scotsman, General Forbes, for the position. Mercer received the appointment. Until mid-January, Stephen supervised improvements on Forbes's road, particularly between Quemahoning Creek and Laurel Hill.[40] General Forbes died in Philadelphia on March 11, 1759, and was succeeded by Gen. John Stanwix.

Byrd's regiment disbanded at the start of the New Year, 1759, as stipulated by law, leaving only the remnants of the 1st Regiment, which Stephen now hoped to command as Washington's successor. But some officers did not like this prospect. Capt. Robert Stewart from Fort Loudoun, Virginia, on December 29, 1758, wrote Washington: "It's whisper'd here that Lt. C. Stephens has receiv'd a Letter from one of the Council intimating the Governor's intention of giving him the Regts whenever you Resign—I need not tell you how alarming this is to the Corps." Again Stephen was disappointed. In January, Governor Francis Fauquier named William Byrd to command the Virginia troops.[41]

Stephen returned to Virginia and helped Byrd organize the new 1,000-man regiment at Fort Loudoun near Winchester. Apparently Stephen's popularity with other officers, not to mention the politicians, had waned. Edward Hubbard, whom Stephen had taken with him to South Carolina and was now a captain of an artificer company, wrote Bouquet in March 1759 that he was "resolved to have the Conduct of Lt Col Stephens examin'd, by the assembly intending to lay before them the many Crimes of which he is Accus'd— which will (perhaps) Require all his Dexterity to Elude."[42] It is not known what Hubbard had in mind, and the assembly did not take up charges against Stephen.

One matter of concern for the Virginia veterans of Grant's defeat in September 1758 was the loss of blankets and shirts left behind in the baggage a few miles from Fort Duquesne; the equipment subsequently was destroyed or captured by the enemy. Stephen petitioned the Virginia legislature to reimburse the soldiers. Washington, now a burgess, supported Stephen's request, and the assembly voted £175 compensation for the loss.[43]

In Philadelphia during March 1759 Colonel Byrd received orders from General Stanwix to send 300 Virginians to Fort Ligonier. Stephen was given the command of this force, which he first led to Bedford, where he arrived on May 2, "after a very fatigueing march from Winchester: occasioned by rainy weather, deep Roads, & high

Rivers." Stephen's immediate task was to forward provisions to Forts Ligonier and Pitt; because Indians interrupted the supply line, the latter post was so short on food that the soldiers were on the verge of eating horses and dogs. Stephen was sure that any further attacks on convoys going to the two forts would compel the abandonment of these installations. He assigned all but twenty of his soldiers to supply escort duty.[44] Stephen also found that his old nemesis, Sir John St. Clair, "acts again on this Quarter," and he inquired of Bouquet "if any further respect is to be paid to him than formerly."[45]

Stephen expected to carry on road work, but as he informed Bouquet shortly after his arrival at Bedford, it was "impossible to do anything toward the heavy repairs necessary on the roads" because of rainy weather and swollen streams and also because he had to employ his men on the convoys, "dispatching Supplies wt the greatest Expedition for the Use of the Trans Alpine Garrisons." By May 17 Stephen had forwarded 42,000 pounds of provisions. He pressed Bouquet, who was then at Lancaster on his way to Philadelphia to confer with General Stanwix, to send more cattle and packhorses. Eventually Stephen had a work party out on the road. He complained of the hardships of his men, especially the constant duty and not having any tents. A convoy under Captain Bullitt coming from Virginia was attacked by Indians four miles from Fort Ligonier on May 23; thirty-six Virginians were killed or missing, all fifty wagon horses were taken or killed, and most provisions were carried off. Stephen requested Bouquet to send reinforcements, even threatening to turn over his command to Capt. Alexander McKenzie if this was not done.[46] Stephen also wanted Bouquet to order more Virginia troops from Winchester to Fort Cumberland, so that they would be in a better position to strike out against the Indians.[47]

Under orders from Bouquet, Stephen led his Virginians and four companies of Royal Americans about June 1 to Fort Ligonier.[48] As commander of this post, Stephen had his biggest test in July. Capt. François-Marie Le Marchand, sieur de Ligneris, who had been the last French commandant at Fort Duquesne and now, at Fort Machault (Venango), had charge of all French troops in the west, planned to make one final effort to dislodge the English from the Pennsylvania frontier. Drawing on soldiers and Indians from the French posts at Le Boeuf, Presque Isle, and even as far away as Kaskaskia on the Mississippi, he collected 1,000 French troops and 1,000 Indians. With 700 of these, Capt. Charles Philippe Aubry, who had come in from the Illinois country, marched for Fort Ligonier. An attack was also to be made subsequently against Fort Pitt. Just before the enemy appeared at Fort Ligonier on July 6, Stephen ordered a party of Royal Americans to Bedford, accompanied through the woods to Laurel Hill by nineteen Virginians. After this group left, the enemy attacked the fort. The "fire on the first Redoubt was the hottest," noted Stephen, but the cannonade against the enemy proved effective. The French and Indians then "retired into the skirts of the Woods, and continued their fire at a distance till night." At the time Stephen had 350 men at the fort. About sunset the Virginia escort returned and joined in some of the fighting. "The party behaved well, fought until they had orders to retreat and got in without the loss of a man." The French and Indians, except for small groups firing from a distance, did not further attack the fort. A convoy with a drove of cattle and provision wagons on the way to Fort Pitt got through. The enemy withdrew, planning to resume the assault, but messengers soon arrived bringing word that Sir William Johnson and a large British and Iroquois force were marching on Fort Niagara. Ligneris decided to evacuate all French soldiers in western Pennsylvania to meet this new challenge.

Stephen could be proud of his victory. As one commentator a century later observed, Fort Ligonier was saved "by the bravery and good conduct of Lieutenant-Colonel Stephens and the garrison under his command." The only casualties among Stephen's men were the death of Capt. Samuel Jones of the Pennsylvania troops and three wounded.[49] Writing eight weeks after the French attack, Stephen informed Richard Henry Lee of this final enemy offensive. "We had a very hard and difficult Campaign untill the reduction of Niagara," noted Stephen. "Nothing was eaten or drunk at this Post or Pittsburg but what was fought for." The French attempt on Fort Ligonier "was well designed but ill executed. Had they succeeded— All was undone! Pittsburgh must have fallen of course for want of provisions. . . . With the Artillery and stores found here, they would have immediately destroyed our Magazines, at Bedford & spread desolation far and wide through the province." The French decision to relieve Niagara was "a most lucky Interposition for us! . . . All our hopes, Our Labours, expence & fatigue for five years would have been blasted and of none effect." Because of the shortage of provisions, Stephen said it was impossible then to have marched to the other abandoned French posts—namely, Le Boeuf, Presque Isle, and Venango. But "the Tempest has now subsisted, all the threatening clouds are dispersed, and we are in perfect tranquility."[50]

At last the battle for control of the Ohio Valley had ended. In September the fate of the French east of the Mississippi and in Canada was sealed on the Plains of Abraham. For five years Adam Stephen had been a participant in the international struggle. He had command in the last engagement with the enemy on the Pennsylvania frontier, a fitting punctuation to the long, arduous, and often frustrating experience. Though the foreign threat had been removed in the west, that of the Indians had not.

FIVE

Veterans, Politicians, and Cherokees

W ith the French gone, Adam Stephen attended to putting
Fort Ligonier into "a respectable state" and was proud
that a new redoubt and an underground magazine had
been built.[1] The construction of Fort Pitt also was far along. A
strong military presence was still needed on the western frontier.
The Indians, "full of discontent & sorrow at our Successes," as
Stephen informed Richard Henry Lee, were still hostile: "They
continue to murder some of our people, and steal all the horses they
possibly can. They are extremely treacherous."[2]

In September 1759 Gen. John Stanwix, now at Pittsburgh, ordered Stephen and his Virginians to march to that post from Fort
Ligonier in escort of a supply train, taking all the construction tools
with them. On September 23 Stephen and 150 Virginians arrived at
Pittsburgh. Much to the delight of residents of the frontier town,
they had with them ninety-seven of the "Largest Bullocks" and
forty-three wagons of provisions. En route Stephen had his men
make repairs on the Three Redoubts and also road improvements.[3]

Stephen seemed to have some rivalry with Col. John Armstrong
of the Pennsylvania provincials, who replaced him as commander of
Fort Ligonier. Armstrong in late October complained that Stephen
had sent to that fort "a parcel of Horses to be loaded Out of the
Publick Store without any Authority, or even a line to me that might
explain the Matter."[4] Stephen had a grievance about Armstrong

himself, concerning the implementation of Bouquet's order that the number of women be reduced at the forts. Stephen wrote Bouquet that he had seen the instructions to Colonel Armstrong "about the fair, I may Say, the foul Sex." Armstrong "has brought up a mere Seraglio with him, and among the Rest, three of our Cast offs. . . . If a person of his Rank and Gravity, a person whose example is so much respected, Connive at these things I fancy the thing will soon gain ground." Stephen also explained that all the women that Stephen had "wanted to get rid of, claim his patronage," and therefore Stephen had "been obliged to Confine a Group of them, for pretending to go down, and then fetching a Compass, and Returning in the night to the Suburbs of Ligonier again."[5] Apparently Stephen's objection had effect; Armstrong decided to do something about the camp followers. Because "no Orders, are Obey'd by the Females I'm beginning to Duck & Drum Out," Armstrong said, "but nothing less than force will persuade them to Visit their Old friend Capt [Lewis] Ourry, by which he will naturally Suspect they have neither true hearts nor Sound Bottoms they are inshort the Bane of any Army, the Devil & two Sticks."[6]

Stephen received a letter from the Virginia governor thanking him for sending news of the Virginia troops. Governor Fauquier added: "I congratulate you on being relieved from the post [Fort Ligonier] which you protected with so much honour to yourself and Advantage to the Colony."[7] Stephen was undoubtedly glad to learn of the departure of Governor Dinwiddie, who had upbraided him for carelessness in duty and insubordination. As a matter of fact, Dinwiddie's brusqueness had alienated many prominent Virginians. The new governor, Francis Fauquier, was regarded as a complete gentleman; he was tactful, dedicated to the public interest, and a man of refinement. Fauquier had arrived in summer 1758, just before the victory in western Pennsylvania, and all that he knew of Adam Stephen was that he was a ranking officer in the successful military operations.

At Pittsburgh, Stephen found a bustling community of soldiers, sutlers, workmen, contractors' agents, and traders. Nearby was an Indian village on the Allegheny River. Though no one as yet was permitted to own property, by late spring 1760 Pittsburgh, sectioned into an upper and a lower town, had 200 residential dwellings, mostly crude huts.[8] Stephen did not like a new Pennsylvania law prohibiting the issuance of licenses to private traders and confining the Indian trade to Forts Augusta and Pitt. He viewed the restrictions as a means to exclude Virginians from the Indian trade. Indians, who could no longer meet traders in their own villages, grumbled about having to travel long distances in order to exchange goods. Merchandise was in such short supply at the two forts that Indians could not find buyers for much of their large quantities of skins and furs. Yet Indian relations did improve somewhat; from 1759 to 1763, 338 white prisoners were delivered at Fort Pitt.[9]

Stephen warned Governor Fauquier that if a Pennsylvania officer was given command at Fort Pitt, the Indian trading law would be fully enforced. Another matter touching intercolonial relations also troubled Stephen. He feared that Virginia veterans of the French and Indian War would be impeded in taking up lands in the Ohio Valley—the 200,000 acres promised by Governor Dinwiddie's proclamation of 1754. Especially concerned also were members of the Ohio Company, consisting mainly of Virginians. Because of the war, surveys by the company in the Ohio Valley had been delayed. The company's members were apprehensive that Pennsylvanians would preempt the best lands, which would also underscore the fact that the company had been negligent in not living up to its contract in promoting surveys and settlement.[10]

The prospect now of entry into the Ohio lands also stirred controversy among the Virginia officers. It seemed that George Mercer and George Washington were about to conbime interests to make a joint claim in the Ohio country. Countering the two were Thomas Bullitt and Stephen. The key to who would get the best veterans' lands depended much upon who would be commissioned by the Virginia governor as surveyor. The appointee obviously would be in a position to appropriate the best lands for himself and his friends.[11]

Stephen took a furlough in Feburary 1760 for the purpose of visiting Williamsburg to report firsthand on the Pennsylvania threat but more importantly to lobby for the appointment of his friend Bullitt as surveyor of the Ohio lands. He used the occasion to meet with a number of Virginia leaders.[12] Mercer did not take kindly to Stephen's intervention and alerted Washington that Stephen had gone to the capital to use his influence on Bullitt's behalf. Stephen "rubs his hands, shrugs his shoulders, and says he knows if Tom gets the Place he will serve a Friend. . . . it woud give Me the greatest Joy imaginable to disappoint these mighty Schemes." Stephen and Bullitt were determined "to have the best Land on the Ohio &c in Partnership—The Plan has been long concerted, and they already think Themselves absolute Proprietors."[13] Washington, however, did not feel the same way as did Mercer and was even willing to support Bullitt, who was appointed the surveyor.[14]

Not only did Stephen warn Virginia authorities about the competition from Pennsylvanians for western lands, he also was concerned that the commander of British forces in America, Jeffery Amherst, would insist that the territory beyond the Alleghenies was a public domain and should be made an Indian reserve. Writing to Richard Henry Lee later in the year, Stephen said, "It is uncertain to me what the Genl Calls the Indian Lands. . . . in my Opinion the Lands which I have taken upon the Waters of Ohio in a Legal manner is as much mine, as the Lands I hold on the Waters of Potomack."[15]

Stephen also used his leave time to put everything in order on his plantation and to attend to seeding crops. He employed several soldiers on leave on his farm and to drive some of his cattle to the troops in western Pennsylvania. He took a few weeks off to visit the Ohio country, searching out parcels of land that he might later claim as military bounty.[16] He added to his Virginia estate by acquiring 890 acres on Opequon Creek from a foreclosure sale and also a lot in Winchester.[17]

One reason Stephen remained in Virginia so long was his expectation of being sent on an expedition against the Cherokee Indians on the Carolina frontier. The Indians were laying siege to the Fort Loudoun there (in present-day Tennessee), and the General Assembly enacted a law to march a Virginia force into the Cherokee country for the relief of that post.[18] It was thought that William Byrd would refuse the command, and Stephen, the second ranking military officer on active duty, anticipated that the governor would name him to lead the expedition.[19] Governor Fauquier wrote Gen. Robert Monckton at Fort Pitt that he considered "Lt. Colonel Stephen in every Respect equal to the Command of the few Men I am empower'd by Acts of Assembly to join to his Majesty's Forces under your Command for the Campaign."[20] But Byrd was willing to serve. For the time being the Cherokee expedition was not organized, and Stephen was ordered to return to Fort Pitt. By mid-August 1760 he had arrived at the Pennsylvania fort with the "recover'd men, recruits & deserters."[21]

During his long furlough in Virginia, Stephen may possibly have married, although there is no evidence that he did. His daughter, Ann, was born the next year. The best conjecture is that Ann's mother was Phoebe Seaman. A letter to an old friend and commission merchant in England (or Scotland) of May 20, 1760, strongly suggests that Adam Stephen had not married, nor was the thought in his mind. To George Gordon he offered congratulations, "on your entering into the respectable State of Matrimony, May Heaven Shower down its best blessings on You & Mrs Gordon." Stephen promised to write frequently and "inform you of my Schemes. . . . I have made an addition to my Estate last winter, which will I imagine turn me about £600 p Annum." Stephen also noted that "I go on one of the most dangerous Enterprises Since the War Commenced, that is against the Southern Indians who have formed a powerful Confederacy agt Georgia & South Carolina." In a postscript Stephen added: "Please to remember my Duty to my Dr Mother."[22] If Stephen had any plans of matrimony or had married, surely he would have made such mention; on the other hand, there is no word of his brothers in America, which would certainly have been of interest to his mother if not the Gordons.

Stephen's new service at Fort Pitt lasted only several months. Governor Fauquier wrote Monckton in October that because the war with the French on the frontier and in Canada was over, the Virginia troops should return to the colony; if any were kept in Pennsylvania, they would not be paid by Virginia.[23] In December, Stephen brought back 300 troops from Pennsylvania, with only a few Virginia soldiers left behind at Fort Pitt and Fort Burd (Redstone, now Brownsville) under the command of Capt. Robert Stewart.[24] The Cherokee campaign would be held in abeyance until early summer. The assembly voted to keep the regiment intact but not to authorize a march into the Cherokee country until General Amherst supplied British regulars to act in conjunction with the Virginia troops.[25] Many Virginia soldiers were allowed lengthy furloughs, with a token force kept at Fort Loudoun near Winchester. Stephen probably only checked occasionally into the fort, which was about twenty miles from his plantation.

There was again time to give full attention to the farm and the livestock. In February 1761 Stephen notified Bouquet that he was driving cattle to Fort Pitt and expressed a desire that the British colonel help promote land speculation. The cattle "will cost me extreamly high in driving at this Season," Stephen said, "besides the risk of losing Some, I am Obligd to load about twenty horses with Corn from Fort Cumberland, to keep them in tolerable heart in passing the mountains." Stephen added that "all my Views are turned towards farming & trade" and that he hoped for Bouquet's "Concurrence & assistance in any scheme which will Raise the Value of our Lands in the Back parts: My present design is to fix a market for the produce of them, and to Establish flour & Hemp our Staple Commodities." Stephen was disappointed with the outcome of his cattle shipment to Fort Pitt, as they did not weigh in as he expected, and he protested to Bouquet, but to no avail.[26]

With respite from army duty, Stephen decided to try his hand at politics. He declared his candidacy as a burgess from Frederick County in the May 1761 election. Stephen felt he had a good chance, especially now being well known to the constituency and having spent so many years in the defense of the colony's frontiers, not the least of which included part of the county. Stephen had a big challenge before him because one of the most prominent men in the colony was in the running—none other than George Washington himself. Washington, though living in Fairfax County, could legally run in Frederick County because he owned land there. Two burgesses were elected from each county, and often candidates paired themselves for mutual advantage. Washington and his associate, Thomas Bryan Martin, had been previously successful, but Martin now took himself out of the race, and Washington combined inter-

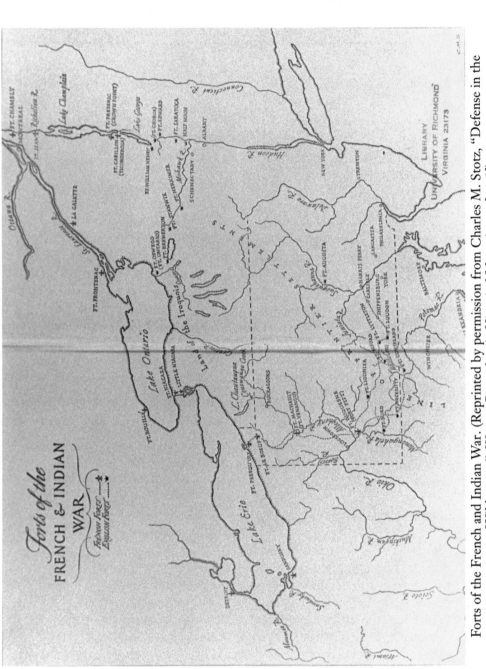

Forts of the French and Indian War. (Reprinted by permission from Charles M. Stotz, "Defense in the Wilderness," *Western Pennsylvania Historical Magazine* 41 [1958])

ests with another candidate, George Mercer. It was from this election that Washington confirmed suspicions that he had already began to have of Stephen's character—namely, that Stephen could behave with impropriety in seeking a goal. Washington, with his elitist temperament, considered that Stephen violated a gentleman's honor as well as Virginia political tradition by being too solicitous for votes. However, Washington himself followed a sort of a double standard; he made the rounds in Frederick County before the election, visiting local planters and attending a wedding and a cockfight.[27] What probably irritated Washington most was that Stephen, a compatriot in arms and longtime second in command of the Virginia Regiment, dared to be a political rival. As early as February 13, 1761, Capt. Robert Stewart wrote Washington from Winchester that Stephen was pursuing a campaign of demagoguery. Stephen, said Stewart, "is incessantly employ'd in traversing this County and with indefatigable pains practices every method of making Interest with it's Inhabitants." His "claims to disinterestness, Public Spirit and genuine Patriotism are Trumpeted in the most turgid manner; it's said he will reduce these shining Virtues to practice . . . by Introducing various Commercial Schemes, which, are to diffuse Gold & opulency thro' Frederick, and prove (I suppose) as Sovereign a Remedy against Poverty and Want as Glen's red Root was in removing hunger and imbelicity from our Horses in Campaign 58." Stephen "has attracted the attention of the Plebians, whose unstable Minds are agitated by every Breath of Novelty, whims and nonsense." By appealing to opportunity for "speculative Wealth" and with "an immensity of Flummery," Stephen "has brought over many," which "gave me extreme uneasiness till I was certain that the Leaders and all the Patrician Families remains firm in their resolution of continuing for You."[28] In March, Stewart again commented on Stephen's electioneering. Stephen "continues indefatigable and I'm inform'd intends to make use of every method to arrive at his point de vue."[29]

The sheriff controlled all the activity at the election, including the opening and closing of the polls. For good measure Washington kept in contact with the sheriff of Frederick County, Capt. Thomas Van Swearingen. Washington expressed his concerns about the election to Van Swearingen three days before the voting on May 18. In the letter, as Douglas Southall Freeman notes, Washington's remarks about Stephen were his first personal attack on any of his officers. As Washington observed, "Col. Stephens proceedings is a matter of the greatest amazement to me. I have come across sundry of his Letters directed to the Freeholders wherein he informs them that he acquitted himself of what was charged to him in the Streets of Winchester while you were present, and goes on to draw Comparisons to prove his Innocence." Stephen's "conduct throughout the whole is very obvious to all who will be convinced, but I find there are some that do not choose to have their Eyes opened." Washington told Van Swearingen that "I hope my Interest in your Neighbourhood still stands good, and as I have the greatest reason to believe you can be no Friend to a Person of Colo. Stephens Principles; I hope, and indeed make no doubt that you will contribute your aid towards shutting him out of the Public trust he is seeking." If "Mercer's Friends and mine" could be "hurried in at the first of the Poll it might be an advantage, but as Sheriff I know you cannot appear in this, nor would I by any mean have you do any thing that can give so designing a Man as Colo. Stevens the least trouble."[30]

Washington's own suggestion that the sheriff should admit pro-Washington voters to the poll before others, thereby possibly influencing the balloting, which was done viva voce and then publicly recorded on a sheet in view of all, certainly approached impropriety. But given the deferential voting patterns in the colony, it was not uncommon for candidates themselves to get their supporters to the polls early. Obviously Washington was a little unsure that both he and Mercer would win. As a candidate Washington did not have much of a record to stand on. He had been pretty much a backbencher as a burgess; in more than two years he had presented only one bill—to curtail hogs running at large within the town of Winchester.[31] Washington's reference to Stephen's getting into trouble on the streets of Winchester in view of the sheriff is unclear; possibly Stephen was thought to be violating election laws by offering "treats" or other rewards for votes.

Although the Washington-Mercer team easily prevailed at the election, Stephen did have a good showing. The results were: Washington, 505; Mercer, 399; Stephen, 294; Robert Rutherford, 1; John Hite, 1; and Henry Brinker, 1. Stephen did not have the advantage of a partner-candidate as did Washington and Mercer. Curiously, Washington's previous running mate, Thomas Bryan Martin, nephew of Lord Fairfax, the proprietor, voted for Stephen;[32] the two were good friends. Probably because he thought the electorate in Frederick County too "plebian," Washington in the next burgess election in 1765 stood as a candidate from Fairfax County.

There was another important matter on Stephen's mind other than the election. The Cherokee Indian expedition would now proceed. In March 1761 the assembly had voted to bring the Virginia Regiment up to strength, to 1,000 men. Col. William Byrd was retained as the head of the regiment, and Lt. Col. Stephen was still the second in command. The Virginia troops were to journey to Stalnakers on the Holston River, where they would build a small fort, and then move downriver to the Great Island. Col. James Grant, with British regulars, South Carolina militia, and Indian auxiliaries in May began a march from the Carolina coast toward the middle towns of the Cherokees.[33]

Stephen had written Bouquet a week before the Frederick election that he was about to march from Winchester. His resumption of military duty and anticipated long absence from the county may have been a factor in his loss of some votes to Washington, who for two years had been a civilian and was available to take a seat in the assembly.

Stephen and his detachment from Winchester joined Byrd at Staunton on May 26.[34] Some of the Virginians were left at Forts Lewis (on the Roanoke River) and Fauquier (at the head of the James River). In all, the regiment had about 750 men, far short of the authorized quota.[35] On July 1 Byrd and Stephen, with the main body of troops, reached Fort Chiswell on Reed Creek (near present Wytheville), about 240 miles from Winchester. Stephen was pleased to hear from the governor that he was now brevetted a colonel. While Byrd took 500 men on to Stalnakers, Stephen remained temporarily at Fort Chiswell to arrange supply trains for flour and cattle. By mid-July he and his 150 men joined Byrd at Stalnakers.[36]

Byrd resigned his commission in late August, and Stephen assumed command of the Virginia expedition. At Stalnakers, Stephen superintended the collection of wagons, supplies, and tools and put his men to "Open the Road." In mid-September Stephen and the Virginia force marched fifty-eight miles to the southwest and made camp eventually on Great Island (at present Kingsport, Tennessee). Stephen wrote Amherst in early October that he had received messages suggesting peace from the Great Warrior (Oconostota), Judd's Friend (Osteneco), and other Cherokee leaders. Some 350 North Carolina troops and 52 Tuscarora Indians arrived at the camp around the beginning of October. Stephen considered that now, with British and provincial forces in the field, the Cherokees would sue for peace.[37]

Grant's army had just fought several skirmishes with the Cherokees and destroyed fifteen Indian towns and crops, coming within 100 miles of the main Cherokee capital, Chota. Stephen thought that although Grant's force was too far away to be much help, it nevertheless was effective in convincing the Indians to cease hostilities. The Cherokees were well restrained: the Virginians threatened from the north and Grant at their eastern flank. The Chickasaws, in lower Tennessee, had switched from ally to enemy of the Cherokees. In late summer the Middle Cherokees started negotiations for peace with Grant, and the Little Carpenter (Attakullakulla) and ten warriors journeyed to Charleston to consult with Governor William Bull. But the parleying dragged on, with talks moved to Fort Prince George, and the Cherokees delayed ratification once peace terms were set. Despite his instructions from General Amherst to bring the Virginia troops to the heart of the Overhill Cherokee country, Stephen, realizing that the Indians were nearly ready for peace, desisted from any further advance.[38] He informed Amherst, in a letter of October 5, that because of the "Submissive messages" he had received from the Indians, he would "take care to promote their good Counsels," but, if necessary, he would conduct "another Stride towards their Country, putting the Crown to as little expence as possible."[39]

While waiting for further responses from the Indians, Stephen erected Fort Robinson, which consisted of a square log fortress, with four bastions, surrounded by a polygonal stockade. Stephen boasted that this installation on Great Island was the only such structure on the far frontier between Forts Pitt and Prince George; it "commands a large River . . . navigable to the Mississippi, & not only awes the Cherokees but Several other Numerous tribes of Indians."[40]

Stephen had knowledge of the pending peace with Grant and the South Carolina government, but he thought it would give greater security to the Virginia frontier to come to separate terms with the Overhill Cherokees. He sent Indian runners through the Overhill country, asking for a treaty conference. Standing Turkey (Connetarke) accepted the invitation and with some 400 warriors headed for Stephen's camp at Great Island. It took this Indian delegation about a month to traverse the 200 miles, because on the way they hunted for subsistence. Finally on November 17 the Indians appeared at Great Island, and a conference ensued over the next several days. Stephen told the Indians "You have escaped very happily!" If they had not sought peace, his troops and those under Grant "must have Effectually ruined your nation." On the twentieth a treaty was signed. It had only two short articles, compared to the much longer twelve-item document waiting to be ratified by the South Carolina authorities and the Cherokees. Stephen's treaty said simply that "the Cherokee Warriors now here, are to bury the Hatchet" and to make "a Firm Peace" with the Tuscarora warriors who were in Stephen's camp; also, "If Murder is Committed by a Cherokee Indian, the Person, or Head of the Murderer is to be Delivered up to the Governor or Commander of the nearest English Fort." The American signatories were Stephen as "Colonel Commandant of the Troops," Col. Hugh Waddell of the North Carolina Regiment, and Virginia captains John NcNeill and Henry Woodward; for the Indians, Standing Turkey and four other Cherokee headmen and two Tuscarora warriors, Colonel Cross and Captain Blunt, signed. Standing Turkey and several warriors traveled to Williamsburg to confer with the governor and council.[41] Thus Adam Stephen on his own initiative brought peace to the Overhill country without a fight, indeed an accomplishment, for other officers might have been more hotheaded and penetrated deeper into the Indian country, causing some bloodshed. Other Cherokees finally ratified the fuller treaty with South Carolina on December 18.[42]

To assure the Cherokees of the good faith of the Virginians, Stephen asked for an officer to volunteer to visit the Cherokee towns. Lt. Henry Timberlake took on the assignment and on his return brought back Judd's Friend, Outacity (Man-killer), Uschefeesy (Great Hunter or Scalper), and other Indians. A few months later, in April 1762, Timberlake and Thomas Sumter led Judd's Friend and a band of seventy Indians to Williamsburg, where they startled the governor and council, who were not expecting them; the Indians were received anyway in the council chamber. Stephen also went to Virginia's capital, at the same time as the Indian delegation, and met with the colony's authorities concerning Indian affairs. Judd's Friend, jealous because his rival, the Little Carpenter, had visited London in 1739–40, insisted that he now be afforded the same treatment. Judd's Friend and several other Indians were sent to England. Unfortunately the interpreter died on the voyage, and in London no one knew the Cherokee language. Nevertheless, they were given royal treatment, being received at court, and had their portraits painted by Sir Joshua Reynolds.[43]

With peace accomplished with the Cherokee Indians, the General Assembly decided not to maintain the fort on Great Island because of difficulty in provisioning it. In early January, Stephen led most of his troops back to Fort Lewis, leaving about 100 men at Great Island and "small parties on the Communication."[44] Stephen had several persons map the eastern Cherokee country as General Amherst had asked him to do. He was pleased to receive a complimentary letter from the British general, forwarded by the governor who noted that Amherst's letter "contains an Approbation of your Conduct; for so able a Commander and so good a Judge."[45] One lasting achievement of Stephen's advance to the Holston was laying a good road, over which thousands would soon travel to the "beckoning land" of southwest Virginia and eastern Tennessee.[46]

It seems that Stephen put up some of his own credit while the army was on the frontier. The expense of conducting the Indian treaty was very great and unexpected because so many Indians had to be boarded. Stephen especially complained that rum "in the wilderness" sold for 8*d*. per gill and five dollars per gallon. There were contingency expenses that he had to meet. While George Washington and William Byrd had a special allowance as commander of the Virginia Regiment, Stephen had none. Stephen even had to give his bond to Adam Hoops, then a subcontractor of Plumsted and Franks, a Philadelphia firm which supplied provisions for the Virginia force. Hoops, whom Stephen said "was a good Sort of Man but a bad Clerk and could Scarcely write his Name," assigned Stephen's bond to Col. John Syme as part of a dowry for Hoops's daughter, Sarah, who married Syme. Apparently the contractors were never fully paid by either the Virginia government or the crown. Many years later Syme sued Stephen unsuccessfully to obtain payment. The suit was again renewed by George Fleming, who had married Syme's daughter. But the bond was "lost," and a key witness, William Murray, who had been an agent for Hoops, had left the United States and was living in Spanish territory. The issue pursued Stephen until the end of his life.[47]

The Cherokee War and diplomacy had broadened Stephen's frontier experience, and he now sought to capitalize on it. He applied for the position of superintendent for Indian affairs in the southern district. The British government had created two such agencies. William Johnson was the northern superintendent. His southern counterpart, Edmund Atkin, had died October 8, 1761. Governor Thomas Boone of South Carolina recommended as Atkin's successor Capt. John Stuart, a Scotsman and Charleston merchant now serving in the South Carolina militia army. Stuart was well known among the Cherokees, who called him "Bushy-head." Maj. Robert Rogers, frontiersman and commander of a ranger company (supported by British funds) during the northern phase of the French and Indian War, also sought the appointment. Stephen recognized the opportunity for financial gain and prestige that the Indian superintendency might confer, and he requested Governor Fauquier to write on his behalf to the Board of Trade. Fauquier perfunctorily complied, telling the board that Stephen "claims some Merit from his long Service and frequent Intercourse with Indians of many Nations, and as I have known him to be a good Officer, I could not deny him this Act of Favor which I hope your Lordships will excuse. But to be well served hereafter, if Occasion should be, I must not refuse to assist Gentlemen on such Applications."[48] The superintendency went to Stuart, who served until the outbreak of the American Revolution. Stephen was not too disappointed. It would not have suited him to spend most of his time among the Indians, at great distances from home. He would have had to treat with all the southern tribes and also keep rein on white traders, most of whom were prohibited by the British "Plan of 1764" from commercial relations with the Indians. Stuart, as it was, found it expedient to make his headquarters at Mobile.

Stephen finally sent General Amherst "a Sketch of the Country towards the Cherokee Country" and also forwarded intelligence, which perhaps showed a gullibility and exaggeration of a kind that would be of concern to George Washington during the Revolution. Amherst thanked Stephen for the map and information but stated "I cannot give Credit to that part of the French having abandon'd the Halboma Fort: Indian News in general are not to be depended on & there is little reason at present to think that the French should be Alarmed in those Quarters."[49]

In February 1762 Governor Fauquier ordered the Virginia force disbanded.[50] The assembly had voted that the troops would receive one year's salary above their regular pay,[51] but the recompense was long delayed. Stephen left Fort Lewis in February to return home. Soon news of Britain's declaration of war on Spain arrived in Virginia. As a result, the assembly decided to retain the Virginia Regiment in service until the final outcome of the European war was known. On April 7, 1762, Fauquier signed into law an act recreating the 1,000-man regiment and, of special interest to Adam Stephen, also providing a levy of 268 troops "to be incorporated in the Regiments of the British Establishment in America."[52]

Having failed to gain the Indian superintendency, Stephen still saw a chance to enter the royal service; this time it would be for a limited period and thus would not compromise too much his farming and other local interests. He believed that if he raised the regular volunteer troops, he would be given their command, or at least that of a company. His point of view was not unlike that of George Washington, who, in accepting the position as a temporary aide-de-camp to General Braddock in 1755, commented that he would have a good opportunity "of forming an acquaintance which may be serviceable hereafter, if I shall find it worth while to push my Fortune in the Military line."[53] Stephen's seeking the appointment indicates that he considered himself at the crossroads between a militiaman and a professional soldier.

Stephen may have been partially motivated by the expectation that a pension would follow a tour of duty as a British regular officer. He was mindful of his brother's experience. Alexander Stephen, serving with the 60th Regiment of the Royal Americans and still suffering greatly from wounds received in Braddock's expedition and in Canada, was now about to retire on half pay. Also, command of a royal company or regiment consisting of Virginians, would give Stephen greater opportunity to sell his flour and livestock to the army at a good price and for hard cash. He had planned to visit General Amherst at his New York headquarters for the purpose of straightening out accounts of the Cherokee campaign, but probably more importantly to lobby on his own behalf for a royal appointment. But with the duty of supervising recruitment in Virginia, he decided not to make the trip.[54]

At Fredericksburg, Stephen discharged troops whose enlistments had expired and at the same time shuffled recruits into the royal service. Stephen's "Scheme" astonished Capt. Robert Stewart, who never missed an opportunity to call George Washington's attention to Stephen's misdoings. Governor Fauquier, Stewart pointed out, was using "his utmost Efforts" to secure for Stephen a royal commission. Stephen's "assurances" from Fauquier were "so strong" that he had already named the subalterns (Charles Cameron, Thomas Gist, and Alexander Menzie) and the sergeants for a royal independent company. But Stewart could not believe that General Amherst would "*give a Compy to a man who has made such a Fortune by the Service* and overlook others who have suffer'd so severely by it." Stewart, of course, was alluding to Stephen's supplying his own flour and beef to Fort Cumberland, the Virginia militia stations, and the western Pennsylvania posts. Furthermore, if Stephen should get a crown military appointment, Stewart noted, "what Perquisites will he not make from his Compy and the Indian Trade &ca."[55]

Stephen continued to direct enlistments for service of both the colony and the crown. The £10 bounty allowed by the assembly applied to provincial and regular enlistment alike. Each recruit was to be properly clothed: a coat, waistcoat, breeches, two shirts, shoes, stockings, hat, comb, and a blanket in addition to a canteen, kettle, knapsack, haversack, and "such usual Necessaries." An officer was afforded 1s. per day subsistence for each recruit "till regularly passed" and 30s. for his own expenses. The enlistees were not to be under age eighteen or over forty, but, as Stephen advised, "You are not to regard the Size of the men provided they be young healthy able Bodie & have good Eyes." Those entering the royal service were to remain on duty until the British troops returned home.[56]

Despite the feeling of many of Stephen's veterans that they had been "defrauded of pay" thus far, the new recruiting program was successful; many of the old soldiers reenlisted. General Amherst ordered tents sent to Virginia to supply all the new troops. Even with an outbreak of smallpox among the recruits at Fredericksburg, Stephen at the end of June forwarded 189 men for the British service, leaving "about 500 good men" at Fredericksburg "besides Several Recruiting parties out." The new regulars embarked from Hampton in a vessel sent from New York by Amherst.[57] The British commander in chief thanked Stephen for his efforts and said that he was sending another ship to pick up additional regulars.[58] Though Stephen was actually reducing the pool of men by signing up recruits for the royal service, he also had some success in getting men to enlist in the Virginia Regiment.[59]

By early August 1762 Stephen considered his recruiting task all but finished. Though the Virginia Regiment numbered only 535 rank and file, this was enough men for the time being, with no military operations pending. For the British service 320 men were enlisted, although Lt. Donald Campbell, whom Amherst sent to Virginia to receive the recruits, refused to accept 80 of them for being undersized. As for the Virginia Regiment, Stephen informed Amherst, it was unlikely that the legislature would raise more money for its support if the "unsteadiness" and "present Temper" of the people continued, "which is a weighty Reason with me for completing the Quota for the British Battalions, as they are irrevocable by an Assembly." Stephen used the opportunity to prod Amherst further about a military appointment, mentioning that he had been at considerable expense in raising the troops.[60]

By December 1762 it was evident that the war with the French and Spaniards was over, with news expected any day of the signing of peace treaties. Thus there was no further need to incorporate provincial troops into the British army. Stephen did not get a royal commission. The Virginia governor ordered the colony's regiment disbanded for the second and last time, and Stephen proceeded to discharge the men and give them their final pay.[61] At Fredericksburg on December 10 Stephen, as he prepared to relinquish his militia command, sent a letter to the Speaker of the House of Burgesses, expressing appreciation for "the extreme genteel Gratuity voted to the Officers." Stephen assured the legislators that in any "future Commotions" he and his fellow officers "will cherfully evince, by the most spirited Exertion of our best Endeavours to maintain the Honor and Safety of the Colony, which we have so long had the Honour to serve."[62]

Like so many veterans of the French and Indian War, who had viewed firsthand the unlimited expanse of virgin territory on the frontier, Stephen hoped to speculate in western lands. He also took advantage of opportunity closer to home. In July 1762 he acquired from the Fairfax proprietary 137 acres at the foot of Bear Garden Mountain along a branch of the Great Cacapon River in Hampshire County and, in February 1763, 1,000 acres "on the Drains" of Opequon Creek and the Shenandoah River. The quitrent was the usual 1s. per 50 acres.[63]

In addition to the lands promised by Governor Dinwiddie's 1754 proclamation, Stephen soon learned that he would be entitled to 5,000 acres, owing to his military service, by the Proclamation of 1763. He also expected additional opportunity for speculative acquisition of western lands. Hoping to make the British government more aware that the Virginia officers deserved to be recipients of frontier territory, Stephen and Andrew Lewis joined with Washington in sending to the king a "Memorial" on behalf of themselves "and the rest of the surviving Officers and Soldiers who enlisted in the Service of your Majesties late royal Grandfather (of beloved memory) for the Defence and Security" of Virginia. The address noted that the memoralists were among the first engaged in the king's service and continued "as long as they were wanted."[64]

Four months before the issuance of the Proclamation of 1763, Stephen had met with Washington and seventeen other Potomac Valley men, probably at the Stafford Courthouse, to organize the Mississippi Company. Stephen, with the others, signed the articles on June 3, 1763. The company was to consist of fifty persons, each of whom should be entitled to 50,000 acres of a 2½ million-acre grant they hoped would be conferred by the king. The territory would be located in the upper Mississippi Valley, bounded on the east by the Wabash and Tennessee rivers and on the west by the Mississippi. Each shareholder had one vote, but he could not dispose of his lands without the consent of the other members. Royal troops were to afford protection from the Indians. The company would be free of quitrents for twelve years, after which time members were to have fully settled the area. Arthur Lee was sent to England to lobby for the grant from the king. It was a bad time to seek such a charter, with the new imperial prohibition on western land settlement included in the Proclamation of 1763; moreover, Lee was temperamentally unsuited for his task, possessing little tact or delicacy. Decision on the Mississippi Company plan was delayed for several years. Eventually Lord Hillsborough, appointed to the new post of secretary of state for the colonies in 1768, refused to endorse the project, and he made it known that no lands would be granted west of a line running from the Kanawha River to Chiswell's mines on the New River near the Virginia–North Carolina border. Lee then proferred a second request that the company would be contented with a different grant, namely between 38° and 42° just west of the Alleghenies. Lee's petition, bearing thirty-six names including that of Stephen's, was read in the Privy Council on December 16, 1768, and then referred to the Board of Trade, which tabled it. Members of the Mississippi Company did not push their plan with the crown authorities because many of them also belonged to the

Ohio Company, which was considered to have a better chance of success.[65] Thus one opportunity for Stephen to become a big speculator in lands faded.

Yet as fate would have it, Stephen would be summoned again to view territory on the Allegheny frontier, not at the behest of land surveys or the like—but because the Indians of the Ohio country were once more on the rampage. There seemed to be no relief from military duty. Though 1763 had witnessed the official end of the French and Indian War, service again called for defense of the northern Virginia frontier against Indian aggression.

SIX

"Such Principles
and Such Behaviour"

J ust as Adam Stephen was becoming accustomed to being a civilian and a full-time gentleman farmer, he again answered a call to arms. Indian hostility flared up throughout the Northwest, along the frontiers of Virginia, Pennsylvania, and New York, in late spring 1763. Stephen would command militia from western Virginia for the purpose of thwarting Indian depredations. The situation, however, differed from the experiences of the past decade; the colony now was reluctant to allow its soldiers to serve beyond its own borders.

War parties of a dozen to fifty warriors from the Ohio country raided isolated settlements along the river valleys of western Virginia. Farther distant, Pontiac's rebellion engulfed the northern frontier, beginning with the siege of Detroit in early May and then followed by attacks on all the posts on the Great Lakes and the western Pennsylvania frontier. Of the forts west and above Fort Pitt, only Detroit and Niagara were not taken by the Indians. Forts Pitt, Bedford, and Ligonier, where Stephen had lodged so much time, were for a period under siege. About every tribe of the northwestern country was involved in the Indian warfare—Ottawa, Wyandot, Chippewa, Potowatomie, Delaware, Shawnee, Mingo, Huron, and Seneca.[1]

Prompted by General Amherst in New York, the Virginia assembly took quick action, calling up 1,000 experienced woodsmen from the militia to serve chiefly on patrols of thirty or more to scout for Indians and pursue them. The field militia consisted of two divisions. Stephen was appointed commander of the troops from the northwest sector of the colony and was authorized to draft men from Hampshire, Frederick, Culpeper, Fauquier, and Loudoun counties for the protection of the frontier from the Potomac River to the southern boundary of the Fairfax proprietary. Col. Andrew Lewis took charge of the southwest militia (from Halifax, Bedford, Amherst, Albemarle, Louisa, and Augusta counties), who would cover settlements from Lord Fairfax's line to the Carolina border.[2] William Greene of Culpeper County congratulated Stephen on his new assignment: "You being appointed to Command on the Frontier in so Dangerous a Juncture, is a Circumstance extremely pleasing to me, & I doubt not must be so to every Lover of his Country."[3] George Washington was less pleased with Stephen's new role. Writing to Robert Stewart, he commented wryly that 500 of the troops were "under the command of Collo. Stephen whose Military Courage and Capacity (says the Governor) is well established. . . . Stephens immediately upon the Indians retiring, advanced to Fort Cumberland with 200 or 250 Militia in great parade."[4]

Washington was not quite correct. On his way to Fort Cumberland, Stephen had to be constantly on the watch for Indian attack. Discovering some tracks at Patterson Creek, he sent out a detachment under Capt. William Crawford in pursuit. About twenty-five miles from Fort Cumberland, Crawford caught up with a warrior party and in the ensuing fight killed and scalped an Indian, wounded several others, and recovered two white prisoners and plunder. Stephen asked the governor to authorize building a fort on Patterson Creek, but Fauquier said there was no money available for the project and that the settlers could erect it themselves.[5]

General Amherst directed Stephen to lead some of his troops to Pennsylvania and there employ them "in keeping open the Communication" between Forts Bedford and Pitt; the men would also be used as "alert partys" to "Act Offensively against any of the Lurking Villains." Help from Virginia was all the more necessary because of inaction by the Pennsylvania government. By Stephen's bringing up troops, Virginia will have "the Honor of not only Driving the Enemy from its own Settlements, but that of protecting those of its Neighbours who have not Spirit to Defend themselves."[6]

About the time that Stephen set out for Pennsylvania with a body of militia volunteers, in mid-August, he received the surprising news that Col. Henry Bouquet had defeated the Indians at what has become known as the battle of Bushy Run on August 5–6. The fight took place along Stephen's old supply route between Forts Ligonier and Pitt. Bouquet, with 400 men (the 42d or Black Watch and 77th regiments), was escorting a large supply convoy for the relief of Fort Pitt. In the two-day engagement, the British lost 50 killed, 60 wounded, and 5 missing; the Indians had 60 dead. Bouquet and his provisions train then continued to Fort Pitt.[7]

Stephen and his detachment of ninety-eight men and ten captains arrived at Fort Bedford on August 19. Capt. Lewis Ourry, who had no liking for the Virginia colonel, commented that Stephen "with the Officers & Lady that accompanied him" barged in at dinnertime "without any previous Notice." Ourry was disgusted that he could not obtain any assistance from the Virginians. None of Stephen's men would volunteer to form an escort for a cattle drive to Fort Ligonier. Stephen's troops were also needed as scouts. Ourry complained: "So after living on the King's Provisions & my Keep 2 or 3 Days they marched back again to cover their Frontiers." It also seemed to Ourry that Stephen's patriotism was affected by a profit motive. Stephen "did not come absolutely for nothing," for he made an agreement with an agent of the army contractors, Plumsted and Franks, to deliver at Fort Bedford fifty or sixty head of cattle by September 20 and 15,000 pounds of flour by October 10, with the total delivery of 45,000 pounds of flour by December 10. Stephen would be paid in cash.[8] This business completed, Stephen led the Virginians back to Winchester.[9] That Stephen had so many officers with him and that they did not object to the brevity of the stay in Pennsylvania suggests that some of them, too, were searching for business arrangements in supplying the army.

At Winchester, Stephen found a welcome letter from the governor. "Your Zeal, prudence, and activity in the Defence of the Frontiers," said Fauquier, "fully answers my Expectations."[10] At least to Stephen's credit he had raised troops. Stephen was gratified that the

Virginia government was willing to keep the men under his command in the field a while longer, because of fear that the Indians might seek revenge along the Virginia frontier for their defeat at Bushy Run.[11] Indeed, there were a number of Indian raids in the backcountry from late August to October.[12] Stephen called for more militia from the counties,[13] and he also asked for volunteers who would assist in protecting the supply line in Pennsylvania and would be available for an expedition into the Ohio country. General Amherst was hoping that Stephen and Virginia volunteers would join the royal troops under Colonel Bouquet at Fort Pitt for a march against the Shawnee towns along the Scioto River.[14]

Stephen was a little rueful that he had missed the battle of Bushy Run and, of course, the glory in which he would have shared. Maybe the Virginians could yet participate in an offensive action. In a letter of September 15 congratulating Bouquet on his victory, Stephen said that he would probably be able to forward some volunteers, but because by law he could not order any militia out of the colony, "it must rest on perswasive means, all that is to be expected from me on the Communication." He also suggested that if a fort should be erected at Redstone Creek, it would be possible that "the Virginians would be prevailed on to maintain it, as it greatly Covers their frontiers."[15]

Bouquet encouraged Stephen to bring up Virginia volunteers so that an expedition could be mounted against the Ohio Indians before winter. The British colonel commended Stephen for his interest in the project. "I had too long experienced and known your Zeal for the Service," he said, "to be surprised at the Intention you express to follow this lucky blow by procuring a Party of Volunteers from the Men under your Command to make some New Attempt that might compell the Villains to Submit." Ammunition, provisions, and boats were on hand to support an invasion of the Indian country. "You would have the Command of the most Promising Expedition that has been Attempted yet against the Savages," Bouquet told Stephen, and would "obtain great Honour to your Government and to yourself by so great and Seasonable a Service." A 700-man force, with one-half of them provided by Stephen, could destroy all the Indian settlements between Fort Pitt and the Wabash

River.[16] Bouquet informed General Amherst that he had complete confidence in Stephen as "a Man of Resolution, and in my opinion very capable of Executing this Commission."[17]

There was no support, however, among the colony's leaders for sending volunteers to join in a western campaign against the Indians. Stephen received no instructions from Governor Fauquier, who was attending an Indian conference at Augusta, Georgia. He sent letters pertaining to the advantages of an Indian campaign to the president of the Council, the Speaker of the House of Burgesses, and various legislators, which brought almost no response. When he did hear from the Council, he was told that members were greatly pleased "to find such a Spirit in the People on the frontiers," but nothing could be done to give Stephen any aid toward an expeditionary force until the governor returned.[18]

Stephen, therefore, acted on his own initiative. He sent 100 volunteers under Capt. John Field to join Maj. Allan Campbell and British 42d Regiment "to assist in carrying the grand Convoy" from Fort Bedford to Fort Pitt. The Virginians could also be used "to forward" the "Designs against the Indian Settlements." Stephen thought he could eventually have 1,000 men for the Indian expedition, but he realized that such a goal could not be accomplished immediately. It would take time to obtain enough volunteer militia from Virginia's frontier counties. Provisions had to be collected. There was still the problem of sending militia outside the colony, and, besides, as he told Bouquet, "the Gentlemen of Rank in Virginia Seem to be turned so great Oeconomists."[19] It was also getting too late in the year to field a full volunteer force for an Indian campaign. Amherst himself informed Stephen that it was now best to wait until spring. Gen. Thomas Gage, who succeeded Amherst in November, expressed the same view; he was willing, however, to have the crown pay for a later expedition that would consist of both British and Stephen's troops. Meanwhile Stephen received orders from the Virginia council to discharge most of the militia and also "a genteel reprimand" for having sent some of them out of the colony; there was also a "hint" that the troops who went to Pennsylvania would not be paid.[20]

If Stephen was having problems in sending Virginia troops to assist British regulars in Pennsylvania, he could, nevertheless, use his army connections to turn a profit. He sent ninety-five head of cattle and some hogs to Fort Bedford, although not exactly to the satisfaction of the representative of the chief army contractor, the firm of William Plumsted and David Franks. He fell far short of the amount of flour promised and missed the October date for the first shipment by one month. In November, Stephen informed Bouquet that he had 100,000 pounds of flour, which he hoped to send between Christmas and April.[21] But because Stephen's initial shipment of flour had not arrived on time at Fort Bedford, Bouquet refused to have any more accepted for the army. This decision led to bad feelings between Stephen and Bouquet, whereas before there had been a mutual respect and admiration between them. Stephen wrote Bouquet on April 16, 1764, voicing his complaint. He said that a large part of his flour had been used by the militia at Patterson Creek, but he had 26,000 pounds at Fort Cumberland, which "lies in a hundred dollars worth of good Bags." If Bouquet would take it, Stephen would "endeavour to Return the favour." The flour "is of good Quality, as any designed for the West Indian Market, & the bags of New Sacking." Stephen intimated that the army's purchase of the new flour would not lead him to seek redress for the flour that had been rejected. "Your Sentiments on this head," he told Bouquet, "will determine whether I shall be Obliged to Wait on the Genl [Gage] about the affair."[22]

Bouquet responded by saying that he was sorry that Stephen became "a sufferer" by Bouquet's refusal to accept the flour, but Stephen had only himself to blame for the delay. Stephen had been given the contract and the promise of a high price "upon express Condition of it being delivered at a certain time at Bedford where it was not wanted for that Post, but to be forwarded with the Convoys to Fort Pitt, and you know that it was but a certain period that I could procure sufficient Escorts."[23]

The estranged relations between the two men undoubtedly tempered Stephen's zeal to field a Virginia volunteer force to assist Bouquet in an Indian campaign. Bouquet, nevertheless, in the spring applied to the Virginia government for militia volunteers. The council insisted that Governor Fauquier not commit any support to troops going out of the colony; if volunteers went, they would not be paid. This policy also meant that Virginia troops also would not be supplied or paid for the escort of provisions "thro' Roads which do not pass thro' the Colony," as Fauquier told Bouquet. "The Militia are calld out merely to protect the Inhabitants of the back Settlements, and can be employed to no other purpose." The 250 men available to Stephen and Colonel Lewis's 450 men were to be used chiefly "to pursue any parties of Indians who make Irruptions into the Colony."[24] Stephen even had to withdraw what militia he had at Fort Cumberland, because this post was located in Maryland.[25]

Renewed Indian hostilities in spring 1764 made it all the more imperative to keep the colony's militia within its borders. In late May a large party of Indians fell upon settlers working in fields near Fort Dinwiddie in Augusta County, with fifteen of the farmers killed, fifteen wounded, and sixteen made captives. There were casualties elsewhere. In early June a man and his wife and child were taken by the Indians within ten miles of Winchester.[26]

Yet there was still a possibility that a Virginia volunteer force could be raised to assist Bouquet in the western Indian campaign. The only legal restriction on Virginia participants was simply that they would not be supported or paid by the colony. Colonel Bouquet on July 5 wrote Stephen requesting that he "give Encouragement to good Woodsmen on Your Frontiers to join as Voluntiers the Troops under my Command"; they would not be paid but would receive provisions and ammunition at Fort Cumberland. The volunteers should march up Braddock's road to Fort Pitt about September 25. Pennsylvania was contributing 1,000 provincials to join the regulars and also providing "a Considerable Reward for Scalps, which no doubt will be a Strong inducement." Only 300 to 400 troops were needed from Virginia.[27]

But Stephen was not willing to endure all the trouble he had experienced the previous fall in attempting to raise a volunteer force. The colony's authorities had given him no support then and would not do so now. Besides, Stephen harbored a grudge against Bouquet for not accepting his flour. Why should he do Bouquet any special favor? It seems that Stephen refused to take any active role in collecting volunteers. Rather, it was now Col. Andrew Lewis who assumed responsibility for fielding a volunteer force. Lewis proposed to lead 300 to 400 Virginia militia to the mouth of the Great Kanawha River simultaneously as Bouquet troops left Fort Pitt to cross the Ohio. The Indians thus would have to face two different bodies of troops at the same time.[28] Maj. John Field wrote Bouquet from Winchester that because Stephen "at the helm of affairs is Discouraging the Expedition greatly," he himself would bring "a large party of Volunteers" to Fort Pitt by September 25.[29]

Capt. Thomas Rutherford of Frederick County complained to Bouquet that Colonel Stephen was doing his utmost to thwart enlistment for the Indian campaign. Stephen and "Some of his Sycofants are constantly bawling out that the Government is capable of undertaking and Executing an Expedition against the Enemy, and then Its Scandalous to Join another," said Rutherford; "this argument Points out the motives of his opinion, it is a thousand pities that Such Principles and Such behaviour could not be examined into and Receive their due Reward."[30] But Stephen denied that he was discouraging recruitment of volunteers for the western Indian expedition. He issued a declaration to the militia of Hampshire and Frederick counties, saying that although he could not promise any pay for those leaving the colony, persons serving in the Indian campaign certainly would be accorded "proper notice" for their efforts.[31]

Rutherford, a justice of the peace for Frederick County, was determined to expose further Stephen's hypocrisy. He collected depositions and sent copies to the governor and council, the House of Burgesses, and Colonel Bouquet. Capt. Jacquett Morgan, one of the deponents, though he had been discharged by Stephen, raised twenty volunteers for the western expedition. He and his men met with Stephen, who used every argument he could to dissuade them "from prosecuting their Design." Later Stephen threatened Morgan that if he persisted on joining Bouquet, he would never again hold a commission. Lt. James Chew testified to the same and said that Stephen "appeared to be in a great passion" and told him "that he and the Rest of the Company were a sett of silly foolish fellows, and that the Scheme was mad." Other deponents referred to similar behavior by Stephen.[32]

Governor Fauquier defended Stephen to Bouquet. Although

Fauquier encouraged the volunteer recruiting, he emphasized that such troops had to be raised under Bouquet's authority and be put in the king's service. The governor could do nothing to obtain pay for the volunteers, nor could he give them any marching orders.[33] To clear any apprehension that Colonel Bouquet might have that he was obstructing the war effort, Stephen went to Fort Bedford to meet personally with the British commander. But Bouquet was away. Stephen left him a note explaining his role thus far in the "Voluntier Scheme." He pointed out that he had retained in militia pay those who planned to go on the expedition, and as encouragement to recruiting he had announced that the colony would give recognition to campaign service and that there would be "the Chance of Plunder, the Reward for Scalps."[34]

It seems that the accusations against Stephen came from men whom he had discharged. Both Stephen and Lewis had orders from the governor to muster out 150 men each. Charges against Lewis for obstructing volunteering also were made, almost exclusively by those who had been dismissed. Governor Fauquier wrote Bouquet that he hoped "the complaints against Colonel Stephen will upon Enquiry turn out as groundless as those against Colonel Lewis did." The governor nevertheless asked the council to look into the Rutherford charges against Stephen.[35] Bouquet did not take Stephen at his word and was still convinced that Stephen was doing all he could to dissuade men from joining the Indian expedition. He notified General Gage of Stephen's alleged conduct, which "is highly blamable," and said that he had asked Governor Fauquier to appoint someone else to Stephen's militia command, "as I can no longer Correspond with, nor place any Confidence in a man who uses his Power" and "his Place" to "obstruct so essentially the Service."[36]

It was ironical that the Virginia authorities would encourage enlistment in the proposed Indian campaign and yet not provide any material support for it. Both the council and the House of Burgesses conducted hearings on the charges that Stephen had obstructed the king's service. But by the time each chamber got around to Stephen's case, the controversy had become moot, because the western expedition had finally taken place. Andrew Lewis and 200 Virginia volunteers joined Bouquet in September 1764. While Col.

John Bradstreet marched from Niagara to relieve the siege of Detroit and subsequently brought the Indians to peace terms, Bouquet and Lewis took their men through the eastern Ohio country, where bloodshed was also avoided, much to the disappointment of the Virginia frontiersmen who had been eager for a fight; the Shawnees and Delawares were also quite willing to negotiate peace. Stephen was happy he had stayed away from the volunteer expedition; not only was there no fighting and therefore no glory, the Virginia government was true to its word and refused to offer any monetary recompense for those who had served.[37]

On November 6, 1764, the council minutes noted: "The Complaint against Colonel Stephen for obstructing his Majesty's Service, in respect to the Expedition carried on by Colonel Bouquet against the Shawnese and Delawares, was this day inquird into; as in the course of the trial Colonel Stephen was accused of some other things." The council called for a postponement of the hearing until April 1765. Rutherford was ordered to deliver in writing his particular charges against Stephen, and depositions were to be taken in the presence of both Rutherford and Stephen in Winchester on March 3, 1765, before justices of the peace Thomas Bryan Martin, John Neville, and Burr (or Matthew?) Harrison.[38] The council, however, seems to have dropped any further consideration of Stephen's case.

The House of Burgesses gave the complaints against Stephen a much more thorough and volatile airing. A motion was made to raise Stephen's militia pay "above that of a County Lieutenant in Service." Rutherford, a member of the House of Burgesses, used this opportunity to introduce a set of charges against Stephen, including peculation. The accusations were threefold. First, Stephen had "by Persuasions, Orders, Threats, and Influence, prevented many Persons from joining as Volunteers in the Expedition commanded by Col. *Bouquet* against the *Indian* Towns the *Ohio*, &c." Second, Stephen had at various times ordered militia out of the colony to Forts Cumberland and Bedford for the purpose of escorting wagons and packhorses, "with Flower and Beeves, his own Property, in Compliance with his own private Engagements, &c"; in doing so, militia serving Stephen in a private capacity left "the several Garrisons from whence they were taken so weak that they were insufficient to protect the Frontiers from the Incursions of the Indians." While the posts were understaffed, Indians "did actually come down within the Settlements, and kill and carry away many of the Inhabitants." Third, Stephen had sent wagons from the South Branch of the Potomac "to *Hite's Mill*, near his own Plantation, for his own Flower, to supply the several Garrisons on the Frontiers, when the same might have been had much nearer, as cheap and as good."

Depositions were ordered by the House of Burgesses to be taken on behalf of both Rutherford and Stephen before the Frederick County court in Winchester on November 26. The occasion was publicly advertised. Many persons attended the meeting, and if Thomas Barnsley is to believed, 100 "oaths" were "taken" against Stephen. Stephen, however, did not appear at the meeting and instead went to the capital to present his side to the legislators; perhaps he was allowed to attend the examination of the case by the House of Burgesses.[39] The Committee on Propositions and Grievances of the house had the responsibility of considering the controversy and reporting its recommendations to the full house. After "three Days strict Inquisition," on December 15 the committee presented its report, which the house approved in its entirety. It was resolved that Stephen "has not fully acquitted himself of the first Article of the said Charge"; as to the second, Stephen "was guilty of a Breach of Duty in sending out Escorts of the Militia under his Command in such Services"; of the third, Stephen "hath acquitted himself." The house voted that Stephen should receive pay of a county lieutenant "only during the Time he was employed in the Service of the Country." Taking note of his overall service, the house finally resolved: "That Col. *Adam Stephen* hath discharged his Duty (saving in the two Instances before mentioned) as a brave, active, and skilful Officer."[40] Nevertheless, Stephen's reputation was impaired because of the proven conflict of interest.

Rutherford got some satisfaction over the house's decision. He wrote Bouquet that he had clearly proved his case against Stephen and "had a very great majority of the House in my Interest." Stephen "is loaded with his own expences" and did not get any more pay than that of a county lieutenant; "the two put together cuts him Short of about four hundred pounds our Currency, which with the light Brand he had Received on the Jounrals of his country I hope will be a warning to him in cases of the like Nature."[41]

Given all the problems he was having, Stephen was glad to put active military duty behind him. Peace had been restored to the frontier. He had achieved one ambition—for a time, command of the colony's army. He still kept some contact with the local citizen-militia by serving as county lieutenant for Frederick County, mostly an administrative post requiring little effort but important politically. He could now devote greater attention to another goal—attaining wealth and thereby entering into the ranks of the upper gentry, with all the accompanying perquisites of power and influence. Particularly, substantial landholdings afforded a mark of genteel distinction.

Stephen expanded his real estate close to home. In April 1764 he bought 212 acres on Mossey Creek and two tracts (170 and 400 acres) along the North River. In 1770 he acquired 255 acres from Morgan Morgan, Jr., along Tuscarora Creek, which he would later develop into a town site.[42] Stephen continued to take up unimproved lands of the Fairfax proprietary, for which his brother Robert was now the collector. In 1765 he received 386 acres on Opequon Creek in Frederick County and, in 1770, 542 acres on Patterson Creek in Hampshire County, as before for the quitrent of 1s. per 50 acres.[43] Stephen, like other settlers in the lower Valley, probably hoped that the westernmost claims of the proprietary might eventually be declared beyond the actual Fairfax grant and hence free from any dues owed the proprietor. Much of the Fairfax lands taken up were intended for speculation, and the grantees were frequently delinquent in paying quitrents.

Stephen and other Virginia veterans awaited confirmation of lands claimed under Governor Dinwiddie's 1754 proclamation and the Proclamation of 1763. The lands were being staked out along the Monongahela, New River, Great Kanawha, Sandy Creek, and adjacent streams. The veterans petitioned the governor and council on December 15, 1769, to issue warrants for the bounty lands. One factor that had caused delay was that the claims lay in the territory prohibited for settlement by the Proclamation of 1763. But in 1768, with the treaties of Fort Stanwix and Hard Labor, the barrier was moved far enough west to accommodate the area intended for the land bounty grants. The officers had to pay for the surveys of the lands they intended to take up, and Stephen contributed some funds toward staking out his claims. Prompted by further petitions from Washington and other officer veterans, the Virginia government validated surveys and claims in the early 1770s. But it was not until 1781 that warrants were finally issued by the state for the lands. Stephen received warrants for 5,000 acres as a field officer in Colonel Byrd's regiment; 5,000 acres for the same under George Washington; 5,000 acres as a field officer and also 3,000 acres as a captain in Colonel Fry's regiment; another 3,000 acres as a captain; and 2,000 acres as paymaster. Stephen would also eventually fall heir to the 2,000 acres given his brother Alexander. As did most of the officers, Stephen seems to have disposed of much of his bounty lands early, though at the time of his death he still held some of the land warrants, which were eventually inherited by his daughter's second husband, Moses Hunter.[44]

Although there was little, if any, immediate profit to be made from these western lands, there could be ample rewards from farming in the fertile lower Valley. Like other Virginians after midcentury, Stephen turned to crop diversification. For the market he raised wheat and hemp, which were especially suited to the rich Valley soils. Instead of fluctuating in price as tobacco did, wheat steadily rose in value, from 3.32s. per bushel in 1720 to 6.42s. in 1775. Even without manuring his fields (most planters did not), Stephen could expect an average yield of twelve bushels of wheat per acre. He usually transported grain in his own wagons and sold directly to wholesalers. Virginia wheat was much in demand at North American coastal communities, especially in New England, and it was also exported to southern Europe, the Azores and Canary Islands, and the West Indies. Usually Stephen brought his flour to Alexandria, where he had a choice of about twenty merchants with whom to deal. The Great Wagon Road passed through Frederick County and Winchester, and Stephen sent grain, hemp, and cattle along this busiest thoroughfare in America to Philadelphia.[45] For goods purchased, Stephen, as did most planters, relied on barter exchange, because sound money was scarce.[46]

Stephen also had business connections at Fredericksburg/Falmouth on the upper Rappahannock. Good roads led from various places in the Northern Neck to this port location. Dr. Hugh Mercer, also a war veteran and Scotsman, handled some of Stephen's transactions with the firm of McLean and Stuart of Philadelphia (for example, for wine and "essence of lemon") and also supplied from his apothecary shop medicinal items ordered by Stephen, such as oil of amber, "Emollient Gargle," manna (a laxative), blistering plaster, almond guiacum, balsam, febrifuge, "Bark in powder," camphor, scopolamine, chamomile, and anodyne in various forms— drops, pills, boluses, or "Mixture." Stephen wrote Mercer in August 1765 that he was ashamed to be so long settling his accounts, but "disappointment & the Dearness of Cash" had caused the delay. "I have hemp enough," said Stephen, "& as soon as I can get it to Market, I will remember you upon Honor." Mercer had to take Stephen to court to collect on the amount of £7.11.6.[47] In 1767 the firm of Stewart and Campbell brought suit for "a Plea of Debt" against Stephen for £68 and £10 damages, which ended up before the colony's General Court. Governor Fauquier signed an arrest warrant for Stephen confining him until the trial in Williamsburg.[48] The resolution of this suit is not known.

Not having to participate in the actual work on his plantation, Stephen found time again to practice medicine, which he had enjoyed doing many years before. As a general practitioner he got to know his neighbors better and perhaps earned a little cash in barter or money. The lower Valley had a scarcity of doctors, and Stephen, with medical and surgical skills, could hardly deny assistance when called upon to ease suffering. That Stephen engaged rather substantially in his former calling is evidenced by the large orders for medicine he placed with Dr. Mercer in Fredericksburg. He regularly made house calls. On one occasion when he was unable to visit a patient, he wrote her husband, explaining what should be done.

I am a good deal hurt by my horse falling down with me, & cannot wait on Mrs Brown today, but I hope to morrow or next day shall be able to ride— She has been kept too warm, and perhaps has taken too [forcing?] things—

You will have her kept off the bed as much as She conveniently Can; let her have free Air, but not expos'd to a draught between doors, or Sitting at a Window—I have her feet bathd at least once a day in Warm Water & bleed her in one or both—The Chillingness is owing to State of her blood; it will be remov'd by moderate Air, and taking the Medicines sent per boy. Give as much as will ly on a pistrine [pistareen, a Spanish coin], of the powder every third hour when well dissolved in Rennet whey; or any Tea She likes—Between every dose of the powder give 20 drops of what is in the phial, in Cool Water or any Tea She likes, give her nothing hot, or Chilly Cold—Please God, She will soon be set to Rights—The State of her blood Makes her low Spirited—The Child's purging & fevers is owing to teething, I will bring something for him; Let her take Nothing from the good Women, before I see her, & I am perswaded she will get well soon.[49]

Stephen probably offered some medical assistance to his brother Alexander, who was partially disabled from the war and in declining health. Alexander frequently visited the nearby Berkeley Springs (then usually called Warm Springs or Frederick Springs), as did the sick and lame from throughout Virginia. The Springs was a popular resort among the able-bodied, too, even though its reputation was somewhat tarnished because it attracted loose women.[50] George Washington had a cottage there, as did the Fairfaxes, and in summertime Washington occasionally would take Martha and the two Custis children, Patsy and Jacky, in tow for a trip to the Springs.[51]

Despite their touchy relationship, Adam Stephen called on Washington at Berkeley Springs, on August 28, 1769, and dined with him and other guests—Lord Fairfax, the Reverend William Meldrum, and a Mr. Allan.[52] Apparently Washington and Stephen patched up some of their differences. The following year when Washington set off for his tour of lands on the Ohio he apprised Stephen of his impending journey. Stephen, of course, had much interest in the western claims and met with Washington at the home of William Crawford, now the official surveyor of the bounty lands. Crawford lived along the Youghiogheny River near present-day Connellsville, Pennsylvania.[53]

Adam Stephen's brother Alexander Stephen died May 8, 1768. An obituary mentioned that he "was a Gentleman of Integrity and Bravery" and cited his military record. Alexander had saved the colors of the 44th Regiment at Braddock's defeat. He was twice wounded in that battle; he had also fought in the English capture of Quebec and Louisbourg and at the unsuccessful attack on Quebec by the French in April 1760. In the latter engagement he "received a dangerous Wound, of which he never perfectly recovered."[54] Three brothers—Adam, John, and Robert—and two sisters in England were the next of kin. John was named executor for the estate and inherited the Virginia lands. The two sisters were to divide £40 that was still in the hands of Alexander's agent in London; another £40 was left to cover funeral expenses. Any money remaining was to go to "Miss Pheby Semans" (Phoebe Seaman), and she also received "my Gold Buttons and my Buckles." It seems Adam and Alexander Stephen may have had some kind of falling out at one time (perhaps including romantic rivalry over Phoebe, Alexander's and then Adam's housekeeper and also the putative mother of Adam's daughter), as suggested by a reference in Alexander's will to Adam which stated that "the Collo had Some trouble with me." Alexander left Adam "my Sword & Sheath if he Choose to accept them."[55] Alexander's military lands probably came to Adam Stephen upon the death of John Stephen.

As a leading planter, Adam Stephen assumed community responsibility and undoubtedly again was looking forward to holding colonywide public office. Persons who were elected burgesses or were appointed to government posts at the colony level almost without exception had served the local constituencies in various capacities. Thus Stephen was a vestryman, justice of the peace, county lieutenant, and sheriff (when the new county of Berkeley was created in 1772). He was a member of the vestry for Norborne Parish, established in 1771 (with boundaries coterminous with present-day Jefferson, Berkeley, and Morgan counties), and served in this position until 1776. Samuel Washington, George's brother, was the senior warden.[56] Among the duties of vestryman were to determine the tax support for the church, verify boundaries, maintain roads and ferries leading to churches, collect debts due the parish, build churches and oversee their upkeep, direct poor relief, and take care of the glebe. The parish at the time had only one town—Mecklenberg (incorporated in 1762 and later named Shepherdstown). Stephen probably attended services at the parish church, St.

George's Chapel (built 1770–72), at Worthington marsh, seven miles southeast of his plantation and a mile and a half from what would later become Charles Town. After the founding of Martinsburg, he most likely attended services in a chapel which was erected there toward the end of the Revolutionary War.[57]

From 1764 to early 1772 Stephen was a justice of the peace for Frederick County. The number of justices varied according to counties, but the average at this time was between ten and fifteen. The office brought no compensation of any kind but conferred power and prestige. The primary function of the justices was to preside over the county court, which had both judicial and administrative duties. Stephen attended the court infrequently, but this was not uncommon because only four justices constituted a quorum, and more than that number rarely were present at any given court session. Because of their busy schedules and the demands of the court on time and energy, the gentlemen justices distributed the amount of attendance among themselves, with the senior members taking the greater responsibility. For hearing matters of major importance, however, a quorum was expected.[58] Among Stephen's varied duties as justice of the peace, besides sitting on the court, were receiving the membership list of the Hopewell Meeting of Quakers in January 1768 (as required by law); taking depositions, such as those regarding proof of age; and, along with other justices, serving in an examiner's court to certify the binding of persons accused of certain felonies over for trial in the colony's General Court.[59]

As county lieutenant, Stephen watched for any potential disruption in Indian-white relations along the sprawling mountainous frontier beyond Frederick County. In 1766 he sent a militia officer to inspect a post on the Lost River.[60] One rough-hewn new militia officer, later destined for military fame, was Daniel Morgan, who in 1771 received from acting governor William Nelson a captain's commission in the Frederick County militia, to serve under Adam Stephen, the "Lieutenant and Chief Commander."[61]

Rumors of a slave insurrection in the making caused alarm in 1767. A large group of blacks had assembled, and the first thought of whites was that a conspiracy to revolt was underway. Stephen, as county lieutenant, ordered Ens. Robert Rutherford with a detachment of thirteen militia to apprehend some of the slaves and bring them before a justice of the peace to be examined. No evidence of a plan for an uprising was found, and the slaves were discharged.[62]

Two years later, in July 1769, Stephen sent a number of dispatches to the governor and council pointing out that some 300 Indians near Fort Pitt exhibited hostile intentions and beyond the Alleghenies settlers were fleeing their homes. The council expressed surprise that the Indians were about to take up the tomahawk so soon after the Treaty of Fort Stanwix and discounted Stephen's information, deciding that it was "merely from report, unsupported by any Affidavit, and they incline to think that the mischief done to the Cattle and Horses if any, was committed by some of the young Indians, who, in their first Sallies out to War, are not always kept within bounds." The council refused to take any action and warned against both unjustly provoking the Indians and illegal settlement beyond the mountains.[63]

In September, Stephen reported that some Virginians had stolen horses from the Indians and "three proligate fellows" had killed an Indian who had come to trade with them and wounded another. Two weeks later Stephen notified the colony's authorities that two more Indians had been murdered by "some of the worthless part of the Inhabitants over the mountains." Col. George Wilson of Hampshire County arrested one of the culprits, who, however, was rescued by "a Banditti." Stephen advised the governor that if the outlawry was not checked, the Indians would seek revenge, which would prove "troublesome to your Lordship's Administration." Stephen suggested that a "person of Weight known to the Indians" visit the tribes in order to assure them that the behavior of the white offenders was not in any way sanctioned by the Virginia government. The governor should immediately issue arrest warrants for the culprits, who would face "condign punishment." Stephen sent the governor the speech of "a noted Indian," which indicated the "sense of that people, who it seems are disposed to live on good terms with us if Our Wicked people would let them alone."[64]

Col. Felix Seymour, sheriff of Hampshire County, wrote the governor about the same problem and warned that war might break out because of the incidents. Seymour, however, thought that the white outlaws were from a gang called the Black Boys from Maryland and Pennsylvania. The sheriff also reported that John Ryan, who had left his family on the Greenbrier River, had murdered two Indians, and farther upriver other whites killed three Indians. The governor and council sent word to the tribes that the whites would be punished and issued a proclamation to this effect, calling specifically for apprehension of several of the known murderers.[65] Stephen was asked to assist in arresting the outlaws.[66]

Stephen reported to the governor in October that one person implicated in the murder of an Indian named Stephen had been captured and was lodged in the Winchester jail until he was rescued by a band of seventy men led by Abraham Fry and his three brothers, Jacob, Joseph, and Benjamin. However, the Fry brothers, who were freeholders in Frederick County, were not convicted for abetting the escape.[67]

With all his many activities in a backcountry county since retirement from the army, Stephen found himself somewhat isolated from a broader world. At least his war experiences had been intercolonial in nature, and he had served in conjunction with British regulars. Although he corresponded with some of the colony's leaders, such as Richard Henry Lee, Stephen felt himself distanced from the vital center of the colony's political life. He was not much inclined nor perhaps could he afford to live in the high style of some of the gentry, who lavishly entertained and traveled. But more fundamentally, Stephen was an outsider to the colony's elite, not only because of the area of his residence but also he was essentially a parvenu and not of the kinship network of old families that since the turn of the century had controlled Virginia's affairs. Moreover, he was a Scottish émigré, and thanks mainly to the sharp practices of Scottish factors in Virginia, Scotsmen were viewed with suspicion. Stephen's own quick success, taking advantage of every opportunity, could be seen as behavior of the typical Scotsman. The ethnic prejudice of some Virginians toward Scotsmen is evident from a piece inserted in the *Virginia Gazette* of October 20, 1774: "A Scotchman, when he is first admitted into a house, is so humble that he will sit upon the lowest step of the staircase. By degrees he gets into the kitchen, and from thence, by the most submissive behavior, is advanced into the parlour. If he gets into the dining room, as ten to one he will, the master of the house must take care of himself; for in all probability he will turn him out of doors, and by the assistance of his countrymen keep possession forever."

As the protest movement against England grew, Valley residents joined in, though, with the lack of major port towns, not as visibly aggressive as elsewhere. Taxation without representation and the closure of the frontier were as volatile issues in the western as in the eastern parts of the colony. Stephen managed to keep up with events from his correspondents and from the Philadelphia and Williamsburg newspapers. He offered no complaint against the Virginia Resolutions of 1765 and 1769 condemning the Stamp Act and the Townshend duties. To a displaced Scotsman, English tyranny could just as well be manifested through Parliament as by the king. The imperial crises of the 1760s left him wondering what course Virginia—and himself—would take in the future.

SEVEN

Premier Gentleman Freeholder

In the 1770s Adam Stephen assumed the role of founding father of local government, both county and town. The rapid settlement beyond the Blue Ridge brought the need for divisions of the two larger frontier counties of Frederick and Augusta. Stephen was instrumental in the creation of Berkeley County and, later in the decade, the town of Martinsburg. As the largest landholder in the new county, Stephen would have a major voice in guiding its affairs.

When Frederick County was formed in 1738, it included the whole northern part of the Valley and extended from the crest of the Blue Ridge Mountains west "to the utmost limits of Virginia." Hampshire County, created in 1754, gave Frederick a fixed western line. But still Frederick County covered a vast area, and for some settlers it took two or three days to travel to the courthouse in Winchester. Stephen was among those who found it inconvenient to journey to the county seat, especially as a justice of the peace and county lieutenant. Not surprisingly, Stephen led freeholders of the northern third of Frederick County (representing a white population of about 9,000, with 2,250 tithables) in petitioning the legislature to carve out a new county. In February 1772 the assembly established Berkeley County (named after the popular governor, Norborne Berkeley, Baron de Botetourt, who had died in 1770) and Dunmore County (honoring the incumbent governor), with

May 15, 1772, as the date for the commencement of the new governments. Adam Stephen now lived in Berkeley County. He was appointed a justice of the peace and almost simultaneously, on April 18, 1772, was issued a commission from the governor to serve as sheriff for the county.[1]

As sheriff, Stephen was the chief administrative official of the court, manager of elections, law enforcer, process server, and collector of taxes. In holding this office he could not act in a judicial capacity, even though sheriffs came from the ranks of the justices of the peace. Usually a senior justice was appointed. Stephen, of course, had been a longtime justice of the peace in Frederick County. A sheriff's term in office did not exceed two years. Limiting the duration of service by a single individual was intended to prevent an overriding political faction in a county. Samuel Washington, the second largest landholder in Berkeley County, was sheriff for 1773, and Stephen again served in this post from 1774 to December 1775, when he resigned to become colonel of the 4th Virginia Regiment.[2]

The Berkeley court first met on May 9 at Edward Beeson's log dwelling, known as the Red House, just north of present-day Martinsburg. At the November court Stephen produced a writ from the colonial secretary's office ordering the court to reconvene at Morgan's Spring, where Stephen owned land. Sessions were held in the home of Joseph Mitchell, and John Neville's house was rented for use as a jail. In 1774 the court then met at the home of Isaac Taylor.[3] Stephen donated an acre of land and some stone for the construction of a courthouse and jail. The jail was completed in 1774, and the courthouse five years later.[4]

Stephen soon owned most of the land in the area of the new county seat. In April 1773 he purchased 563 acres from George William Fairfax for £200, adjoining the estate he had obtained from Morgan Morgan, Jr., in 1770. This new tract straddled Tuscarora Creek, and the Great Wagon Road passed through it, linking up nearby with Bull Eye's Road that led to Warm (Berkeley) Springs. Stephen began constructing a stone house for himself which was not fully completed until 1789. Within a few years he had erected a saw mill, distillery, and armory on his new property and also was grazing cattle on the surrounding rich meadowland.[5] In all, Stephen would

own 5,381 acres in Berkeley County (including the Bower plantation). In 1774, 4,000 acres, claimed as part of the Proclamation of
1763 bounty grants, were surveyed for him in Fincastle County (in
northern Kentucky).[6]

It was Sheriff Stephen's responsibility to attend to the imprison-
ment and physical punishment of persons sentenced by the court.
Fortunately, it seems he did not preside over any hangings. Except
for slave felons, all criminals arraigned for capital crimes were tried
before the General Court in Williamsburg, and upon conviction,
executions took place there. For capital offenses involving slaves,
however, the cases were tried before special courts of oyer and
terminer, consisting mostly of members of the county court, and
the slaves would be put to death in the county. In April 1773 Governor Dunmore commissioned eighteen Berkeley residents, including
Adam Stephen, as a court of oyer and terminer.[7] Many offenses
tried on the county level resulted in corporal punishment. Stephen
probably left the whippings to his deputy sheriff, Samuel Oldham.
The first criminal conviction recorded in Berkeley County concerned hog theft, with the accused being slaves; the four convicted
each received thirty-nine lashes.[8] Several months later, the court
ordered Stephen to mete out the same punishment to a convicted
forger.[9]

Stephen's rivalry with Jacob Hite threatened to disrupt law and
order in Berkeley County. The Hite family had been prominent in
the Valley for forty years. Jacob Hite had accompanied his father,
Jost Hite, to the Valley in 1731–32. Jacob had served as sheriff
twice for Frederick County and also as justice of the peace for that
county and now for Berkeley. His son Thomas at age twenty-two
entered the House of Burgesses in 1772.[10] Bad blood had been
brewing between Stephen and Jacob Hite. There had been a misun-
derstanding over an arrangement whereby Hite would take timber
from Stephen's land and in return Stephen's wheat was to be ground
at Hite's mill. They also had their differences as to the location of
the new county seat. Hite had expected Hite's Town (later named
Leetown), east of Opequon Creek in what is now Jefferson County,
would be selected. Hite and some of his fellow justices of the peace—
Thomas Van Swearingen, Thomas Rutherford, William Morgan,

Robert Stogdon, James Seaton, James Strode, and William Little—filed a petition with the Virginia council complaining that the courthouse, "not being Centrical," should be transferred to the land of John Strode. The council, however, declared it was "well satisfied with their former Choice" and advised the governor against removal of the county courthouse. Furthermore, it noted that because the opposing justices of the peace "had entered into a Combination" and had engaged in "an indecent Attempt to overawe the Deliberations of the Board," they should no longer serve "in the Commission of the peace." Hence Hite and his "confederates" were purged from the court, and their militia commissions were revoked as well. A new slate of justices of the peace was installed. Stephen was among the justices of the peace who were not supporters of Hite and were retained.[11]

As sheriff of Berkeley County, Stephen executed a judgment of the Frederick Court against Jacob Hite, which resulted in a fracas that almost led to bloodshed. Hite had lost a suit brought against him in 1772 by James Hunter for a debt of £1,641.6.2 and refused to pay the judgment. Stephen and several deputies went to Hite's plantation, seized fifteen of Hite's slaves and twenty-one of his horses, and brought them to the county jail and stable to put them up for auction.

Hite wrote newcomer Horatio Gates, a justice of the peace, that he would stop the sale or sue anyone who bought his property, but also suggested that Gates and others might do the purchasing, and Hite then would buy back the slaves and horses at the price that had been paid. Gates advised Hite to sue those who were "active in plundering him." Hite, however, decided first to take matters into his own hands. A friend of Hite's, who was the constable, Daniel Hendricks, assembled a posse—including Jacob's son Thomas Hite, Vachel Dorsey, Daniel Grant, Daniel Bradley, Daniel Pearce, Joseph Hite, Francis Mosley, William Murphy, Robert Job, Francis McKenny, Charles Hazle, and "many others"—and marched to the courthouse area, where they seized and tied up the jailor, John Nelson, and a guard. Nelson would not deliver up the keys, so the gang chopped the jail door down with axes and broke the lock on the stable door. The fifteen slaves and twenty-one horses were then released, as were also Marty Handly, a prisoner for debt, and a runaway servant.

Seven of the Hite posse—Thomas Hite, Daniel Hendricks, Vachel Dorsey, Daniel Grant, Daniel Pearce, Joseph Hite, and Francis Worldley—were arrested "on suspicion of Feloniously & Rioting breaking open the Gaol." Before Gates and other justices of the peace, they were tried for breach of the peace but acquitted, though they had to go bond to guarantee their good behavior for twelve months. Tempers flared even more. Hite and his cohorts filed court action against Stephen and other officials. But Stephen realized, as his lawyer, James Mercer, advised him, that if he did not "save" the "estate" to satisfy the debt owed Hunter, he might become liable himself for a suit for recovery of the debt. Stephen got intervention from the General Court, which upheld the execution of the original judgment against Hite, thus vindicating Stephen's actions. The General Court agreed to make a complete determination on the whole situation. Hearings, however, were postponed from time to time mainly because records kept by Gates were lost when forwarded to Williamsburg. Mercer threatened Gates with a contempt proceeding. The General Court refrained from any further decision. Yet the personal feud between Hite and Stephen would become even more venomous.[12]

The Hite affair only momentarily disrupted Stephen's friendship with Horatio Gates, who had just settled in Berkeley County, about four miles from Stephen's residence and also not far from Hite's Hopewell plantation. Gates, who had served with Washington and Stephen in the Braddock campaign, had retired from the British army at half pay in 1765. In England he had financial reverses and was regarded as a "red hot Republican." Seeking a more favorable political climate and greater opportunity for attaining wealth, he and his wife, Elizabeth, decided to come to America, after first sounding out George Washington on the advantages of settling in Virginia. The Gates family had arrived at Hampton by late 1772 when Stephen wrote Gates, encouraging him to take a look at western Virginia. Conditions were much improved since Gates had been in America, Stephen pointed out, and "the Ohio is Settled very thick" seventy miles below Fort Pitt. Lord Hillsborough "before he went out gave Orders for dismantling Fort Pitt, which is executed Accordingly—Here ends our Bleedings, Aches, & Watching—Do not be in a hurry Settling farther."[13]

Gates visited Berkeley County, and Stephen tried to interest him in 659 acres near Opequon Creek, which Joseph Grabel was willing to sell for £1,653. Gates looked at the property, and shortly afterwards Stephen wrote him that he had met Grabel on the road; as he was "passing him, the Old Dunker kindly ask'd me to drink Some of his Beer, you know Old Soldiers Refuse Nothing that is Good." Stephen then went to the Grabel house and informed Mrs. Grabel that Gates and his wife would return in a few days to view the property again. "I ordered the Frow [Frau]," said Stephen, "to have a Turkey Roasted for you, & a Clean Cover for the Table. Be sure it Should be So! the Old Woman Replied . . . Now Sir, I can perceive that they are in the Humour to Sell—I request you that you would not lose a hog for a ha'p worth of Tar. . . . All I can Say, upon honour, is that it is the Most Suitable place for you that I know for Sale at this time."[14] Gates followed Stephen's advice and bought the Grabel estate, which he named Traveller's Rest. By mid-March 1774 the Gates family moved into their new home, a solid one-and-a-half-story limestone house (standing today, now in Jefferson County).[15]

Soon Charles Lee, another British major retired on half pay, also took up an estate in Berkeley County. Lee had fought at Braddock's defeat and then served in the northern theater of the French and Indian War. Colorful and eccentric, the bachelor Lee could count among his exploits being accepted into the Bear clan of the Mohawks under the name of Ouewaterika (Boiling Water) and having "married" Seneca chief White Thunder's daughter, who bore him twins. After leaving the British army in 1763, he became a soldier of fortune, with the rank of major general in the Polish army. Returning to America in 1773, Lee two years later purchased 3,284 acres of Jacob Hite's Hopewell plantation for £5,504. He first called his thick limestone-walled house Prato Verde and later Prato Rio.[16] Although Lee's new plantation was only several miles from Stephen's Bower farm, Stephen never really got to know Lee, who did not settle on his estate until 1779 after his suspension from the army. Except for Lee's brief command in Virginia in early 1776, the paths of the two men during the Revolutionary War rarely crossed.

Of the three future Revolutionary War generals from Berkeley County—Gates, Lee, and Stephen—only Stephen participated in the military warm-up in Virginia, the Indian campaign of 1774. Lord Dunmore's War, a punitive campaign against the western Indians, excited a martial spirit in the colony and tested both raw recruits and the veteran officers of the French and Indian War. Although there was a growing number of small encounters between Indians and frontiersmen in the early 1770s, the murder of the family of Logan, a Mingo chief, at the mouth of Yellow Creek along the Ohio on April 30, 1774, brought on severe retaliation by Logan and his followers. In June, Indians raided along the Greenbrier River. Governor Dunmore sought to check their entry along the northern Virginia frontier. He ordered Maj. William Crawford, with men from the Monongahela and Youghiogheny valleys, to construct Fort Fincastle at Wheeling and Col. Andrew Lewis and Augusta militia to build a post at the mouth of the Kanawha River. From Fort Fincastle, Col. Angus McDonald marched with 400 troops into the Shawnee country. Though burning villages and destroying crops, McDonald and his men could not find the enemy. The foray aroused further Indian hostility, and the governor decided to lead an expedition himself. The army would consist of two divisions: Col. Adam Stephen would accompany Dunmore with militia from Frederick, Berkeley, and Hampshire counties and proceed to Fort Dunmore (Fort Pitt) and from there down the Ohio; Col. Andrew Lewis, with men collected from Augusta, Botetourt, and Fincastle counties, would journey overland to the mouth of the Kanawha or elsewhere on the Ohio to join forces with Dunmore. The combined troops then would invade the Ohio country.[17]

As colonel and county lieutenant of Berkeley, Stephen had orders from the governor to have 400 to 500 militia ready to march. Stephen expected that Horatio Gates, who had accepted a lieutenant colonelcy, would join the expedition. On August 20 Stephen wrote Gates that Dunmore had ordered him "to have a field officer ready" to take charge of the Berkeley contingent; "You will therefore be so good as hold your self in Readiness to march as soon as His Lordship directs."[18] Gates, however, balked at serving in the expeditionary force, and he informed the governor that taking troops outside the colony was illegal. Dunmore replied that there was no such legal sanction. Stephen again wrote Gates to assume command of the Berkeley troops,[19] whereupon Gates pleaded that he was ill but upon recovery would join the expedition.[20] Gates's apparent reluctance may have been due in part to a sense of honor as an officer; having held a high commission in the British army, he did not want to be outranked in the field by a provincial officer. Stephen himself was not very excited about the pending Indian campaign; he wrote Richard Henry Lee on August 27 that Dunmore had ordered him to the Ohio "to endeavour to put matters on a footing to establish a lasting peace with the brave Indians; who, in my opinion, would behave well were they not poisoned by the blackguard traders allowed to go among them."[21]

Dunmore and Stephen, with the militia of Frederick and Berkeley counties, left Winchester on August 27 and soon were joined by the Hampshire troops. The ragtag infantrymen, attired in hunting shirts, buckskin leggings stretching halfway up their thighs, and fur caps, carried flintlock rifles, scalping knives, and tomahawks. Stephen and the other officers were prepared for an Indian fight, too; besides their swords they each had a tomahawk and scalping knife. From Fort Cumberland the little army marched over a road that had been opened by Abraham Hite, Thomas Rutherford, and James Wood through the mountains to the mouth of Redstone Creek on the Monongahela. At Fort Dunmore the Virginians linked up with Maj. John Connolly and 200 men of the "West Augusta Battalion." A British regular at Fort Dunmore, Lt. Col. Augustine Prevost, dined with Dunmore and Stephen several times, once commenting that Stephen was one "who had seen some service during last war, who bears a worthy good character." Prevost also observed that on September 16 "We alighted at the tavern, where I fetched Colo. Stevens" and three days later mentioned that "this morning his Lordship came up the Alighany in two boats accompanied by Colo. Stevens & Maj. Co—y [Connolly], a couple French horns & a S—tch piper, with the Union Flag desplayed." Stephen and his men went to Fort Fincastle, where Dunmore and the rest of his force joined him on September 30. Including the 1,500 militia under Lewis, the Virginia expeditionary army numbered 2,700. Dunmore now decided to rendezvous his and Lewis's troops across the Ohio at the mouth of the Hocking River. Dunmore moved his force immediately to this point, where he had a stockade built, naming it Fort Gower.[22]

Lewis and his division had made camp at Point Pleasant, a half mile from the confluence of the Kanawha and Ohio rivers. At this site, Col. William Fleming, a Scottish physician and seasoned veteran of frontier warfare, was "agreeably surprized" to receive a letter from Stephen. Fleming replied that "to know you was so near, and that we were to make an excursion again together after so long an Interval of ease, rousd in my breast sentiments . . . warmer than common lifeless Friendships contracted in indolence or over a bottle A Soldiers connections in this light may be compaired to Gun Powder which keapt dry, will with a spark kindle into a blaze."[23]

At Point Pleasant on October 10, Lewis's Virginians were beginning to break camp at dawn when they were attacked by 1,000 Indians, under the great Shawnee chief Cornstalk, who had crossed the Ohio quietly during the darkness. Fierce combat lasted most of the day. Finally, troops under Evan Shelby and others flanking the enemy and the arrival of men under Col. William Christian (which gave the Indians the impression that even more soldiers would be joining Lewis) caused the Indians to withdraw. The battle of Point Pleasant was a costly victory for the Long Knives, as the Indians called the Virginians—46 killed and 80 wounded.[24]

Dunmore and Stephen in the meantime had proceeded deeper into the Indian country, leaving 100 men to garrison Fort Gower. Lewis, as he had been ordered, with 1,000 men crossed the Ohio on October 17. But there was little need for this division to continue farther. The spirit of the Indians had been broken, and Cornstalk was ready to sue for peace. Stephen met with several Delaware and Mohawk chiefs and asked Captain Pipe, a Delaware chief, what he knew of the intentions of the Shawnees. The Indian leader replied that he had met with some of the Shawnees, and "after having cleared their eyes and opened their ears, in the common form . . .

they had a great dance," after which they declared a desire for peace. Dunmore parleyed with Cornstalk at Camp Charlotte, as the new Virginia encampment was called, and preliminary peace terms were agreed upon. The treaty would be completed at a conference at Fort Dunmore in the spring. Dunmore sent a dispatch to the approaching troops under Lewis that they should now return to Virginia. The men under Dunmore and Stephen, except for a detail of 25 sent to Fort Fincastle and 100 to Fort Dunmore, returned to Fort Gower.[25]

During the campaign Stephen was anxious for information on the growing colonial protest against the Coercive Acts recently passed by the British Parliament. Before he left on the expedition, a Virginia convention had met in early August at Williamsburg and had agreed to call for a boycott of English goods and to send representatives to the pending Continental Congress in Philadelphia. At Fort Gower, before returning home, Stephen picked up "disagreeable news" from Boston that General Gage had seized cannon in Cambridge and 100 hogsheads of powder at Charlestown, Massachusetts, and had fired on the populace.[26] Amazingly, this version of the "Powder Alarm," a totally erroneous rumor, had spread quickly to the far frontier.

At Fort Gower the Virginians also undoubtedly learned of Congress's actions, particularly the adoption of the Suffolk Resolves, which called for Massachusetts to be in a state of military preparedness, and the "Declaration and Resolves," a bold statement of colonial rights and complaints. On November 5 Stephen and other officers met "for the purpose of considering the grievances of British America" and drew up resolutions to be published in the *Virginia Gazette*. In the preamble, the officers asserted "that we are a respectable body is certain, when it is considered that we can live weeks without bread or salt; that we can sleep in the open air without any covering but that of the canopy of Heaven; and that our men can march and shoot with any in the known world." Endowed "with these talents, let us solemnly engage to one another, and our country in particular, that we will use them to no purpose but for the honor and advantage of America in general, and of Virginia in particular." The officers then submitted two resolutions, "maturely considered . . . nemine contradicente." The first expressed allegiance to the king, "whilst His Majesty delights to reign over a brave and free people." But "as the love of liberty, and attachment to the real interests and just rights of America outweigh every other consideration," the officers pledged that "we will exert every power within us for the defense of American liberty, and for the support of her just rights and privileges; not in any precipitate, riotous or tumultous manner, but when regularly called forth by the unanimous voice of our countrymen." The second resolution exonerated Governor Dunmore from a charge that he had started an Indian war in order to divert attention from the imperial crisis; the governor had acted "from no other motive than the true interest of his country."[27]

The language of the "Fort Gower Resolutions" and especially the Latin phrase, which was a device that Stephen often employed as punctuation, suggest that he was a principal author of the document. The fusing of a military stance and the rhetoric of liberty in the "Fort Gower Resolutions" at this time is significant, anticipating the *rage militaire* in a little more than a year and the "Spirit of 76." The document exudes the officers' confidence in their military ability and their sense of fraternal pride. It expresses unstinted patriotism, which was intended to counter apprehensions of the dangers of calling forth a strong regular army.

Stephen assumed the position that the American protest should not be compromised, and he was ahead of most Virginians in expecting a military solution. His views were comparable to those of Richard Henry Lee, a "radical conservative" from Westmoreland County and one of the seven-member delegation from Virginia to the Continental Congress. Just as he was setting out on the Dunmore expedition, on August 27, 1774, Stephen wrote Lee, who was preparing to journey to Philadelphia to attend Congress. The Indian campaign, said Stephen, "prevents my attending the general Congress, where I would expect to see the spirit of the Amphyctions shine, as that illustrious council did in their purest times, before debauched with the Persian gold. The fate of America depends upon your meeting, and the eyes of the European world hang upon you, waiting the event." Stephen mentioned that he objected to the Quebec Act, which established "Depotism, and the Roman Catholic religion" in Canada. He could just as well have mentioned that implementation of the Quebec Act would nullify Virginia's claim to lands north and west of the Ohio River and possibly also lead to restrictions on the bounty land grants. Stephen also commented on the Administration of Justice Act (one of the Coercive Acts). "Can we be said to enjoy liberty," he asked, "if the villain who ravishes our wives, deflours our daughters, or murders our sons, can evade punishment, by being tried in Britain, where no evidence can pursue him?" For "a governor to suppose me guilty of a crime, and tell me that there can be no fair trial in America; that is, there are not honest men to be found in my country to try me, he must send me home to rot in Newgate, is shocking to human nature. Could I get within musket shot of him, I would put him to death; he should never attempt to send home another." Stephen then pointed out that Congress should make arrangements to supply arms and ammunition to localities. He wished that "the united wisdom of America" would prevent war, but he expected that given the "determined system of arbitrary power at home . . . matters will come to extremity. . . . they intend to irritate America into rebellion, and then govern us like a conquered people." Stephen advised that Congress should "try all fair means" to avoid armed conflict "but be prepared for the worst as soon as possible. . . . Let us be provided with arms and ammunition, and individuals may suffer, but the gates of hell cannot prevail against America."[28]

After Stephen returned home from the Indian expedition, he learned that all thirteen colonies had responded to Congress's summons for an "Association" to bring economic sanctions on Great Britain. By joining the Association, the colonies agreed to nonimportation of goods from Great Britain and Ireland and a selective boycott of certain items from the West Indies, beginning December 1, 1774. Nonexportation of American-produced goods would commence September 10, 1775, provided that by then Parliament had not rescinded the Coercive Acts. Stephen and other Shenandoah Valley planters, however, were glad that even if nonexportation went into effect, they could still send wheat to the very important markets in southern Europe.[29]

To enforce the Association, localities established committees of safety; fifty-one Virginia counties had done so by summer 1775. Stephen chaired the Berkeley County committee, which met in Mecklenberg (Shepherdstown). Committees of safety were most active in counties with port towns, although everywhere they engaged in the vital role of raising volunteer militia companies.[30]

A few public matters interested Stephen other than the rising revolutionary cause. The failure of the legislature to compensate the troops who went on the recent Indian expedition irked him. Stephen asked Richard Henry Lee to help pressure the assembly to vote the money. "In these troublesome times," said Stephen, "it is absolutely necessary that you pay the men employed in the expedition; they have done honour to our country." Unless the veterans "are paid off directly, their certificates will be sold for a fourth part of their value to Pedlars and Storekeepers." Commissioners should be appointed to settle the accounts.[31]

Stephen also concerned himself with a grand design to open the upper Potomac River for navigation from Fort Cumberland eastward to the tidal water above Mount Vernon. The Virginia assembly had given its approval, although action from Maryland was also required. Stephen, Washington, and others subscribed to a plan for the creation of the Potomac Company, and Stephen probably attended an organizational meeting at Georgetown, Maryland, on November 12, 1774. John Ballendine, one of the subscribers, and a few laborers began work on the locks at the lower falls on the Maryland side of the river. A lottery was approved, with 20,000 tickets at £5 each. Nothing further immediately developed, with the war intervening, but the Potomac Company was revived after the Revolution and was chartered by Virginia and Maryland in 1785. Also of interest to Stephen and other Valley planters was expectation of navigational work on the Shenandoah River connecting with the Potomac.[32]

As the New Year came, Stephen's thoughts turned all the more to the revolutionary movement in Virginia. Writing to Richard Henry Lee on December 27, 1774, he emphasized the military quality of the Virginia citizen soldier. During Dunmore's War, said Stephen, it was demonstrated "that a few Brave men, on the Conclusion of Harvest, laid down their Sickles, & Pitch forks, took up their Riffles

& Tomahawks, march 300 miles without Noise or parade, took position in the Enemy's Country, chastised them"; they "imposd on them more humiliating Terms, than before could be done by all the Kings forces ever employd against them—Established the peace of the Country & returned again, to the plow after the antient Roman manner." Therefore, "let the Enemies of America hear this & Tremble! All of this was done without a farthing of money advancd either for pay or provisions." Stephen thought that the Virginia assembly should consider means to provide saltpeter, which "may be made in Virginia & Maryland to Supply an Empire. . . . I wish every person who had a Tobacco house were obligd to make Some." Great quantity of this mineral compound, used for making gunpowder, could be obtained in Virginia's mountains; on the north side of a hill one could "sweep up half a Bushel of dirty Saltpetre in One place." In reference to a request by the Continental Congress and the Virginia Convention that colonists produce more wool, thereby replacing Britishers as a source of this commodity, Stephen pointed out that sheep raising hitherto had been infeasible in his region because of the prevalence of wolves.[33]

Stephen writing to Lee in February 1775, advocated the renewal (with amendments) of the soon-to-expire militia act, a topic which would become very heated at the second Virginia Convention in March 1775 and which elicited Patrick Henry's fiery oratory in demanding that the Convention take upon itself to pass a new law. Such an ordinance, Stephen told Lee, should include provision for a 100-man horse unit in every county. As to courts-martial, "let a majority present determine any matter; and during an attack, or in battle, let the men be subject to the Articles of War." Until firearms could be provided to all soldiers, they should be furnished with spears and tomahawks. Stephen also called Lee's attention to the British ineptness during the last war: "six broken Regiments from France, withstood, for five years, all the force of British Fleets and Armies from home, and fifteen or twenty thousand Americans, every campaign. . . . What can we do, if united? We only want a Navy to give law to the world, and we have it in our power to get it." The time for decision was at hand. Though Stephen hoped that the "New Parliament" might make appropriate concessions to the colonies, he said that "I must acknowledge my dread to hear from them." He had been informed by "Several Sensible men lately from England" that "the people Seems but little affected with our dispute, & that they without thought or Consideration declare that America ought to be tam'd." Lord North "has declared that he has a Rod in piss for the Colony of Virginia & province of Maryland— Could I see him in America! in Spite of all the Armies of Commissioners, Custom house officers & Soldiers, I would make the meanest American I know, piss upon him."[34]

Stephen held this letter for over two weeks before sending it to Lee, not wanting to "trouble" him with it, but he finally put it in the mail, with a brief cover note, dated February 17, in which he again commented on the need for Congress to vote some pay for Virginia soldiers, including those of the past Dunmore campaign. All that Congress had to do, for the present, was to "resolve to acquaint the men employed in the last Expedition, that they would be paid as soon as the general commotions are settled, it would keep them in heart." Stephen warned that "it would be highly imprudent to disgust a body of such useful men at this important era; for, by what I can hear, it will come to the shedding of blood, unless Providence interferes in a very special manner." Stephen then described his personal solution, much like the life he had already created for himself: "For my part, before I would submit my life, liberty, and property, to the arbitrary disposal of a corrupt, venal aristocracy, the wanton and effeminate tools of power, I would set myself down with a few friends, upon some rich and healthy spot," 600 miles westward, and "there form a settlement, which, in a short time, would command attention and respect."[35]

Despite this impulse to flee the current problems, Stephen was ready to take an active role in the colonywide revolutionary movement. The Virginia Convention was scheduled to reassemble on March 20, 1775, and the counties were again to be represented by two delegates each. Stephen and Robert Rutherford were selected to be the Berkeley members. It was quite evident that the process was under way of replacing the House of Burgesses with the Convention. Of special interest to Stephen, the next meeting of the Convention would have military affairs as a primary item on the agenda. Like other delegates he would have to look to the future consequences of any actions they took. He was already all but convinced that there would be war. Parliament was adamant in refusing to repeal the offensive measures. Stephen believed, along with Patrick Henry, that the time was approaching when "we must fight!" He recognized that the experiences in frontier warfare of twenty years were valuable assets for defending American liberty.

Unquestionably Adam Stephen was warmly attached to the Revolutionary cause. The Scottish intellectual training of his youth had left him imbued with concern for the rights of a free people. Not at all to be discounted, however, were other factors contributing to Stephen's bellicose patriotism. From a military point of view, Stephen perceived the need for vigilance against potential threats of foreign foes. The French aggression had ceased and also, for the time being, that of the Indians. Great Britain in violating the rights of the colonists as freeborn citizens, was now the common enemy. Motivated by personal reasons more than he was wont to admit, Stephen certainly could expect further army advancement. There would be opportunity not only to achieve further military distinction but also to pursue economic gain.

Fort Necessity (reconstructed). Reprinted by permission from Charles M. Stotz, *Outposts of the War for Empire: The French and English in Western Pennsylvania: Their Armies, Their Forts, Their People, 1749–64* (Pittsburgh: University of Pittsburgh Press and the Historical Society of Western Pennsylvania, 1985), p. 21.

Braddock's Defeat. Painting by Edwin Deming. (Courtesy of the State Historical Society of Wisconsin)

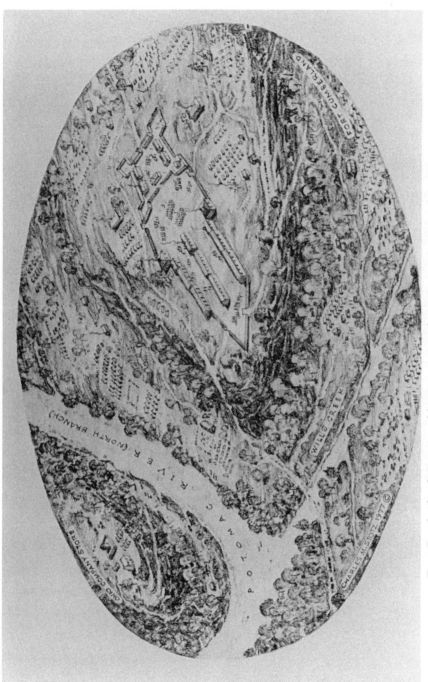

Fort Cumberland. Reprinted by permission from Stotz, *Outposts of the War*, p. 91.

Governor Robert Dinwiddie. (Courtesy of the Virginia State Library and Archives)

Sir John St. Clair. Painting by John Singleton Copley. (Courtesy of the Historical Society of Pennsylvania)

General John Forbes. Copy from painting in possession of the Royal Scots Greys Regiment, Aldershot, England. (Courtesy of the Historical Society of Pennsylvania)

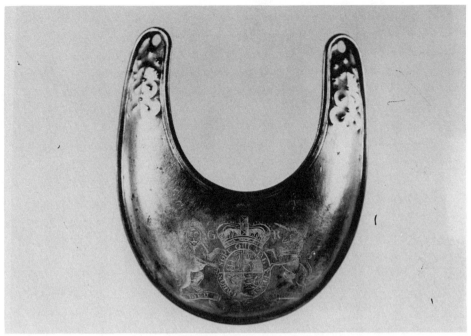

Brass gorget (decorated with the British coat-of-arms) worn by Adam Stephen during the French and Indian War. (Smithsonian Institution photo no. 30729B)

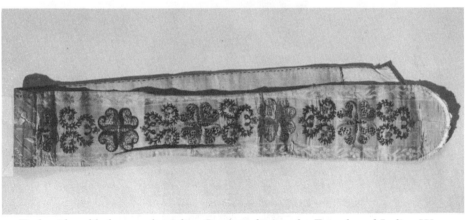

Embroidered belt worn by Adam Stephen during the French and Indian War. (Smithsonian Institution photo no. 47008)

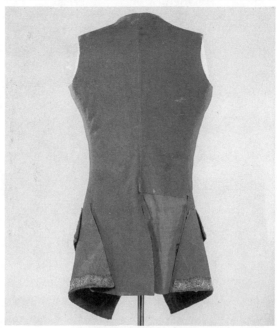

Uniform scarlet waistcoat (gold-laced) worn by Adam Stephen during the French and Indian War. (Smithsonian Institution photo nos. 61200A and 61200B)

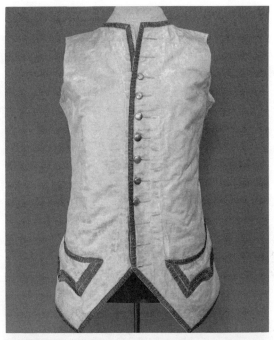

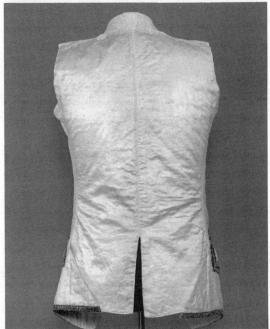

Uniform white waistcoat worn by Adam Stephen. (Smithsonian Institution photo nos. 67464 and 67466)

Fort Ligonier (scale model). (Courtesy of the Fort Ligonier Association, Ligonier, Pa.)

Colonel Henry Bouquet. Painting attributed to John Wollaston, 1758.
(Courtesy of the Historical Society of Pennsylvania)

George Washington. Painting by Charles Willson Peale, 1772.
(Courtesy of the Washington/Custis/Lee Collection,
Washington and Lee University, Virginia)

General Horatio Gates. (Courtesy of the Virginia State Library
and Archives)

Traveller's Rest. (Courtesy of the Virginia State Library and Archives)

General Charles Lee, in caricature. (Courtesy of the Virginia State
Library and Archives)

Adam Stephen mill, Martinsburg (destroyed). (Courtesy of the General Adam Stephen Memorial Association)

Adam Stephen house, Martinsburg. (Courtesy of the General Adam Stephen Memorial Association)

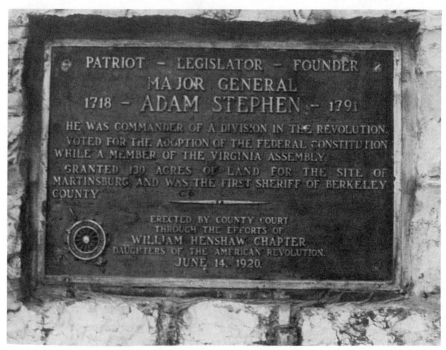

Plaque on Adam Stephen monument, Martinsburg. (Courtesy of the General
Adam Stephen Memorial Association)

Adam Stephen monument and grave, Martinsburg. (Courtesy of the General
Adam Stephen Memorial Association)

The Revolutionary War Begins

The war that Adam Stephen knew was inevitable came closer with the meeting of the second Virginia Convention, March 20–27, 1775, at St. John's Chapel, a little frame structure overlooking the town of Richmond. As a delegate from Berkeley County, Stephen could realize an ambition. He had failed fourteen years earlier to win a seat in the colony's assembly; now he could take his place alongside the burgesses in the extralegal representative body. The second Convention, like the first, consisted largely of members of the House of Burgesses, who were eligible to serve as delegates if they so desired. It seems that Adam Stephen substituted for Thomas Hite, an elected burgess. Apparently Hite had declined to serve, and Stephen was selected by the county committee of safety as the alternate. As sheriff, county lieutenant, militia colonel, and chairman of the committee of safety, he was the likely choice.

Because the reassembling of the Convention had been announced January 28, 1775, in the *Virginia Gazette*, western delegates had ample time to make arrangements for attending the meeting. For many of them, however, travel over the some 150 to 200 miles took longer than expected. Stephen was two days late when on Wednesday, March 22, he took his seat at the Convention. He was one of 17 of the 120 delegates who were not also burgesses.[1]

The Convention had been moved from Williamsburg not as a

convenience for western members but to make it less accessible to Governor Dunmore, who, with royal marines and sailors, might cause trouble and even attempt to arrest the Convention's leaders. Dunmore unwittingly had abetted the importance of the Convention by delaying to summon the assembly. The House of Burgesses would not meet until June 1, 1775, and then for only three weeks, without the cooperation of the governor. Two other legislative sessions were aborted, March 7 and May 6, 1776, because of the lack of quorums.

Stephen appeared at the Convention just as it started to consider the main issue: whether or not to pass an ordinance to fill the void left by the expiration of the militia law of 1738. Debate over resolutions submitted by Patrick Henry for the Convention to assume this responsibility grew intense. There were those who thought that a militia enactment would have implications of rebellion. Henry and his followers, with Stephen certainly among them, were suspected of wanting to create a separate government. Conservatives and moderates such as Richard Bland, Benjamin Harrison, Edmund Pendleton, and Robert Carter Nicholas opposed any measure beyond economic sanctions that might deepen the imperial crisis.

Pendleton was among those who spoke against the Henry resolutions. Congress had sent a petition to the king, he pointed out, and any action on whether to exercise extralegal authority should be deferred until a reply was received. How could several militia regiments, he asked, resist the splendid army and navy of Great Britain? Americans were without arms, industry, and revenue. There was no certainty of foreign support. A number of delegates added their forensic skills in arguing both sides of the question. With Adam Stephen nodding his head in approval, Henry declared that war was imminent and that the colony must be prepared militarily for defense. The oratory of the Hanover delegate emotionally charged the Convention. A Scottish factor, James Parker, in Norfolk several weeks later, commented: "You never heard any thing more infamously insolent than P Henys speech he Called the K— a Tyrant, a fool, a puppet & a tool to the ministry" and "said there was now no Englishmen, no Scots no Britons, but a Set of wretches Sunk in Luxury. . . . he could not have been more compleatly scurrilous if he had been possessed of John Wilks Vocabulary."[2] Stephen, who himself had a flair with words, probably refrained from debate. Some prominent men, such as George Washington, were silent throughout the Convention. Richard Henry Lee spoke persuasively on behalf of the Henry resolutions, and Stephen, a great admirer of the congressman from Westmoreland County, most likely deferred to him as to any speech making. He could not top Henry's oratory, and moreover, as a legislative newcomer it was more or less proper for him to be, at least for a while, a backbencher.

Henry's resolutions narrowly passed. The Convention then ordered the colony to engage in defense preparations. Stephen served on the committee to draw up a plan for military organization; other members of the group included Henry (chairman), Richard Henry Lee, Robert Carter Nicholas, Benjamin Harrison, Lemuel Riddick, George Washington, Andrew Lewis, William Christian, Edmund Pendleton, Thomas Jefferson, and Isaac Zane. As recommended by the committee, the Convention voted on March 25 that each county should establish a volunteer company, to be kept in constant readiness. For the support of these military units the county committees should collect arms and ammunition and provide a tax levy.

Stephen was heartened by resolutions of the Convention that praised the men who went out to fight in Dunmore's War. Pay was promised to the veterans "so soon as Opportunity permits." Other actions of the Convention also interested Stephen. Courts were temporarily closed to civil suits in order to bring pressure on English creditors. Virginians were urged to help make the colony more self-sufficient. The Convention called for greater production of flax, hemp, and cotton and the manufacture of gunpowder and steel. Having anticipated the colony's need for weapons, Stephen had already established an arms manufactory on his property.

Hardly had Stephen returned to the Valley when news arrived of an event that indeed might plunge the colony into war. During the night of April 20–21, Governor Dunmore's marines transported twenty kegs of gunpowder from the Williamsburg magazine to an armed schooner lying in the James below the capital. In response to a petition from Williamsburg citizens to return the gunpowder immediately, Dunmore threatened to unleash Virginia's slaves and burn the capital. About the time that Stephen learned of this crisis, he also had news of the fighting at Lexington and Concord in Massachusetts.

To compel the governor to surrender the gunpowder seized at Williamsburg, Patrick Henry and 150 volunteers from Hanover County on May 2 headed for the capital; they were joined on the way by militia from New Kent, King William, and Charles City counties. The rabble army halted near Williamsburg. Henry met with Carter Braxton, son-in-law of Col. Richard Corbin, the colony's receiver general, and was given a bill of exchange as compensation for the gunpowder. Satisfied, Henry and his troops returned home. One result of the episode was to spark the counties into organizing their independent companies.[3] Governor Dunmore declared Henry an outlaw and proclaimed that he and his "deluded followers" had, by taking up arms and marching out of their counties, "put themselves in a posture of war." Dunmore called upon all persons to withhold aid to any "unwarrantable combinations."[4] For safety, Dunmore and his family took up residence on HMS *Fowey*.

The crisis now turned into an impasse, with the governor and the colony's citizens watchfully waiting. Stephen was surprised at two measures adopted by the House of Burgesses during its brief nonlegislative session in June 1775. First, that body issued a call for the third Virginia Convention. It also appointed Adam Stephen, Thomas Walker, James Wood, Andrew Lewis, and John Walker as commissioners to complete peace terms with the Ohio Indians.[5] Dunmore had not taken any steps to finalize the Treaty of Camp Charlotte or return Indian hostages, and it was suspected that the governor's neglect was calculated to bring about the renewal of Indian hostilities. The commissioners would travel to Fort Dunmore (Pitt) and reopen negotiations with the Indians.

Stephen followed closely the work of the second Continental Congress, which convened on May 10. That body took charge of the armed resistance in New England and made it a united effort of all the colonies. In a letter to William Fleming of Cumberland County, on May 31, 1775, Stephen reported the quick-developing events. At Congress, he said, "they have great dependence on us Virginians—Men will be raisd, Regimented & regularly paid in every province." Stephen was aware that Congress, as a first step in forming an army, would call for rifle companies, and he asked Fleming to use his influence to encourage enlistment in such units. Stephen was also thinking continentally. Because Forts Ticonderoga and Crown Point had been captured by the Americans, if a "Naval force" could now be put in Lake Champlain, the British would be prevented from making "any Inroads" from Canada into New England and New York. "If we now take Niagara," Stephen said, "& get shipping on Lake Ontario, we will Reduce Canada to its Antient Limits, & Annihalate the Canada Bill [Quebec Act]."[6]

Stephen's prediction that a call for Virginia riflemen soon would be forthcoming was borne out in a congressional resolution of June 14 requesting six rifle companies from Pennsylvania and two each from Maryland and Virginia. Immediately the Virginia quota was raised: a company in Frederick County, under the command of Capt. Daniel Morgan, and in Berkeley, led by Capt. Hugh Stephenson. So many volunteers showed up that marksmanship contests had to be conducted to select the riflemen. Washington was consulted on the appointments of officers, but Stephen, who headed the Berkeley committee, which made the selections for the local company, probably had the last word in choosing that county's officers. Stephenson had fought in the French and Indian War and had led a company in Dunmore's Indian campaign.[7]

Although his public responsibilities and involvement in the revolutionary movement made demands on his time, Stephen gave attention to plantation affairs and his new industries—a distillery and a weapons manufactory. As in the past, Stephen viewed war as creating opportunities for profit. A scheme of a different sort, in which he gambled on the future growth in the backcountry, was the promotion of a town site on his property. During 1774–75 he managed to sell about a dozen lots and hence already had a nucleus for a town he would later name Martinsburg.[8]

By midsummer 1775 full-scale war had erupted. The battle of Bunker Hill on June 17 removed any doubts. Washington assumed command of the Continental army in early July. The third Virginia Convention, scheduled to begin in Richmond on July 17, would be confronted with momentous decisions in determining Virginia's participation in the war effort. Delegates were now to be chosen by freeholders at large, similar to the burgess elections.

As sheriff, Stephen set the date for voting on delegates from Berkeley County. Normally, for the selection of burgesses, a sheriff received a writ from the governor ordering an election, which was returnable six to eight weeks later. The sheriff then decided on the date for opening the polls, usually giving several weeks' notice and fixing the time to coincide with a court day. The governor, of course, did not recognize the extralegal Conventions, and Stephen assumed the full responsibility for arranging the Berkeley County election.[9]

On Sunday, April 24, 1775, just before services, Stephen attached to the door of St. George's Chapel an announcement that both the county committee and the vestry would meet on the following Sunday, and on the next day, May 2, a general muster and the election for delegates to the Convention would be held. Thus he allowed only eight days' notice for the election, almost too brief a time for all the citizens of the county to learn of it. Furthermore, as the Reverend Daniel Sturgis, rector of Norborne Parish, later testified, Stephen did not bother to place similar bulletins at three other chapels in the county.[10]

Holding the election on the same day as the general muster afforded Stephen an opportunity to influence the balloting. As colonel and commander of the county's militia, Stephen marched the militiamen to the polls and allegedly requested that they vote for him. Many Berkeley citizens were infuriated that the election had not been sufficiently publicized and that so short a notice was given. There was very little voting in the two other precincts of the county. Stephen's high-handedness accentuated his continuing feud with Jacob Hite. A petition protesting Stephen's actions signed by 104 county residents, with Hite heading the list and including Horatio Gates, was sent to the Convention, asking that the election be nullified and that a new one be scheduled. Stephen was accused of taking upon himself the sole power of setting the time of the election and affording inadequate notice; not only did many persons not learn of the election but for those who did there was no time to appraise "the merits and abilities" of the candidates. Citizens had requested that the balloting be extended at least one day. Stephen, however, refused; he "imperiously declared that he viewed himself as duly elected and whatever might be the Opinion of the County was determined to attend whenever a Convention should be summoned." The petitioners considered Stephen's election procedure "to be a most daring and violent attack upon their Liberty of Suffrage at a time when the publick Voice in all matters referred to them ought to be collected in the most free open and unbiassed manner."[11]

The petitioners' charges were also brought before the Berkeley Committee of Safety, which was headed by Stephen. The fifteen members in attendance on June 8 concluded that Stephen had done nothing improper and that by calling other meetings for May 1–2, he had enhanced voter participation. Stephen had acted upon the advice of several committee members in fixing the time of the election, and actually "a Numerous & Respectable body of the Freeholders" showed up at the polls; there was "a fair Election." The criticism against Stephen was "groundless and only tends to create Jealousies and Divisions in the County."[12]

But Jacob Hite was determined to even scores with Stephen. For good measure, Hite went to the public print to let people know what kind of man Adam Stephen really was. By publishing a lengthy indictment of Stephen's handling of the Hunter debt case in the *Virginia Gazette* on July 6, 1775, he hoped to disparage Stephen's character before the Convention, which would be an added factor toward a decision to have Stephen disqualified as a delegate. Hite, in the newspaper piece, accused Stephen of not only forcibly taking his property to satisfy the Hunter debt and selling some of it at less than half value but also getting an injunction from the General Court "to stop whatever monies were in his or his deputy's hands, belonging to me, for the satisfaction of Mr. Hunters demands against me" at the same time that Hite had suits before the local court for amounts greater than the Hunter debt. Whenever Hite sought to recover from the sheriff money due him, "I am silenced by producing the injunction! . . . Mr. Sheriff is ordered to retain all money which is or shall come into his hands, but is not ordered to pass a receipt for any part of it." Hite accused Stephen of converting the escrow funds for his own use.[13] This charge of Hite's appears blantantly false; no evidence was presented to this effect; nor did Stephen face any legal prosecution for having appropriated to himself any of the money in question.

With his honor thus impugned before all of the citizens of the colony, Stephen decided nearly three months later to print a rebuttal in the newspaper. Why he took so long is not known, but there were the matters of attendance as a delegate to the Virginia Convention and also service as an Indian commissioner during the intervening period.

In a letter to John Dixon and William Hunter, published in their *Virginia Gazette* on September 30, 1775, Stephen presented his side of the dispute. Because Stephen was serving as an Indian commissioner when he wrote the letter, he said a complete review of the case would have to wait his return. In the meantime it would suffice to inform the public certain facts. Stephen's deputy sheriff had committed him to security of £1,600 "by trusting to JACOB HITE's Word for Delivery of the Effects on the Day of Sale," which would satisfy the debt owed by Hite to James Hunter. Stephen admitted that "I did necessarily interfere in that Affair, on Purpose to have Justice done to an honest Man, as well as to save my own Character and Estate," but not "until several *Venditions Exponas* had been issued" and "I had at last procured a Number of Purchasers, with ready Cash." The prospective buyers "assembled at the appointed Day of Sale, and the Effects might have been sold to the greatest Advantage, but JACOB HITE would not produce a single Article that had been executed."

Stephen pointed out that Hunter had given Hite ample extension of time to pay the debt. Stephen also recounted how he had seized slaves and horses belonging to Hite and how Hite with an armed band had broken into the jail and stable and released the seized chattel, which he then sent to his new estate in South Carolina to avoid further attachment. Stephen mentioned that the part of Hite's estate "that came to my Hands was sell sold," in spite of Hite's "designing to buy every Thing at an under Rate himself." Hite, "in Order to defraud the Creditor," forbade "the Purchasers to buy, and sued every one of them as soon as they had purchased. Near an

Hundred Suits are not depending on Account of that affair." Hite "seems uneasy, least Mr. HUNTER has not received the Money for the Sales. I wish he would pay Mr. HUNTER the £1000 which yet remains due on that Judgment. Mr. HUNTER is in Possession of all the Sheriff's Returns and Account of Sales, and can best tell what Money is due upon that Account." Jacob Hite was "so void of Honour and Integrity that he is not to be bound by Promise, either in Word or Writing. . . . He seems to promise only with a View to deceive"; besides "the groundless Imputations thrown out against me with licentious Virulence," Hite had also accused the General Court of "Partiality" and "the Court of FREDERICKSBURG with being arbitrary." Stephen concluded by apologizing to the readers; "I am sorry to be obliged to give the Public the Trouble of attending to private Disputes." It would seem, on the balance, that Stephen simply had been carrying out his duties as sheriff, though perhaps with more haste and persistence than he would have in other similar cases. The bitter feud between Hite and Stephen would soon end. Stephen would go off to war, and Hite, upon returning to his new home in South Carolina, was killed by a band of Cherokee Indians.[14]

Meanwhile, Stephen and Robert Rutherford, the two Berkeley delegates, traveled to Richmond to attend the third Convention. They knew that this body, like the House of Burgesses, claimed the right to be a judge of the election of its members. The petition of the local residents protesting the Berkeley County election was turned over to the Committee on Privileges and Elections. With the support of the Berkeley County committee, Stephen thought it would only get a perfunctory hearing. But the large number of petitioners could not be discounted. On July 27 the committee submitted its report, and the Convention passed a resolution declaring the election of the Berkeley County delegates "irregular" and calling upon the county to conduct a new poll.[15]

Thus both Stephen and Rutherford were disqualified from serving in the Convention. Because it adjourned on August 26, there was not enough time for new delegates to be returned. When the election was held, Rutherford, who probably had nothing to do with Stephen's calling the hasty May election, regained his seat, and he served in the next meeting of the Convention, commencing in

December. Stephen probably did not stand for election because he still had a major duty to perform as an Indian commissioner. William Drew, clerk of Berkeley County, replaced Stephen. Drew had not been a signer of the petition against Stephen and probably was a member of the county committee that had absolved Stephen of any misdoing. Drew later was reelected to serve in the fifth and final Convention of May–July 1776.[16]

Before his ouster, Stephen had an important role in the Convention, which on July 19, 1775, resolved "that a sufficient armed Force be immediately raised and embodyed, under proper Officers for the Defense and protection of this Colony." Stephen was one of seventeen persons appointed to prepare and bring in an ordinance. The Committee for Raising and Embodying a Sufficient Force for the Defense and Protection of This Colony wasted no time in settling down to work. It met each day from 7 to 9 A.M. before the Convention assembled and, as George Mason reported, also in the evening "immediately after dinner and a little refreshment" until 9 or 10 P.M. The resulting ordinance, which passed August 21, provided for the raising of two regiments for the Continental army, two companies of 113 men and officers for frontier defense, and for each military district one or more companies of 68 militia each and one battalion of 500 "minute men," who could instantly take to the field.[17]

It is possible that Stephen before or after his Convention service in summer 1775 visited Philadelphia, perhaps to consult with some of the congressmen and to check out marketing connections. Dr. Benjamin Rush many years later recalled a conversation with Stephen allegedly in Philadelphia during summer 1775. The famed physician may have confused the particulars when he noted in a letter to John Adams in February 1812 that in summer 1775 "I dined in company with General, then Colonel Stevens on his way from Virginia to the camp [Stephen, of course, did not go on to Cambridge]. I sat next to him. In a low tone of voice he asked me who constituted General Washington's military family." Rush replied that Washington's aides were Col. Joseph Reed and Maj. Thomas Mifflin, both of whom were serving as military secretaries to the commander in chief in July and August 1775.

"Are they men of talent?" said he.

"Yes," said I.

"I am glad to hear it," said the General, "for General Washington will require such men about him. He is a *weak man.* I know him well. I served with him during the last French war."[18]

If Stephen did go to Philadelphia after leaving the Convention, he did not have much time at home on his return. The Convention had not countermanded the General Assembly's appointment of the Indian commissioners. In early September, Stephen along with the other Virginia commissioners (Andrew Lewis, James Wood, and John and Thomas Walker) left for Fort Pitt and, "after a very disagreeable, wet and fateagueing Journey," arrived there on the tenth, the date for opening the Indian conference. "Scarcely any Indians" had showed up, and runners were sent to hurry them on. Tribes invited to the parley were the Delawares, Shawnees, Wyandots, Mingoes (Ohio Iroquois), Senecas (from the upper Allegheny River), Ottawas (from near Detroit), and Pottawatomies (from the northwestern Ohio country). Stephen and the other Virginia commissioners jointly wrote a letter to Thomas Jefferson, who was serving in Congress, reminding him of "the unhappy territorial dispute" between Pennsylvania and Virginia. Both colonies claimed jurisdiction over the Fort Pitt vicinity and had established rival county governments. Already physical intimidation had occurred between the Pennsylvania and Virginia factions. Capt. John Neville with 100 men, by orders of the Virginia Convention, had officially taken possession of Fort Pitt. The commissioners told Jefferson that Congress should refuse to consider a Pennsylvania petition concerning the contested jurisdiction; but if they did, Jefferson and the other Virginia congressmen should object to the surrender of any territory west of Laurel Hill to Pennsylvania.[19]

To confuse matters at the Indian conference, there were several American delegations. Besides Stephen and his associates, there was a six-man commission sent by the Virginia Convention to settle accounts with the Indians. James Wilson, Lewis Morris, and Thomas Walker (also a Virginia commissioner) served as emissaries of Congress.[20] Walker was named chairman of "the Joint Commission," consisting of the congressional and Virginia treaty delegations. An

English tourist at Fort Pitt at the time commented that the various commissioners were all colonels, majors, or captains "and very big with their own importance." He was also dismayed at the intercolonial friction. "Disputes," he said, "are very high between Virginia and Pennsylvania and if not timely suppressed will end in tragic consequences. . . . Nothing but quarrelling and fighting in every part of the town."[21]

When more Indians had not arrived by September 12, Stephen and his fellow commissioners dispatched John Gibson, a Virginia trader, and Allaniwisica (probably Cornstalk's son) with a message to prod the Delaware and Shawnee delegations to move a little faster.[22] Three days later many Indians appeared, and the treaty conference officially began, lasting thirty-four days, until October 19. As one writer has mentioned, the Fort Pitt treaty conference was "by far the largest deliberative congress of Indians that ever assembled in the valley of the Ohio." Although there was no new agenda, every detail of the Camp Charlotte agreement was thoroughly discussed. Probably at no other time in early America were there so many great chiefs together at one place. On September 26 Cornstalk and Blue Jacket with the Shawnees arrived to the beating of drums, the flying of colors, and a salute of musketry. The White Mingo and his Indians appeared four days later, and on October 7 Captain Pipe and Custaloga with the Delawares. There were also the Half-King of the Wyandots and Shaganaba, son of the renowned Ottawa warrior Pontiac. Each group of Indians contained a number of chiefs. One of these was Blue Jacket, who was a white man. Formerly Marmaduke Van Swearingen of Fauquier County, Virginia, this young man four years earlier at age seventeen voluntarily had gone off with a Shawnee hunting party. He was adopted by the Indians; as Blue Jacket he became the principal Shawnee chief and the terror of the Ohio-Kentucky settlements during the later Indian wars.[23]

With so many Indians at the conference there was bound to be some altercations with the local whites. Stephen and other commissioners on one occasion visited the Indian camp to straighten out a quarrel and discovered that the Indians "had Misapprehended the White People from their small Acquaintance with the Language."

One problem—the burning of a fort and some houses at the mouth of the Kanawha River—by young Shawnees threatened to disrupt the treaty. Cornstalk, however, to demonstrate his sincerity, brought the first news of this outrage to the conference and condemned it.[24]

What bothered Stephen most was evidence that the Indians were leaning toward an alliance with the British. He pointed out to Richard Henry Lee, in a letter of September 23, that the British at Detroit, Niagara, Albany, and Caughnawaga (near Montreal) were holding consultations with emissaries of various tribes. What Stephen observed was the beginning of a contest between the Americans and the British for the loyalty, or at least the neutrality, of the western Indians; it was a struggle which would not end until some forty years later. The British had told the Indians, Stephen noted, that the Americans could not fight for long because they lacked gunpowder. "I can see that the Indians are very jealous, greatly divided, and at a loss how to act," he said. Stephen thought that the invasion of Canada by American troops then under way should convince the Indians to refrain from any alliance with the British. "General Schuyler's success will settle the matter," said Stephen. "But an unsuccessful attempt will determine the greatest part of the western Indians against us; perhaps make it necessary to take possession of Niagara and Detroit."[25] Lee forwarded Stephen's comments to Washington, noting that the Indians "evidently appear to be waiting the event of things in Canada, when they will surely according to custom join the strongest side."[26] The American commissioners did not know that the British at Detroit had sent Peter Drouillard, a Frenchman and Indian trader, to spy on the conference. Drouillard did not enter Pittsburgh but at a concealed position about ten miles from the town met from time to time with Indians who were attending the treaty.[27]

The commissioners sought to impress upon the Indians that they represented a whole nation, not just individual colonies. Lewis Morris, in a speech of October 7, emphasized this point: "what we may now say is from all the Wisemen of all our United Colonies who are as one Man and that Virginia is one of them and as the right Arm." The Indians, said Morris, should "not believe those who tell you that the Virginians are a Distinct People. The Country of your Brother Onas [Pennsylvania] is also one of the thirteen United Colonies and it is in his great Town where the Wisemen from Virginia and all the other Provinces now sat in our Council."[28] Many speeches were given by the chiefs, who reciprocated in expressions of friendship and said they recognized the unity of the colonies.[29] Thomas Walker and his son, John Walker (on one occasion), appear to have been the only Virginia commissioners who made addresses for the record.

The Fort Pitt conference ratified the Camp Charlotte agreement, specifically recognizing the Ohio River boundary and requiring the Indians to surrender all captive persons and horses. Also, the Indians pledged neutrality in the British-American war. Two white men were permitted to accompany each group of Indians on their return and visit the Indian towns to see that the terms concerning the hostages and horses were implemented. Stephen, Lewis, Wood, and Thomas Walker signed the new agreement on October 21 and then departed for Virginia. John Walker had left the conference about ten days earlier.[30] The Treaty of Pittsburgh proved significant. The Indian pledge of neutrality lasted two years, thereby aiding the American prosecution of the war. Thomas Walker, accompanied by a young son of the Indian chief Bawbee, brought the treaty to Williamsburg.[31]

Although Virginians breathed more freely with the assurance of peace on the frontier, there was cause for alarm from a different source. As Adam Stephen discovered upon his return to the Valley after a two months' absence, war clouds had darkened in the colony. Several hundred Virginia volunteers from the county independent companies had encamped on the outskirts of Williamsburg during summer 1775. Governor Dunmore, aboard HMS *Fowey*, now in the company of other British war vessels, was determined to defeat rebel militia in the lower Tidewater. The third Virginia Convention in August 1775 sent troops to defend Norfolk and Portsmouth against Dunmore's motley army of British seamen and marines, blacks, and loyalists. The governor repulsed militia at Kemp's Landing on November 17, but on December 9 at Great Bridge, twelve miles below Norfolk, his force lost a hard-fought battle. Although having taken Norfolk, Dunmore now put all his troops on ships in the city's harbor. Col. William Woodford, with 1,000 men, marched into Norfolk on December 14. Except for cannonading there was little action until January 1, 1776, when Dunmore's marines and sailors, under effective cover of ship artillery, landed at the waterfront and set afire the buildings at the wharf. Flames spread, and soon most of the city was in ashes. Woodford's force and North Carolina troops under Col. Robert Howe continued to occupy Norfolk until early February, with skirmishing and firing between the British and Americans in and around the city. Upon orders from the Virginia Convention, Norfolk was evacuated, and the American troops were then posted at various places, including Kemp's Landing, Great Bridge, and Suffolk, awaiting Dunmore's next move. The fourth Virginia Convention, which had convened on December 1, 1775, called for six additional regiments in the field, to make the total eight; the Virginia troops were now to enter into the Continental line, under the authority of Congress. On January 12 the Convention elected Adam Stephen commander of the 4th Virginia Regiment, at the rank of colonel. Stephen was ordered to take post immediately at Suffolk.[32]

Stephen did not get into the field until early May. He may have been waiting for his regiment to be fully raised and to see what arrangements Congress would make in receiving the Virginia regiments into the Continental line, especially what seniority would be given him. On February 4, 1776, he reported to Congressman Richard Henry Lee that the two companies ordered from Berkeley County were completed and ready to march. "If they are so active throughout the Colony the Levies will soon be Completed," he commented. Stephen again offered Lee suggestions as to the policy-making of Congress. That body should apply for foreign aid, "as the Bloody Violence of K—g & Ministry & the Apathy of the people of Britain, seem to me incurable. Every Sinew must be Exerted! Nothing but plentiful bleeding by Successful opposition, will bring them to their Senses." Stephen also advised that Congress should make efforts to obtain from France supplies and naval protection of American merchant vessels. Americans, however, could depend entirely on their own manpower.

Stephen reminded Lee of his claim to a senior military status by virtue of his long experience, dating back twenty-two years. He reiterated the steps in his army career, concerned that men who had been junior to him in rank during the French and Indian War would now be given preference over him. "Col Hugh Mercer Served but 58, 9, & 60," Stephen pointed out, while "I have Served Eleven Campaigns, & have nothing to reproach my Self . . . Heaven was pleasd to bless me with Success—Were I not of Abilities, & Experience equal to any; Who pretends to the Command of our troops, I would not mention this to you, Whom I look upon as Concerned in my Conduct."[33] Stephen's reference was to Col. William Woodford, who had emerged from the last war as only a captain. He may also have had Andrew Lewis in mind; Lewis would soon be appointed commander of all the Virginia troops.

The Virginia field officers, from the war's start, displayed a high degree of sensitivity about their seniority in rank. Stephen's expression of his apprehension as to his own status was justified, for Congress as a whole was not always well informed about the background of the men whom it gave rank in the Continental army. Certainly in provincial service Stephen had the greater depth of experience and seniority over Lewis, Mercer, and Woodford. Stephen's credentials as a military officer also had been enhanced since the French and Indian War. While honing his plantation management skills, he served as colonel and county lieutenant of the local militia and again had led troops in the field in the Indian expedition. As sheriff, justice of the peace, head of the county committee of safety, delegate to the Virginia Convention, and Indian commissioner, Stephen had gained further experience in leadership and diverse personal relations.

Congress accepted the Virginia regiments into the Continental line, and on February 13, 1776, it elected the officers for these units, in effect confirming the appointments that the Virginia Convention already had made.[34] Thus, in the Continental establishment, the commissions of Stephen, Mercer, and Woodford bore the same date. On March 1 Congress elected Lewis a brigadier general. As colonel in the army of the United Colonies, soon to be the United States, Adam Stephen not only would have a broader obligation of military duty than he had ever before but also would find himself in a different kind of warfare, one taken out of the woods and put into a context of large armies maneuvering and fighting according to European tactics.

NINE

"Rejoice! Let Us Rejoice!"

At last, in May 1776, Adam Stephen reported to Maj. Gen. Charles Lee, commander of American forces in the southern department, and Brig. Gen. Andrew Lewis at Williamsburg to assume his regimental command. Lee was temporarily in Virginia to help organize the colony's defenses. Stephen's first assignment was to lead his 4th Regiment to Suffolk, to join the 2d and 5th regiments there and relieve Col. John Peter Muhlenberg and his 8th "German" Regiment so that they could accompany General Lee to Charleston, South Carolina. A British expeditionary force under Gen. Henry Clinton had reached the North Carolina coast and, reinforced by a fleet and troops from England, was ready to move against the South Carolina port. Muhlenberg and his regiment left for Charleston on May 16, and Stephen assumed command of the Virginia troops in the Suffolk area.[1] Just about everything was in disorder among the Virginia soldiers at Suffolk. The food was bad; the sick, dispersed about the town had no physician to attend them; the men were ill-disciplined; and many of them were without arms.[2]

Stephen, however, did not stay long in Suffolk, which had been considered a good staging area for operations should Dunmore and his fleet remain at the head of the Elizabeth River near Norfolk and Portsmouth. The enemy had entrenched at Tucker's Mill Point (today Hospital Point) near Norfolk. Thick breastworks offered cover for Dunmore's ships from the land side, and local tories supplied the British force with flour and provisions. But Dunmore's position became increasingly precarious. The Americans were greatly superior in manpower and were collecting numerous small craft. Reinforcements that Dunmore had expected from England did not arrive. Furthermore, he was deprived of much of his loyalist support when the Virginia Convention ordered the evacuation of the inhabitants of Norfolk and Princess Anne counties. On May 22 Dunmore abandoned his camp at Tucker's Mill Point, and the British war and merchant vessels sailed out of Norfolk harbor into the Chesapeake Bay. From May 23 to May 26 the British ships anchored at Hampton Roads, and then they moved to Gwynn's Island, near the mouth of the Rappahannock.[3]

Just after the British left Tucker's Mill Point, Stephen led a detachment to view the evacuated works. He reported to Edmund Pendleton, president of the Virginia Convention, that he kept his men distant from the interior of the former British camp, "as it is certain that pestilential disorder Raged in the fleet"; 300 "fresh graves" were discovered, "some of them large enough to contain the Carcasses of a Corporals Command." Stephen himself reconnoitered the vicinity of Norfolk and Portsmouth and sent a detachment to Craney Island, at the mouth of the Elizabeth River, "in order to protect the Inhabitants & Stock on that Quarter; as well as take advantage of any Accidents that should befall so numerous a fleet, passing a narrow channel." Stephen went into Norfolk and was shocked with what he saw; the destroyed city "is a standing monument of the Weakness of our Counsels, & feeble Efforts; before we were rous'd to a just sense of our Danger and Interests." The "promiscuous Ruin" of the churches, the courthouse, and "the convenient & Elegant habitations of our friends as well as foes, produce feelings which Humanity cannot with propriety withhold." Stephen advised Pendleton that the former British breastworks should be strengthened by the Americans in the event of a new invasion by Dunmore. They formed "the most advantageous post the Enemy can possess in Virginia for prosecuting their piratical War. . . . We can have our Strength collected at one or two places Contiguous; which will command respect from our Enemy, & establish better Orders and discipline." If the enemy could be kept out of the Elizabeth River, they would "have no place to the South-ward of Halifax to clean & repair their ships." Also, Stephen recommended that the completion of a "large ship on the Stocks" and the building of "Row-galleys, floating Batteries, & fire boats" would serve to "secure" the Elizabeth River.[4]

Stephen wrote in a similar vein to Dudley Digges, a member of the Virginia Committee of Safety. It was important to erect fortifications on the Elizabeth River, said Stephen, and "I am impatient & anxious to have it done." Stephen also informed Digges that he had "taken possession of the Grounds at the New distillery & Town Point" at Portsmouth, where "we will have it in our power to blow a Ship out of Water, or under Water, as you Gentlemen shall think proper to Command."[5] For several weeks Stephen supervised construction of fortifications at Portsmouth. He acted independently of General Lewis, who, because he had not himself inspected the area, did not take offense that he was not consulted.[6]

July 3 brought back memories of the defeat at Great Meadows in 1754, and Stephen thought this would be a good time to write his commander in chief. Washington was also nostalgic, and his reply to his old comrade in arms, on July 10, seemed to offer a reconciliation between the two men. Washington thanked Stephen for his "kind congratulations on the discovery of the vile Machinations of still viler Ministerial Agents," in reference to the nipping of an alleged assassination plot against Washington in New York City. Washington brought Stephen up-to-date on his own military situation. Howe had landed nearly 9,000 troops on Staten Island and was expecting reinforcements that would bring the British army up to 20,000 men. Washington hoped that after harvest his own military force would increase. Washington, too, reflected on the past campaigns. "I did not let the Anniversary of the 3d. or 9th. . . . . pass," he said, "without a grateful remembrance of the escape we had at the Meadows and on the Banks of Monongahela." The "same Providence that protected us upon those occasions will, I hope, continue his Mercies, and make us happy Instruments in restoring Peace and liberty to this once favour'd, but now distressed Country."[7]

Instead of renewing an offensive, as Stephen had expected, Lord Dunmore and his fleet and little army remained stationary at Gwynn's

Island. General Lewis and the other field officers decided it was time to take the war to the enemy. Lewis, regimental commanders Stephen, Mordecai Buckner, George Weedon, and William Christian, and several other officers went down to the American camp across from Gwynn's Island. The forward Virginia force consisted of six companies of the 1st and four companies of the 2d regiments. Arriving at night on the eighth, the officers found that the *Dunmore* "had exposed herself very prettily." Lewis immediately ordered two American 18-pounders to open up on the *Otter* and *Dunmore*. Cannonading was renewed at 8 A.M. the next morning and continued for an hour and a half. The *Otter*, almost a mile away, was struck "between Wind & Water," and four volleys pounded the *Dunmore* on the sides and another hit her in the stern. Three British sailors were killed, including the boatswain, and Dunmore himself was slightly injured. As Stephen commented, the first cannonade against the *Dunmore* "destroyed his Lordships China, & Spoild his dancing by driving a splinter into his Leg." At noon the firing resumed, with artillery concentrating on the smaller British vessels. Lewis had neglected to collect boats, but by the next day, the tenth, enough canoes and small craft had been secured to effect a landing on the island. Lewis sent over a detachment under Col. Alexander McClanachan, but before these troops reached the island, Dunmore had gathered all his force shipboard and had pulled anchor on the four warships (*Fowey, Otter, Dunmore,* and *Roebuck*) and the many smaller vessels. The fleet headed up the Chesapeake and into the Potomac. Lewis and the Virginians did manage to capture a British sloop and schooner. The only rebel casualty during the "battle" of Gwynn's Island was the death of Capt. Dohicky Arundel, occasioned by the bursting of his new-style mortar.[8] Stephen had little to do but observe the artillery firing, but nevertheless he was party to an important event: the uprooting of Dunmore and his force from their last base in Virginia, thereby putting an end to the governor's invasion of his own colony.

A grisly sight awaited the American troops who crossed over to Gwynn's Island: dead and dying blacks strewn along a path for about two miles. Smallpox had taken a heavy toll among Dunmore's "Ethiopians," the slaves who had answered the governor's emancipation proclamation offering liberty on condition of military service. Hundreds of blacks died, including women and children who had also fled to the protection of Dunmore's fleet. Although inoculation reduced smallpox among the whites in Dunmore's army and fleet, scurvy and typhus were rampant among both seamen and soldiers.[9]

Stephen was jubilant over the withdrawal of Dunmore. He wrote Gen. Charles Lee, who was at Charleston, an account of the affair and other news, while offering encouragement to Lee in facing the onslaught of British forces in Charleston harbor. Stephen had heard that the British attack on Fort Sullivan was stalled. Stephen told Lee: "In the words of that zealous Grecian, who run himself to death, to announce at Athens the Successful Event of the Battle of Marathon; I do most Cordially congratulate you; Chairite! Chairamen! Rejoice! Let us Rejoice! Upon which expression, the Athenian expired; but there I beg leave to be off; and will patiently wait, to hear more Joyful news from you."[10]

Besides contending with Lord Dunmore during summer 1776, Virginians faced another threat. The Overhill Cherokees exhibited a "hostile Disposition" along the southwest Virginian and North Carolina frontiers. The new Virginia state government asked Stephen's advice on what should be done, because he had commanded the Cherokee expedition of 1762–63. The council adopted Stephen's suggestions that Virginia supply 1,200 men for an Indian expedition and that North Carolina be called upon to contribute 300 troops from its frontier counties. Stephen believed that Cherokees from the lower towns, hard-pressed by local militia, would move into the Overhill villages, thus making it possible for a large Indian force to conduct "a formidable attack on the Troops on Holstan River."[11]

Stephen apprised Congressman Thomas Jefferson of the Indian situation and, of course, cited his own role in the last Cherokee War. He also commented on the Revolutionary War in the north and in Virginia. "It is with dread, and dispondency that I look towards New York," he said. "I wish all the Virginia Troops were with Genl. Washington, to give him One Weeks Work and help out with the dead lift. I heartily Sympathize with him: there is great difference between the Number of Men, and Soldiers." As if to emphasize his own ability for military command, Stephen told Jefferson

that the Americans could have seriously damaged British ships passing through the Narrows at the entrance of New York harbor by
making use of water batteries to assist the ground artillery. Stephen
noted that in Virginia he had taken such a precaution, emplacing
artillery at Portsmouth and Windmill Point "to clear the Har-
bour." He also reported the ascent of Dunmore's fleet up the Potomac. A British party had landed near Dumfries and burned a plantation house. "The Poltroons, the Militia of Stafford," ran away.
The enemy group then sought to destroy a mill, "but 30 of the P.
William militia happily arrivd, advancd with good Countenance,"
and drove the intruders back to their boats. Then the Prince William
militia "went to look for the Runaways, and making briskly up
to them, the Stafford men Squatted in thickets, imagind it to be
English men, and run them selves almost to death, to avoid falling
into the hands of the P. William Militia. Pudet hoc Opprobrium
Nobis." [12]

While Dunmore's fleet cruised the Potomac, Stephen and companies of the 4th and 5th regiments returned to work on fortifications at Portsmouth. Stephen also directed construction of six
boats. [13] He was prepared to dispute any British landing in the Portsmouth vicinity. After anchoring off St. George Island, the British
fleet reentered the bay, arriving at the Capes on August 4. Stephen
claimed that a small detachment which he sent to Cape Henry "repulsed" a British landing party. [14]

It was impossible for Dunmore to restage an invasion. Disease
had left him with only 150 effective troops. The unsuccessful Clinton
expedition on its return from Charleston harbor bypassed Chesapeake Bay, thereby denying the last faint hope for reinforcements.
Capt. Andrew Snape Hamond of the *Roebuck* commented on the
decision that had to be made: "[I am] myself most heartily tired
of carrying on a sort of Piratical war, that tended in no degree to
benefit his Majestys Service," and "his Lordship" was "equally desirous of quitting a situation that was every day growing more &
more distressing." [15] On August 5 Dunmore's fleet sailed from the
Virginia Capes in two directions. The *Otter* and a convoy of mostly
small loyalist craft headed for Saint Augustine and Bermuda. Dunmore and Hamond, with the *Fowey*, *Roebuck*, and *Dunmore*, accom-

panied by five transports with a number of small vessels, got under way for New York.[16]

After Dunmore's departure, Stephen, in order to guard against any future invasion, remained in Portsmouth looking after defense preparations. Richard Henry Lee later wrote Jefferson that "Stephen tells me that the works he laid out at Portsmouth will put (if properly gunned) that place in a state of security from any Seaforce that can come against it."[17]

Congress fully recognized Stephen's services, not in small part because of the backing that Stephen had from Virginia congressmen. Richard Henry Lee and Thomas Jefferson were gratified to receive Stephen's witty and newsy letters, which also displayed military knowledge. Stephen, personally, now had occasion to "rejoice." He would soon be taking part in a larger war with an expanded command. Congress on September 3, 1776, ordered three more regiments from Virginia "to reinforce the army at New York, of which that commanded by Colonel Stephen to be one." The 1st and 3d Virginia regiments had already left for that city in August, arriving in time for the battle of Harlem Heights on September 16. Stephen was delighted to learn that Congress, on September 4, had unanimously elected him a brigadier general in the Continental army.[18]

Stephen had maintained a warm rapport with the officers of his 4th Regiment, and they were glad for his good fortune. They presented him with an "address," expressing their "heart-felt satisfaction." It was a promotion "justly due to your merit." Furthermore, "when we reflect, Sir, on the kind, the indulgent, though manly treatment, we have received whilst under your immediate eye" and "consider with what facility you established amongst us that discipline and order so essential to the preservation and glory of an army, we are at a loss which most to admire, the polite Gentleman, or the accomplished officer." The officers, "with hearts replete with gratitude and respect," implored divine guidance for Stephen's safety in future service. Stephen graciously acknowledged the commendation. "In the course of all my service (and this is the twelfth campaign)," he said, "I have seldom met with officers so warmly attached to the service, or so anxious and attentive to study their duty." Stephen declared that he would always be interested "in the behaviour of the 4th battalion" and he was confident that the unit would continue to perform with honor and distinction.[19]

Praise of Stephen was also expressed by residents of Norfolk and Princess Anne counties, in an unsigned notice printed in the *Virginia Gazette*. The local citizens offered Stephen "their warmest, sincerest, and most heart-felt acknowledgements, not only for the military operations which he carried on at Portsmouth with so much spirit and judgment for their protection and safety, but the politeness, humanity, and benevolence, which he has been pleased to shew on all occasions, to all ranks of people." Stephen's service, they pointed out, contrasted with that of officers who previously commanded in the area, when there was disregard of citizens's rights and property; indirect references were made to the army's attempt, before Stephen's arrival, to relocate persons and to its having put the final torch to Norfolk in February 1776.[20]

Stephen prepared to join Washington's army near New York City. Gen. Andrew Lewis, commander of all Continental troops in Virginia, notified Congress on September 10 that he had directed the 4th, 5th, and 6th regiments to march speedily northward. The three units, forming Stephen's new brigade, were headed respectively by Colonels Thomas Elliot, Charles Scott, and Mordecai Buckner. Because of illness, with half of the brigade sick, and logistical problems, including insufficiency of arms, the Virginia troops were not on their way until the first week in October.[21]

Now, as a general in the Continental army, Stephen would have no time to oversee his farming, industries, and real estate concerns. Anthony Noble managed the new arms manufactory during Stephen's absence. The muskets and bayonets were delivered by wagon to Williamsburg to supply the Virginia militia. The gunnery employed some thirty workers. Noble, in a progress report on November 14, 1776, noted many labor problems: work slowdowns, grumbling and complaints, employees taking "French Leave," and difficulty in retaining skilled workers. Yet work continued. The "Guns and Cocks" made at Stephen's plant, Noble said, "are equal . . . in Goodness work and Beauty" to those produced at James Hunter's arms manufactory at the outskirts of Fredericksburg.[22]

Because of inadequate cost effectiveness, Stephen's arms manufactory made little profit. Noble sent Stephen reports over the next year. The costs of materials and labor increased drastically, and as Noble wrote in April 1777, "every thing hear is nearly double to what it used to be." Despite "unavoidable delays" and "unforeseen accidents," efficiency at the gunnery improved somewhat. Noble observed that he was about to send 100 stand of arms to Williamsburg; when all the employees "all stick at their work (which is very difficult to make them) we can turn out 18 Stand a week, but they may be averaged at 15 a week."[23] Four months later Noble wrote Stephen that he was sending another 100 stand of arms to the Virginia capital.[24] After delivering 138 stand of arms in October, Noble reported that the price was good, and in the future it could be expected that each musket would bring £8. Labor relations, however, had deteriorated. When Noble returned to the gunnery, he "found the Hands all Idle, standing out for more wages, and not a single Gun made. The wages they already have are more than we well can afford to give, considering the high prices of materials and the great expence the works are carried on at." Noble, therefore, was "Determined not to advance the prices a single farthing—I have told them this; and in consequence of which some of them have left me." Half of these workers soon returned to their jobs. Noble commented that gunnery workers "in general are a parcile of Villains, they are eternally a plotting, and throwing everything into confusion, and the more one hurries them the worse they are. I know no way to manage them, but to turn the grumbling rascalls out of doors."[25]

Noble also looked after the flour mill and distillery, which had problems similar to those at the gunnery. The distiller was "fractious" and "ill natured," but because "there are more of them" who had "failings," Noble said that he "had to put up with him"; the pay was 10*d.* per gallon of the whiskey manufactured plus provisions. The supply of rye and wheat was almost exhausted, but Noble pledged that "the stills shall be keped Constantly a going let the price of grain be what it will." The miller had quit, and the new one "is now laying for death. I think it will be impossible for him to recover." Noble also noted that "there are now in the Mill something better than 3 Hhds of whiskey. The man whom Major Hunter

had employed to carry two Hhds to Camp never came for them."²⁶
It seems, therefore, that some of Stephen's whiskey was destined for
Washington's army. Ephraim Gaither managed Stephen's business
affairs, chiefly selling lots for the new town, and Jonathan Seaman
looked after the Bower plantation. Labor, of course, was scarce, but
at least some of the men at the gunnery, despite a certain amount of
feuding with local militia officers, were exempted from the draft.²⁷

Thus, with all his enterprises administered by persons in whom
he had confidence, Stephen gave full attention to his military duties. While readying his troops for the journey northward in autumn 1776, Stephen wound up the quasi-naval activities that had
been thrust on him while commandant at Portsmouth. A number of
boats were completed. The Virginia government decided to extend
defense preparations at Portsmouth, and Stephen and Lewis were
summoned before the council to get that board's recommenda-
tions.²⁸ But Stephen could not now be concerned with local defense, for it was urgent that he and his troops join Washington's
army. Partly on Stephen's recommendation, James Maxwell, a merchant and seamaster, was placed in charge of all ship construction in
the state.²⁹

As suggested by Washington in order to speed on the Virginia
Continentals, Stephen's force traveled by water up the bay to Head
of Elk, Maryland.³⁰ By October 5 Stephen and the 4th Regiment
(the 5th and 6th followed a week later) had reached Annapolis. On
the following day, a Sunday, he had to answer a charge placed
against him in the Maryland Council of Safety that he had illegally
impressed a black pilot at Annapolis to guide his boats to the Head
of Elk. Stephen apologized, though pointing out that the had obtained the consent of the slave's owner. The Council of Safety was
sympathetic and obtained another pilot for him.³¹

There was a change of plans as to the destination of Stephen's
troops. Washington's army, except for a sizable force at Fort Washington, had left Manhattan Island. It was questionable what General Howe and the British army would do next. With Philadelphia
vulnerable, Congress took upon itself to order that the Virginia
troops remain temporarily along the Delaware River. Stephen and
the 4th Regiment camped at Chester, and the 5th and 6th at Wil-

mington. Yet New Jersey was defenseless against the enemy. If Howe intended to take Philadelphia, his army most likely would move through that state from New York. Gen. Charles Lee, now commanding the middle department of the American army, advised Congress that "the sooner the Virginia battalions march, at least as far as Brunswick, the better."[32]

The congressional Board of War ordered Stephen and his brigade to move upriver to Trenton. The three regiments linked up at that town and a week later were directed to advance farther into New Jersey. Stephen left 324 sick men at Trenton, informing Congress that these "Convalescents could take a brush with the Enemy occasionally." Congress now left the disposition of the Virginians to Washington. On November 9 the commander in chief wrote Gen. Nathanael Greene, who commanded all patriot troops in New Jersey, to deploy Stephen's brigade and Hugh Mercer's "Flying Camp" as he saw fit. Stephen headed for the port town of Amboy, where he expected to join up with General Mercer's special mobile unit. On the way he wrote the Board of War, "If any thing can be done on Staten Island—I will Rejoice at the Opportunity." Greene asked Mercer to send Stephen's Virginians northward, and he informed Washington that Stephen's troops would be stationed at Aquackanock, a pass in the Highlands (at Passaic). Apparently any orders given to Stephen in this respect were countermanded, and, of course, the American army was soon in full retreat southward through New Jersey. When Stephen and his men reached Amboy on November 16, Mercer and his light troops had left.[33]

The war took a change for the worse. Howe had doubled back after the battle of White Plains on October 28 and captured Fort Washington on November 16. Cornwallis and 6,000 British troops then crossed the Hudson, as did Washington with a force half that size. Fort Lee, across from Fort Washington, had to be evacuated. The American troops now had to link up in New Jersey and either retreat or confront Cornwallis's army in battle. But with his army outnumbered and moving along the flat coastal plain, Washington really had one option—to retreat. Stephen waited at Amboy to form a junction with the rest of the American army. At this location, at the mouth of the Raritan, Stephen's men prepared to resist any attempt of the British to land. General Lord Stirling's eight regiments were close at hand at New Brunswick and could afford assistance to Stephen.[34]

On December 1 Stephen's brigade had 572 men present and fit for duty out of a total of 661. Many of the troops were new recruits. They certainly did not make a good impression, as one person noted of the soldiers of the 6th Regiment when they were earlier encamped at Leesburg, Virginia: they were "a set of dirty, ragged people, badly clothed, badly disciplined and badly armed." Stephen was dissatisfied that so many of his men were riflemen, who would not be too useful in close combat. He asked the Board of War to send him muskets and bayonets as replacements for rifles.[35] Stephen, to some degree, was responsible for the quality of his officers. Congress on November 1 resolved that commissions be granted to fill the vacancies in the 4th, 5th, and 6th regiments "agreeable to the list given in to the Board of War by General Stephen." Stephen was to fill in the dates on the commissions for the captains and subalterns.[36]

In New Jersey, Stephen and his men were disillusioned to find support for the British among the local citizenry. His Virginians apprehended five alleged tories and several British seamen as they were breaking loose a grounded British vessel in Amboy Bay. The collaborators were also charged with giving the enemy intelligence. Stephen had the "parcel of Tories" and seamen escorted under guard to Burlington, where the New Jersey government was then sitting. He advised Governor William Livingston that "some method of punishment" should be found to make the captured tories "useful to the State." Perhaps they could be inducted into the navy; but "at any Rate prevent their Return. Insignificant as they are, should they be permitted to Return the Soldiery will put them to death." Stephen's men, "greatly irritated at finding a Number of disaffected & mischevous persons, daily supplying the Enemy," should not be expected, if this practice continued, "to rough the Rigours of War, & forgo Domestic Felicity; to fight the Battles of a People, who are not willing to distinguish their Friends from their Foes." Under Congress's orders, Stephen's loyalist prisoners, along with a number of Pennsylvania tories, were sent to Frederick, Maryland. They later were returned to New Jersey for examination before that state's

Council of Safety on charges of aiding the enemy, whereupon three were acquitted.[37]

While at Amboy, Stephen learned that the grand army was coming his way. Washington's force lingered at Newark for five days and resumed the retreat on November 28. At New Brunswick, General Stirling's troops joined with the army. When Cornwallis approached the town, Washington withdrew across the Raritan, destroying the bridge behind him. By next morning advance units of the American army were in Princeton. Stephen and his Virginians probably connected with Washington's troops enroute from New Brunswick to Princeton. Stephen's contingent was welcomed, especially since New Jersey and Maryland militia had gone home. Stirling's and Stephen's brigades formed the rear guard as the American army headed for Trenton, where there were soon reinforcements—Col. John Cadwalader's Pennsylvania militia and Col. Nicholas Haussegger's German Regiment. Howe joined Cornwallis at New Brunswick, and now the British army stepped up its pace. Washington, who viewed his present objective as the defense of Philadelphia, decided to enter Pennsylvania.[38]

The Americans made the Delaware crossing on December 7–8. Stephen's troops, still a part of the rear guard, were among the last to leave the east bank. A Hessian detachment of jägers, sent out to catch some of the American rear guard in early afternoon of the eighth, came within 300 paces of the final boat shoving off into the river. American artillery shells, flying over the heads of the troops in midstream, dispersed the Hessians at the river's edge. Because Washington had seized all river craft, Cornwallis's army was unable to continue pursuit. On the Pennsylvania side of the river, Washington spread out four brigades (Stirling, Mercer, Stephen, and Fermoy) and smaller units for a distance of twenty-five miles, from Yardley's Ferry to Coryell's Ferry. Howe returned to New York, and Cornwallis's army now took post at various places in New Jersey—Hessians at Bordentown and Trenton and British units at Princeton, New Brunswick, Maidenhead, Kingston, and Amboy.[39] Should boats be secured or the Delaware freeze over, the British could with ease attack Washington's army in Pennsylvania. But from all appearances, the British army was entering winter cantonment.

In mid-December arrived the distressing news of the capture of Maj. Gen. Charles Lee at Basking Ridge, New Jersey. Lee had been holding back nearly 4,000 troops from Washington's army but at last had decided to join his commander in chief along the Delaware. Gen. John Sullivan eventually would bring in 2,000 of Lee's force to the Delaware encampment.[40] Stephen, who thought it his duty to report events and intelligence to Congress, wrote Thomas Jefferson of Lee's capture and of his own observations. The taking of Lee was an absurdity, Stephen said. "The Enemy like locusts Sweep the Jerseys with the Besom of destruction," Stephen also told Jefferson. "They to the disgrace of a Civilized Nation Ravish the fair Sex, from the Age of Ten to Seventy. The Tories are Baneful in pointing out the friends to the American Cause, and giving Notice of every Motion we make." Though being careful not to reflect adversely on his commander in chief, Stephen did have veiled criticism of Washington's reliance on some bad advice from his generals, with Gen. Nathanael Greene obviously in mind. "The Enemy have made greater progress than they themselves expected," Stephen declared, "owing to the Weakness of our Counsels and our Attempt to maintain The Forts Washington and Lee." Greene had persistently argued for the retention of Fort Washington. Stephen also alerted Jefferson to problems that should concern Congress. "Our Salvation under Heaven," Stephen said, "depends on our Raising an Army Speedily. Every lover of Liberty should with Spirit promote the Recruiting Service." As to strategy, "if we lose Philadelphia and let it Stand, it will go near to Ruin us. They will open the port, give great prices for Wheat and flour and Seduce the Body of the People." Stephen mentioned that conducting secret business before Congress as a whole was risky, as information always leaked out. He referred to a British frigate which had given chase to a vessel on which Benjamin Franklin was aboard. "Must they not have had Intelligence from a member of Congress?" asked Stephen. "Would it not be adviseable to open the doors of Congress and have the Debates in public?" The "Secret Business," however, should "be done, by a Committee, or the Boards of Admiralty and War; after the plan has been Settled by Committees of the Whole house in Secret. We should then have a better Chance of distinguishing the Spirited from the Languid Members."[41]

One important Philadelphian at this time thought that the ill success of the army thus far was owing to the inferior caliber of the generals. Dr. Benjamin Rush had met Stephen and seems to have been attracted to him. Rush always liked people who were talkative, and besides, both men were physicians educated at Edinburgh. On December 21, 1776, Rush put in a good word for Stephen with Congressman Richard Henry Lee. "Since the captivity of General Lee," Rush said, "a distrust has crept in among the troops of the abilities of some of our general officers high in command. They expect nothing now from heaven-taught and book-taught generals." Rush hoped that "in our next promotions we shall disregard seniority. Stevens [Adam Stephen] must be made a major general; he has genius as well as knowledge."[42]

If Stephen's standing as a military officer seemed to be enhanced among members of Congress, prospects for the army were not encouraging. Indeed, it was a time that tried men's souls, as Thomas Paine, who had accompanied the army across the Delaware, observed in his *American Crisis*. Underclad and hardened by camping in the wintry air in the woods, the American troops looked like scarecrows. Troops under Generals St. Clair and Gates joined the army on the Delaware. Though the commander in chief had a paper army of 10,804, he actually had on hand 8,000 men, only 6,000 of whom were effective for duty. Stephen's brigade of three regiments had dwindled to 520 men, of whom only 404 were present and fit as of December 22.[43]

Stephen and other generals met with Washington periodically at the William Keith farmhouse and on December 20–23 at the Thompson-Neely home, which was General Stirling's quarters.[44] It is not known if Stephen had much to say about operational planning. He did, however, draw up a proposal for bringing on more troops from Virginia. Stephen's "Memorandum," which Washington sent to Congress on December 20, proposed that the 2d and 7th Virginia regiments, convalescents who had been left behind but were now well, and all new recruits should be marched immediately to Washington's army. Stephen suggested the routes to be taken from the respective Virginia military districts. Washington merely endorsed Stephen's proposal by saying that Congress "will please to adopt in whole, in part, or reject," as would be "consistent" with "their Plans, and Intelligence."[45]

One subject that increasingly came up in the war conferences was the opportunity for an assault on the Hessian troops at Trenton. The river so far had been relatively free of ice, though that situation was soon expected to change. By December 23 the decision had been made to attack. The General Orders for the twenty-fourth stated that Stephen's brigade was to serve as an advance party. A council of war met the same day at Samuel Merick's house to work out the final details. Attending were Major Generals Greene and Sullivan; Brigadier Generals Stirling, Fermoy, Mercer, Stephen, and St. Clair; and Colonels Paul D. Sargent, John Stark, John Glover, and Henry Knox. The assault on Trenton would be three-pronged: Washington and Greene leading a division of 2,400 men from the north; Gen. James Ewing and 700 militia crossing at Trenton; and Gen. John Cadwalader with 2,000 Pennsylvania militia and Continentals landing twelve miles below the town. Ewing and Cadwalader, however, were detained because the river now was heavily ice-clogged at their points of transit.[46]

Shortly after dusk on Christmas Day, the division commanded by Washington and Greene paraded and then marched to McKonkey's Ferry. The plan was to complete the crossing by midnight. Throughout the evening Durham boats conveyed troops to the east bank. Eighteen cannon were brought along. The crossing took longer than expected, and all the troops were not over until about 4 A.M. Adam Stephen's brigade, the first troops to reach the Jersey side, formed a chain of sentries around the landing place. Some nine miles above Trenton, the army divided into two columns: Washington, Greene, Fermoy, Stephen, and Mercer took the upper road directly to Trenton, and Sullivan and St. Clair marched along the river road to enter at the middle of the town. Stephen's brigade continued in the advance.[47]

Plodding through snow changing to sleet, Washington's division saw no indication that the enemy had been alarmed. But there was a surprise. Off to the side of the road, wandering through a field, were fifty soldiers of Stephen's 4th Regiment, led by Capt. George Wallis. They had been sent out at twilight on Christmas Eve to test the enemy's outer pickets and also, as Stephen said later, to exact revenge on the Hessians for having killed one of his men in a boat. The group had encountered Hessian guards and, according to Stephen, had killed four and wounded eleven of them; the German account however, claimed that six Hessians were wounded and none killed. A Hessian horse patrol under Lt. Andreas Wiederhold had pursued the Americans, who escaped by running through fenced fields. Washington was astonished and enraged at stumbling upon Wallis's party. He allegedly sent for Stephen and exclaimed: "You, sir, may have ruined all my plans." Washington was afraid that the whole Hessian camp was now alerted. The commander in chief, however, soon calmed his temper and, realizing that the soldiers of the search party were fatigued, assigned them to the rear of the march. Stephen's "blunder," instead of spoiling the element of surprise, had the reverse effect. The Hessian commander, Col. Johann Rall, had been warned of an impending action by the Americans and concluded that Wallis's party was what had been alluded to. All that Rall did was to send out Wiederhold's men; he waited until the next morning to investigate the encounter further.[48]

With no sign of the enemy, Washington's bedraggled force trudged along the road to Trenton. Just after dawn, Stephen's brigade, in the advance, made contact with Wiederhold's pickets, and the firing began. The Hessians retreated into the town, with Stephen's men in close pursuit, halting only at the intersection of King and Queen streets, where Knox's artillery pieces were put in place to enfilade each street. Stephen's and Fermoy's brigades moved past the entrance to the town eastward and formed a line closing a gap between the Princeton Road and Assunpink Creek to block an escape route. Meanwhile, the rest of Washington's troops poured into the town, firing from hedges and houses. The startled Hessians were quickly in the field of battle. Sullivan, approaching from the west of the town, also soon got into the fray. The 3d Virginia Regiment, including young Lt. James Monroe, did heroic duty in capturing the enemy's cannon in King Street. Some of the enemy sought to gain the Princeton Road, only to find their way blocked by Stephen's and Fermoy's troops. The two generals, in order to prevent further bloodshed, ordered their men to cease firing and called upon the Germans to throw down their arms and surrender. Lt. Col. Frankziskus Scheffer and Maj. Ludwig von Hanstein agreed to the demands. The Hessians lowered their standards and grounded their arms; the officers, indicating submission, placed their hats on the points of their swords. Some of the enemy soldiers, however, threw their weapons into the woods or broke the locks of the guns. In all, of the Hessian force of 1,586 at Trenton, 918 became prisoners of war; the rest, excepting the battle casualties, escaped because they were either south of the Assunpink when the action started or were able to get away along the creek bed.[49]

Stephen took the victory rather nonchalantly. A week later he casually mentioned it in a letter to Jonathan Seaman, the overseer of his plantation. "We had a Christmas frolick at Trenton," Stephen said. "I could tell you a great deal about Shooting, if I had time— You never Saw so many good Shot made in your life time—We drove the Enemy from their Cannon in our Shooting." Stephen told how one "brave" German remained at his artillery piece "& was loading her by him self after the Rest had left him—A Virginian as brave as he, would not let him but run up knockd him down wt the butt of his Gun & took him prisoner—We have killd & wounded the most of three Regimts of Hessians." Stephen also reported the Wallis incident.[50] Stephen also informed Congressman Richard Henry Lee of the battle of Trenton. Lee, in reply, signing himself as "I am, as of old, your affectionate friend," offered praise. "Nothing could have happened more opportunely," said Lee, "than the drubbing you have given the Hessians at Trenton. . . . The *genius* of *America* seems now to be awakening from profound sleep."[51]

Since going off to war eight months before, Adam Stephen had participated in two victories: the expulsion of the British from Virginia and now the triumph at Trenton. The watchwords for the Trenton operation, "Victory or Death," had a special meaning for him as they did for others in Washington's army, which was almost to the point of extinction, with many enlistments expiring at the first of the year. The Trenton victory was a counterpoise to the loss of New York City, the surrender of several thousand troops at Fort Washington, and the humiliating retreat. Now the world would witness that the Americans could not only fight and win but even outsmart the enemy. For Adam Stephen himself there was a professional satisfaction. As a general he had commanded part of the military force that bested seasoned European troops in a coup de main.

TEN

"A Certain and Considerable Advantage"

Success at Trenton tempted Washington to continue with a war of posts in New Jersey. Fortunately, the army was still intact, owing in large measure to the bonuses for reenlistments that Congress provided. Washington estimated that there was a "fair Opportunity" for "drawing the Enemy entirely from, or at least to, the extremity of the province of Jersey." The American army, which had retired to Pennsylvania after Trenton, recrossed the Delaware on December 27–29 and took position on a ridge overlooking Assunpink Creek and Trenton. But a chance to attack another of the enemy garrison-posts in New Jersey became remote when General Howe again decided to take the initiative. Cornwallis, having collected 8,000 troops, was now poised at Princeton, ready to march against Washington and engage him in battle.[1]

To intercept a 1,200-man British van along the Princeton Road, Washington sent out a strong detachment consisting of Charles Scott's 5th Regiment in Stephen's brigade, Col. Edward Hand's riflemen, several regiments of Fermoy's brigade, and Colonel Haussegger's German Regiment. These units on January 2 made a stand against British light infantry and Donop's jägers at Shabbakonk Creek and then conducted an orderly withdrawal back to Trenton, where they crossed the bridge over the Assunpink to Washington's lines. The main British army had moved slowly because of deep mud in the roads from the heavy rain the night before. Cornwallis's army nevertheless was at Trenton by dusk. The British commander decided to wait until morning to do battle. He was confident that he could pin the Americans against the Delaware and, by cutting off any avenues of escape, totally annihilate Washington's army.[2]

Adam Stephen attended a council of war with other general officers at St. Clair's quarters (Alexander Douglass's house) on the night of January 2. There were several options: retreat down the Delaware Valley and into Pennsylvania, fight at the present position, or steal around the British army. The latter alternative won approval. Using decoys an American work party, which was left behind, and with campfires burning throughout the night, Washington and his army silently slipped away and headed for Princeton.[3]

As the American force approached Princeton, the British 17th, 40th, and 55th regiments, commanded by Lt. Col. Charles Mawhood, were marching out of the town on the way to join Cornwallis. Mercer's brigade and 300 of Cadwalader's Pennsylvania militia headed directly toward Princeton. Sullivan's division wheeled around the town to the right, and two brigades circuited Princeton to the left. The rest of the army, including Stephen's brigade, halted at the side of the road, about 1 ½ miles from Princeton. Charles Scott's 5th Regiment, in Stephen's brigade, provided cover to the army baggage and supplies. Mercer made accidental contact with British troops in an orchard, and in the bloody clash he was mortally wounded. The rest of Washington's army moved toward the site of the fighting. Mawhood escaped by taking the back roads, though 200 of his men were captured. Stephen's brigade apparently saw little or no action, at most perhaps making brief contact with some of the fleeing troops.[4]

Washington hoped that by keeping distance from Cornwallis's army, he could attack the British post at New Brunswick. But, as artillery chief Henry Knox noted, the Americans were too exhausted, "without either rest, rum, or provisions for two nights and days." If there had been 1,000 "fresh men" at Princeton "to have pushed for Brunswick, we should have struck one of the most brilliant strokes in all history."[5] After encamping briefly at Pluckamin and Somerset Courthouse, Washington's army on January 16 entered into winter quarters at Morristown. Stephen and his brigade served as a rear guard on the march from Princeton to Morristown, again watching after the baggage of the army.[6]

Morristown and vicinity made an ideal location defensively and offensively. On a plateau surrounded by rugged hills and a mountain ridge, the site was equidistant from the British posts at Newark, Amboy, and New Brunswick. Most of the Virginia troops were stationed as light infantry below Morristown at Quibbletown and Chatham. Because the Virginia ranks were so depleted, Washington ordered Stephen to send his officers not immediately needed home to recruit.[7] Stephen's brigade was now to be engaged in constant harrassment of enemy detachments in search of food and forage. Washington, who had just been given "dictatorial" powers in the impressment of goods, ordered the Americans in the field to collect all the beef, pork, flour, and spiritous liquors that were not needed for subsistence by local residents; payment was guaranteed to the owners. Also, the light troops were to remove out of enemy reach all horses, wagons, and beef cattle. Force could be used to compel compliance with these directives.[8]

Frequently Stephen's Virginians had brushes with the enemy. On January 23 Col. Mordecai Buckner and his 6th Regiment intercepted two British regiments escorting a wagon train from New Brunswick to Amboy. Buckner held part of his 700-man force in reserve, and only those led by Lt. Col. Richard Parker attacked the convoy. Buckner inexplicably rode away to his quarters one mile distant. As it was, Parker and his men inflicted heavy casualties on the enemy.[9] Afterwards Buckner was cashiered from the army for cowardice.

Another major skirmish of Stephen's troops occurred on February 1—the engagement known as the battle of Drake's Farm (near Metuchen). Col. Charles Scott with 500 Virginians and Connecticut infantry ran across a British foraging party of 1,000 troops under Gen. Sir William Erskine, the British quartermaster general. Scott led 90 men to attack 230 enemy soldiers loading hay and "made a push for the wagons." Bullets "flew like hail" for ten minutes; then Hessian grenadiers reinforced the beleaguered foragers, and Scott's men had to fall back. During the fighting neither the other Virginians nor the Connecticut troops under Col. Andrew

Ward came to Scott's aid. Nevertheless, the action was considered a victory for the Americans. After the skirmish, Stephen boasted: "My brigade has behaved to admiration, most of the officers like heroes, and in a campaign or two will surpass any troops in the world." Scott's losses at Drake's Farm were nine killed and fifteen wounded. Unfortunately, seven Americans—two of them officers—had to be left on the field of battle. Several British soldiers "dashed out their brains with their muskets and ran them through with their bayonets, made like sieves." Lt. William Kelly, adjutant to Scott's 5th Regiment, was one of the officers murdered. Wounded in the thigh, he surrendered and was immediately clubbed to death with his own musket.[10]

The brutal killing of Kelly and the other officer led to a bitter correspondence between Stephen and Erskine. Three days after the fight at Drake's Farm, Stephen, from Chatham, wrote a barbed letter to Erskine. Stephen expressed the disbelief that "a Gentleman Officer so eminently distinguished for Bravery & Experience, should allow the Troops under his Command, to murder the wounded after the manner of Savages—Untill this time, it was unequivocally allowed that Humanity was a certain Concomitant of Valour." It was now apparent "that Britons unhappily divested of many excellent qualities peculiar to their Ancestors, are become Strangers to Humanity, & deaf to the Intreaties of the Brave." Stephen cited the brutality involved in the death of Lieutenant Kelly and also that of Gen. Hugh Mercer. "It gives pain to a generous Mind, Sr. Willm," Stephen stated, "to see you tarnish the Laurels, so honourably obtained last War, by permitting such Savage Barbarity." Stephen warned that if such conduct continued, it would stir an inveterate hatred of "Britons." Stephen said that even the Indians after Braddock's defeat "could not be prevailed on to butcher the wounded, in the manner your Troops have done, untill they were first made drunk." Stephen also pointed out that "we have beat the Indians into good Humour, & they offer their Services—It is their Custom in War to Scalp—take out the Hearts of their Enemies—and mangle their Bodies." If the British officers "do not restrain their Soldiers from glutting their Cruelty with the wanton destruction of the Wounded—the United States will be compelled, contrary to

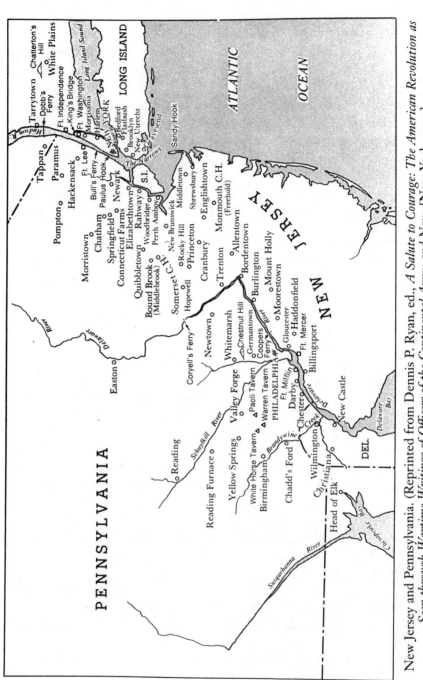

New Jersey and Pennsylvania. (Reprinted from Dennis P. Ryan, ed., *A Salute to Courage: The American Revolution as Seen through Wartime Writings of Officers of the Continental Army and Navy* [New York, 1979], p. 54. Copyright © 1979 Columbia University Press. Used by permission)

their natural disposition, to employ a Body of ferocious Savages, who can with an unrelenting heart, eat the flesh & drink the Blood of their Enemies." Stephen told Erskine that he well remembered when in 1763 Lt. Francis Gordon of the Royal Americans and eight other British soldiers "were roasted & eaten up by the fierce Savages, who now offer their Service." The Americans had treated wounded and captured British soldiers "with that Civility & tenderness natural to a brave & generous People: Should the inhuman Cruelty of your Men compell the American Army to retaliate; Let it be remembered, that the British Officers stand answerable to the World & to Posterity for the many dreadful Consequences."[11]

Stephen told Washington, without asking for clearance, that he was going to write this letter, stating that he would warn Erskine that unless the atrocities stopped, the American soldiers would not be restrained from making retaliation. Washington, who did not offer any advice one way or another to Stephen, nevertheless informed Congress of the letter. Also, to Samuel Chase the commander in chief wrote: "Genl Stephens sent a Flag to Sir William Erskine, complaining of this Savage Manner of Carrying on War; but I do not know his Answer. I have heard that orders were given at Trenton to make no Prisoners, but kill all that fell into their hands, but of this there is no proof."[12]

Erskine, in reply to Stephen's accusations, said that he was "extremely obliged" for "the good opinion you seem to have of my past character, but as much hurt at the unmerited charge you lay against me at present. It is unnecessary for me to answer minutely every paragraph of your letter, which is wrote in a style & language I have not been accustomed to." Erskine pointed out that he had "never countenanced an Act of Barbarity" in his lifetime, "nor can I think any Gentleman in the British Service equal to it—We on the contrary wish to treat prisoners with Lenity & to take all possible Care of the wounded." But "it is not to be wondered at if our soldiers are a little exasperated, considering the many cruelties that have been of late committed on them & their Officers, *even unarmed* passing singly from Quarter to Quarter."[13]

Washington also sent Governor William Livingston of New Jersey copies of the Stephen-Erskine correspondence, along with the

"necessary Affidavits." Livingston replied: "If nothing else will restrain their Barbarities, it may not perhaps be improper to let loose
upon them a few of General Stephen's Tawny [Indian] Yagers, the
only Americans that can match them in their bloody Work."[14] The
Erskine-Stephen controversy found its way into the newspapers,[15]
but otherwise the issue was dropped between the two principals.
Washington was troubled at other times with the question of retaliation, but with each side having an equal capacity to inflict it,
neither the British army nor the Americans condoned excessive
brutality.

Later, in April, when the enemy burned the house and laid waste
the farm of Capt. John Conway of the 1st New Jersey Regiment,
Stephen wrote Washington that he and Gen. William Maxwell
planned retaliation, "yet, Suspecting that we might have been Accused of doing it wantonly, as we had not Consulted Your Excellency—We have hitherto let it alone." Washington vetoed any such
action. "I lament Capt. Conway's loss," he informed Stephen, "but
tho' my Indignation at such ungenerous conduct of the Enemy,
might at first prompt me to Retaliation, yet Humanity and Policy
forbid the measure. Experience proves, that their wanton Cruelty
injures rather than benefits their cause."[16]

While keeping track of his troops acting as light infantry, Stephen
was delighted to learn that he had been promoted to major general,
with the command of a division. Congress on February 19 named
five major generals; besides Stephen, Lord Stirling, Arthur St. Clair,
Thomas Mifflin, and Benjamin Lincoln.[17] Stephen would now rank
ninth below Washington. He had strong support for his elevation
in rank from prominent Virginians, especially Congressman Richard
Henry Lee and Governor Patrick Henry. Writing to Lee on January 9, Henry pleaded: "I beg you'll tell me what is the best method
for doing justice to Gen. Stephen as to his rank. I think he ought to
be raised above his present rank."[18] The debates in Congress leading to the appointments lasted a week and, as North Carolina delegate Thomas Burke complained, were "perplexed, inconclusive, &
irksome."[19] Instead of relying on seniority, Congress adopted new
guidelines for the selection of general officers. There were three
main criteria: seniority, number of troops furnished by a candidate's
native state, and merit.[20]

It would be interesting to know how Stephen would have fared under a plan that Richard Henry Lee had proposed: the election of major generals by the general officers of the army. Stephen's quick promotion, only six months after being commissioned a brigadier general, ruffled the sensibilities of other brigadier generals who had outranked him. Andrew Lewis was one, and he resigned in April because he was not on the promotion list, though ostensibly giving his reason as ill health. Washington sought to soothe Lewis and said he was disappointed that Lewis had not been promoted (implying a preference of Lewis over Stephen). Benedict Arnold protested in being passed over by those whom he had outranked; with Washington's backing, however, he was named major general in May, with the stipulation that he outranked Stephen and the other four new major generals. Benjamin Lincoln had been promoted directly from the militia.[21] The new promotions (including the arrangement of seniority within grade), along with Congress's grant of commissions to foreigners over the heads of American officers, so affected the pride and sense of honor of those who were slighted that Congress for the next year found itself with the difficult task of making adjustments.

Richard Henry Lee sent Stephen his commission from Congress. Stephen thanked Lee for the "particular mark of your friendship," and he said that Lee's "Exertions" to "restore my Rank are very obliging, & will always be acknowledged." In a postscript Stephen indicated that he could return the favor. "Please to Recommend a parcel of promising young men, Some of your friends, for Commissions," he said. "We have a great many Vacancies—I am ashamd to tell you that Some of our Officers have deserted—that is gone home wtout leave."[22]

Stephen's rapid rise in the army seems to have brought out a greater vanity, even a flippant air, in him and also stirred his old sensibilities as a politician. He supplied information to the newspapers, with the implications of his own importance, as, for example, in a letter to the publishers of the *Pennsylvania Journal*, printed in the March 26 issue. "Movd by Duty to my country," said Stephen, "& from a grateful respect for merit, I desired to acquaint the public" that Col. James Potter and Maj. Thomas Robinson, "with the officers and men of the Northumberland militia . . . have distinguished themselves in the most assiduous and active service . . . and that they have deservedly received the repeated thanks of General Sullivan, General Maxwell, and my self; under whose more immediate command, they have so faithfully served."[23]

Stephen engaged in some braggadocio when he wrote Angus McDonald, entreating him to accept a lieutenant colonelcy in the Continental line. McDonald, a Scottish immigrant, as a private had fought with Stephen at the battle of Great Meadows in 1754, had led the expedition into the Shawnee country in 1774, and had served as sheriff of Frederick County. Stephen urged McDonald not to decline the commission as "it is more honorable than if you had been appointed by convention or Committee." Stephen said that "I desire you only Remember that in February I was nothing in a Military way—in less than a year I was a col—Brigadier—& Major General—Had not my attachment to the Interests of America been Superior to all Scrupulosity—I would have now been poaking at home about the Mill." Aware of McDonald's "Highland pride," Stephen told him that "should you be obstinate—G—d forbid— Write a polite letter to General Washington thanking his excellency for his notice and making the best excuse you can." Stephen's postscript also is revealing: "Fighting is now become so familiar that unless it is a very great affair we do not think it worth mentioning. . . . my Division is an Excellent School for a young soldier— We only fight eight or ten times a Week—in short I have got my men in such Spirits that they only ask where the Enemy come out, & where they are, without enquiring into their Numbers, & so fall on." McDonald wrote Washington on April 20 that he was refusing the army commission because it would entail financial hardship in the support of his family.[24]

Stephen maintained his headquarters at Chatham during March and April. Although he exaggerated the number of encounters with the enemy, the light infantry under his command and those under Sullivan, Maxwell, and Lincoln held tight rein on British detachments leaving their posts at Amboy and New Brunswick. Robert Forsyth reported on February 15 that Charles Scott's brigade, in Stephen's division, had "engaged the enemy's strong foraging parties" twice since the Drake Farm skirmish on the first.[25] Stephen's troops probably participated in the heated actions near Quibble-town (now New Market) on February 8 and 21. Often the light in-fantry in the field were drawn from Stephen's division and William Maxwell's brigade. In a letter to a Virginia general (probably Wood-ford), Stephen noted two actions involving his and Maxwell's troops on March 9–10. He mentioned that Washington had been "ex-treamly ill," but "by the great Attention" of physicians, particularly that of Dr. (Maj.) Theodorick Bland, had recovered. Stephen also told the general, who had gone home, that "we shall want Some pretty young men for Subalterns in the Virg. troops—I want young men possessed naturally of a head in impulse for Military Achieve-ments—& None of your Milk Sops, that Will languish for hash & hominy."[26]

Stephen's troops were not involved in the engagement of April 13, when Benjamin Lincoln's detachment of 500 men went up against 2,000 troops led by Cornwallis and were forced to retreat to the hills. But Stephen got in some accounting for Lincoln's defeat. He wrote Richard Henry Lee that he had "resolved the Enemy should make a Compensation for their Excursion to Bound Brook [Lincoln's for-mer camp]"; his troops, therefore, surprised an enemy picket, which, according to Stephen, resulted in killing seven and capturing six-teen. Washington put the figure a little lower, at thirteen prisoners.[27]

Light infantry was playing an increasingly important role in the war, as the armies were hesitant to engage in pitched battle. Wash-ington designated one company from each Continental regiment as light infantry. Usually several of these units would join together for a mission of skirmishing with enemy pickets or detachments in the field. They were designated as light infantry because they traveled with the minimum of equipment and arms, unlike mounted infan-try, or dragoons. When completing an assignment, light infantry returned to their regiments. Stephen's and other light infantry kept relentless pressure on British foragers and pickets. The tactics of the light infantry created a healthy respect by the British for the American soldier.[28] The constant harassment led to the drastic re-duction of provisions and forage for the British garrisons, where in-sufficient diet caused scurvy and other illnesses, even contributing to a high mortality rate. Without the availability of hay, the enemy's horses were also affected.[29] Not only did Stephen's and Maxwell's light infantry successfully limit British access to the countryside, but the hit-and-run tactics proved a valuable training experience. Moreover, the effectiveness of the light infantry missions raised the morale of the American soldiery while adversely affecting that of the British and, not the least, demonstrated to the local population the viability of American arms.

Despite the use of light infantry as a corps to attack the enemy, small parties often were combing the New Jersey plains, and it was difficult to control their movements. Stephen called Washington's attention to the problem. In a letter of April 14 he said: "I go on the out posts today, and do not approve of the mens being so dispersed as not be able to Support one Another." Two weeks later he notified Washington that he had ordered "that no project Shall be Undertaken without the Approbation of the Officer Commanding the Corps." [30] Washington, who usually gave leeway to his forward light infantry commanders to conduct operations much as they pleased, recognized the problem and sought to tighten the chain of command. Writing to Stephen on April 26, he said: "It ever was against my inclination, for an Officer to attempt any thing against the Enemy, without the Knowledge and Consent of the Officer immediately commanding him." Washington had particularly in mind a captain of a New Jersey regiment who went out on a patrol simply on his own authority and was captured. The commander in chief had heard that there was much the same situation among Stephen's troops. "Here I must take the liberty to inquire," he told Stephen, "whether the orders I some time past sent you, directing an immediate inquiry to be made into the cause of some of our parties retreating on the approach of the Enemy, have been complied with." Because Stephen and Maxwell both "thought that there was misbehaviour somewhere," Washington had expected that "the inquiry would meet with no delay. Disappointed in this, I must insist that it be made without loss of time, and sent up, that punishment, if deserved, may be inflicted." Furthermore, Washington told Stephen that "I am very sorry that my orders have been too frequently unattended to, and most sincerely wish that in future no cause for a Similar Complaint may exist." [31]

It seems that Stephen, as a division commander, with part of his troops engaged in light infantry operations along with those from Maxwell's brigade, had difficulty in keeping track of all that was going on. His own reports, more often than not, indicate knowledge after the fact. He perhaps was negligent in not requiring closer ties between himself and officers who were serving in a light infantry capacity. The blame more probably belonged to Scott and others who actually commanded light infantry in the field. Yet because Stephen himself voiced complaints about officers acting insubordinately and shirking duty, he should have attempted to hold some persons to account. Stephen would yet have to learn that to raise questions about the conduct of his men meant that it was incumbent on him to seek the answers. Strict accountability was certainly a maxim with Washington. But the commander in chief had himself somewhat to blame for confusion in the chain of command regarding light infantry operations in New Jersey. Precision in the planning and employment of forward army movements was never a strong point with Washington—as evidenced in one later example, the preliminary operations leading to the battle of Monmouth in 1778. Yet Washington was correct in reprimanding Stephen for not following through on his complaints.

A major problem that Stephen and other general officers faced was the turnover and insufficiency in the number of officers. Many had gone home, even without leave. To curtail the practice of unauthorized absences, Washington's general orders for April 7 stipulated that all officers of the 1st, 3d, 5th, 6th, and 9th Virginia regiments who had left without permission from himself or Stephen and were not on special assignment or involved in recruiting were to return immediately to the army. [32]

During winter 1776–77 an intelligence network for the army began to materialize, and Adam Stephen, as he had done during the French and Indian War, collected what information he could about the enemy, although, as before, he exhibited an easy credulity. Soon after he arrived in New Jersey with his troops in late 1776, Stephen began submitting intelligence. On January 8, 1777, he informed General Lord Stirling that from "my man from New York," he had learned that General Howe intended to march soon toward the

Delaware and then to Philadelphia with 7,000 men. Stirling forwarded Stephen's information to Robert Morris and a committee of Congress. As a result, Congress requested Washington to have General Ewing move his force to Bristol and Trenton Ferry to guard "the passage of the River should it be attempted by the Enemy."[33]

Washington expected his generals in the field to be on the alert for any intelligence. Fiscal accounts of the commander in chief indicate that special funds were provided officers for use in paying informers. Stephen received $200 in May for this purpose. Most of the secret service involved operatives around New York City, where the coming and going of British troops and ships best revealed General Howe's future actions.[34]

General Maxwell sympathized with Stephen in the difficulty of obtaining accurate information. Addressing a note to Stephen from Westfield on April 10, Maxwell said that he had "pity" for Stephen for "want of Intelligence"; apparently Stephen had been duped by incorrect news from one of his informers. "I know now how you must feel," said Maxwell, "as I suffered Just in something the same way my self by the Scoundrel that remained in and about Newark." It "is impossible for a man to divine these things in our degenerate days and he that will go blindfolded into such Matters is worse than a fool. We have a very difficult card to play," and "we have often to act by the Moon or twialight and leave the World to Judge of it in clear sunshine."[35]

Stephen considered it his duty to forward to the commander in chief all intelligence that came his way, without attempting to discern its truth or falsity because most of the information was uncorroborated. Stephen claimed to have contacts at New York City, Paulus Hook, Bergen, and Staten Island.[36] In mid-April he reported that a large enemy force was being collected at Bonhamtown and that an attack on his troops at Chatham might be expected. Washington had the forward units put on alert.[37]

Stephen told Washington in late April that he had intelligence that the British planned "A Certain Conquest of America" before October and that "Betts of 100 Guineas" were being taken in New York that Howe would be in Philadelphia by May 1. Stephen included information on the economic situation in New York and gave various data on the British ships and troops. Many British sailors were sick from having subsisted on a salted diet. Stephen alerted Washington to be on the lookout for a British spy, Thomas Long, "not an American, nicknamed Bunk Eye, for his prominent Eyes"; the suspect was 5½ feet tall and over forty years old, wore white clothes, and had a "fair complexion." Stephen added that Long, a schoolmaster from near Rahway, "is gone for Philadelphia as a spy. . . . He associates with Quakers."[38] Washington forwarded Stephen's intelligence to Congress and told that body that he had asked Stephen to hire persons to go to New York City and New Brunswick. Washington advised Congress that although he did "not put intire confidence in the whole" of Stephen's intelligence, nevertheless "measures" should be taken to apprehend Thomas Long.[39]

Patrick Henry continued to seek advice and information from Stephen, who, however, did not always agree with the Virginia governor's views, particularly that more troops should be sent to the frontier. Henry was grateful that Stephen had been keeping him posted on matters relating to the army. "You tell me, my dear General, more in a paragraph, than others do in a page," wrote Henry on March 31. Henry told Stephen that he feared an eruption of war with the Cherokees and the Ohio Indians. In the latter case, Fort Pitt would be endangered. Henry asked Stephen how many troops should be stationed at that post in order to make it secure from Indian attack. In closing his letter, Henry said: "Adieu, my dear Sir. May we live to see the happy Days of Victory, & safety. . . . May you long live in the full enjoyment of that Happiness you so nobly struggle to give your country."[40]

Stephen not only disapproved of strengthening frontier defense, as Henry wanted, but also disagreed with the recommendation of some Virginians who wanted to keep more troops in the state to thwart any British invasion. He wrote Congressman Richard Henry Lee, cautioning against the siphoning off of any soldiers destined for the Continental army. "The sending Americans to their antipodes," Stephen said, "was as wicked and extensive a plan, as the agents of the devil could form on earth." Any "intended attack" on Virginia was merely "a creature of the volatile Burgoyne, engendered on Lady Dunmore or his Lordship, who doubtless will attend with his council, in order to add some more oderiferous beauties to his Ethopian seraglios." Should the British obtain enough troops to invade Virginia, "which I reckon impossible, they may distress individuals, but can do nothing towards conquering our country. To prevent this attack, and obviate all difficulty, our present object ought to be the destruction of their army in the Jerseys." As for frontier defense, all that was needed was to organize western militia and provide them with ammunition. "The clouds which threaten from Canada and the savages, and all other *petites*" would be "dispersed, yea, dissolved like meteors, upon the destruction of Howe's army." Indeed, the British force in New Jersey could be crushed if the northern states would do their full share in providing troops. "Virtue is certainly wanting," Stephen told Lee, "or we should have had men enough to have effected it before this time. The Virginians, with a few Jersey men, and as few Pennsylvanians, are likely to bear the burden of the day; the myriads of the north; the great warriors, who were to do the business, if we found money, seem cloyed of fighting, and are wonderfully backward in turning out." [41]

Not only was Stephen critical of lack of support for the main army, but he thought that operations in New Jersey should be more aggressive, not just nipping at the British foraging parties and the like. Stephen was almost alone among the general officers in advocating attacks on the enemy outposts. At a council of the general officers on May 2, the question was raised: "Will a general attack" upon "Brunswick and the neighboring Posts be adviseable?" Although Stephen's vote made for an unanimous negative, he held out for an attack on British camps at Bonhamtown and Piscataway (both locations about halfway between the enemy posts at Amboy and New Brunswick). [42] Stephen would have his way. The next week, without authorization from Washington, he ordered an attack on the British at Piscataway. Here were stationed the 42d Regiment (the famous Highlander "Black Watch") and six companies of light infantry.

On Saturday, May 10, Stephen mustered 800 men, collected from different regiments, at Col. William Cooke's quarters, about nine miles from Metuchen meetinghouse. In the afternoon, the corps marched over "Dismal Swamp" and approached the enemy's picket outside Piscataway. The British had fully observed Stephen's advance and had 300 troops waiting at the location of the picket. What exactly happened next is not clear, as Stephen's account differed widely from that of the British and even of some American officers. Reports in several Philadelphia newspapers (and also later in the *Virginia Gazette*) reflected Stephen's version and undoubtedly were supplied by Stephen or his aides and also drawn from a report that Stephen sent Congressman Richard Henry Lee. According to the newspaper accounts, which varied in some details, Stephen's troops, after a fight lasting 1½ hours, "repulsed" the enemy "with considerable slaughter." When the British were reinforced, the Americans retreated "in excellent order." The casualty estimates, following Stephen's account, were put at about 3 killed and 24 wounded for the Americans and about 70 killed and as many as 120 wounded for the British.[43]

British accounts saw the battle quite differently. Capt. Archibald Robertson, in the royal corps of engineers, said that 2,000 troops under both Stephen and Maxwell (who, however, appears not to have been involved) attacked at Piscataway, "where the 42d Regiment is cantoned, who beat them back for near 3 miles to their Camp on the heights near Metuchen," with the American casualties at 2 officers and 9 enlisted men killed, 17 wounded, 33 captured, and 73 missing. The British, according to Robertson, had only one sergeant wounded.[44] A Hessian officer reported that Stephen's force made two attacks, one in the morning and the other in the evening; he gave American losses as 26 killed and 35 captured, and 9 dead and 22 wounded for the British.[45] Another Hessian soldier saw Stephen's onslaught as "a disorderly attack"; despite their superiority in numbers, the Americans "continually exposed either their right or their left wing" and, therefore, had "to fall back with great loss." Light infantry then pursued the Americans. He estimated 48 Americans killed and "many wounded"; for the British, 1 officer and 6 men killed and 21 wounded.[46] The tory *New York Gazette and Weekly Mercury* on May 19 reported that at the battle, after heavy firing, the Americans retreated "in the greatest Confusion toward their Left," where they fell in with the light infantry. "The Whole of the Rebels now gave Way, and fled with the utmost Precipitation, our Troops pursuing them close to their Encampment. . . . The Ardour of the Troops was so great, that it was with difficulty they could be restrained from storming the Encampment; but Night coming on, they were ordered to return to their Cantonments." According to this report the British had 2 officers and 26 men killed and wounded; as for the Americans, "upwards of 40 were found next morning in the Woods, besides an Officer and 36 Men taken Prisoners." [47]

On May 12, two days after the battle, Stephen reported to Washington. "I can now with propriety Congratulate your Excellency on a Certain and Considerable Advantage gaind over the Enemys best troops; by the Continental Troops of My Division," he said. Troops from the Continental lines of other states had joined with Stephen's select corps. Stephen said that soldiers of the 1st Pennsylvania Regiment under Col. William Cooke began the attack; they "behaved well," and Captains James Chambers and James Parr "distinguished themselves." Capt. Noah Phelps of Col. Andrew Ward's Connecticut troops also "behaved well & the few men that were with him did honour to the Corps." Stephen said that "the Combatants in the first Onset were within 50 yards. Some of them nearer, & None further off than 100 yards." The initial fighting lasted half an hour; the enemy retreated, leaving 3 officers and 39 men dead. Then "the Continental troops Supported by 150 Virginians Compelld them to give way again," with "Considerable loss." But after this second engagement had continued for about an hour, "our Videt discovered about 2,000 men within a quarter of a Mile, on their way from Brunswick." Thus, "the troops were prudently withdrawn, in the very Nick of time." Stephen put the American losses at 3 killed, 15 wounded, 5 captured, and several "Straglers," who had been "plundering the dead," missing. He estimated the total enemy casualties as 200 killed and wounded. "It was a Bold Enterprise. It was the time & Rapidity of the Attack that Secured us the Success we met with." [48]

Washington, replying on the same day, rebuked Stephen for apparently inflating his claims. The "account of the attempt upon the Enemy at Piscataway is favourable," Washington declared, "but I am sorry to add, widely different from those I have had from others,

(Officers of distinction) who were of the party." Washington said that he could not learn from them "that there is the least certainty of the Enemy's leaving the Slain upon the Field . . . that instead of an orderly retreat, it was (with the greatest part of detachment) a disorderly route, and, that the disadvantage was on our side, not the Enemy's, who had notice of your coming and was prepared for it, as I expected."[49]

Stephen, however, insisted on the credibility of his report and told Washington point-blank that the commander in chief had relied on the wrong sources—namely, those who were not a part of the action and some who were even cowards. "Your Excellency has not seen an Officer that was in the Action Saturday Night," Stephen declared. "They were of the party; but to their Staying at Such a distance from the Scene of Action The Surviving Highlanders owe their Existence." Stephen said that he had taken "delight in mentioning the Troops to your Excellency who distinguished themselves," but now "the Reverse gives me pain; hoping that time, Attention, & habit, will improve us—Whether owing to the order in the field, or to what, I am uncertain—but one half of the troops were not Engaged, & never had the ground gaind from the Enemy." The soldiers "who Stayd a Quarter or near half a mile in the rear must needs have run damnd hard to retreat by the way the troops engaged did—But the fighting troops were halted a Considerable time on a Rising ground untill they had an Opportunity of Coming off." As if to emphasize his own indispensability in commanding the forward troops, Stephen gave Washington intelligence that he regarded "of the Utmost importance"; Howe had abandoned his plan to take Philadelphia, the British intended an attack on Bound Brook, Cornwallis and other generals were reconnoitering "the ground about Drakes farm," and the enemy were "forming a Bridge of Boats at Brunswick." In the postscript Stephen implied criticism of Washington. "I beg your Excellency will not countenance the Story of Officers at Morristown whose Rgts were on the Lines," Stephen said, "nor permit Officers to go home without ordering them of my division to Acquaint me."[50]

The Piscataway affair strained the always uneasy relations between Washington and Stephen. Never before had the commander in chief so questioned the credibility of a general officer. There would be a doubt in Washington's mind now as to not only Stephen's reliability but also his usefulness in the army. Washington, of course, had not forgotten Stephen's remissness and alleged improprieties while in past military service. Yet it seems that Washington himself overreacted. Stephen had only claimed an "advantage" over the enemy, not a victory, and he did acknowledge a precipitate retreat. His report on American losses were essentially correct, though he estimated enemy casualties at two to three times their actual number.[51] But guessing enemy losses at more than they actually were, immediately after an action, was a common practice. There was probably truth in Stephen's claim that some of the officers refused to lead their troops into the fight. Of course, the hesitation would have been due in part to being aware that the enemy had been forewarned and were prepared to do battle. Stephen's fault was his rashness in bringing his troops into an engagement. Yet the Piscataway affair was one of a series of skirmishes that would convince the British of the futility of occupying northeastern New Jersey.

For several weeks after the Piscataway fight, Stephen energetically put himself into his work. He called to Washington's attention problems that needed to be remedied, and he also prodded the commander in chief to initiate an offensive in New Jersey. It was as if Stephen was seeking to redeem himself to Washington. On May 15 Stephen reported on courts-martial for officers who had been absent without leave. Upon the acquittal of Lt. Samuel Gill, Stephen gave vent to his exasperation: "With what Countenance Can Soldiers be punished for neglect of Duty, if the Officers escape wt impunity? Gill had not done duty for Six months." Stephen also had news and suggestions. "The Tory Regiment made an Excursion as far as Acquaquennonk & two Nights ago Carryd off Capt Marinus & several others," he said. "I take a tour to day by Newark & Elizabethtown, for Intelligence &c. I have a great passion to wait upon the Tory Regiment, who are so mischievous to that Neighbourhood." Stephen advised that Gen. Nathaniel Heard of the New Jersey militia "should move his Quarters frequently—Taking post for a short time about the Hackensack, Then down on Barbados Neck, Then to his old post again. The men will be more healthy, &

the Enemy more puzzled." From his "Confidential Servant," Stephen learned that British officers at New Brunswick were going back to England because they "are tired of the Service." The informant also heard while playing a game of quoits with British soldiers that "there were numbers of Rebels in England, that one half of the City of London, was the same way of thinking wt the Americans."[52]

Stephen sent Washington other intelligence two days later, emphasizing that the enemy now seemed to be making no preparations in New Jersey that would indicate a pending offensive. Stephen said that he had detained a deserter at Chatham, "but he is so drunk, I have ordered him to sleep." He added that "I hope a parcel of these deserters will be hanged, one on Every Road leading to the Enemys posts." Then Stephen caught Washington off guard with a proposal to attack the tory regiment quartered at Bergen. "It must be Attempted to morrow night," he said, "or the Tide will not Answer again for a Week. Can so many men be spared from the Lines?"[53] Tench Tilghman, aide to the commander in chief, without consulting Washington, sent a note to Stephen asking for more specifics and how many men would be needed. He also advised Stephen to consult with Maxwell and other general officers as to what number of men would be "prudent to draw from the Lines."[54] As soon as Washington received Stephen's plan, however, he found it infeasible. Writing Stephen quickly on the seventeenth, the same day that the Bergen proposal was submitted, Washington gave his reasons, rather pointedly, why he was refusing to allow the attack. Because of the "known disaffection of the Country," as soon as a select corps assembled, the enemy would know of the plan, and either "they would prepare themselves to give you a reception" or "they would retreat from Bergen to Powles Hook, and after they got beyond the Hills, it would be impossible for you to follow them." An attack "must be effected by Surprise or not at all, and I have no conception that Boats sufficient for the purpose could be collected, and such a Body of Men embarked without the Enemy's having notice of it."[55] Stephen persisted with the idea of attacking the tory regiment at Bergen, and Washington again vetoed the plan for the same reasons as before.[56]

Not to be deterred, Stephen had other suggestions for attacking enemy posts in New Jersey. What he did not realize was that Washington had decided to abandon the strung-out forward line, in anticipation for a larger confrontation with the enemy. From Chatham on May 24 Stephen wrote Washington that he wanted to attack the British camp near Amboy, "before they had all left the Town, or could get the Camp fortified." The enemy's departure from Amboy would be "of very extensive Consequence. It gives the Enemy Command of the Country." Furthermore, "traitors have no interruption in Corresponding with, or Supplying the Enemy with provisions." Stephen feared that the British "may make themselves masters of Westfield where we have Some Stores—of Springfield where we have an hospital," and they "will Certainly overrun Newark & Elizabethtown. . . . the Enemy taking possession of these places again tho' of no great importance, Will make a figure in their pompus Announciations at St. James." [57]

Thus Washington and Stephen differed fundamentally as to tactics in New Jersey. The commander in chief patiently explained to Stephen why it was impractical to extend operations in the state, doing so censoriously but not coming down too hard on his dissenting general. "To protect every Town, and every individual on this wide extended Continent . . . is a pleasure that never can be realized," Washington said. Because "our dispersed Situation, is neither formidable for defence, or Offence, it becomes me to place the Continental Troops in such a manner as to answer a more valuable purpose than to give the Shadow (for it is no more) of security, to particular Neighbourhoods." Troops were to be recalled from Springfield, Westfield, and "likewise from the other Posts, upon the communication. Some Men will be sent to possess the Pass of the Mountain, on some advantageous spot, between Springfield and Chatham." Stephen's "compliance" in assisting these measures was expected. Washington also said that Stephen's "apprehensions of the Enemy taking possession of New Ark and Elizabeth Town, with a view of holding them, does not strike me at all." The British had already "experienced the evil of multiplied Posts, as we shall do, if they should be seized with a Spirit of Enterprize." Maintaining posts "can give no effectual opposition to the Enemy, if they were disposed to move, and the Country is too much drained by both Armies, to afford much support." [58]

Looking forward to a summer campaign, Washington rearranged the army on May 20 into five divisions: Greene, Stephen, Sullivan, Lincoln, and Stirling. The brigades of Scott (4th, 8th, and 12th Virginia regiments and the Additional Continental regiments of William Grayson and John Patton) and Woodford (3d, 7th, and 13th Virginia regiments) formed Stephen's division. The other two Virginia brigades (Weedon's and Muhlenberg's) served under Greene.[59]

On May 28 Washington moved the army to Middlebrook, in the foothills of the Watchung Mountains. The new encampment was about eight miles from New Brunswick and in a position to intercept a march by Howe to Philadelphia. Stephen was again at odds with Washington's decisions, disapproving the collection of all the troops at Middlebrook. It seems Stephen found a sympathetic ear in Gen. John Sullivan, to whom he expressed his dissatisfaction on both June 1 and 4. Stephen said that he doubted that Howe "intended a vigorous attack" on Washington's army. Meanwhile, "we shall get languid here. The enemy are in possession of a fine country, well supplied with greens, lamb, veal, beef, mutton & pretty girls. My sentiments are to form companies of Light Infantry, and let them and the Riflemen, under active officers keep constantly in their [the enemy's] skirts."[60] In the second letter, Stephen rather clearly disputed Washington's military judgment. "I know as little of the reason of our present disposition as General Sullivan does," he said. "Yea, they were so polite as to order the Troops under my command off the Lines without my knowledge." This "happened at the same time that I was concerting an attack on the enemy's camp near Amboy and encamped on the heights, and wanted to get about their house before they got settled, or had all moved out of town. I solace myself by Pope's maxim, 'Whatever is, is best.' The same person [probably meaning Greene] who advised another grand affair, I take to be the author of this." Stephen said that "I would not have moved from M—s t—n [Morristown] unless the motion of the enemy had compelled me untill I had it in my power to make the day of my movement memorable in the annals of America."[61]

But Washington's position at Middlebrook did make sense after all. On June 12 Howe collected nearly his whole force, some 18,000 troops, in New Jersey. The British army, with pontoons, evidently to be used in crossing the Delaware, established a line from Somerset Courthouse to New Brunswick. Howe sought to lure Washington out of the hills by feigning a retreat, but the American army stayed put. The only major engagement occurred when two British columns unsuccessfully sought to catch in a pincers the troops under General Stirling, who had come down from Washington's encampment. Stirling's men, however, were able to find refuge in the passes. With Washington's army not offering battle on British terms but still in a good defensive position to contest an advance of Howe's force by land to Philadelphia, the British general withdrew his troops to Amboy and then crossed to Staten Island on June 30. From now on, there was a guessing game as to what Howe planned next. Would he move up the Hudson to assist Burgoyne, cross New Jersey to Philadelphia, take that city via the Delaware or Chesapeake Bay, or possibly conduct an invasion in the South? For several weeks in July, British transports were loading off New York, and on the twenty-fourth Howe's fleet set sail—but to where? Washington decided that the British general's objective was to move up the Hudson to aid Burgoyne, and consequently he marched the American army through the New Jersey highlands to Smith's Clove near West Point on the Hudson. Stephen's and Lincoln's divisions were sent to Chester, New York. The fleet did not arrive, and Washington then marched the enemy southward through New Jersey. Benjamin Lincoln was ordered to join the northern army under General Gates, and Stephen was given temporary command of Lincoln's division as well as his own. Stephen and the two divisions made a "forced march" along the back roads to Howell's Ferry on the Delaware, covering ninety-five miles in four days. Soon the rest of the army came up, and Washington waited for word of Howe's moves. The morning of July 31 Washington received an express from Congress that the British fleet was near the mouth of the Delaware River. Washington started the army toward Philadelphia, only to learn that the British fleet again had set sail and were next seen off the Capes of Virginia. On August 21, at the Neshaminy encampment, Washington met with his general officers (including Stephen), who voted that the army should march immediately toward the Hudson River. Washington then sought to clear this decision with Congress. But the next day word came that the British fleet had entered the Chesapeake, and it was now ascertained that the enemy would debark for a march on Philadelphia. The American army trekked southward to counter the new invasion.[62]

On the return trip from New York, Stephen alienated several of his junior officers, which later would have an adverse impact on his career. Capt. John Chilton of the 3d Virginia Regiment noted in his diary: "To return to my disagreement with Genl. Stevens [Stephen] some days ago, I had just gone up to drink our friends health in grog, the retreat beat . . . a sergeant and file of men came and informed me we must go to the Genl. I went down very angry." Stephen asked Chilton if it was possible that he had been "out of your duty." Chilton replied that there was a possibility but that he "could not submit that it then was, that the strictest discipline had been maintained, that all regulations allowed 5 minutes but that I had not taken 2, that I knew my duty and had done it and admitting I had made a slip thought it too triffling to be sent for in that way." Stephen then said that he did not know they were officers, "asked our pardon, asked us to drink grog, which we refused to do and went very angry away. The next day he called to me quite across a platoon of men to know 'how I did' seemed sorry for what he had done, so I even thought it was best to be on good terms again."[63] Later charges indicate that Stephen may have been inebriated. Chilton however, was not present at a later court of inquiry investigating Stephen's alleged drinking too much on the march from New York, for he was killed at the battle of Brandywine.

Stephen also got into a minor controversy of a different kind while on the New Jersey–New York marches. Fort Ticonderoga fell to the British during this time, and Stephen wrote Congressman Francis Lightfoot Lee stating that the fort had been abandoned because of lack of support from New England. Whereas 8,000 troops were necessary to retain the post, New England had supplied only 3,000; "for Want of the Quota the Place is lost & they stand answerable for the consequences." Stephen's remarks were passed on to other congressmen and stirred Yankee blood. Samuel Adams entered into the argument. He wrote Richard Henry Lee that "it is natural for Parties to shift the Fault from one to the other; and your friend General Steven . . . seems desirous of clearing his Country-

men from Blame, in a letter to your Brother. . . . The General for-
gets that five of the ten Regiments ordered from Mass. Bay were
countermanded and are now at Peekskill." [64] What Stephen was for-
getting, too, was that while Virginians made up a large part of the
main army, as Washington's force was often called, the northern
army, then challenging Burgoyne's invasion from Canada, consisted
mostly of New England and New York troops.

Thus far Stephen's experience in the war had been that of participation in limited engagements and maneuvers. The war of outposts
in New Jersey was now in the past, and it no longer mattered whether
Stephen was right or wrong in insisting that the Americans had
missed opportunities to give the enemy crippling blows. If a clash of
armies should come, Stephen's abilities as a division commander
would be severely tested.

ELEVEN

Flight from Victory

The two grand armies struck a collision course. As British troops debarked at the head of Chesapeake Bay, forty miles from Philadelphia, Washington's force marched rapidly southward to gain a position to contest the enemy's advance. By August 25 the American army reached Wilmington. Stephen's and Greene's divisions made camp four miles south at White Clay Creek Bridge.[1]

Howe on September 3 dispatched 3,000 British troops toward Iron Hill, four miles below Stephen's and Greene's camp. Maxwell and 800 selected light infantry were sent to check the British advance and took position at Cooch's Bridge. During the fighting that ensued, Stephen's and Greene's divisions marched two miles "and posted ourselves, waiting for the enemy till some time in the afternoon." Scott's and Woodford's brigades of Stephen's division were sent to aid Maxwell. It seems, however, that only the 12th Regiment of Scott's brigade arrived in time to give Maxwell any assistance. Stephen commented that the Americans at the battle of Iron Hill (Cooch's Bridge) were beaten "in detail." On September 4 Sullivan's division took possession of the front lines, while Stephen's troops moved about one mile to the new American encampment near Newport.[2]

Washington now expected to meet the whole enemy army in battle. Trying to avoid direct confrontation, Howe directed his force toward Newark, Delaware. So as not to be outflanked, Washington moved his army back across the Brandywine and posted troops on the heights at Chad's Ford, overlooking the main road to Philadelphia. The American line stretched from two miles eastward to four miles westward. Stephen's, Stirling's, and Sullivan's divisions formed the right (west) wing, from Brinton's Ford to Painter's Ford. On September 10 the Americans were busy preparing to make a stand, while the British army camped at Kennett Square, six miles from Chad's Ford.[3]

The morning of September 11, the British army advanced. Knyphausen led a strong detachment to attack the American units at Chad's Ford. About 2 P.M., Cornwallis and 6,000 British troops, in a wider flanking movement than Washington had expected, crossed the creek six miles above Chad's Ford. Stephen's, Stirling's, and Sullivan's divisions, under the wing command of Sullivan, were immediately ordered up the Brandywine to oppose Cornwallis. The British, however, with the greater number of troops, were able to extend their line beyond Stephen's and Stirling's divisions; Sullivan's division, having taken a circuitous route, arrived after the fighting started. Eventually the three divisions sought to hold ground on the slopes of Birmingham Meetinghouse Hill. About 4 P.M. Cornwallis's troops pressed toward the hill. The battle around and on Birmingham Meetinghouse Hill, involving the divisions of Sullivan, Stirling, and Stephen, lasted two hours. The Americans were able to get small artillery to the top of the hill and send an effective barrage against the British attackers. Woodford's brigade, in Stephen's division, protected by a stone wall and trees near the meetinghouse, enfiladed the British left with small-arms fire. On the west end of the hill, however, the second Maryland brigade under General Preudhomme de Borre, in Sullivan's division, fought desperately in a narrow lane with Hessian grenadiers but was soon put to flight. De Borre three days later would resign upon charges of cowardice. Fighting seesawed back and forth, principally with Stirling's and Stephen's troops being engaged with the enemy. But the Americans' ammunition was running low, and they were forced from the hill and retreated through the woods to another eminence in the rear. Here they gave the enemy stiff resistance, but

Scott's brigade, in Stephen's division, was struck on the flank by British infantry and Hessian jägers and was thrown into confusion. Meanwhile, Washington ordered up Greene's division. Arriving as Stephen's, Stirling's, and de Borre's troops were retreating, this reinforcement helped to stem the tide. Especially Weedon's brigade made a heroic stand in a plowed field, covering the American retreat. As it was now dusk, Cornwallis halted his army and at 8 P.M. was joined by Knyphausen's troops, who had finally gained the heights at Chad's Ford. With the British occupying the battleground, Washington's army retreated to Chester.[4]

The battle of Brandywine was a clear victory for the British. Estimated casualties for the Americans were 200 killed, 500 wounded, and 400 captured; the British had 90 killed and 448 wounded.[5] Yet the British missed an opportunity to crush Washington's army. As a Hessian officer commented, "Had General Howe set out two hours earlier, or marched faster, Washington's army would have been caught between two fires, and could have been cut off from the Schuylkill and completely destroyed."[6] Despite the delay in synchronizing the three divisions placed under Sullivan to check the large British force crossing the upper Brandywine, the Virginia troops distinguished themselves. The 3d Regiment in Weedon's brigade (Greene's division) was the last to leave the field, and most of its officers were killed. Woodford's brigade, in Stephen's division, had fought hard and was the last unit to leave Birmingham Meetinghouse Hill. Woodford was wounded. Charles Scott's brigade, also in Stephen's division, had fought heroically, despite Stephen's later assertion of the ineptitude of its commander. A Boston newspaper, in printing a letter from a Philadelphian, reported on October 2 that Weedon's and Woodford's brigades "behaved admirably. They sustained a close and heavy fire from the enemy for a long time, without starting an inch. . . . Many others (Virginians especially) . . . behaved in a manner that would do honor to veteran troops."[7]

Whereas Washington could have been faulted for his failure to assess the possibilities open to the British in an attack (particularly the wide flanking movement), it was Gen. John Sullivan who bore the brunt of criticism for the defeat at Brandywine. Thomas Burke, who had witnessed part of the battle, and other congressmen charged that Sullivan, who had been stationed on the right of the army before the battle, engaged in improper reconnaissance and forwarded inaccurate intelligence of the British flanking movement. Sullivan also was denounced for taking his troops into battle late because he had made an indirect march, covering two miles unnecessarily. Sullivan acknowledged the delay but said it was because he did not know the location of Stephen's and Stirling's divisions. Even so, Sullivan claimed, he was soon able to get all three divisions into the battle. On September 14 Congress voted to suspend Sullivan from command until a court of inquiry could determine the issue. Washington, however, managed to convince Congress to hold back on the recall. Yet the commander in chief did not vigorously defend Sullivan because he had not been in that general's sector of the battle. The inquiry was delayed indefinitely, and in October Sullivan was cleared of another charge, that of botching an attack by his division on British troops on Staten Island on August 22, 1777.[8]

Like Stephen, Sullivan had something of a reputation as a free-wheeler, braggart, and one who was always pestering his superiors.[9] Stephen had an inkling that Sullivan's predicament could also be his in the future, for generals' actions in battle often came under review. It was important, however, to stand up to any assault on military honor in its earliest stage, especially that which involved the meddling of politicians. One congressman was already impugning the character of two generals as alcoholics; he possibly had in mind Stephen and either Sullivan, Maxwell, or Stirling. The latter two were definitely known as hard drinkers but had never been held to account for this propensity interfering with their duty. There were rumors that Stephen had been imbibing too much, even to the extent of clouding his judgment at the battle of Brandywine. Congressman Charles Carroll expressed his concern to Washington on September 27: "two officers in high command in our army are said to be much addicted to liquor: what trust, what confidence can be reposed in such men? They may disconcert the wisest and best laid plans"; such persons "ought to be removed from their command & the army, for their example, besides the mischief which may be occasioned by a clouded & muddled brain, will have a pernicious influence on others."[10]

Adam Stephen offered his support to Sullivan. In a letter of September 20 to the New Hampshire general, he declared that he was "astonished, at a Report in Camp, whispering, that you are Suspended, by a Resolve of Congress; and That your Intention is to resign.—It is alarming to me, and I suppose to ev'ry Officer of Spirit, & Reputation." Stephen said that Congress, to retain respect, must pursue "a steady, & Uniform Conduct, keeping constantly in View the Principles, on which we set out." Stephen praised Sullivan for his composure and "Coolness" during the military actions of 1777, including the battle of Brandywine. He advised Sullivan that if he persisted in wanting to leave the army, he should also "reflect" on his "noble Retreat from Canada, which does you . . . the greatest Honour—I scarcely know a retreat that is superior it exceeds Marshall Broglios from Prague."[11] Stephen, who had been critical of New England's war effort, now staunchly supported the general from New Hampshire. At least he was giving assurance personally to Sullivan, though it may be suspected he was not so enthusiastic in defending Sullivan among the officer corps. If Sullivan was cleared of incompetence at Brandywine, it might follow that Stephen's own behavior in that engagement would come under closer scrutiny. It appears that Sullivan did not reciprocate in extending friendship between himself and Stephen.

Although the Brandywine fiasco dampened hopes of ending the war, neither Congress, Washington, nor the army suffered from any lack of confidence. The commander in chief was determined to draw the British into another battle. On September 15 the American army recrossed the Schuylkill from Germantown and the next day was close to the enemy at Warren Tavern, twenty miles northwest of Philadelphia. Howe's force was on the way to Goshen (West Chester) when he learned of the American position nearby. The British took to sloping ground near the White Horse Tavern, expecting the Americans to attack. Washington stationed his men along the crests of the South Valley Hills. Both armies, extended for three miles, faced each other. Scott's brigade was ordered to skirmish with the enemy but was unable to do so because of the weather. Rain "poured" down vehemently" and incessantly. The musket cartridges of soldiers of both armies were soaked. Washington, also concerned about difficulties in protecting the rear of his army, declined combat. During the night of September 16, the Americans marched down from the hills through ankle-deep mud. By dawn they reached Flatland Ford, where they encamped. Thus what might have become a major confrontation of the war resulted only in a maneuver, otherwise referred to as the "battle of the Clouds." [12]

Washington on the nineteenth crossed to the north side of the Schuylkill, still intending to block passage of the British army over the river at the upper fords. Wayne's division, left behind near Paoli, was attacked during the night of September 21 by three British regiments under Gen. Charles Grey and suffered heavy casualties. Howe crossed the Schuylkill twelve miles below the American position, and now the way was clear for the British to march directly to Philadelphia. But the British commander refrained from taking all his army immediately into the city. With 9,000 men he encamped at Germantown, while Cornwallis led the rest of the British troops into Philadelphia. Howe did not fortify his camp, considering this would be a sign of weakness; nor did he expect an American attack. At camp near Pottsgrove, Washington and his general officers met and decided not to advance on the enemy until reinforcements and Wayne's troops arrived. Washington moved the American army to Pennypacker's Mill, some twenty miles above Germantown, where on September 28 another council of war voted against going immediately into battle, although it was agreed that the army should be brought closer to Germantown. Stephen sided with the majority in the decision that upon receiving reinforcements an attack should be made on the British at Germantown. Following his council's advice, Washington took his army to Metuchen Hill and vicinity on Skippack Creek, about fourteen miles above the enemy. On October 3 Washington and his general officers now decided that during the night a swift march would be made to Germantown, with columns of the army using different roads. They hoped to catch the British army totally by surprise about dawn. [13]

About 7 P.M., October 3, the American army started for Germantown. Stephen's and Greene's divisions, with McDougall's brigade in the flank, composing the left wing, headed down Lime Kiln Road, with the objective of engaging the enemy's right. Sullivan's and Wayne's divisions, preceded by Conway's brigade, taking a direct

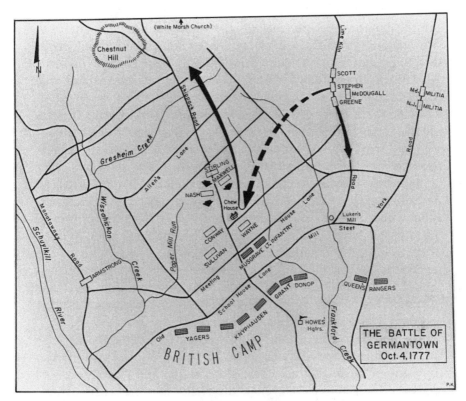

Battle of Germantown. (Drawn by Paul Kersey, Richmond)

road, would enter into the center of the town. Stirling's division (Maxwell's and Nash's brigades) formed a corps de reserve. Maryland and New Jersey militia under Smallwood would make a circuit and come upon the British right and rear; on the other side Armstrong's Pennsylvania militia would do the same. For the broad pincer movement it was of the utmost importance that the advance be synchronized to the greatest precision so that the American units would attack at once. But a guide led the American left wing down the wrong road. Although the troops of Sullivan, Wayne, and Conway "halted a considerable time," Conway's brigade came upon the first British picket post and the fighting began, with other British

troops immediately entering into the action. There were difficulties
for the Americans at the outset: light horsemen had been unable to
maintain communications among the several columns, the troops
had to go into battle fatigued from the long march, and a fog made
visibility no more than fifty yards. When the battle commenced at
dawn, the British set fire to buckwheat fields, which further contributed to the dark haze. Stephen commented that his and Greene's
divisions "formed the line of battle at a great distance from the British, and marched far through marshes, woods, and strong fences,
[so that they were] mixed before we came up with the enemy."[14]

Sullivan's, Wayne's, and Conway's troops drove the British about
two miles to the center of the town. The Americans gained "possession of the enemy's different encampments," their baggage, and "a
great part of their Artillery"; there was "the utmost reason to think
they would have obtained a complete and glorious victory." But
confusion prevailed. Adj. Gen. Timothy Pickering, who was with
Sullivan's and Wayne's troops at the time, observed that "we could
not hear of the left wing's being engaged, for the smoke and fog
prevented our seeing them, and our own fire drowned theirs."[15]
Howe was able to reform his army. Colonel Musgrave and six British companies made a stand at the Chew house. Knox's artillery was
brought up to breach the thick stone walls, but without success.
Maxwell's brigade was delayed by the exchange of arms fire with the
British defenders at the house. Meanwhile, Stephen's troops broke
away from those of Greene and headed toward the Chew house,
obliquely across the left rear of Wayne. Stephen had heard firing
in that direction and thought his men were needed there. From
the Chew house Stephen sought to catch up with Wayne's advancing troops. Wayne's and Sullivan's divisions had separated. Wayne,
hearing the noise of the firing at the Chew house and fearing that
Sullivan was flanked by the British, ordered his troops to reverse
direction and retrace their steps. Wayne mistook Stephen's men for
the British and had his men fire on them; Stephen's troops replied
in kind. At the same time British soldiers fired on the Americans
from the fields at the end of the town. Greene's troops continued
the attack in Germantown but without support from Stephen or
Wayne, and with Sullivan at the edge of the town impeded by

fences and walls, they had to retreat. Also, there was no assistance from the militia forces at the far flanks. By 10 A.M. the battle was over. What was thought would be a great victory when the fighting started now became a general retreat. The full element of surprise had been lost. The adverse weather conditions had lessened the opportunity for victory. The American troops withdrew too quickly after the confused situation developed in the vicinity of the Chew house. Adam Stephen perhaps bears a major responsibility for bringing about the retreat. Although "the Unfortunate retreat," wrote Walter Stewart a week afterward, "cannot yet be accounted for," Stephen "certainly gave the orders to the left wing." [16]

No one initially faulted Stephen for his role at Germantown. Wayne, who had the most reason to find someone to blame other than himself for the disaster near the Chew house, did not take any issue with Stephen's exercise of command. In writing his wife two days after the battle, Wayne charged the defeat to an unlucky set of circumstances. "We had now pushed the enemy near three miles," he said, "and were in possession of their whole encampment, when a large body of troops were advancing on our left flank, which being taken for the enemy, our men fell back, in defiance of every exertion of the officers to the contrary, and after retreating about two miles, they were discovered to be our own people." This mishap and the fog "prevented us from following a victory, which in all human probability would have put an end to the American war. General Howe for some time could not persuade himself that we had run away from victory, but the fog clearing off, he ventured to follow us with a large body of his infantry, grenadiers, and light horse." [17]

Wayne's and Stephen's divisions retreated simultaneously. Upon leaving "the field of Battle," as Wayne reported to Washington, those "who took the Upper Rout were formed at White Marsh Church under Genl Stephen—it was thought Advisable to Remain there for some time in Order to Collect the Straglers from the Army." Wayne came up nearby. Upon the appearance of a detachment of British light horse and some 2,000 infantry, with two field pieces, the two generals thought it best to retreat farther. Wayne said that he "took the Liberty" to have Colonel Bland cover the rear "with the Horse aided by some of the Infantry." But "finding the Enemy Determined to push us hard," Wayne "Obtained a field officer from Genl Stephens and taking the Advantage of a hill that overlooked the Road we marched on—they met with Such a Reception as Induced them to Return back over the Bridge they had passed."[18] Wayne makes no mention of an accusation to be made by Gen. Charles Scott that Stephen, paying no attention to the advice of any of his officers, refused to have his troops reform and post artillery to check the enemy's pursuit; rather Stephen, according to Scott, went to reconnoiter the area, leaving the men of his division to fare on their own.[19]

Washington did not parcel out any blame on his division commanders for the defeat at Germantown. The commander in chief thought the major problem was the fog, which made American troops cautious and allowed time for the enemy to recover. Furthermore, it "served to keep our different parties in ignorance of each Others movements" and hindered "their acting in concert." The fog also "occasioned them to mistake one another for the Enemy, which, I believe, more than any thing else, contributed to the misfortune which ensued." Despite the many casualties (152 killed, 500 wounded, 438 captured), Washington considered that the surprise attack upon the British army at their encampment demonstrated the capability of American troops to defeat the British army.[20] Meanwhile, Washington's army rested on the west bank of Perkiomen Creek (opposite Pennypacker's) and, after several moves, camped in Whitpain Township.[21]

Nathanael Greene, as much as anyone, could have been taken to task for being late in arriving at Germantown, and his troops also hastily joined the retreat. In his division orders of October 7, Greene mentioned that the commander in chief "has the mortification to assure the Troops they fled from Victory" and that in the future the soldiers are advised not to mistake "a particular Retreat" (one of maneuver) for a "general" retreat.[22] It was one thing for Washington or Greene to describe the whole army as having "fled from Victory." But it was another matter for Stephen, who undoubtedly referred to retreat from victory in his own division orders. The younger, ambitious officers of Stephen's division did not want any criticism from Stephen. Accusations of misconduct on the part of

Stephen during and after the battle began to circulate widely in camp. Dr. James Wallace, a surgeon with the Virginia troops, noted that many officers had told him "that when they were ordered to retreat they were then pursuing the enemy, who were flying before them; they were astonished to the last degree when they retreated from the highest expectations of success."[23] Stephen thought the main source of the discontent was Charles Scott, whom he apparently had taken a dislike to since the early New Jersey fighting. Scott, eighteen years younger, had worked his way up through the enlisted ranks dating back to the French and Indian War and was barely educated. Scott had demonstrated courage and resourcefulness but, like Stephen, seemed to lack the perseverance and judgment for successful command in actual battle.

Stephen's ire got the best of him, and on October 9 he addressed a long letter to Washington, desiring that his name be cleared and, if necessary, that a court of inquiry be held for that purpose. Stephen was not mindful as yet of the gravity of charges he might face, such as being intoxicated in battle and even abandoning his troops in the retreat, which if proved in the extreme could be a capital offense. It was certainly a mistake for Stephen to write the kind of letter that he did, especially in venting his petulance toward Scott. Scott was very popular with his Virginia troops, and Stephen only further alienated Washington and the Virginia officers as well. Stephen's remarks to Washington were unusually direct and frank. "I understand that Many Officers of My Division are highly disobliged," he began, "at my Saying the troops which I commanded in an Attack on Saturday last the 4th Inst, fled from Victory by which Expression I by no means intended to charge them with Cowardice, many of them I know to be of experiencd[?] Bravery. But in order to do justice these Officers as well as my Self I am obligd to intreat your Excellencys patience to hear the Circumstances." Stephen mentioned the difficulties that his and Greene's troops had with the terrain just before the battle. He recorded how several units under his command quickly made contact with the enemy. He himself led his troops "on to the Attack." Stephen stated that the regiments of Oliver Spencer and John Patton advanced and "pushed the Enemy so Closely, that I calld to them to give them the bayonet—Upon hearing this, The Enemy officers on horse back rode to their Rear out of Sight; Many of their men running after them; whilst a party Run towards our troops crying Quarters." At this moment "a large Corps dressed in blue, mistaking the Enemy which had Surrendered, for a party coming up to charge them . . . Took the Start—I hollowerd from the front that they were running from Victory, & hastend to them, to Stop them but to no purpose."

Stephen cited the gallantry of certain officers in his and Greene's divisions. He, however, had no praise for Gen. Charles Scott, whom he blamed for starting rumors against him regarding the battle of Brandywine as well as that of Germantown. "I am Compelled to inform your Excellency, that General Scot has been an incumbrance to me for Some time," Stephen declared. At the beginning of the battle of Brandywine, Scott delayed in pressing his troops into action, as Stephen had ordered; he claimed that he was waiting for orders from Washington. Furthermore, after the fighting was underway, the troops of Scott's brigade secured favorable ground, "most of them Entrenched to the Chin in the Ditch of a fence Opposite to the Center of the Enemy," but then, to Stephen's "great Surprise," Scott marched off his brigade "from that Advantageous position without my Orders or Knowledge." Stephen said that it then "took a long time to form them in tolerable order, as the Enemy were firing upon them . . . I am Confident by this unseasonable Manoeuver the Enemy escaped Considerable Loss, & it shortend our Stand." Stephen also referred to the near engagement of September 16: "when drawn up in order of Battle, waiting your Excellencys Orders—Genl Scot Movd off with his Brigade without my Knowledge." Stephen said that he "had great inclination to let all these things pass hoping that the least Reflexion" would have led Scott "to alter his Conduct; but besides Aspersing me to your Excellency, he goes through the Division alienating the affection of the officers, & breeding bad blood." Stephen requested that "wherever my Conduct is Suspected I would be Obligd to your Excellency to order a Speedy & Strict Scrutiny."[24]

Other generals besides Stephen faced examination of their behavior. Stephen could take comfort that they fared very well, gaining acquittals. Serious charges were placed against Wayne for the disaster at Paoli. Upon his own request Wayne was tried by court-martial, of which General Sullivan was president, and acquitted on November 1. A court of inquiry dismissed charges against General Maxwell, brought by Lt. Col. William Heth, a Virginia officer, except that it found "that it appears he was once during said time disguised with liquor in such a manner, as to disqualify him in some measure, but not fully, from doing his duty; and that once or twice besides his spirits were a little elevated by spiritous liquor." It was recommended that Washington use his "better judgment" whether or not Maxwell should face a court-martial. Washington decided that the drunkenness charges were severe enough, and from October 30 to November 1 a court-martial, with General Sullivan presiding, heard the case, which ended in acquittal.[25]

Undoubtedly, as Stephen saw it, officers were given too much leeway to bring charges against their superiors, without being held responsible for their recklessness in attempting to fix blame. Later, in November, Wayne, Maxwell, and Sullivan, in a joint letter to Washington, complained bitterly of the lack of accountability for officers who brought charges. The three generals insisted that the commander in chief reprimand officers who had made accusations that were demonstrated in a judicial process as having no substance.[26] Washington did not act on this recommendation.

Not only did Stephen have to face criticism of his decisions made on the battlefield, but the gossip was turning ugly. Word was being spread that Stephen was drunk at the battle of Germantown. Of course, it was common knowledge that Stephen enjoyed a spiritous drink once in a while. This could be said of virtually all the generals, and especially of those from Virginia. Even the soldiers had their daily rations of either whiskey or rum. Stephen, however, undoubtedly was tippling a little more of late, fortifying his constitution wearied by the long marches and heavy responsibilities. But he had never been held to account because of his imbibing before. Probably there was more common knowledge of Stephen's propensity for hard liquor than was admitted publicly, but it is also not difficult to imagine how a vicious rumor, in a camp beset with frustrations over the recent campaign, could be magnified out of proportion to the actual facts.

There is no evidence that Stephen was drunk at the battle of Brandywine to the extent he was unable to perform his duties, the charge placed by George Washington's nephew three-quarters a century later notwithstanding. George Washington Parke Custis was prone to write anecdotes into his *Recollections* that enhanced his narrative but had slight or no bearing on fact. As to the battle of Brandywine, according to Custis, Lt. Benjamin Grymes, of Washington's personal guard, found Stephen (whom Custis was careful not to mention by name) lying on the ground at a fence corner, drunk. As the story went, Grymes grasped Stephen "by the collar, placed him on his legs, and bade him go and do his duty." [27]

The rumor that Stephen was intoxicated at the battle of Germantown persisted and wound its way to Congress. Charles Carroll of Carrollton, who had already remarked on the excessive drinking by the general officers, wrote his father on October 12: "We hear that several officers in General Steven's division have lodged complaints agt. him. I believe them to be well founded for Stevens (entre nous) drinks." [28] Even the president of the Congress, Henry Laurens, was pessimistic about Stephen's situation; he wrote John Wells on October 20 that "Your friend General Stevens is highly censured for malconduct the 4th Inst." [29]

The man who had helped Stephen win his promotion to major general, Dr. Benjamin Rush, now seemed to turn against him. Six days after the battle of Germantown, Rush dined with Washington and about the same time jotted down his impressions of some of the general officers. Perhaps Rush had plied from the commander in chief some tidbits of information. In a notation written in October 1777, under the heading, "State and Disorders in the American army," Rush commented on four major generals—Greene, Sullivan, Stirling, and Stephen: "The 1st a sycophant to the general, timid, speculative, without enterprise; the 2nd, weak, vain, without dignity, fond of scribling, in the field a madman. The 3d, a proud, vain, lazy, ignorant, drunkard. The 4th, a sordid, boasting, cowardly sot." [30] Rush, who was now a staunch temperance advocate and had just been asked by the Board of War to republish his pam-

phlet on army health, which included warnings on the evils of spiritous liquors, had no use for any high officer in the army who was in
his cups.[31]

One interested bystander to Stephen's predicament was the marquis de Lafayette. Having only entered the American conflict in
summer 1777, Lafayette, not yet twenty years old, had been commissioned a major general but without command. If Stephen was
removed, this would solve the dilemma of what to do with the
youthful marquis, who as a volunteer had been wounded at Brandywine. Lafayette casually suggested to Washington on October 12
that "if i was to be at the head of a division and your excellency
would be master of it, (as I am told that Stephens gives his dismission), I can not help to tell you that a division of Virginians as they
are, principally with General Woodfort would be the most agreable
for me."[32] Lafayette later in the first edition of his *Mémoires* noted
that about August 1777 Stephen was "a general always drunk,"
which, upon republication, he changed to "a general often drunk."[33]

Alleviating his despondency for the moment, Stephen found himself in charge of the military tribute honoring the defeat of General
Burgoyne along the Hudson River. The news had come prematurely that the British general had capitulated on October 14 (actually the event was three days later). Washington scheduled the victory celebration for the eighteenth. "The Major General of the day
will superintend and regulate the *feu-de-joy*," read Washington's
general orders. Stephen was that officer, and he must have had
mixed emotions, a sense of great pride yet saddened by the rumors
that sought to blacken his reputation. In the late afternoon appointed for the festive occasion, the troops were assembled, with
Stephen at their head. The chaplains presented "short discourses"
to their respective units, after which thirteen cannon boomed from
the artillery park; then, successively by each brigade, the soldiers
fired their weapons without bullets.[34] One North Carolina infantryman many years later recalled the celebration. "We rejoiced with
great shouting and firing all day," said Hugh McDonald, who was
about fifteen years old at the time, "our officers being more joyous
than the common soldiers . . . and I think more so than was necessary—prancing and capering about everywhere on their horses,

and in all places in camp." The horses were scared by the artillery fire. General Stirling had a bad fall. "After lying for some time, he got up and shook himself like a great water dog."[35]

A week later, acting upon Stephen's request, Washington announced there would be a court of inquiry. The next day, October 26, five officers—Generals Greene, Smallwood, and Knox and Colonels William Richardson of the 5th Maryland Regiment and William Russell of the 13th Virginia Regiment—met to deliberate the charges against Stephen. Greene served as president for the hearing, which extended to six days, as numerous witnesses were heard. Stephen certainly was uncomfortable in that Greene, whom he had on several occasions indirectly criticized, headed the commission. The court of inquiry, as requested in the commander in chief's after orders of the twenty-fifth, was to evaluate Stephen's conduct "on the march from the Clove to Schuylkill falls," at the battle of Brandywine, and "more especially in the action . . . at and about Germantown, on which occasions he is charged with 'Acting unlike an officer.'" Stephen also was to answer to a "charge against him for 'Drunkenness, or drinking so much, as to act frequently in a manner, unworthy the character of an officer.'"[36]

Rarely were minutes of either courts of inquiry or subsequent courts martial made public, a notable exception being that of Charles Lee in 1778. Although the court of inquiry held for Stephen did not identify particular testimony of witnesses, the report, rendered on November 1, was explicit as to the issues, though vaguely defined. The conclusions of the hearing, which served much like a grand jury in determining whether there was cause for prosecution, were unfavorable for Stephen.

The court of inquiry, in reference to the first charge, found that "there are several unquestionable Evidences of their being great confusion upon the march from the Clove to the Delaware, that General Stephens frequently contradicted by verbal orders his own written ones." Furthermore, "on this March the Genl was often seen intoxicated, which was generally supposed the cause of the confusion and disorder which pr[e]vailed. At Howels Ferry the General was seen in open view of all the soldiers very drunk taking snuff out of the Boxes of strumpets." To rebut "these positive Evidences," Stephen "produced many positive ones of good repute, who say they were with the Troops on that march and neither saw the confusion afforementioned or the General in the least intoxicated with Liquor, altho they saw him at the very places where he was said to be drunk. Most of his Family and several others who frequented his Table declare they have not seen the General intoxicated this Campaign."

Similarly, the court of inquiry, even finding some of the testimony of Stephen's own witnesses implicitly damaging, upheld the other charges. The "Evidences" concerning Stephen's behavior at the battle of Brandywine "all serve to prove the General did not pay that general attention to his Division which might be expected from an officer of his Command." Also, as to the "Action of Germantown," the "Evidences . . . all serve to prove that the General was not with his Division during the Action. The Evidences also prove their stand might have been made on the retreat at White Marsh Church, and that it was necessary to cover straglers which were coming in." Stephen "was the oldest Officer on the Ground to whom application was made by General Scott and others to have the Troops formed and to post some Artillery to check the Advances of the Enemy"; but Stephen "went off under pretence to reconoitre ordering off the Artillery at the same Time and left his Division behind; for want of this necessary Disposition tis supposed many Stragglers fell into the Enemys Hands." It was acknowledged, however, that Stephen "produced many Evidences to prove he did not shrink from danger" at Brandywine and Germantown and "that he always appeared cool and delivered his orders with deliberation and firmness becoming the dignity of an Officer" with "no uncommon fear of personal Danger."[37]

Despite attending the court of inquiry, Stephen and the officers on the panel found time to keep up with their other responsibilities. Stephen joined other generals in a council of war on October 29. The group voted against any attack on the British in Philadelphia. It was decided that the army make camp at Whitemarsh. Other questions as to location for a winter cantonment and those dealing with problems relating to the commissary, inspection, the manual of arms, and prisoner exchange were deferred.[38]

Upon receiving the report of the court of inquiry, Washington concluded there were grounds for further action and ordered Stephen to be tried by court-martial. The trial had to be delayed a day, as the army on November 2 marched to Whitemarsh, thirteen miles north of Philadelphia. Ironically, this was the very place where, according to the major indictment, Stephen had allegedly been most negligent in his duty. At 9 A.M., November 3, General Stephen appeared at General Sullivan's headquarters to attend the proceedings that either would vindicate him or end his long military career in dishonor.[39]

TWELVE

"Dismission from the Continental Service"

G en. Adam Stephen warily greeted the officers of the court-martial. The only major general was John Sullivan. Two of the four brigadier generals were Virginians, John Peter Gabriel Muhlenberg and George Weedon, both of whom were serving in Greene's division. Muhlenberg, son of German immigrants, had settled in the Valley in 1772 and became the pastor of a large German Lutheran congregation, even though he had been ordained an Anglican minister. He had entered the Continental army as a commander of the 8th Virginia "German" Regiment. Weedon, a portly, easygoing innkeeper from Fredericksburg, had more of a proclivity for horse racing than for overindulgence in liquor. Of the two, Muhlenberg had the more level head, but he had his foibles, too: at the battle of Germantown it was said that he had fallen asleep on horseback while waiting for some of his men to tear down a fence. Neither men had much opportunity for independence of command. Weedon could be very spiteful, and his fit over being outranked by other Virginia brigadiers in a congressional reshuffle of rank in 1778 led to his retirement from the army, though he returned to military service as a commander of militia during the British invasion of Virginia in 1781. Weedon had served with Stephen during the French and Indian War. Unlike Stephen, he was an admirer of Greene, almost bordering on sycophancy. Both Muhlenberg and Weedon had seen hard action at Brandywine, where at a heavy cost in casualties to their brigades they both had protected the retreat of Stephen's and other troops; hence they may have harbored some resentment toward Stephen's conduct at that time. Stephen probably had little familiarity with another brigadier general on the court, Jedediah Huntington of Connecticut, who had held his present rank only since May 1777.

The fourth brigadier general on the court, the Irish-French interloper Thomas Conway, was resented by all the general officers for having been appointed by Congress to his rank upon unproven merit. It was rumored that Congress was about to name Conway a major general, as indeed he was six weeks later, on December 13, 1777. John Laurens wrote his father, the president of Congress, that Conway had been accused of cowardice at the battle of Germantown, on grounds that he had disobeyed orders and for a time was separated from his brigade. However, Conway, unlike Stephen, was lucky. Washington, as John Laurens observed, "thinking that a public investigation of this matter set on foot, by him, might be attribut'd to motives of personal resentment, suffer'd it to pass over." [1]

Five colonels sat on the court-martial: Edward Stevens of the 1st Virginia Regiment, Elias Dayton of New Jersey, Alexander McClanachan of the 7th Virginia Regiment, Philip Burr Bradley of Connecticut, and Walter Stewart of Pennsylvania, who was regarded by some as the most handsome man in the American army. Stephen thought it was beneath the dignity of a court trying a major general to have three lieutenant colonels on the bench, namely William Davis and James Thackston of North Carolina and William De Hart of New Jersey (Stephen would say afterwards that there were four). [2]

Besides Conway, of the twelve-man panel there were five Yankees and six southerners (four of whom were Virginians). A wide disparity in age separated the defendant and members of the court. Stephen was fifty-six, and on the court-martial the generals' ages averaged slightly less than thirty-six years old and, for the colonels, a little less than thirty.

General Sullivan, of New Hampshire, was the court's president. Stephen had no reason to question Sullivan's impartiality. However, Sullivan, who had a little sectional bias, as did Stephen, earlier in the year had made a statement which has a ring of poetic justice. In February, Sullivan, miffed that New England troops had not been given credit due them in actions such as the battle of Trenton, had told John Adams that "I have been much pleased to see a Day approaching to try the Difference between yankee Cowardice and Southern valour. The Day has or Rather the Days have Arrived . . . that the yankees Cowardice assume the Shape of True valor in the Field" and "Southern Valor appears to be a composition of boasting and Conceit." [3]

It was irregular that the court was the same which had heard the cases against Wayne and Maxwell. Washington, however, in his general orders of November 2 explained that he had not established a new panel because he wanted to avoid a delay and it would be difficult to find general officers who had not served on the court of inquiry. [4] Stephen's court-martial convened intermittently from November 3 to November 17. The trial, but one of the "infinite resulting courtmartials," as General St. Clair called them, put a strain on the army, with the judicial service infringing upon the regular duties of the officers. Stephen made use of his right to call his own witnesses and cross-examine those of the prosecution. His disappointment at not having more high-level officers on the court was not particularly well grounded, because courts-martial trying general officers could include those with rank as low as major. [5]

Although a record of the court-martial has not been preserved, it seems that damaging testimony came from Stephen's own brigade commanders, Woodford and Scott. Certainly Scott was a leading witness for the prosecution, in view of the accusations that he had already made openly against Stephen. Woodford, who had been wounded in the hand at the battle of Brandywine, appeared at camp about October 20 after a recuperation at the officers hospital in Bethlehem. Woodford had resigned when Stephen was made a brigadier general over him in September 1776 but had returned as a brigadier general in February 1777. He was not at the battle of Germantown. Woodford, who had led a gallant fight at Meetinghouse Hill during the battle of Brandywine, may have been displeased with Stephen's actions at that time, though there is no direct evidence. Yet, Stephen's later disparagement of Woodford in a letter to

Richard Henry Lee in which he discussed his trial seems to indicate that Woodford testified against Stephen at the court-martial.[6]

Stephen was tried on three charges: "1st Unofficerlike behaviour on the march from the Clove; 2nd Unofficerlike behaviour in the actions at Brandywine and Germantown; 3rd. Drunkenness." The court found Stephen guilty "of unofficerlike behaviour, in the retreat from Germantown, owing to inattention, or want of judgement and that he has been frequently intoxicated since in the service, to the prejudice of good order and military discipline; contrary to the 5th. article of the 18th Section of the articles of war." The sentence was dismissal from the army. The court did not find Stephen guilty "of any other crimes he was charged with." Thus Stephen was convicted of misbehaviour during the withdrawal from Germantown and for general conduct that exhibited too much drinking over a period of time. The charges arising from the court of inquiry involving Stephen's command duties on the march through New Jersey and at Brandywine obviously were not proved sufficiently for conviction, and that of taking snuff with some of the camp followers was frivolous at best. Washington approved the sentence, which was announced in general orders three days after the court-martial adjourned.[7]

The charges on which Stephen was convicted lacked specificity. A distinction was made between Stephen's conduct at Germantown and that of excessive drinking. The court did not state that his "inattention and want of judgment" at Germantown was owing to inebriation. "If drunkenness was proven at Germantown," writes Robert Lisle, "clearly that finding would have been used to strengthen the wording of 'frequently intoxicated since in the service.'" The charge of failing to collect and rally his troops once they had fled the battlefield at Germantown is also defined in general terms. The question is raised that because the retreat from Germantown was disorderly and became a rout for all units, were not other commanding officers culpable? Indeed, four other Virginia officers, less than general grade, were tried on charges involving the battle of Germantown, of whom three were acquitted and one (Lt. Col. John Markham) was cashiered. But, as to Stephen, the inexplicit charges, arising from those presented at the court of inquiry, covering the period from July to October, attest that Stephen's overall behavior was the main issue. It is significant that Stephen was not proved drunk during any battle action—or, at least the judges gave him the benefit of the doubt. But excessive drinking did contribute "to the prejudice of good order and military discipline."[8]

In extreme cases, officers who were cashiered had to attend a parade whereupon their swords were broken over their heads, and efforts were made to publish notices of the dismissal in newspapers in the culprit's home area and in the vicinity of the army.[9] Such was not the situation with Adam Stephen. His punishment was simply a "dismission" from the army. Stephen had only to pick up his effects, at his leisure, and leave the camp.

Stephen appealed the verdict to Congress, which had the power to overturn it. He wrote the president of Congress, Henry Laurens (whose name Stephen mispelled as "Laurence") on December 6. Stephen's denunciation of Washington in the letter, though coming at a time when dissatisfaction with the commander in chief supposedly was beginning to surface among the politicians, did not help his cause. The rancor that Stephen bore toward Washington and his other alleged persecutors is quite evident. "It has been my misfortune to become the Object of hatred of a Person of high Rank [Washington]," Stephen said, "for no other reason that I know, but for delivering my Sentiments on the Measures pursu'd this Campaign, with that Candour & Boldness which becomes an old officer of Experience, who had the Interest of America at heart." By Washington's orders "I have been tryd, after Serving thirteen Campaigns with reputation; for unofficerlike Behaviour on the march from the Clove to Sculkill, unofficerlike behavior in the Action of Brandywine, & unofficerlike behaviour more particularly in the Battle of Germantown—& for Drunkenness." Stephen pointed out that the court-martial proceedings reveal "that my Conduct in both Actions merited Applause instead of Censure"; the testimony of Stephen's aide-de-camp "and other Gentlemen more Conversant with me" indicates "that I have not been drunk since I enterd the Service of the States; & that I was Sober at the very hour & place where some mistaken people Swore I was drunk." It should also be noted "that I acted like an Officer of attention & Judgment on the retreat from german town and I have reason to believe that all the officers of Experience & Judgment on the Court were of that Opinion"; most members of the court were officers "of one or two Campaigns Standing: There were four Lt Colonels which is unprecedented in any Service." Stephen left no doubt that he considered that Washington was most responsible for the miscarriage of justice. "Your Excellency will be pleasd to Observe," he told President Laurens, "that the General descends to No particular Charge, but that of Drunkenness; that instead of a Court Martial it was a Court of Inquisition, unparalleled in any Army to the Westward of Asia. Without doubt the General did not Consider how dangerous it was to himself to Establish such a Precedent." Stephen assured Congress "that although I am justly disgusted with the Malevolence of Certain Persons yet I am zealously Attachd to the American Cause & when to vindicate my Own Character I publish My Case to the World, I may be naturally led to Expose the Weakness & partiallity of Some Commanders—yet I hope to be Acquitted of Any Intention of hurting the Interests of America—None of her Officers are willing to go further lengths to Save her." [10] Stephen's letter to the president of Congress was read during the session of December 8, simply for the record, and no action was taken. [11]

Stephen was one of two major generals dismissed from the Continental army during the war. Except for the drunkenness charge, there are striking similarities between his predicament and that of Maj. Gen. Charles Lee: the strained relationships with Washington, the accusations against them for evading command responsibility, the failure to rally their troops against the enemy, and the course of the court-martial proceedings. Lee was held to account for not converting retreat into an advance at the battle of Monmouth on June 28, 1778. Both men had criticized Washington's judgment and decisions, indirectly claiming that the commander in chief relied too much on the wrong men for advice. Both Lee and Stephen had long experience in military command, and each in his own way had been a rival of Washington. Both men believed that young, ambitious officers, eager to assert loyalty to the commander in chief, had misrepresented the cases against them. Both Lee and Stephen were held blamable for confusion in retreat. Gen. Charles

Scott was a major prosecution witness against both men in their courts-martial. The charges against Lee, however, were more grave than those against Stephen: Lee was tried for disobeying Washington's explicit orders, misbehavior before the enemy in allowing a retreat, and disrespect for the commander in chief. Convicted on all three counts, Lee was suspended temporarily from the army, a light sentence compared to Stephen's. Like Stephen, Lee wrote a letter to Congress severely critical of Washington, for which he was then dismissed from the army. When Stephen wrote his letter, he, of course, had already been ordered to leave the military service. It was in Congress's power, however, to reinstate both Stephen and Lee. Like Lee later, Stephen spoiled any chance for a favorable hearing from Congress by writing the kind of letter that he did.[12]

Adam Stephen lingered at the Whitemarsh camp several weeks before leaving for home, in itself an indication of a lack of harsh enmity toward him among the officers and men as a whole. From Whitemarsh, Stephen on November 25 sent Richard Henry Lee a copy of the verdict of the court-martial, with some evaluative comments of his own. "Annexed, you will see my dismission from the Continental Service," Stephen told his old friend who had been instrumental in his promotion to major general. "I do not sink in my own Esteem by it, & when the proceedings of the Court are seen I am firmly perswaded that I shall rise in the Esteem of my friends." Stephen noted that he expected that the court record would be published, and then "let the World Judge—It will appear that the greatest inveteracy could not prove me once drunk since I enterd the Service—And it will appear that my Attention & Judgment in the Retreat from German Town Action Savd great part of the Army." Stephen advised Lee that "you will please to Observe the Court has avoided telling that they had considered the Evidence—It will appear . . . that they have paid but little regard to the Evidence." It was "an unprecedented Court ordering an inquisition into my Conduct Since I enterd the Service—I would tell my mind freely & I seemd to be in the way, & to do my Self Justice shall be oblige to Expose the weakness & Principle[?] of a great many officers of Rank." Leaving no doubt that he thought that General Woodford, who apparently had testified against him, was prejudiced, Stephen reminded Lee that he had been promoted over that officer; he also mentioned that the "inhabitants" of Norfolk and Princess Anne counties had sent a letter to him while he on the way to join the main army in fall 1776 which alluded to Woodford's incompetence as commander of troops in the lower Tidewater of Virginia.[13]

Stephen was probably still at camp when his successor was named, the marquis de Lafayette. The young Frenchman had been mending his wounded leg at the officers hospital in Bethlehem; he returned to active duty about November 1. Lafayette sat in the council of war on the eighth.[14] Two weeks later he went with Greene's division to contend with an army under Cornwallis, which had crossed the Delaware into lower New Jersey. Both Greene and Cornwallis avoided a fight, and the British and American troops soon were back at their respective camps. But on the excursion, Lafayette with 400 militia and 170 men of the "rifle corps" attacked and routed a picket of 300 Hessians at Gloucester on November 25. Greene's dispatch to Washington declared: "The Marquis is charmed with the spirited behaviour of the militia and Rifle Corps." He "is determined to be in the way of danger." Several congressmen were soon echoing this assessment.[15]

Washington, in late November, recommended to Congress that Lafayette be given a division command. Lafayette had been pressing hard for such an appointment, Washington noted, and "I fear a refusal will not only reduce him to return in disgust, but may involve some unfavorable consequences. There are now some vacant Divisions in the Army." Washington said that he was convinced that Lafayette "possesses a large share of that Military order, which generally characterises the Nobility of his Country." The commander in chief also repeated Greene's comment: "The Marquis is determined to be in the way of danger."[16] Lafayette got his wish. On December 4, 1777, the general orders announced that Lafayette was assuming command of the division formerly headed by Gen. Adam Stephen.[17]

Rather surprisingly, Stephen's dismissal aroused very little comment among the public in general. It was easy to believe that the old soldier, who was known to drink amply, could have been inebriated at times, and anyone with a drinking problem should not be allowed to hold a command position in the army. In Stephen's case, the verdict was simply accepted. There was almost no discussion among congressmen about the dismissal. Two New England delegates wrote Joseph Trumbull, a newly elected member of the Board of War. Elbridge Gerry merely said that "General Stevens is broke for drunkenness," and James Lovell, formerly a supporter of Stephen, commented: "Genl. Stevens is dismissed with several inferior Officers by sentence of Court martial *approved* by Genl. Washington, which looks a little like firmness and rising Discipline. Cowardice, Theft & Drunkenness must take warning."[18] Lovell made similar remarks to General Gates.[19]

General officers followed a code of silence. Lafayette, however, later in his *Mémoires* stated that now he "ceased to be a volunteer, and replaced Stephen (the old drunkard) as commander of the Virginians."[20] In writing to Greene in February 1778, recalling the battle of Germantown, Gen. Alexander McDougall gave implied praise to Stephen: "I did not see the least indication of your [Greene's] want of activity or spirit in carrying on the Troops that day but the contrary. Those of your and Genl Stephens Divisions marched so brisk or ran to the charge that they were some minutes out of sight of my Brigade."[21]

The view from the soldiers was mixed, of which there is only very scant testimony, long after the fact. Richard T. Atkinson, in filing a pension claim many years later, commented that Stephen had appeared drunk at the battle of Germantown and, probably confusing him with someone else, said that Stephen had tried to set fire to the Chew house.[22] Hugh McDonald, late in life, recalled the battle of Germantown, though not too accurately; for example, he said that Lee was in command (actually Lee at the time was still a prisoner of war). The former North Carolina infantryman remembered that during the morning after the battle Virginia troops were at Whitemarsh tavern, commanded by "Gen. Stephens, a Scotchman, who no doubt had a feeling for his king. . . . An express was sent to Gen. Stephens, who was drunk when it came, to come to our assistance"; instead, Stephen "ordered his men to retreat to Long Oaks, which cowardly, base, or drunken movement frustrated our intention of driving the British from Philadelphia that day."[23] Yet it can be as-

sumed that some officers and men serving with Stephen were unhappy at their commander's removal. The biographer of George M.
Bedinger, who served with Stephen as a captain of a Virginia rifle
company, interviewed members of the Bedinger family and other
descendants of Revolutionary War veterans and concluded that
there had been dissatisfaction among Stephen's troops over his
ouster. The officers, "according to tradition in the family, brought
in a verdict that 'he did not have more liquor on board than a
gentleman ought.'"[24]

Virginians back home reflected little on Stephen's dismissal. After
all, he was getting up in years, and drinking could well have affected
his judgment. Washington needed younger men anyway, especially
those with clear heads. Edmund Pendleton, former president of the
Virginia Convention and now a member of the House of Delegates,
made an acerbic comment in a letter to his friend and neighbor,
General Woodford. "I doubt not the old Heroe [Stephen] will muster all his Arts to Parry the Attack upon him," he said, "and he will
have Partizans to support him; I care not for my part how Gently
they let him down, so he does not continue in the Army, to keep a
better man from a Post of consequence, which he filled to so little
(to say no more of it), in the late Actions."[25]

Stephen's removal created a problem for Governor Patrick Henry
of Virginia. Back in late 1776 Stephen had been appointed by Henry
to be in charge of reenlistments in the Continental army in Virginia. Of course, there was little that Stephen could do while constantly in the field with Washington's army, but he could keep track
of officers on leave and have them spur recruitment in the state.
Governor Henry wrote Washington on the subject on December 9,
enclosing an extract of a letter from Stephen, by which "it appears
considerable progress was made by him in that Business." Henry
said that he had heard that Stephen was "no longer in Service," and,
therefore, he asked Washington to send him "a state of the Inlist-
ments that are made of those Troops, that some means may be
thought of for supplying such Deficiency as may happen by the refusal of some of the men to reinlist." Henry said that he had written
to Generals Woodford, Weedon, and Muhlenberg, asking them "to
proceed in finishing so much of that Work as General Stephen left

unfinished." Henry inquired of Washington if he had any recommendations.[26] All that Washington knew about this subject was
Stephen's plan in December 1776 concerning the forwarding of
more Virginia troops to the main army, which Washington had sent
to Congress, and a letter from Stephen on the subject in April 1777.
Washington's reply to Henry expressed surprise that the governor
had officially authorized Stephen to superintend recruiting in Virginia. "I do not recollect ever to have heard," said Washington,
"that Genl. Stephen was employed or that he had interested himself
to reinlist the Troops before the receipt of your favor. But however
this may have been, It is evident, his Success was not very great."[27]

Historians have disagreed to what extent there was a movement
after the battle of Germantown either to remove Washington as
commander in chief or to limit his command. That there was a
Conway cabal involving certain congressmen and military person-
nel, including those army members of the new Board of War, has
been almost totally discredited. Gen. Thomas Conway worked himself into a corner in trying to extricate himself from a charge that he
was attempting to form a conspiracy to oust Washington; the accusation was based mainly on a paragraph which may have been inserted into a letter that he had written. Conway nevertheless resigned from the army. There was discontent, to be sure, over the
ill successes at Brandywine and Germantown, but it never grew
into any organized attempt to overthrow Washington or, for that
matter, reached the point of a formal inquiry into Washington's
own conduct.

If a cabal was under way, it would have likely made use of Adam
Stephen by one or both of two means: an investigation into Stephen's
grievances against Washington or, conversely, citing Stephen and
others as examples of the incompetence of Washington's general
officers. The possibility of the latter was suggested in the correspondence of several congressmen who were known not to be en-
thralled with Washington's leadership. Thomas Burke of North
Carolina wrote Governor Caswell on November 4 that the battle of
Germantown had been a "miscarriage," which "sprung from the
usual source—want of abilities in our superior officers and want of
order and discipline in our army." Samuel Adams wrote Richard

Henry Lee on January 1, 1778: "We have indeed suffered no shameful Defeats, but a promising Campaign has however ended ingloriously. To what are we to attribute it? I believe to a miserable Set of General Officers." [28] Although the generals were appointed by Congress, their conduct could be related to Washington's own leadership and ability as commander in chief. Benjamin Rush, a former congressman and now surgeon general of the middle department, was almost alone in siding openly with Conway. "For God's sake do not suffer him [Conway] to resign," he declared. "Some people blame him for calling our generals fools, cowards, and drunkards in public company. But these things are proof of his integrity and should raise him in the opinion of every friend of America." [29]

As Gen. Adam Stephen prepared to go home, it seemed everything was in chaos among the troops and the officer corps. Perhaps the main error of Stephen and the other generals had been their lack of diligence and persistence in training and drilling the soldiers. Stephen had concerned himself primarily with the generality of command and issuing the routine marching and bivouac orders. From the French and Indian War he understood drill tactics, but probably he did not appreciate the need of drumming in such skills while the army was highly mobile and in anticipation of battle. Many of the junior officers had little if any previous professional military experience. As did other generals, Stephen delegated regular leadership duties to the brigade and regimental commanders. There was seldom joint training for more than one regiment. The fluctuation of troop strength and the frequent regrouping of units had also hindered training and the promotion of an esprit de corps. Tougher and more professional discipline, however, would emerge from the Valley Forge encampment, thanks largely to the army's new drillmaster, Baron von Steuben. Among Steuben's reforms were blending Prussian, British, and American methods of training and creating a more personal liaison between company commanders and their troops. If concession is made to a measure of doubt as to Adam Stephen's own culpability leading to his dismission, it may be argued, albeit tenuously, that had there been greater proficiency of the troops in the campaigns of 1777, Stephen possibly might have remained a major general.

Stephen, of course, was bitter, thinking that he had been singled out for blame for the compounded errors of the recent campaigns. But it must have been of some relief to be going home in "retirement," leaving behind all the cares of military life. One of his regrets was that he would not reap any material rewards for his service in the Revolutionary army, while other officers at the end of the war would be given large land grants. But there now would be plenty to keep him busy, looking after his farm and industries and developing the new town of Martinsburg. Even while he endured the humiliation of the court-martial his thoughts turned to his plantation in Berkeley County. On November 7 he wrote his overseer, Jonathan Seaman, a good-humored note, which was conspicuous in its omission of mention of his trial and any reference to military affairs. This must have struck Seaman as curious, for Stephen usually had something to say on army campaigning. "Dear Jonathan," Stephen said, "if Opportunity offers, Sell my Cattle before they Eat up my Hay—Beef Sells here at four pounds Ten Shillings p hundred weight. . . . I want my Calves & philleys well taken Care of; & for that Reason would Save my hay—If you do Sell them take good Care of the Cash—My Compliments to the Girls—The Homely Toads; I have not heard from them this long time." [30]

By mid-December Stephen had returned to his Valley farm. It must have been disconcerting to greet all the folks, who had taken pride in their hero, one of the highest-ranking generals in the country, now dishonored by being expelled from the army. Most of Stephen's neighbors understood, though. Perhaps drink did do him in, or he had just a stroke of bad luck. There seems to have been little or no enmity toward him because of his ouster. What hostility there was must have decreased when the other generals who had been a source of pride for the people in the lower Valley met much the same censure as did Stephen. Charles Lee was dismissed from military service. Horatio Gates saw his army totally annihilated at Camden, South Carolina, in August 1780. Though disgraced, he was cleared by a court of inquiry and regained military command. Had Gates not been an able adjutant general at the start of the war, president of the congressional Board of War, and, of course, the victor at Saratoga, he might also have faced punishment. The three

major generals from the lower Valley could take consolation in that
each had incurred disrepute because of a battle: Stephen at Germantown; Gates at Camden; and Lee at Monmouth. An anecdote,
most likely apocryphal, about the three generals getting together
back home appeared in a Maryland publication in 1798. Supposedly
Lee said: "You, Stephen, was broke for getting drunk when every
man should be in his senses; I for not fighting when I was sure to
be beat; and you Gates, for being beat, when you had no business
to engage." [31]

Stephen intended to publish his side of the story of his dismissal.
But he never did. As time wore on, he realized that any attack upon
Washington and other generals would be counterproductive. After
all, Washington was, as General Weedon would comment, the nation's "Christ." Undoubtedly a major factor in Stephen's not pressing his case was the lesson of Thomas Conway, who was crushed
even by his alleged remote impugning of the character and ability
of Washington. Stephen soon discovered, too, that Congress showed
no interest in the letter that he had sent them. Perhaps he was for-
tunate that he had not been excoriated for the criticisms of Washington that he had made to Congress. Yet immediately after his return home, he did allow his resentment to show and for a while
entertained the idea of going public. On December 15 Stephen sent
a letter to Robert Carter Nicholas, formerly the colony's treasurer
and still a powerful leader in the state. Although Stephen's purpose
in writing was to thank Nicholas for his role in a financial transac-
tion, he took the opportunity to complain about his dismissal. "If
my Conduct has been such as to Sink me in my own Esteem,"
Stephen said, "or in that of any person of Integrity & honour I
would not have wrote you—I am Conscious that Since I enterd the
Service I have Served the United States, as faithfully and Effectually
as any officer in it of whatever rank or denomination." Stephen said
that he intended to publish "my Case as soon as I get it ready." Then
the public could judge "whether the Army or my Self, sustaind the
greatest dishonour by my dismission." Stephen observed that "there
has been a great Many faux pas Committed this Campaign—But I
need to Convince the public that they are not with justice to be

Charged on me, & that had my Sentiments been adopted, Matters in all probability would have been in a way more favourable for America."[32] But Nicholas, now a member of the House of Delegates, did not offer Stephen any encouragement. Recognizing that his case had been settled in the minds of members of Congress and even among the state leaders, Stephen let the matter rest. If he had been a sacrificial lamb on the altar of liberty, so be it.

Stephen, however, maintained some military contacts. In August 1779 he wrote Gen. Anthony Wayne, congratulating him for the "late Noble Achievement in Reducing the Strong Post on Stony Point without the use of Powder—You have added dignity to the American Arms & acquired immortal Renown."[33] From February to June 1780 Stephen regularly wrote General Gates, who had returned to his Valley farm after a year commanding the eastern department of the army at Boston. Stephen refrained from discussing the army but had news relating to England and Europe, the price of crops, congressional proceedings, and aspects of the Virginia war effort.[34]

Stephen still had western land claims (7,000 acres of which were now in Kentucky), by virtue of his French and Indian War service. Writing to Col. William Fleming, one of the Virginia land commissioners, at Boonesborough, Kentucky, in April 1780, Stephen reviewed the latest news and took the opportunity to criticize Washington's current military leadership. "We are in great anxiety," he told Fleming, "to hear of the Result of the Attempt Genl Clinton has made by this time on Charleston S. C. The people are greatly disturbed that more Vigorous Measures were not pursu'd to save that important City. . . . It is asked why the Commander in Chief did not March with the main force of America to Oppose the Br. C. in chief with the British Army."[35] Stephen was suggesting that Washington should have brought his army southward, as he would later do at Yorktown. Charleston was under siege, defended by a force of mostly militia under General Lincoln. Of course, the conditions that Washington's army would have faced at the southern port would have been much more disadvantageous than those later confronted on the York-James peninsula.

Despite his resentment toward Washington, it was to Adam Stephen's credit that he could put his bitterness and frustrations behind him. As far as he was concerned—and so it seemed also among the local citizenry—his honor was intact. He found much to keep him occupied, in private and public capacities. It was not so much that Adam Stephen was creating a new life, but returning to one that he had already known, and making the most of it.

THIRTEEN

Civilian and Citizen

U pon settling down again in the Valley, Adam Stephen could give close attention to his farm and industries and help guide the development of his new town. With no local acrimony toward him for his forced retirement from the army, he entered into public affairs, reminiscent of his earlier decade of civilian life. Perhaps unexpectedly, he was again called upon occasionally to ply his long unused medical and surgical skills.

Only several months after he had returned home, Stephen got a call from the Winchester area to attend a patient who had a severe case of gangrene in his left leg. The sufferer was John Hunt, one of twenty Quakers who had been exiled from Philadelphia and interned in Winchester because of pacificist/tory views. The refugees soon had been allowed to reside with the Hopewell community of Quakers, about six miles from Winchester. Hunt was being cared for at the large stuccoed house of the widow Elizabeth Jolliffe, on the Great Valley Road (Martinsburg Pike), by a Winchester physician, Dr. Robert Mackey. With amputation the only way to save Hunt's life, Mackey decided that he needed the assistance of another physician-surgeon. Someone suggested that Dr. Stephen had just returned to the Valley and that he had a reputation as a competent surgeon and had been trained at Edinburgh. Saturday night, March 14, 1778, a messenger was dispatched to fetch Stephen, some twenty miles distant. Early Sunday morning, William Smith, one of the Quaker exiles, awakened Stephen, who agreed to help. Reaching the Jolliffe house, Stephen found that the patient's condition had worsened and the blood vessels in Hunt's leg were so relapsed that it would be impossible to stop the bleeding if an amputation was undertaken. In a few days the gangrene had temporarily halted its spread and the patient seemed improved physically. Stephen and Mackey agreed to operate. On Sunday morning, March 22, Hunt was placed on a table between two windows, to insure maximum light. With all the necessary surgical equipment assembled—a saw, nippers, shears, thread, bandages, a tenaculum, knives, and other tools—Stephen performed the operation, assisted by Mackey. Hunt showed uncommon fortitude during the ordeal. Either Stephen or Mackey remarked to him afterwards, "Sir, you have behaved like a hero"; to which Hunt replied, "I have endeavoured to bear it like a Christian." Stephen and Mackey stayed on several days more to attend Hunt. Unfortunately the patient's strength had been so sapped that he died March 31.[1]

Stephen hitherto had definitely let it be known that he did not like Quakers. But, having been misunderstood himself by his own countrymen in war and now seeing what decent people the Friends were, he had a sympathetic attitude toward them. Stephen kept in touch with one of the Quaker exiles after they returned to Philadelphia. In August 1779 he wrote James Pemberton, thanking him for his "good, Sensible, & friendly Letter." Stephen probably developed a trade connection with Pemberton. Commenting apparently on an economic regulatory issue of the time, Stephen said that "It is a delicate affair to meddle with Trade & Money Matters—Men of Experience think they Regulate themselves best." Stephen offered consolation upon the death of James's brother, Israel Pemberton, who had also been one of the exiles: "His Integrity, Experience, & Benevolence were of Extensive advantage to his fellow Citizens."[2]

One advantage of being home permanently was that Stephen could assist in promoting the development of the town of Martinsburg. Since 1772, when Berkeley County was established, people slowly but surely were moving into the village along Tuscarora Creek. Located on Stephen's property, 120 lots had been laid off on

130 acres. The land parcels had been selling for about £20 and by the mid-1780s for £50 in Virginia currency. The county courthouse and jail were located at the corner of King and Queen streets.[3]

While Stephen had been away in the army, residents on May 4, 1777, petitioned the legislature for town incorporation.[4] The Virginia General Assembly complied in October 1778. The affairs of the town, including the distribution of house lots, were now administered by trustees, though Stephen would still receive the moneys from purchases. Purchasers of lots had to agree to build a dwelling at least 20 feet long and 16 feet wide, containing a brick or stone chimney, within two years of the date of sale.[5]

Stephen had named the town Martinsburg (also at times previously known as Martinstown and Martinsville) after his friend Col. Thomas Bryan Martin, nephew of Thomas, Lord Fairfax. At the time of incorporation Martinsburg already had several taverns and stores, a blacksmith shop, and a shoemaker, in addition to Stephen's grist and saw mills, in or bordering the town.[6] Upon motion of Stephen, the Berkeley County court, on August 20, 1779, ordered that the plat of Martinsburg be recorded.[7] At the southern part of the town, Stephen laid out Norborne (Parish) Cemetery, officially recognized by the legislature in 1778.[8]

Stephen applied some finishing touches to his eight-room stone house at the east end of the town, off John Street; begun as early as 1774, it bears a datestone of 1789. Probably during most of the 1780s Stephen continued to live on the Bower farm. The Martinsburg house (today maintained by the General Adam Stephen Memorial Association and since 1970 listed in the National Register of Historical Places) has four rooms and a center hall on each floor, plus a basement and large attic, where beams show Roman numerals. There are two fireplaces, one in the kitchen and the other in another main-floor room. The flooring is of pine, and most of the house was put together with wooden pegs. The walls are twenty-one inches thick, and the plastering in the interior was probably made of burnt lime, pulverized red clay, and animal hair.[9]

As Berkeley County's largest landholder, Adam Stephen had the full respect of the local populace. This was evidenced by his election to the House of Delegates in May 1780. He served until Janu-

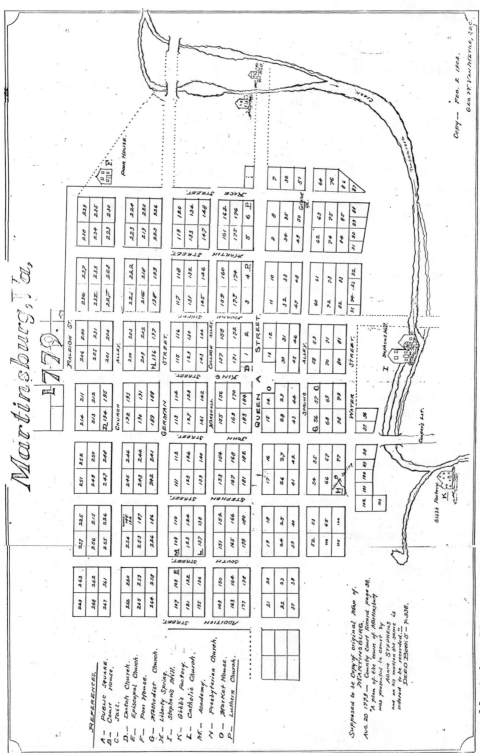

Martinsburg, Va., 1779. (Courtesy of John W. Small, Jr, County Clerk, Berkeley County Court, Martinsburg, W.Va.)

ary 1785, being succeeded by Philip Pendleton. For this period, the other Berkeley delegate was Stephen's future son-in-law Moses Hunter, except in 1782 when Dolphin Drew was the county's other representative. Stephen, however, did not take his legislative responsibilities very seriously and attended a very small part of the sessions of the General Assembly. He may have faced some ostracism among some delegates because of his expulsion from the army, even perhaps among those whom he had regarded as friends, such as Richard Henry Lee. Richmond, the new capital, was 170 miles distant. Stephen and Hunter, like other members, often were dilatory in attendance at the legislature. As was customary for delinquent delegates, the House of Delegates on several occasions had to order Stephen taken into custody by the sergeant of arms to insure his presence. Stephen then was admitted to his seat upon paying the costs for the summons. Several times he arrived only just before adjournment. Stephen was prompt once—in May 1783. During the spring 1783 legislative session the few recorded roll calls indicate he supported bills that passed for the better supervision of sheriffs' collections of taxes and the transfer of £1,800 from the Chesapeake defense fund and £1,200 from moneys reserved for recruiting to use as increased compensation for the delegates. The latter act passed only after heated debates, as the revenue came from import duties collected mainly in the eastern part of the state. Stephen, in the minority, voted against postponement of a bill for the relief of debtors and joined the majority to quash a proposal to move the capital back to Williamsburg. Apparently Stephen did not attend the legislature at all in 1784. During his tenure, he received no assignments to any of the House's half dozen standing committees, which was not unusual for a junior delegate, but perhaps, after several years of service, he resented not being placed on a committee.[10] On the local level, in 1786 Stephen was elected an overseer for the poor for Berkeley County.[11] Previously vestrymen, of which Stephen had been one, had charge of indigents, but the responsibility was placed entirely on a public basis with the postwar disestablishment of the Anglican church.

Of the two other war-weary generals who had returned to the Valley, Stephen struck up a camaraderie with one and only had contacts at arm's length with the other. Maj. Gen. Horatio Gates was back at his plantation, Traveller's Rest, late 1779 until summer 1780, when he assumed command of the southern army. After the defeat at Camden in August 1780, Gates returned to the Valley for a while, joined Washington's army outside New York City, and then came home to stay in mid-1783. Gates lived in Berkeley County until 1790, when he freed his slaves, sold his property, and moved to New York City.

In June 1782, in a letter conveying reports on Greene's army and an Anglo-French naval battle, Stephen expressed a local concern to Gates: "Some malignant devil put it in the Peoples head that there was a plan before the House for dividing Berkeley County. I never heard a Whisper of it untill Dark [William Darke] came down with a petition against it . . . perhaps he was not so bright as to call upon you." [12] Stephen, of course, was opposed to a division of Berkeley County, which had his Martinsburg as its seat (not until 1801 was a new county, Jefferson, created from part of Berkeley, with the Bower plantation in the new jurisdiction).

Gates, who had gone to Philadelphia and then to New York City on some business, in July 1784 chided Stephen for not writing and asked him to pass on instructions for the overseer at Traveller's Rest. [13] Stephen and Gates had many reminiscences to share, for they had fought together in the French and Indian War. Stephen visited Traveller's Rest on July 9, 1782, the anniversary of Braddock's defeat, in which both men had participated. Scotsman George Grieve, translator of the 1787 edition of the marquis de Chastellux's *Travels in North America*, and a companion happened by in time for dinner at this occasion and from the two generals learned "many curious particulars" about the 1755 battle on the Monongahela; "nor was the wonderful revolution in the affairs and minds of men, the subject of less anxious discussion with them." [14]

Maj. Gen. Charles Lee finally settled in at Prato Rio, ten miles from Martinsburg. On his 2,800-acre estate Lee tried his hand at farming, horse breeding, and the usual plantation industries, but not very successfully. Except for an initial social call, Stephen probably met with Lee only when the two of them visited Gates. Lee was more eccentric than ever, preferring the companionship of his dogs to that of humans. His house, a low barnlike dwelling, also dubbed "the Hut," had no walls in the interior, only chalk markings to designate rooms. Lee eventually became persona non grata with Gates and his wife, Elizabeth (who died in June 1783; Gates married Mary Vallance, a wealthy heiress, in July 1786). Lee always quarreled with the first Mrs. Gates one time calling her a "Medusa."

Late summer 1782 Charles Lee went to live in Philadelphia, where he died in October. In his will he declared: "I desire most seriously that I may not be buried in any church or churchyard, or within a mile of any Presbyterian or Anabaptist meeting-house; for since I have resided in this country, I have kept so much bad company when living that I do not choose to continue it when dead." [15] Had Lee lived a little longer, he might have included in his list of undesirables the Methodists, who were making great inroads into the religious communities of Martinsburg and Berkeley County. There were also sizable numbers of Lutherans and German Reformed adherents in the area.[16] When Lee's estate in the Valley was advertised for sale in a New York newspaper after his death, one attraction mentioned was that the plantation was near the homes of George Washington (more correctly the residences of Samuel and Charles Washington), Adam Stephen, and Horatio Gates.[17]

Adam Stephen, presumably all his life a bachelor, enjoyed some semblances of family life. His younger brother, Robert (born 1746), lived in Martinsburg (in the section later called Boydsville). Phoebe Seaman, sister of Jonathan Seaman, who had looked after Stephen's plantation in addition to his own off Warm Springs Road near Opequon Creek,[18] kept house for Adam at the Bower farm. For want of any evidence to the contrary, it may be assumed she was the mother of Stephen's daughter, Ann, who in early summer 1779 married a dashing young artillery officer. Stephen's daughter first met Capt. Alexander Spotswood Dandridge when she and her father attended a military celebration in Winchester. Dandridge was immediately struck with the beauty and charm of Ann Stephen, nearly eighteen years old and attired in a red riding habit. It was love at first sight. Dandridge, twenty-five years old at the time, was the son of Nathaniel West and Dorothea Spotswood Dandridge and a grandson of Virginia's governor Alexander Spotswood. The young Dandridge was a second cousin of Martha Washington and had served on General Washington's staff. His father had given him a small plantation in Hanover County.[19]

Patrick Henry, who had married Dandridge's sister Dorothea did what he could to further the prospect of matrimony between Ann Stephen and Dandridge. Henry, who was about to step down as governor, on June 10, 1779, wrote Adam Stephen for the first time since Stephen had left the army, testifying to the fine qualities of his brother-in-law. Henry added that Dandridge could expect an ample inheritance from his father and that he also held 3,000 acres of military lands in Kentucky. Dandridge had lived with Patrick Henry for several years before the commencement of the war. Unquestionably, the marriage, Henry told Stephen, would be "highly pleasing to his Father & all his Friends, & if it takes place I hope will prove lastingly happy to all concerned. My connection with the young man & his Family & my acquaintance with you will I trust be my apology for so much Freedom in this Affair."[20]

Adam Stephen provided the newlyweds, as his daughter's dowry, a tract of 600 acres off Warm Springs Road and adjacent to the Bower plantation, to be known as Hazelfield. He also built a house for them, which still stands.[21] After a lingering illness, Alexander Spotswood Dandridge died about April 1, 1785.[22] Besides the Hazelfield plantation, Ann inherited 618 acres in Hanover County. One son survived, Adam Stephen Dandridge, born December 5, 1782 (died 1821, age thirty-nine); he married Sarah Pendleton, daughter of Philip and Agnes Patterson Pendleton on January 1, 1805, and they had seven children.[23]

Ann married Moses Hunter on April 26, 1787. Hunter was then the clerk of Berkeley County. The *Baltimore Journal* of May 1, 1787, in noting the event, mentioned that Ann was the "daughter of Major General Stephen, a lady of Great Merit With a handsome fortune."[24] The couple lived at Hazelfield and had three children. Moses Hunter died in 1798, and Ann, who did not remarry again, died at Hazelfield on September 29, 1834, age seventy-three.[25]

Aside from family affairs, Adam Stephen could take pride in his growing wealth, most of which was in real estate. Stephen, however, sold some of his lands in Berkeley County. From 1782 to 1788 the tax assessment showed his holdings to be 2,570 acres, of which

1,690 formed the Bower plantation. Samuel Washington now surpassed him as the largest landowner in the county, with 3,368 acres. Stephen owned lots in Martinsburg and had 135 acres in Hampshire County.[26] He still had two tracts of military bounty lands (French and Indian War) in Kentucky: 1,000 acres on Hickman Creek near Lexington and 1,100 acres along the Ohio River, six miles north of the mouth of the Kentucky River.[27] As he had always done, Stephen leased out some of his lands.[28] A tax inventory for 1783 indicates that Stephen had about thirty slaves; for ratable purposes he had fifteen slaves over sixteen years old and nine younger, presumably age twelve to fifteen. It became the practice in the 1780s not to make assessments on slaves below the age of twelve. Also in 1783, Stephen was listed with fifty cattle, nineteen horses, and eighteen stud horses.[29]

Because of his own involvement with French and Indian War bounty lands, Stephen was occasionally called upon for advice pertaining to claims of other veterans of that war. In 1785 Thomas Jefferson, then minister to France, asked Stephen to check out the status of the French and Indian War bounty lands that had belonged to William Polson, now deceased. Polson's brother and heir, John Polson, who had gone to England during the war, feared that they might have been confiscated. Stephen informed Jefferson that the lands were not taken by the state and also pointed out their location and likely prices that they would bring. John Polson wrote Stephen in 1790 thanking him for his "kindnesses."[30]

Stephen and other Valley farmers specialized more after the war, particularly in the growing of wheat. Stephen's flour mill on Tuscarora Creek continued in use, even after his death, when it was referred to as "the Generals old mill." Indeed, the Valley became one of the most important wheat- and flour-producing regions of the South. Although the state established thirty flour inspection stations in 1787, none were in the Valley, and Stephen, therefore, sent his flour to Alexandria, the nearest mercantile town with such a facility. Because he transported his own commodities, Stephen dealt directly with factors (external wholesale merchants): among others, Hooe and Harrison, Daniel and Isaac McPherson, and Hartshorn and Donaldson in Alexandria. Besides flour, Stephen also sent wheat to Alexandria, which along with Richmond was witnessing the rise of substantial flour-milling industries. Prices for wheat and flour continued to rise until the end of the century, although sometimes prices in the export market radically fluctuated. In the mid-1780s Stephen received about 3s. to 4s. per bushel of wheat and 4s. to 16s. per hundredweight of the better grades of flour. In 1790 he was getting 80¢ per bushel of wheat; in 1786 a barrel of flour brought $4. In one year Stephen delivered 158 barrels of flour to one Alexandrian agent. Barrels at the time held 196 pounds of flour. When market conditions were unfavorable, the wholesaler would store the flour and grain for him, adding presumably to the usual 2 percent commission on the sale price. Storage in the summertime, however, was avoided as much as possible because of the tendency of the flour to turn moldy or sour.[31]

In eliminating the middle man, Stephen used his own wagons. Each vehicle was pulled by four horses and hauled about 450 bushels of wheat or 10 to 12 barrels of flour.[32] Usually Stephen received goods for his commodities instead of cash, such as medicines, oysters, shad, herring, sugar, coffee, tea, spices, farm and mill equipment, and salt. One time, however, Hooe and Harrison wrote him: "In future be pleased to give yr Waggoners orders for Cash instead of Goods & then they will be pleased to lay out their Money where they think best."[33]

Stephen went extensively into horse breeding and continued to raise cattle for shipment to market. Western drovers passed through the Valley in September and October, with some livestock going directly to market but the rest staying to be fattened for a year on clover, corn, wheat, and hay. Stephen sent cattle to Alexandria, but after 1783 he probably drove them the short distance to Winchester, which by then was becoming a major collection and distribution point for cattle going to Richmond, Baltimore, or Philadelphia. The growing of timothy hay in the rich soils of the Valley, supplemented by the lush bluegrass that abounded everywhere, greatly aided Stephen's endeavors at livestock and horse raising.[34] Although he phased out his arms manufactory when demand decreased after the war, Stephen remained in the distillery business. Undoubtedly he was experiencing a change of mind about the time of his death,

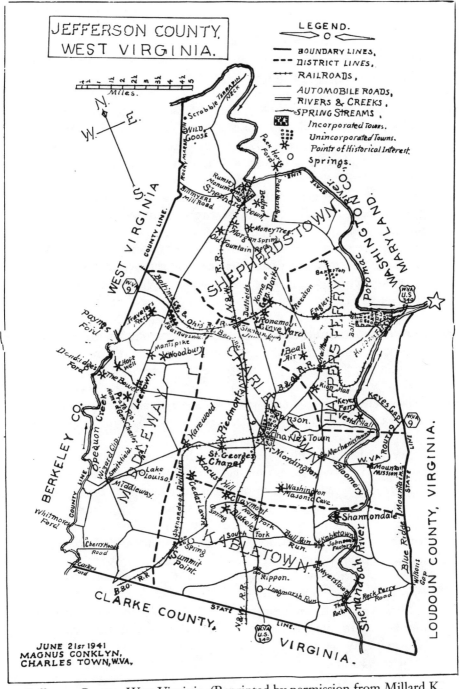

Jefferson County, West Virginia. (Reprinted by permission from Millard K. Bushong, *Historic Jefferson County* [Boyce, Va., 1972])

when the new federal government placed a tax on stills. Stephen had difficulty in marketing his whiskey because of competition from so many other farm distilleries and, as one of his agents wrote him, "owing to the people at large being scarce of money." [35]

Stephen, like his neighbors, looked forward to opportunities for the expansion of trade. The opening of a channel for navigation in the upper Potomac River would provide an easy outlet for goods from the Valley. At last, a decade after its inception, the Potomac Company was chartered by Maryland and Virginia in 1784–85, with Washington as president. Envisioned also was the creation of a great water route to the Northwest via the Potomac and its branches, the Monongahela, and the Ohio. As it was, much of the Ohio country trade, controlled by British fur trappers on American soil, moved up to the St. Lawrence River. Blasting and removal of boulders for the first section of the Potomac channel began in summer 1785 at Seneca Falls and Shenandoah Falls (Harpers Ferry). Another prospective improvement in navigation also caught Stephen's attention. James Rumsey, engineering superintendent for the Potomac Company, successfully demonstrated at Shepherdstown on December 3 and 11, 1786, a steam-powered boat, which proceeded up current at about four miles an hour. Stephen may have been among the spectators, who included prominent persons of Berkeley County such as Gates, Maj. Henry Bedinger, Gen. William Darke, and Philip Pendleton. [36]

Because of increasing gout, Stephen, however, did not get around as much as he used to. Yet he had a lively interest in the events of the time, especially western political development, Indian affairs, and the Constitutional Convention of summer 1787. In August of that year, Stephen wrote Isaac Shelby, the hero of King's Mountain, who had settled in Kentucky and was the leading political figure there. Stephen congratulated Shelby for his role in the third Kentucky convention, which sought statehood. "How do you hold it— take the first Opportunity to inform me," said Stephen, "that I may take my chance in such a manner." Perhaps he had in mind a future West Virginia. Stephen also thanked Shelby "for the Civilities Shown to the young men I sent after my horses—They apprehended the thief and brought home the horses." Stephen reported to Shelby on world news. "There is a hot Civil war in Holland," he said. The United States had made a treaty of peace with the dey of Algiers "which will open Several Channels of trade in the Mediterranean."[37]

Although favoring Kentucky statehood, Stephen was troubled that frontiersmen had created the state of Franklin, illegally carved out of western North Carolina (eastern Tennessee). The new jurisdiction impinged upon the rights of the Cherokee Indians. He informed James Madison, Virginia's rising political star who had recently returned from the Philadelphia Convention, that he was afraid that such action by the overmountain men might ignite an Indian war. "It appears that the Wild men of Franklin State have an intention to drive the Cherokees out of their Country," Stephen told Madison. The Cherokees "are a well behaved people" and had abided by the treaty that Stephen had made with them in 1761, "untill our People broke it, by wantonly killing Some of their Hunters." Should a Cherokee war ensue, "we shall have all the Southern Indians against us—and among other Evills they will infect the Navigation of the Mississippi, which would greatly distress our people settled on the Waters of the Ohio." If John Sevier, governor of Franklin, did not restrain white intruders, 100 rangers, "under a discreet Officer of insinuating Manners and Address," should be posted "at some Convenient place between the Inhabitants and Indians"; this would insure that "the people of Franklin" observed the Treaty of Hopewell (1785), "which had set a line of demarcation between Indian hunting grounds and the area open for white settlement." Stephen thought Congress should assume more responsibility for what he regarded as the public domain. "The Western Territory belonging to N Carolina is extensive and Valuable," Stephen said, "and well disposed of, may help the U States to discharge their debts. It merits attention as well as the Country N W of Ohio."[38]

Stephen had keen interest in the new proposed Constitution of the United States. Upon receipt of that document in Virginia, opposition to it mounted rapidly in several areas of the state,[39] but not in the Valley. Stephen had no trouble at all in making up his mind whether to support ratification. He emphatically told James Madison, in a letter of November 25, 1787, that "the General Convention exceeded my Expectation. I hope the plan will be adopted as it is. When the defecets appear they can be mended. When America is so happy as to have it established, Congress Will have as many Ambassadors, as Augustus Caesar had, when he first came to the imperial throne." If "we are happy to have men of Abilities and patriotism at the head of Affairs for one twenty years—Few States in Europe will command equall Respect." [40]

Stephen well understood that a strong national union would tend to put all sections, even within a state, on an equal ground. As did most western Virginians, he felt that the Piedmont and Valley had always been discriminated against by the tidewater aristocracy, which had controlled the state government. He also expected that a new government under the Constitution would provide for an ample and sound money supply. The Valley farmers needed good money; there was a large indebtedness to British mercantile firms, and paper currency of the time, especially Virginia's, could not be used to extinguish the obligations. Under the Constitution, internal improvements would certainly be promoted. Furthermore, Valley farmers anticipated expanded opportunities in interstate and world commerce; federal authority would establish central control of trade, offering protection against interstate tariff discrimination and foreign competition, and, through the treaty-making power, would open new trading channels. Late 1787 had seen the plunge in prices for American exports to the West Indies. Also, a strong government would force the removal of the British garrisons that had been retained in American western territory contrary to the treaty of 1783; the British presence added to the Indian threat and reduced land values. Closer to home, Stephen and other Virginians feared that if a new government was not soon forthcoming, anarchy would spread; already in summer 1787, upon the heels of the Shaysite uprising in the North, a riot had occurred in the western county of Greenbrier, and courthouses had been burned in King William and New Kent counties by mobs. [41]

Berkeley County citizens enthusiastically supported the Constitution, with Stephen in the fore in organizational activity for that purpose. On September 28, 1787, less than two weeks after the Constitution was submitted to the states, a large assembly of county residents met in Martinsburg. A vote of appreciation was given to those who had served in the Federal Convention. It was requested that two persons present at the county gathering visit clergymen and ask them to preach a sermon expressing "thanks in a special manner to Almighty God, for inspiring the members of the memorable Convention, with amity, wisdom, and unanimity to form a foederal government, with so great judgment, and sound policy, amidst so many and various interests." The group resolved "that the members of the present meeting do pledge themselves to one another, to contribute all in their power, to establish and support the plan of foederal government . . . as it appears sufficient and well adapted to secure *peace, liberty* and *safety* to the citizens of the United States." [42]

On October 25, 1787, the Virginia legislature summoned a "convention of the people" consisting of delegates from the counties and the corporations of Williamsburg and Norfolk, to assemble at Richmond on the first Monday in June "for the purpose of a full and free investigation, discussion and decision upon the plan of Federal Government for the United States." [43] Stephen immediately let it be known that he would gladly accept the honor of being elected one of Berkeley County's two delegates.

Stephen expressed to General Gates, in December 1787, his anxiety over the pending contest for ratification of the Constitution in Virginia. Gates at the time was on a trip northward. He told Gates that Robert Rutherford was "Antifederal" and was a candidate to be a delegate to the ratifying convention. Also "the Demagogues agt the Federal Govermt at Richmond Gain Ground." Stephen was worried that "there is not so much money in the County as will pay the taxes next year—Without the Federal Govermt is adopted we are undone." Stephen had other news for Gates. The legislature had denied a petition to divide Berkeley County, and Governor Edmund Randolph had pardoned a murderer, John Price Posey, "Prot! Temporar pro Mores Prot." Stephen, who did not have much regard for Gates's second wife, commented: "As soon as I get Clear of the Gout, I intend to go to the Hague and Congratulate the Princess of Orange on her Return there—If you will be pleasd to permit I will do my self the honour to Wait on Mrs Gates across the

Atlantic for the Same purpose as She is a friend of the House of Orange."[44]

Delighted with the Constitution but apprehensive that his own state might defeat it, Stephen mustered all his energy to help lead the fight for its ratification in Virginia. He had thought that he was out of politics for good. He again would come to the defense of his country, in order that a viable federal union might be achieved, the ultimate accomplishment of Independence.

FOURTEEN

"Where Is the Genius of America?"

On court day, March 18, 1788, freeholders of Berkeley County elected Adam Stephen and William Darke to represent them at the Virginia Convention, which would decide whether or not to ratify the Constitution. Horatio Gates had been expected to be named with Stephen but for some reason was not a candidate.[1] Darke, like Stephen, was a large farmer and had a long military career.[2]

Stephen was privileged to serve, as the biographer of John Marshall has stated, in "the greatest debate ever held over the Constitution and one of the ablest parliamentary contests of history."[3] Patrick Henry's grandson was to write of the convention: "As the eye wandered over the body, the spectator saw before him such a collection of men illustrious in the annals of their country, as was probably never under the same roof before."[4] The state's most prominent citizens were among the delegates, excepting George Washington, who nevertheless had a powerful behind-the-scene influence, Thomas Jefferson (in France), the dying Thomas Nelson, and Richard Henry Lee. Stephen was probably glad that the latter did not attend, as he was undoubtedly still bitter that Lee, whom he once regarded as a good friend, had not come to his defense when he was being ousted from the army. Lee, a staunch Antifederalist, had already published several powerful tracts denouncing the Constitution. Both supporters and opposers of the Constitution counted among them men of great ability, including, for the Federalists, James Madison, John Marshall, Edmund Pendleton, Edmund Randolph, and George Wythe and, for the Antifederalists, Patrick Henry, John Tyler, James Monroe, George Mason, and Benjamin Harrison.

Of the 170 delegates, 104 were war veterans, and as a group they were almost equally divided as to the support of the Constitution.[5] All fourteen members from the seven Valley counties (Berkeley, Botetourt, Augusta, Frederick, Rockbridge, Rockingham, and Shenandoah) were Federalists. To the west, most of the delegates from counties that are now in the state of West Virginia (Hardy, Hampshire, Randolph, Ohio, Monongalia, Greenbrier, and Harrison) favored the Constitution. The fourteen-man Kentucky delegation, however, opposed ratification, although three members changed their minds when time came to vote on the Constitution.[6]

Stephen and the other delegates sensed the urgency and extreme importance of the convention. Seven states were known to have ratified, and South Carolina's approval was imminently expected. Virginia's ratification would meet the quota of nine states required to put the Constitution into operation. The New York convention, where it was anticipated the Antifederalists would prevail, was scheduled to start on June 17, and that of New Hampshire the following day. James Madison was confident that the Constitution would be approved in Virginia. On April 22, 1788, he wrote Thomas Jefferson that he thought that a majority of the delegates were "friends to the Constitution." At least "the superiority of abilities . . . seem to lie on that side. The characters of most note which occur to me, are marshalled thus," and Madison listed such persons by name, including Adam Stephen.[7]

Patrick Henry, who vehemently objected to the Constitution and was the most pervasive figure at the convention, thought four-fifths of the members opposed the Constitution. Another Antifederalist, William Grayson, was more close to the truth, observing that "our affairs in the convention are suspended by a hair; I really cannot tell you on which side the scale will turn."[8]

The proceedings of the Virginia Ratification Convention began June 2, 1788, promptly at 10 A.M., at the Old Capitol, a three-storied wooden structure at the corner of Cary and Fourteenth streets. The new Roman-styled Capitol, undergoing finishing touches, was not yet ready for use by an assembly. The next day the convention moved to more ample quarters at Alexander Quesnay's Academy, a large frame building designed as a theater on Shockoe Hill near the new Capitol. Hundreds of spectators jammed the hallways and doors. It was hoped that the convention could finish its business by June 23, when a session of the General Assembly of Virginia was scheduled to begin. Whether Adam Stephen arrived in time for the start of the convention is not known, but his enthusiasm and the honor of his selection makes it likely that he was even present to hear the opening prayer. The chaplain, the Reverend Abner Waugh, would continue to give an invocation each morning, after which a bell rang signifying it was time to get down to business. With a majority of the delegates present on the first day, Edmund Pendleton was elected president of the convention. However, George Wythe, as chairman of the committee of the whole, would do most of the presiding. David Robertson, a nondelegate from Petersburg, with an assistant, had the responsibility of transcribing the debates. The two reporters, however, were not allowed to sit in front of the speaker's stand, and Robertson, assigned "an ineligible seat," had difficulty in hearing the profuse flow of oratory and on occasion had to reconstruct or summarize passages. He did the best he could, using shorthand, and he and his assistant left a remarkable record. Very few delegates participated in the debates, and no wonder, with Patrick Henry a one-man show himself. Henry's speeches form one-fourth of the record; one time he spoke for seven hours, and on one day alone he delivered eight speeches. James Madison, John Marshall, and George Nicholas were effective rebutters to Henry. Considering that the debates were preempted by the main leaders, it is noteworthy that Stephen gave two speeches.[9]

Neither Stephen nor other Valley delegates received appointments to the convention's three committees: privileges and elections, reporting on the form of ratification, and the preparation of amendments. Part of the first week was consumed in deliberating on the reports of the committee of privileges and elections concerning several contested elections of delegates.

On June 4 the convention began its evaluation of the document.

A committee of the whole was formed, which would be the procedure on subsequent days of debate. George Nicholas opened the
discussion with a long speech. He covered at random the basic features of the Constitution and concluded that it was "founded on the
strictest principles of true policy and liberty." Patrick Henry immediately took the floor, claiming that the Federal Convention in
Philadelphia had exceeded its authority by proceeding to write a
new constitution. Henry, during the ensuing debates, emphasized
that the adoption of the new frame of government would pose a
danger to the liberties of individuals and of the states; particularly
he referred to taxation and the roles of the executive and the judiciary. George Mason, who next to Henry proved to be the main
Antifederalist debater, on the first day outlined the theme of his opposition: the "concurrent powers" of the federal and state governments "cannot exist long together; the one will destroy the other,"
and the "general government being paramount to, and in every respect more powerful than the state governments" would usurp the
powers belonging to the states. Governor Edmund Randolph, who
had refused to sign the Constitution in Philadelphia, startled the
convention by announcing his unequivocal support of the Constitution. Randolph stated that the only reason he had hitherto not come
out for ratification was that amendments were needed.

As the debates progressed, what galled Stephen most about Henry's
oratory was his constant emphasis on how a new government under the Constitution would betray western interests. The votes of
the western delegates could spell the margin of victory or defeat.
Henry frequently harped on the theme that northerners and eastern-
ers would dominate the new government and would continue to
concede Spain's right to close the Mississippi for transport of western products. Stephen was also at odds with Henry on virtually
every other issue. On June 23 Henry, as usual dominating the debates, stressed the danger of a federal judiciary and the need for a
bill of rights. Stephen listened intently as Henry wound up his
speech. "By the bill of rights of England," the Hanover delegate
pronounced, "a subject has right to a trial by his peers. What is
meant by his peers? Those who reside near him, his neighbors, and
who are well acquainted with his character and situation in life. Is

this secured in the proposed plan before you? No, sir." Henry asked "what is to become of the *purchasers of the Indians?*—those unhappy nations who have given up their lands to private purchasers; who, by being made drunk, have given a thousand, nay, I might say, ten thousand acres, for the triffling sum of sixpence!" Furthermore, Henry declared, if amendments to the Constitution were not obtained, "the trial by jury is gone. British debtors will be ruined by being dragged to the federal court, and the liberty and happiness of our citizens gone, never again to be recovered."

When Henry had finished, Stephen rose and gained recognition. The record affords only several passages of his speech. "Mr. Chairman: the gentleman, sir," Stephen declared, "means to frighten us by his bugbears of hobgoblins, his sale of lands to pay taxes, Indian purchases, and other horrors," which "I think I know as much about as he does. I have travelled through the greater part of the Indian countries. I know them well, sir. I can mention a variety of resources by which the people may be enabled to pay their taxes." Stephen then gave a brief description of the western country, its Indians, and articles that could be secured through the Indian trade. Then, looking at Henry straight in the eye, Stephen unkindly scolded him. "I know, Mr. Chairman, of several rich mines of gold and silver in the western country," Stephen said, "and will the gentleman tell me that these precious metals will not pay taxes? If the gentleman does not like this government, let him go and live among the Indians. I know of several nations that live very happily; and I can furnish him with a vocabulary of their language." [10]

The next speaker, George Nicholas, brought the discussion back to more level ground, with Henry, Monroe, Grayson, and Mason extending the debate. Stephen's speech, though largely irrelevant and somewhat chimerical, was nevertheless refreshing. Henry, who later claimed that Stephen had insulted him, might have taken Stephen to task on the floor, but there was more important discussion at hand. Probably much of Stephen's speech was inaudible and lacked a progressive development which made it hard to follow, as indicated by the brevity of the reporters' transcription. Judge St. George Tucker, present as an observer, later remarked to William Wirt that Henry presented a "fine image" of Virginia "seated on an eminence and holding in her hand the balance in which the fate of America was weighing. Old General Stephen attempted to parodize and burlesque it, but I think he failed."[11]

At last both the Antifederalists and Federalists had their say. There seemed to be an understanding that the Constitution would have no trouble being ratified if amendments were made a condition of acceptance. Such action, however, would entail a second federal convention, which Federalists believed would end up in scuttling the Constitution altogether. On the last full day of debate, June 25, the convention examined primarily the need for a conditional ratification pending the adoption of amendments. Nicholas, Harrison, Madison, and Monroe spoke briefly, followed by James Innes, who represented Williamsburg and had been relatively silent. Innes argued that the Constitution should be accepted as it was. Antifederalist John Tyler then presented a contrary view. Tyler closed his long speech with: "I shall say no more, but I wish my name to be seen in the yeas and nays, that it may be known that my opposition arose from a full persuasion and conviction of its being dangerous to the liberties of my country."

Adam Stephen then rose and spoke at length, and this time went into a more pertinent discourse than in his previous speech. He talked in such a low voice, however, that many of his words were scarcely distinguishable. Stephen described fervently "the unhappy situation of the country, and the absolute necessity of preventing a dismemberment of the confederacy." He said that he could support amendments if they were necessary in order to secure ratification, but he had heard no convincing arguments at the convention to that effect. Amendments could be added later after the new government commenced, when there would be more reasoned judgment. Stephen pointed out:

In all safe and free governments, there ought to be a judicious mixture in the three different kinds of government. This government is a compound of those different kinds. But the democratic kind preponderates, as it ought to do. The members of one branch are immediately chosen by the people; and the people also elect, in a secondary degree, the members of the other two. At present we have no confederate government. It exists but in name. The honorable gentleman asked, Where is the genius of

America: What else but that genius has stimulated the people to reform that government which woeful experience has proved to be totally ineffi-cient? . . . I expected that filial duty and affection would have impelled him to inquire for the genius of Virginia—that genius which formerly re-sisted British tyranny, and, in the language of manly intrepidity and for-titude, said to that nation, Thus far, and no farther, shall you proceed!

What has become of that genius which spoke that magnanimous lan-guage—that genius which produced the federal Convention? Yonder she is, in mournful attire, her hair dishevelled, distressed with grief and sor-row, supplicating our assistance against gorgons, fiends, and hydras, which are ready to devour her and carry desolation throughout her country. She bewails the decay of trade and neglect of agriculture—her farmers dis-couraged—her ship-carpenters, blacksmiths, and all other tradesmen, un-employed. She casts her eyes on these, and deplores her inability to relieve them. She sees and laments that the profit of her commerce goes to for-eign states. She further bewails that all she can raise by taxation is inade-quate to her necessities. She sees religion die by her side, public faith pros-tituted, and private confidence lost between man and man. Are the hearts of her citizens so deaf to compassion that they will not go to her relief? If they are so infatuated, the dire consequences may be easily foreseen.

Stephen made several other remarks; particularly he entreated that Virginia live up to its preeminent role among the states. He con-cluded by declaring that the convention must now decide whether Virginia should be one of the United States or not.[12]

Stephen thus felt that the Constitution had to be ratified at any cost, even on the condition of attaching amendments. More signifi-cantly, as in the Fort Gower resolutions thirteen years before that he and his fellow officers drew up, he evoked images of the despair that had characterized the colonies under English rule on the eve of the Revolution. Without the Constitution, the Union would be lost, and the Americans would suffer from the same distresses as they did when abandoned by England.

In his speech making, Stephen was greatly tempted to allude to how military force had secured the liberties of Americans. It was an army that had expelled the French and later won for America its independence. Unquestionably, Stephen's own views on national union were largely shaped by his military experiences. But he could not speak as did Henry Lee, who had emerged from the war a hero. "It was my fortune to be a soldier of my country," Lee declared during one of the debates. Lee made the most of Patrick Henry's lack of actual military service. Though discussion on the army issue was scant at the convention, several of the debate participants were enjoined over the question whether the new Constitution provided for a national army that could be used to support despotism or overthrow the government. Lee, Randolph, Pendleton, and Wilson Cary Nicholas, for the Federalists, emphasized the limited authority of Congress to employ state militia. Patrick Henry and George Mason voiced apprehension of the potential in the powers of Congress and the executive for establishing a standing army and using military force to subdue the people.[13] Adam Stephen, in past discussion of public affairs, had always eagerly drawn upon his military experiences. But to do so at the convention, in view of his dismissal from the Continental army, would detract from his credibility and also would arouse fears of the tendency toward recklessness of a professional soldiery. Thus Stephen relied chiefly on his own familiarity with western problems.

Stephen's speech was followed by one given by Zachariah Johnston of Augusta County, apparently the only other Valley delegate to address the convention. Johnston argued forcibly for adoption of the Constitution without amendments, pointing out, like Stephen, that it was imperative to save the Union and that any deficiencies in the Constitution could be corrected later. Patrick Henry again spoke on the necessity of amendments before final ratification. Governor Randolph had the parting word, declaring that, with eight states having ratified, upon Virginia lay "the single question of *Union or no Union.*" Thus ended the debates, with Stephen having been honored by delivery of one of the final speeches. Perhaps allowing Stephen and Johnston so much time at the end of the debates was a stratagem by the Federalists to conciliate the Valley bloc.

Edmund Pendleton "now resumed the chair." Resolutions passed by the committee of the whole in favor of ratification without amendments were read. A last-ditch effort, coming on a motion in effect calling for the adoption of amendments and sending the Constitution to a second convention, failed, 80 ayes to 88 noes. Adam Stephen sided against the intended resolution. Then balloting took place whether to ratify the Constitution as it was, with the result in the affirmative, 89–79. Stephen and all the other Valley delegates voted in favor of ratification. A committee then was appointed to draw up a declaration of rights and amendments to be considered in the future by Congress and the states. On the twenty-sixth, an "engrossed form of the ratification, containing the proposed Constitution of government was read" and signed by the president on behalf of the convention. A resolution passed that official notification of the convention's acceptance of the Constitution be sent to Congress. On the final day, June 27, the convention endorsed a declaration of rights with twenty-one articles and a proposal for twenty amendments to be considered in the future.

Thus ended the historic convention. Stephen had done his part toward the preservation of the Union. As Hugh Grigsby, in his study of the convention, stated, Adam Stephen made a contribution at least to the tone of the debates with "a highly figurative strain of eloquence."[14] Ironically, the day after adjournment, it was learned that New Hampshire and not Virginia had been the ninth state to ratify the Constitution (June 21, 1788). The Virginia ratification, however, had immeasurable influence in shifting the New York convention in Poughkeepsie toward a narrow approval.

As an ardent nationalist, Stephen followed closely the policies of the new federal government and the debates in Congress. He made his views known whenever he could. Especially Stephen felt that the rising glory of America lay in the ordered development of the western part of the country. He was still observing the events unfolding in Kentucky, where so many Virginia war veterans had moved to claim bounty lands and where he himself had property. In writing to Robert Lawson, a Virginia militia general during the war who had recently settled at Lexington, Stephen expressed the desire that Kentucky would soon become a state "and be no more an Appendage of the Ancient Dominion."[15]

Stephen thought efforts should be undertaken to organize western territory. "Proper attention to that country is Absolutely Necessary," he wrote Congressman James Madison in September 1789. "In time it will give law to America. . . . The Middle States could do better without the Territory to the East of Hudson River, than without the friendship and intimate Coalition with the Inhabitants of the Trans-appalachan Country." In "the Cities, and on Tidewater, Commerce, Agriculture, Speculation, pleasure and dissipation Seem to engross the Minds of the People. The Strength and Vigour of the United States lie in the Mountains and to the Westward."

A few days before sending this letter, Stephen had a lengthy conversation with Henry Lee, who had brought his family to Berkeley Springs. Both men agreed on the great importance of locating the capital on the Potomac. Thus Stephen commented on the subject to Madison. "Our Coasts are as liable to be insulted and Ravaged as those of the Spaniards were less than a Century ago," said Stephen. "For that Reason the Seat of Government . . . is not Safe on Tide Water. . . . In the discussion of this affair we shall discover whether our Confederacy is well or ill combined." Stephen said that he hoped "that the matter may be postponed to a future day, perhaps till after the next Election, when men will be better acquainted with the General Interests of the rising empire." [16] Stephen and especially those Virginians like Henry Lee who had speculative holdings along the upper Potomac became vociferous advocates for locating the new seat of government near the Great Falls on that river.

In late summer and autumn 1789 the first session of Congress heated up with debates on the issue of fixing a permanent capital of the United States. Almost every town of any size between Trenton, on the Delaware, and Georgetown, on the Potomac, and even far away Pittsburgh were suggested as the proposed site. Shepherdstown in Berkeley County was a contender. By the time Congress adjourned on September 29, no legislation had been accomplished. [17] Sectional animosity had run at a high pitch. Three factions in Congress had formed in regard to the subject: New Englanders, the Middle States men, and southerners. James Madison had pushed persistently for the Potomac site. The strong opposition to that location was led by several Federalist congressmen, chiefly Fisher Ames and Theodore Sedgwick of Massachusetts, Jeremiah Wadsworth of Connecticut, and John Laurance of New York.

Stephen followed the debates in Congress carefully and was particularly incensed by the arguments of the northern "junto," as his own publication on the subject would reveal. The northerners were making a strong case for establishing the capital on the Susquehanna River. Like the Potomac scheme, they contended, this river could be the start of a navigational waterway leading to Pittsburgh by channel development of the Juniata branch of the Susquehanna, several of that stream's tributaries, and Kiskeminitas Creek, which flowed into the Allegheny River. Also, if the nation's capital was on the Susquehanna, it would be equidistant from Delaware and Chesapeake bays. During the debates in Congress, Richard Bland Lee of Virginia infuriated the northern bloc when he said that his state would not have ratified the Constitution if the hostility toward southern interests had been fully known. Wadsworth, in kind, argued that if the capital was situated along the Potomac, New Englanders would consider the Union destroyed. It was even alleged that a Potomac environment was unhealthy, as witnessed by the lack of trade and industry among southerners and the reliance upon slavery.[18]

Both the Maryland and Virginia legislatures agreed to donate land for a ten-mile-square federal district on the Potomac for the seat of government. The acts noted the advantages of such a site: centrality and convenience as to population distribution and geography, availability for communication with the western country, and the fertile soil and healthy climate of the area.[19] Stephen, in collecting his own ideas about the advantages of a Potomac site, concurred with the legislatures' appraisals. Alexander White, a congressman from the Valley, had urged Stephen to send him "a particular description of the River Potomack" from Georgetown to the upper branches of the river.[20] This request and the fact that others were consulting him led Stephen to become involved in the controversy over the location of the capital. Politicians were publishing various letters and tracts pertaining to the question, and Stephen tried his hand at it also. He wrote *The Expostulation of Potowmac*, dating it November 20, 1789, and had it printed as a broadside in early 1790. He wrote James Madison in March 1790 that "the expostulations of Potowmack will make their appearance, after the Treasury and Militia Business is finishd," and in a letter of

April 25 he enclosed a copy for Madison. Apparently Stephen expected to write a sequel or two, as the plural title in the letter to Madison indicates.

The Expostulation of Potowmac is a curious document but is illustrative of Stephen's intellectual and literary capabilities, underscoring those qualities he had often revealed in the past. It is a rambling and somewhat incoherent discourse on the merits of a Potomac River site for the nation's capital. It is derivative to the extent of parodying the remarks in Congress of northern Federalist leaders, namely, Ames, Sedgwick, Wadsworth, and Laurance, and also reflects some of the arguments used by James Madison in propounding the southern site. Stephen was aware of Ames's admiration of ancient Republican Rome, and hence he made some classical allusions of his own. Stephen, in the *Expostulation*, anticipated the opening of a water route from the Potomac to the Ohio; thus a Potomac site would be best suited, considering future patterns of population growth and economic shifts. He especially denounced the placing of the capital on the Susquehanna. As he had often done in the past, striving for literary flair, Stephen allowed for a flight of fancy toward the end of the piece in which he depicted the Potomac anthropomorphically. Potomac tells how great a stream "he" is, and, to answer northern objections, how healthy "he" and the environs are, with people in "his" vicinity living vigorous lives and to extreme old age. *The Expostulation of the Potowmac* does not merit literary plaudits, but it does capsulize the issues and arguments, with some trenchant wit. Stephen sent copies of his broadside to New England and New York newspapers. As he wrote Madison when he enclosed the piece, Stephen hoped "the people of N England will See their Interest so plainly that they will give instructions to their Delegates in favour of Potowmac." But he had "a Suspicion that the Restless Massachusettians, are entering into new plans of Government. They have taken upon them to dictate more Amendment. Our Constitution at this Rate is to change Annually."[21]

Despite tending to hold Yankee politicians suspect, Stephen had no quarrels with the Federalist (Hamiltonian) program. In his letter of March 3, 1790, to Madison, Stephen commented on Alexander Hamilton's first report on the public credit. The secretary of the treasury showed a "great extent of Comprehension," said Stephen. "He with great facility develops and simplifies the most Complicated Subjects." The assumption of states' debts "is a masterly Stroke of Policy, and will establish The Federal Government in the Hearts of the People. The Resources of the Nation stand more Clear, to be adapted to General purposes, as the Excegencies of Govermt may require." Stephen said that "reflecting on the feeble Attempts of the different States to establish a Revenue, and observing them repealing or Altering the Laws every Session, and giving so great advantage to Sheriff or Collector to prey upon the Poor" moved him to "apply to Hamilton what Mr Pope did to the Immortal Newton—

> Resources and Revenue Laws lay hid in Night
> 'Twas said Let Hamilton be! and all was right."

Stephen noted that Hamilton's report "has already advanced the Credit of the Nation, and It is the general Wish of the people within my Circle, that it may be adopted." [22] In his April 25 letter to Madison, Stephen again urged assumption, which "would greatly contribute to the establishment of the Fœderal Government." Stephen feared that the foundation of the national government was still too shaky; at least assumption would serve to strengthen the bonds of union. If a breakup of the new federal system should occur, southern states would be at a great disadvantage economically because "the N Englanders have such a Coasting Trade that Their imposts and Tonnage into the Southern States would amount to a Large Sum." Curiously, as if presaging the inevitable, Stephen added: "We had a Report here that the Se[c]retary of the Treasury was killed in a duel, and were all in Mourning." [23]

In his support for federal assumption of states' debts, Stephen was at odds with many Virginians—including Madison. Unlike the New England states, Virginia had been able to discharge much of its war indebtedness through western land grants. Assumption was voted down in April. The famous compromise of pairing assumption with the location of the capital on the Potomac came later. When the act concerning the capital was passed by Congress in July 1790, Stephen, of course, doubly applauded.

Amidst all his interest in the affairs of the new nation, Stephen's health was rapidly declining, and he became crotchety in personal relationships. He had a falling out with his neighbors, Horatio Gates and his wife, just before they moved to New York. Stephen acquired an aversion to the second Mrs. Gates, reminiscent of Charles Lee's dislike of Gates's first spouse. "Mrs. Gates certainly insulted two of her best friends," Stephen wrote Gates in May 1790. "But Experience Confirms us, that when we fail in one principle affair, the Sine Qua None of the Sin, we must knock[?] under in other matters." Stephen told Gates that he "did right to creep into your hole, and Say Nothing—this will make no difference between you and me— Madam hollow'd so loud, that I was at a Loss, being deaf, whether it was really her or Yourself, for I did not hear a Word—I am with former Respect." [24]

In his last years, Stephen continued his farming and milling. He was still receiving payment for lots sold in Martinsburg. In 1790 he owned 1,970 acres in the county. [25] Stephen still sent flour to Alexandria. The firm of Hartshorn and Donaldson wrote him in April 1791 that some of the twenty barrels received were short of weight, and four had to be condemned, "which in future must be attended to, else a heavy fine will accrue." [26] There were a few litigation problems, some old and some new, and occasionally an overdue bill. [27]

As physical infirmity drew on, Adam Stephen began to reflect about religion. In his papers is found transcribed a long sermon, which must have affected him, based on 1 Peter 4:18: "And if the righteous scarcely be saved, where shall the ungodly and the sinner appear?" The preacher meted out a heavy dose of hellfire-and-brimstone and, in one response to the scriptural query, said, "Let me add that after death every mans worth under go an impartial & just trial . . . tried by fire." The discourse was not very comforting, but at least there was assurance that in the last judgment there would be justice, which Stephen well knew was not always forthcoming among mortals. [28]

Adam Stephen died July 16, 1791, at his Martinsburg home. Several Virginia newspapers carried similar obituaries. Reference was made to Stephen's presence at Braddock's defeat. He had become "a man of respectability and opulence." At the beginning of the Revolution, "he quitted the sweets of domestic retirement, for the more busy and tumultous scenes of war, in behalf of this Land of Freedom, and he had the satisfaction to see the Standard of Liberty firmly erected before he put his sword up into the scabboard." Stephen's "character as a soldier, a politician, a citizen, and a friend, are too well known to need a comment; suffice it to say, that as he lived respected, so is his death sincerely regretted by all who had the pleasure of his acquaintance."[29] A New York magazine, in its obituary column, stated: *"In Virginia*—At Martinsburgh, Adam Stephen, Esq.; a gentleman highly distinguished for his medical talents, industry, learning, and mental endowments."[30] One acerbic remark came from John Mark, who was residing at Traveller's Rest. Writing Horatio Gates in New York, he said: "I Suppose the Publick papers . . . has Informed you of the Death of Genl. Stephen. Fame Says no Mourners but Phebe and the Negroes."[31]

It has been assumed that Adam Stephen was buried at the southern edge of Martinsburg, off South Queen Street (next to the Martinsburg High School grounds). This site was on Robert Stephen's property, which later became part of the estate of West Virginia senator Charles J. Faulkner. Robert Stephen, Adam's brother, and his wife later were interred at the same burial place. Sometime in the early nineteenth century, a monument was erected—a rectangular pyramid, twenty feet at the base, from which the height to the vertex is nine feet. Siliceous mountain stones were used in the construction, the largest being twenty feet in length. In time, part of the monument was destroyed, leaving the height at only four feet, but the full structure was restored to its original state, with a pyramid of Civil War cannonballs placed at the top, in 1920 by the William Henshaw Chapter of the Daughters of the American Revolution.[32]

Adam Stephen's will, dated June 5, 1791, with a codicil attached afterwards, was proved in Winchester District Court on September 6, 1791.[33] James Wilson, Robert McKnight, James Lawson, and Robert Cockburn witnessed the will. Stephen made his eight-year-old grandson, Adam Stephen Dandridge, his principal beneficiary. He gave him all his lands, with the exception of 500 acres which had been purchased from John Stroud, lands in Martinsburg, "which includes my old and new mills," 130 acres below the mills,

200 acres "adjoining Moses Hunter where negro Jack a freeman lives," 113 acres of which "I am at this time contracting to sell to Adam Aldridge," the Kentucky lands, and a small tract on the Bower plantation. Adam Stephen Dandridge also received "all my stock of horses cattle sheep and hogs two cows only excepted," plantation utensils and tools, and all slaves except three women and their offspring. Until his grandson reached age twenty-one, his guardians were to apply profits from the inheritance to his maintenance and "the best education that can possibly be procured," with the surplus to be deposited in "the Frederick or State Banks." If Adam Stephen Dandridge should die before age twenty-one, Adam Stephen's brother Robert would succeed to this inheritance.

Adam Stephen, of course, did not forget Phoebe Seaman, presumably his common-law wife. Phoebe received an annuity of $100 for the rest of her life, two milk cows, a slave woman and her child, and "a comfortable House," which the executors were to build on the Bower plantation; the residence was to have two brick chimneys and two rooms abovestairs and two rooms below, "with the land sufficient for a yard and garden."

Robert Stephen inherited 1,100 acres in Kentucky and £500 Pennsylvania currency, payable in bonds. The executors were to dispose of the 500 acres purchased from John Stroud, "my new Mill," and the 130 acres "before excepted," and the money from the sales was to be vested in Baltimore or Philadelphia banks for the payment of debts, after which Robert Stephen would receive the principal. Robert Stephen's son Alexander received some 1,000 acres on the Ohio River in Kentucky, 130 acres in Hampshire County, and £100 in Pennsylvania currency, payable in bonds. Robert's second son, Adam Stephen, was given £2,000 Pennsylvania currency, also payable in bonds. Moses Hunter, Stephen's son-in-law, was bestowed £500 Pennsylvania currency, payable in bonds, and the 200 acres where "negro Jack" lived. Stephen's granddaughter, Ann Evelina Hunter, was given two women slaves (and the offspring of one) and $1,000, to be paid on the day she married. Daughter Ann Stephen Hunter received five guineas, and if the Hunters had a son, £90 Virginia currency was to be vested in Baltimore or Philadelphia banks until the amount reached £450, which would be paid to the son when he reached his twenty-first birthday. Profits from the old mill and rents in Martinsburg were to be invested for funds to be set aside for future children of Stephen's daughter and his brother Robert. The executors of Stephen's estate were Robert Stephen, Ephraim Gaither, David Hunter, and Moses Hunter.

Thus, at threescore and ten, the old physician-soldier passed on, a man of wealth and honorable reputation. Yet there was a negative side. During his military career Stephen was given to exaggeration, self-partiality, conflict of interest, and recklessness. His flamboyance often alienated others, and as he said of himself, he tended to be outspoken. He was fond of strong drink—not an uncommon vice among officers and soldiers alike during military campaigning and long tedious garrison duty. Yet, alcoholism was probably a major factor in the deterioration of Stephen's relationship with his brigade commanders and certain other officers and contributed to a flippant attitude unbecoming a general in the Revolutionary army. It seems to have affected, to some degree, his decisions while on military duty. On the balance, however, Stephen was an able soldier, if not especially suited for high command. He had a detachment of mind and was often creative and probative in his views. He had an odd intellectual flair about him that, at least in contrast to his peers, was refreshing. It is to Adam Stephen's credit, amidst crushing personal defeat, that he maintained his dignity and self-esteem, putting aside vindictiveness. Despite deficiencies in character and motives of self-interest, Adam Stephen was a dedicated patriot and a contributor to the long series of events that shaped American independence and nationhood.

Abbreviations
Notes
Bibliography of Unpublished Materials
Index

Abbreviations

ASP-LC Adam Stephen Papers, Library of Congress.

A-WP W. W. Abbot, ed. *The Papers of George Washington. Colonial Series.* 6 volumes to date. Charlottesville, Va., 1983—.

CJCLS Church of Jesus Christ of Latter-day Saints Archives. Genealogical Department: microfilm collection of courthouse records.

F-WW John C. Fitzpatrick, ed. *The Writings of George Washington, 1745–99.* 39 vols. Washington, D.C., 1931–44.

HBP S. K. Stevens et al., eds. *The Papers of Henry Bouquet.* Vols. 2–5. Harrisburg, Pa., 1951–84.

HSP Historical Society of Pennsylvania.

JCC Worthington C. Ford, ed. *Journals of the Continental Congress.* 34 vols. Washington, D.C., 1904–37.

JHB John P. Kennedy et al., eds. *Journals of the House of Burgesses.* 6 vols. for 1752–76. Richmond, 1905–9.

JP Julian P. Boyd, et al. eds. *The Papers of Thomas Jefferson.* 22 vols. to date. Princeton, N.J., 1950—.

NYHS New-York Historical Society.

NYPL New York Public Library.

PCC Papers of the Continental Congress, National Archives.

PMHB Pennsylvania Magazine of History and Biography.

RV Robert L. Scribner and Brent Tarter, eds. *Revolutionary Virginia: The Road to Independence.* 7 vols. Charlottesville, 1973–83.

VHS Virginia Historical Society.

VMHB *Virginia Magazine of History and Biography.*

VSL Virginia State Library and Archives.

WMQ *William and Mary Quarterly.*

WPHM *Western Pennsylvania Historical Magazine.*

WP-LC George Washington Papers, Library of Congress.

Notes

CHAPTER ONE

1. William R. Brock, *Scotus Americanus: A Survey of the Sources for Links between Scotland and America in the Eighteenth Century* (Edinburgh, 1982), 15, 68–71; Mary S. Kennedy, *Seldens of Virginia and Allied Families* (2 vols., New York, 1911), 2:426–29; P. Hume Brown, *History of Scotland to the Present Time* (3 vols., Cambridge, Eng., 1911), 3:203; *The Survey Gazetteer of the British Isles*, 9th ed. (Edinburgh, 1952), 573; Samuel R. Gardiner, ed., *A School Atlas of English History* (New York, 1899), 33. On the quality of land and agriculture in Scotland, see James H. Leyburn, *The Scotch-Irish: A Social History* (Chapel Hill, N.C., 1962).

2. Virginia Colonial Records Project Survey Report 4913, Principal Probate Registry, Probate Book 1770—Will of Alexander Stephen, VHS; Samuel Johnson, *A Journey to the Western Islands of Scotland*, ed. Mary Lascelles (New Haven, 1971), 161–67.

3. Peter J. Anderson, ed., *Officers and Graduates of University & King's College, Aberdeen, 1495–1860* (Aberdeen, 1893), 233. The graduates listed include, for March 27, 1740: Master of Arts "Mr. Adamus Stephen, Aberdeen . . . ex parochia de Rhinnie [Rhynie]." See also Brown, *History of Scotland*, 3:37, 191.

4. Brock, *Scotus Americanus*, 90; Victoria E. Clark, *The Port of Aberdeen: A History of Its Trade and Shipping* (Aberdeen, 1921), 70; James Scotland, *The History of Scottish Education* (2 vols., London, 1969), 1:12, 151; Adam Stephen, "The Ohio Expedition of 1754: 'Col. Stephen's Life Written by Himself for B. Rush in 1775,'" *PMHB* 18 (1894): 43 (MS in the Library Company of Philadelphia); Caroline Robbins, "When It Is That Colonies May Turn Independent: An Analysis of the Environment and Politics of Frances Hutcheson (1694–1746)," *WMQ*, 3d ser., 11 (1954): 233–39.

5. Douglas Guthrie, *Extramural Medical Education in Edinburgh and the School of Medicine of the Royal Colleges* (Edinburgh, 1965), 9; D. B. Horn, *A Short History of the University of Edinburgh, 1556–1889* (Edinburgh, 1967), 43–44.

6. Majorie Robertson, Assistant Librarian, Edinburgh University Library, to Francis Silver, Feb. 14, 1979, Berkeley County Courthouse file. Stephen later demonstrated surgical skills.

7. Quoted by Brock, *Scotus Americanus*, 124.

8. Stephen, "The Ohio Expedition of 1754," 43–44; Thomas E. Van Metre, "Adam Stephen—The Man," *Berkeley Journal* 2 (1970): 13; R. H. Mahon, *Life of General the Hon. James Murray: A Builder of Canada* (London, 1921), 44–45; H. W. Richmond, *The Navy and the War of 1739–48* (3 vols., Cambridge, Eng., 1920), 3:25–32.

9. Charles H. Haws, *Scots in the Old Dominion, 1685–1800* (Edinburgh, 1980), 43–45.

10. Mary V. Mish, "General Adam Stephen, Founder of Martinsburg, West Virginia," *West Virginia History* 22 (1961): 63. That Stephen continued to live in Stafford County rather than Fredericksburg is borne out in various documents, e.g., Virginia State Land Office, Northern Neck Grants, Book H, March 9, 1753, VSL; "Indenture . . . Between Doctr Adam Stephen of Stafford County . . . ," July 20, 1751, S/John Harrow and Andrew Campbell, Misc. Adam Stephen Papers, University of Pittsburgh Library.

11. Stephen, "The Ohio Expedition of 1754," 44; Wyndham B. Blanton, *Medicine in Virginia in the Eighteenth Century* (Richmond, 1931), 19.

12. Virginia Colonial Records Project Survey Report 4913, Will of Alexander Stephen, VHS; Northern Neck Grants, Book H, 184–85, 274, 398, VSL; Philip P. Dandridge to Lyman Draper, Sept. 8, 1848, Draper Collection 8ZZ39, Virginia Papers, State Historical Society of Wisconsin; "The Account of Alexander Stephens Relating to Losses he sustained by the French . . . ," in Kenneth P. Bailey, ed., *The Ohio Company Papers, 1753–1817, Being Primarily Papers of the "Suffering Traders" of Pennsylvania* (Arcata, Calif. 1947), 153, 353; J. Estelle King, *Abstracts of Wills, Inventories, and Administration Accounts of Frederick County, Virginia, 1743–1800* (Berryville, Va., 1982), 56; Millard K. Bushong, *Historic Jefferson County* (Boyce, Va., 1972), 61, 65. Stephen's lands along Opequon Creek were: 270 acres (1750); 252 acres (March 1753); 813 acres (May 1753); 400 and 332 acres (separate grants, Aug. 1753)—total 2,067 acres. Before his move, Stephen had engaged in minor land transactions around Fredericksburg, e.g., Aug. 21 and Nov. 7, 1749; see William A. Crozier, ed., *Spotsylvania County Records, 1721–1800* (Baltimore, 1955), 2:10, 181. In 1749 a friend, John Allen, died and left Stephen a 10-volume edition of Charles Rollin's *Ancient History*, which the frequent classical references in his letters indicate he made good use of.

13. Alfred P. James, *The Ohio Company: Its Inner History* (Pittsburgh, 1959), 219.

14. Purchase Agreement with William Williams, Aug. 1753, Misc. Adam Stephen Papers, University of Pittsburgh Library; "Memoirs of Generals Lee, Gates, Stephen, and Darke," *Harper's New Monthly Magazine* 17 (Sept. 1858): 408; Bushong, *Jefferson County*, 61; Chester R. Young, "The Effects of the French and Indian War on Civilian Life in the Frontier Counties of Virginia" (Ph.D. diss., Vanderbilt University, 1969), 20.

15. Van Metre, "Adam Stephen—The Man," 12.

16. Ann Miller to Stephen, Feb. 26, 1753, ASP-LC.

17. Douglas S. Freeman, *George Washington* (7 vols., New York, 1949–57), 1: 271–72.
18. Stephen, "The Ohio Expedition of 1754," 44.
19. "A Roll—Service before the battle of the Meadows, July 3, 1754," WP-LC; Young, "Effects of the French and Indian War," 33–34, 154; James R. W. Titus, "Soldiers When They Chose to Be So: Virginians at War, 1754–1763" (Ph.D. diss., Rutgers University, 1983), 71; Bernhard Knollenberg, *George Washington: The Virginia Period, 1732–1775* (Durham, N.C., 1964), 17; Freeman, *Washington,* 1:339, 351. One-third of the officers were natives of Scotland—Stobo, Stephen, Hog, Polson, and Craik (Robert C. Alberts, *The Most Extraordinary Adventures of Major Robert Stobo* [Boston, 1965], 77). Stephen was named captain on Feb. 25 and received his commission March 8.
20. George Mercer, *The Virginia Soldiers' Claim to Western Lands Adjacent to Fort Pitt, Memorial by Colonel George Mercer, First Virginia Regiment to the King, in 1763* (n.p., Sept. 1766), "A Proclamation, Feb. 19, 1754," VSL.
21. Washington to Dinwiddie, March 20, 1754, to [Adam Stephen?] March 22, 1754, *A-WP,* 1:78, 81; Instructions to Joshua Fry, March 1754, in Archer B. Hulbert, *Washington's Road (Nemacolin's Path): The First Chapter of the Old French War* (Cleveland, 1903), 123–24; Stuart E. Brown, Jr., *Virginia Baron: The Story of Thomas 6th Lord Fairfax* (Berryville, Va., 1965), 130; Donald H. Kent, ed., "Contrecoeur's Copy of George Washington's Journal for 1754," *Pennsylvania History* 19 (1952): 10–11; William A. Hunter, *Forts on the Pennsylvania Frontier, 1753–58* (Harrisburg, 1960), 53; William B. Hindman, "The Great Meadows Campaign and the Climaxing Battle at Fort Necessity," *West Virginia History* 16 (1955): 67; Knollenberg, *Washington: The Virginia Period,* 18.
22. *F-WW,* 2:358n.; Stephen, "The Ohio Expedition of 1754," 45; Hunter, *Forts,* 53.
23. Washington to Dinwiddie, May 18, 1754, Dinwiddie to Washington, May 28, 1754, *A-WP,* 1:98–99, 102–3; Dinwiddie to Washington, May 25, 1754, R. A. Brock, ed., *The Official Records of Robert Dinwiddie* (2 vols., Richmond, 1883–84: vols. 3 and 4 of the *Collections of the VHS*), 1:172–73; Freeman, *Washington,* 1:360–61.
24. *Pennsylvania Gazette,* Sept. 19, 1754; "Deposition of John Shaw," in J. C. Harrington, *New Light on Washington's Fort Necessity: A Report on the Archaeological Explorations at Fort Necessity National Battlefield Site* (Richmond, 1957), 129–30; Hayes Baker-Crothers and Ruth A. Hudnut, eds., "A Private Soldier's Account of Washington's First Battles in the West: A Study in Historical Criticism," *Journal of Southern History* 8 (1942): 32–39; Stephen, "The Ohio Expedition of 1754," 46–47; Knollenberg, *Washington: The Virginia Period,* 19–20; Hulbert, *Washington's Road,* 135–42; Kent, "Contrecoeur's Copy," 16. Stephen, however, gave the number of prisoners as 22.
25. "Letter of Col. John Banister [Jr.], of Petersburg, to Robert Bolling," May 12, 1755, *WMQ,* 1st ser., 10 (1902): 104; Hunter, *Forts,* 55.
26. Washington to Dinwiddie, June 12, 1754, *A-WP,* 1:134; *Maryland Gazette,* Aug. 29, 1754, also printed in Charles H. Ambler, *George Washington and the West* (Chapel Hill, N.C., 1936), 214–16; Knollenberg, *Washington: The Vir-*

ginia Period, 23; Baker-Crothers and Hudnut, "A Private Soldier's Account," 29–31, 39–41.

27. Account of George Washington and James Mackay of the Capitulation, July 19, 1754, *A-WP,* 1:159–65; *Maryland Gazette,* Aug. 29, 1754; Baker-Crothers and Hudnut, "A Private Soldier's Account," 44–47; Hunter, *Forts,* 58–59.

28. *Maryland Gazette,* Aug. 29, 1754; "Articles of Capitulation," in Ambler, *Washington and the West,* 216–17. For a critique of Washington's journal, March 31–June 27, 1754, which was captured with Washington's letters, see Freeman, *Washington,* 1:540–47.

29. Stephen, "The Ohio Expedition of 1754," 49–50.

30. Account of Washington and Mackay, July 19, 1754, *A-WP,* 1:160; Hulbert, *Washington's Road,* 167; Ambler, *Washington and the West,* 88.

31. Pay in the Virginia Regiment, May 29–July 29, 1754, WP-LC; *JHB* (1752–55), Aug. 30, 1754, 198; Harrison Bird, *Battle of a Continent* (New York, 1965), 21.

32. Dinwiddie to Washington, Aug. 3, 1754, John Robinson to Washington, Sept. 15, 1754, *A-WP,* 1:182, 209; *Virginia Gazette* (Hunter), [Adam Stephen letter?], July 19, 1754; J. M. Toner, ed., *Journal of Colonel George Washington, Commander of a Detachment of Virginia Troops, Sent by Robert Dinwiddie, Lieutenant Governor of Virginia, across the Alleghany Mountains in 1754* (Albany, 1893), 165–66, 169, 199; Dinwiddie to Col. Innes, Aug. 1, 1754, William L. Saunders, ed., *The Colonial Records of North Carolina* (10 vols., Raleigh, 1886–90), 5:134; Ambler, *Washington and the West,* 89.

33. Dinwiddie to Stephen, Aug. 1, 1754, Brock, *Records of Dinwiddie,* 2:263.

34. Hindman, "Great Meadows Campaign," 89.

35. Printed Orders of George II of England, Nov. 12, 1754, in Murtie J. Clark, comp., *Colonial Soldiers of the South, 1732–1774* (Baltimore, 1983), 302–3; Ambler, *Washington and the West,* 89–90; Freeman, *Washington,* 1:437–39; Knollenberg, *Washington: The Virginia Period,* 29; Hunter, *Forts,* 30–31.

36. Dinwiddie to Stephen, Oct. 5, 1754, ASP-LC; also in Brock, *Records of Dinwiddie,* 1:345–46.

37. Dinwiddie to Stephen, Dec. 12, 1754, ASP-LC; Dinwiddie to Stephen, Nov. 18, 1754, to Sharpe, Dec. 17, 1754, to Capt. Polson, Dec. 20, 1754, Brock, *Records of Dinwiddie,* 1:411, 427–28, 435; Freeman, *Washington,* 1:134.

38. At a Court held for Frederick County, March 8, 1780, "Journals of the Council of Virginia in Executive Sessions, 1737–1767," *VMHB* 16 (1908): 136n.; Richard L. Morton, *Colonial Virginia* (2 vols., Chapel Hill, N.C., 1960), 2:664.

39. Dinwiddie to Stephen, Jan 1, 1755, Brock, *Records of Dinwiddie,* 1:446; Dinwiddie to Stephen, Feb. 10, 1755, BR Box 257(2), Huntington Library.

40. Dinwiddie to Sharpe, Jan. 7, 1755, to Stephen, Jan. 1, 1755, Brock, *Records of Dinwiddie,* 1:446, 450.

41. Stephen to Washington, [late Dec. 1754], *A-WP,* 1:236.

42. John R. Alden, *General Gage in America* (Baton Rouge, La., 1948), 22; Harry M. Ward, *"Unite or Die:" Intercolony Relations, 1690–1763* (Port Washington, N.Y., 1971), 58; Hunter, *Forts,* 31.

43. Dinwiddie to Stephen, March 7, 1755, ASP-LC; Freeman, *Washington,* 2:6–8, 10.

44. *Major General Edward Braddock's Orderly Books* (Cumberland, Md., 1878); Franklin T. Nichols, "The Organization of Braddock's Army," *WMQ*, 3d ser., 4 (1947): 128, 131.

CHAPTER TWO

1. Stanley Pargellis, "Braddock's Defeat," *American Historical Review* 41 (1936): 257n.
2. W. H. Lowdermilk, *History of Cumberland, Maryland* (Washington, D.C., 1878), 123–27; Peter E. Russell, "Redcoats in the Wilderness: British Officers and Irregular Warfare in the Europe and America, 1740 to 1760," *WMQ*, 3d ser., 35 (1978): 640; Nicholas B. Wainwright, *George Croghan: Wilderness Diplomat* (Chapel Hill, N.C., 1959), 88–91.
3. Braddock to Duke of Newcastle, June 5, 1755, Egerton MSS 3249: 194, British Museum, Virginia Colonial Records program, VSL; "A Seaman's Journal," in Archer B. Hulbert, *Braddock's Road and Three Relative Papers* (Cleveland, 1903), 100–101; "William Johnston to Frank ——," Sept. 23, 1755, *English Historical Review* 1 (1886): 149–50; Freeman, *Washington*, 2: 58–59.
4. Roger Morris to Washington, June 23, 1755, *A-WP*, 1: 315.
5. Stephen to John Hunter, July 13, 1755, Egerton MSS 3249: 277–80, British Museum, Virginia Colonial Records program, VSL; Charles P. Hamilton, ed., *Braddock's Defeat* (Norman, Okla., 1959), "Halkett's Orderly Book," July 5, 1755, 119; *A-WP*, 1: 316n., 328n.; Lee McCardell, *Ill-Starred General: Braddock of the Coldstream Guards* (Pittsburgh, 1958), 234–35; Freeman, *Washington*, 2: 60 and n.
6. Russell, "Redcoats in the Wilderness," 644.
7. Letter from Fort Cumberland, Sept 20, 1755, *Public Advertiser*, "British Newspaper Accounts of Braddock's Defeat," *PMHB* 23 (1899): 316–17; Robert Orme to William Shirley, July 18, 1755, Charles H. Lincoln, ed. *Correspondence of William Shirley* (2 vols., New York, 1912), 2: 208; Charles M. Stotz, ed., "A Letter from Will's Creek: Harry Gordon's Account of Braddock's Defeat," *WPHM* 44 (1961): 132–33; McCardell, *Ill-Starred General*, 238–39; H. Hopper to Horatio Sharpe, June 25, 1755, *Pennsylvania Gazette*, July 10, 1755; Guy Frégault, *Canada: the War of the Conquest*, trans. Margaret M. Cameron (Toronto, 1969), 95–96; *A-WP*, 1: 332n.
8. Extract of a Letter from Fort Cumberland, *Public Advertiser*, Sept. 20, 1755, "British Newspaper Accounts," *PMHB* 23 (1899): 317; "Seaman's Journal," in Hulbert, *Braddock's Road*, 163–64; McCardell, *Ill-Starred General*, 251; Freeman, *Washington*, 2: 67–72; Alden *Gage*, 24–25; Bird, *Battle of a Continent*, 55–57.
9. Elaine G. Breslau, "A Dismal Tragedy: Drs. Alexander and John Hamilton Comment on Braddock's Defeat," *Maryland Historical Magazine* 75 (1980): 123; Freeman, *Washington*, 2: 73–75.
10. Alexander Hamilton to Baillie Hamilton, Aug. 1755, in Breslau, "A Dismal Tragedy," 127, 140; Extract of a Letter from an Officer at Fort Cumberland, July 18, 1755, *Pennsylvania Gazette*, July 31, 1755; marquis de Chastellux, *Trav-*

els in North America in the Years 1780, 1781 and 1782, trans. and ed. Howard C.
Rice (2 vols., Chapel Hill, N.C., 1963), July 1782, 1:265n.; Stanley Pargellis,
ed., *Military Affairs in North America, 1748–1765: Selected Documents from the
Amherst Papers in Windsor Castle* (New York, 1936), 284; Freeman, *Washington*,
2:86. Alexander Stephen was given a commission in Nova Scotia as an ensign,
Nov. 27, 1756.

11. Stephen to John Hunter, July 18, 1755, Egerton MSS 3249:277–80, British
    Museum, Virginia Colonial Records program, VSL. An undated copy of this
    letter was enclosed in a letter of Thomas Pownall, in the Hardwicke Papers,
    British Museum Add. MSS 35593:234, and was also extracted in *Pennsylvania
    Gazette*, July 31, 1755. The Hardwicke Papers copy was published in Paul E.
    Kopperman, *Braddock at the Monongahela* (Pittsburgh, 1977), 226–27; see also
    Kopperman's commentary, 228.

12. Newcastle to Holderness, Aug. 26, 1755, Egerton MSS 3249:274, British Mu-
    seum, Virginia Colonial Records Project, VSL; see Pargellis, "Braddock's De-
    feat," 263–65, for analysis of the tactical errors; Kopperman, *Braddock at the
    Monongahela*, 225.

13. Col. Dunbar to Gov. Morris, July 16, 1755, in Samuel Hazard, ed., *Minutes of
    the Provincial Council of Pennsylvania, Pennsylvania Colonial Records* (vols. 6–9,
    Philadelphia, 1851–52), 6:499; Hulbert, *Braddock's Road*, 131, 134.

14. Alexander Hamilton to Baillie Hamilton, Aug. 1755, in Breslau, "A Dismal
    Tragedy," 136–37.

15. *Pennsylvania Gazette*, Aug. 21, 1755; Leonard W. Labaree, ed., *The Papers
    of Benjamin Franklin* (vols. 1–11, New Haven, 1959–67), 6:111n., 112n.;
    Frégault, *Canada*, 98–99; Hunter, *Forts*, 32.

16. Washington to Dinwiddie, July 18, 1755, "Additional Manuscripts of the
    French and Indian War," *Transactions of the American Antiquarian Society* 11
    (1909): 176; Extract of a private letter . . . , Aug. 18, 1755, in *Public Advertiser*,
    Oct. 3, 1755, "British Newspaper Accounts," *PMHB* 23 (1899): 319.

17. Dinwiddie to Stephen, Aug. 11, 1755, Stephen Papers, Maryland Historical
    Society.

18. Dinwiddie to [Virginia officers], Aug. 25, 1755, ASP-LC; Lowdermilk, *Cum-
    berland*, 201–2; Knollenberg, *Washington: The Virginia Period*, 36–37; William
    W. Hening, comp., *The Statutes at Large: Being a Collection of All the Laws of
    Virginia* (vols. 6–13, Richmond, 1819–23), 6: Aug. 1755, 520. The General
    Assembly voted Washington £300 and each captain, including Stephen, £75,
    lieutenants £30, and privates £5. Seven officers, with Stephen at the head of the
    list, petitioned the House of Burgesses for reimbursement for loss of horses,
    tents, and other items—"in short all our Field Equipage" at Braddock's defeat.
    The house tabled the petition (*JHB* [1752–58], Aug. 7, 1755, 300–301).

19. Orders at Fort Cumberland, Sept. 17, 1755, in Nichols, "Organization of
    Braddock's Army," 133.

20. Washington to Stephen, Sept. 11, 1755, *A-WP*, 2:27, 7n., 57n.

21. Charles H. L. Johnston, ed., *Journal of Charles Lewis of Fredericksburg, Virginia*
    (n.p., n.d.), 14; Lowdermilk, *Cumberland*, 193, 198; John R. Alden, *Robert Din-
    widdie: Servant of the Crown* (Williamsburg, Va., 1973), 98.

22. Washington to Stephen, Sept. 20, 1755, *A-WP*, 2:56.

23. Stephen to Washington, Sept. 25, 1755, ibid., 62–63, 63n. Stephen estimated

the French had only 200 men at Fort Duquesne (Stephen to Bouquet, Sept. 15, 1755, in Sylvester Stevens and Donald H. Kent, eds., *The Papers of Henry Bouquet* [mimeographed, Harrisburg, 1941], no. 21643, 170–71.)

24. Stephen to Washington, Sept. 27, 1755, *A-WP*, 2:64, 64–65n.
25. Ibid. Stephen kept prominent Virginians informed of the military situation, as indicated in Landon Carter's letter to Washington, Oct. 7, 1755 (ibid., 82).
26. Dinwiddie to Stephen, Oct. 3, 1755, Stephen Papers, Maryland Historical Society.
27. Stephen to St. Clair, Sept. 3, 1755, John Forbes Papers, St. Clair Letter Book, University of Virginia Library; Washington to Dinwiddie, April 27, 1756, *A-WP*, 3:59, 62n.
28. St. Clair to Stephen, Oct. 24, 1755, John Forbes Papers, St. Clair Letter Book, University of Virginia Library.
29. Stephen to Washington, Oct. 4, 1755, *A-WP*, 2:72–73, 74–75n.; *Maryland Gazette*, extract, Oct. 9, 1755, in Lowdermilk, *Cumberland*, 193.
30. Stephen to Washington, Oct. 4, 1755, Washington to Stephen, Oct. 29, 1755, Washington to Alexander Boyd, Nov. 1, 1755, *A-WP*, 2:72–73, 146–47, 152, 83n., 132n., 144n., 250n., 252n.; Brown, *Virginia Baron*, 137; Thomas Walker to Washington, Nov. 26, Dec. 4, 1755, Archibald Henderson, "Dr. Thomas Walker and the Loyal Company of Virginia, *Proceedings of the American Antiquarian Society*, n.s., 41 (1932): 124–26.
31. Washington to Dinwiddie, Oct. 8, 1755, *A-WP*, 2:83–84.
32. Ibid.: Washington to Stephen, Nov. 8, 1755, ibid., 172–73, 174n.; Hening, *Statutes*, 6:559–64.
33. Stephen to Washington, Nov. 6, 7, 22, *A-WP*, 2:156–60, 177–78, 36n., 73n.; Johnston, *Journal of Lewis*, 15; Freeman, *Washington*, 1:282n.
34. Stephen to Washington, Nov. 9, 1755, *A-WP*, 2:157.
35. *Pennsylvania Gazette*, Nov. 20, 1755, quoted in Hunter, *Forts*, 190–91.
36. Washington to Stephen, Nov. 28, 1755, *A-WP*, 2:184–85.
37. Stephen to Washington, Nov. 29, Dec. 3, 1755, ibid., 190, 195.
38. Ibid., 211n.
39. Washington to Stephen, Dec. 3, 1755, Dinwiddie to Washington, Dec. 14, 1755, ibid., 195, 215.
40. Stephen to Washington, Oct. 4, 1755, ibid., 72–73, 74–75n.; *F-WW*, 1:249n.; Dinwiddie to Washington, Jan. 23, 1756, Brock, *Records of Dinwiddie*, 2:326.
41. Washington to Stephen, Nov. 18, 1755, *A-WP*, 2:172–73, 173n.; Freeman, *Washington*, 2:138–39, 153–54.
42. Freeman, *Washington*, 2:145–47.
43. Stephen to Washington, Dec. 23, 1755, *A-WP*, 2:226–27, 228n.
44. *Virginia Gazette* (Hunter), Dec. 12, 19, 25, 1755; Freeman, *Washington*, 2:149.
45. Stephen to Washington, Dec. 26, 1755, *A-WP*, 2:233; Johnston, *Journal of Lewis*, 21.
46. Henry Woodward to Capt. John Dagworthy, n.d. (ca. Dec. 26, 1755), in C. H. B. Turner, comp., *Some Records of Sussex County, Delaware* (Philadelphia, 1909), 323; *A-WP*, 2:233–34n.; Annibel Jenkins, *Nicholas Rowe* (Boston, 1977), 37–52; George O. Seilhamer, *History of the American Theater before the Revolution* (rept. New York, 1968), 69–70, 94, 102, 130, 159, 243, 309.

CHAPTER THREE

1. Memorandum, Jan. 7, 1756, Orders, Jan. 8, 1756, Address, Jan. 8, 1756, *A-WP*, 2:254–58, 254–56n.
2. Orders, Jan. 9, 1756, ibid., 259–60.
3. Washington to Stephen, Jan. 9, 1756, to Thomas Waggener, Jan. 9, 1756, ibid., 263–66.
4. Stephen to Washington, Jan. 18, Jan. 31, 1756, Washington to Dinwiddie, April 22, 1756, ibid., 2:286–88, 288–90n., 305–7, 3:34, 35n.; *Pennsylvania Gazette*, March 25, 1756 (concerning Williamsburg item, Feb. 13, 1756).
5. Washington to Stephen, Feb. 1, 1756, *A-WP*, 2:310–11.
6. Extract of a letter from Governor Dinwiddie to Gen. Shirley, Jan. 23, 1756, in William H. Browne, ed., *Correspondence of Governor Horatio Sharpe, Archives of Maryland* (vols. 6 and 9, Baltimore, 1888, 1890), 6:349; *A-WP*, 2:211n.; Freeman, *Washington*, 2:145, 153–56, 165–66.
7. Stephen to Washington, March 29, 1756, *A-WP*, 2:325–27.
8. Washington to Dinwiddie, April 16, 1756, Dinwiddie to Washington, April 25, 1756, and "Proposal for Frontier Forts," enclosed in Washington to Dinwiddie, Nov. 9, 1756, ibid., 3:1–3, 3n., 55, 4:10; *Pennsylvania Gazette*, May 13, 1756; Mabel H. Gardiner, "History of Martinsburg and Vicinity, 1778–1926" (M.A. thesis, West Virginia University, 1930), 10; Alexander S. Withers, *Chronicles of Border Warfare*, ed. Reuben G. Thwaites (Cincinnati, 1895), 81, 81n.; Otis K. Rice, *West Virginia: A History* (Lexington, Ky., 1985), 23–24; Otis K. Rice, *The Allegheny Frontier: West Virginia Beginnings, 1730–1830* (Lexington, Ky., 1970), 50; Knollenberg, *Washington: The Virginia Period*, 39–40.
9. Stephen to Washington, Aug. 1, 1756, Dinwiddie to Washington, Aug. 19, 1756, Washington to Dinwiddie, Sept. 23, 1756, *A-WP*, 3:309–10, 311n., 358, 415.
10. Washington to Stephen, Aug. 5, 1756, ibid., 337, 184n.
11. Stephen to Washington, March 29, 1756, ibid., 2:325.
12. Stephen to Washington, May 19, 1756, ibid., 3:165.
13. Stephen to Washington, July 25, Aug. 1, 1756, ibid., 294–95, 310.
14. Washington to Stephen, Sept. 6, 1756, ibid., 388–89.
15. John Robinson to Washington, [ca. April 2, 1756], ibid., 2:329; Dinwiddie quoted in Knollenberg, *Washington: The Virginia Period*, 42. For the civil-military friction, see Titus, "Soldiers When They Chose to Be So," 211–14.
16. "The Virginia Centinel, No. X," *Pennsylvania Journal*, in Worthington C. Ford, ed., "Washington and 'Centinel X,'" *PMHB* 22 (1898): 438–42.
17. Officers of the Virginia Regiment to Stephen, Oct. 6, 1756, *A-WP*, 4:22–23; Freeman, *Washington*, 2:221–22.
18. See William Peachey et al. to Washington, Nov. 12, 1756, *A-WP*, , 4:21–22n., for further comment by the officers on "Centinel X."
19. See Ford, "Washington and 'Centinel X,'" 445–51, for reproduction of this document; *A-WP*, 3:437n.
20. Stephen to Washington, May 29, May 31, 1756, *A-WP*, 3:182–84.
21. Lowdermilk, *Cumberland*, 210–12.
22. Ibid., 213.
23. Stephen to [Pennsylvania Council], Sept. 30, 1757, copy in Penn Papers, IA,

vol. 2, HSP, printed in Hazard, *Minutes of the Provincial Council of Pennsylvania,*
7:289–90; Hunter, *Forts,* 410, 414–17. For Stephen's other intelligence and
recommendations on the use of patrols, see Extract of a letter from Colo.
Adam Stephen . . . , Nov. 14, 1756, in John Armstrong to Gov. Denny, Dec.
22, 1756, Gratz Collection, HSP.

24. Extract of a letter from Fort Cumberland, [Oct. 1756], *Pennsylvania Gazette,*
Dec. 30, 1756; Sharpe to Lord Baltimore, Nov. 1, 1756, Browne, *Correspondence of Sharpe, Maryland Archives,* 6:503–4; *A-WP,* 4:9n.; Lowdermilk, *Cumberland,* 219.

25. Stephen to Dinwiddie, Oct. 16, 1756, Huntington Library.

26. Dinwiddie to Stephen, Oct. 26, 1756, Brock, *Records of Dinwiddie,* 2:530.

27. Dinwiddie to Lord Loudoun, Oct. 28, 1756, ibid., 533–34. The rank and file at
the end of the year numbered 655, scattered among the various posts. See A
Return . . . Virginia Regiment, Jan. 1, 1757, *A-WP,* 4:76.

28. E. Douglas Branch, "An Unpublished Washington Document from the Bouquet Papers," *PMHB* 61 (1937): 204–13, and "Correction," ibid., 62 (1938):
120; *JP,* 19:436n.

29. Dinwiddie to Washington, Sept. 30, Oct. 26, Dec. 27, 1756, Washington to
Stephen, Oct. 23, 1756, Adam Stephen's Council of War, Oct. 30, 1756, and
Washington's Comments, Nov. 5, 1756, Washington to Dinwiddie, Dec. 10,
1756, *A-WP,* 3:424, 443, 4:71; 3:440-41, 447–52, 453n., 4:49; Lowdermilk,
Cumberland, 221–22.

30. Stephen to John Dagworthy, Dec. 9, 1756, "Notes and Queries," *PMHB* 31
(1907): 249.

31. Extract of a letter of Stephen to William Denny, April 9, 1757, Huntington
Library; Stephen to Dagworthy, Feb. 14, 1757, Turner, *Records of Sussex
County,* 321; Washington to Dinwiddie, April 16, 1757, *A-WP,* 4:135, 136n.,
8n., 73n. *Pennsylvania Gazette,* May 19, June 2, 1757. Stephen had sent Indian
messengers to enlist Catawba support. When a scouting party of two Catawbas and four soldiers all were reported killed, Stephen erected a large square
post, with a pyramidical top, about 100 yards from the fort. A lead plate, with
an inscription at the bottom of which was "In Premium Virtutis Erigedum
Curavit   Adamus Stephen," was nailed to the post commemorating those
who had allegedly fallen. The scouts, however, returned unharmed. The monument remained intact for many years.

32. Dinwiddie to Washington, May 16, 1757, *A-WP,* 4:154, 128n., 345n.; Sharpe
to Dinwiddie, March 30, April 5, 1757, Browne, *Correspondence of Sharpe,
Maryland Archives,* 6:537; Benjamin J. Hillman, ed., *Executive Journals of the
Council of Colonial Virginia* (6 vols., Richmond, 1925–66), 6: April 4, 1757,
35–37; Lowdermilk, *Cumberland,* 222; Knollenberg, *Washington: The Virginia
Period,* 432. The 2,000-man force was to include: 5 companies of regular
troops, 500 men; 3 independent companies, 200; South Carolina provincial
troops, 500; North Carolina, 200; Virginia, 400; and Pennsylvania, 200. In
May Washington had 450 Virginia troops; in Sept., 700, including draftees.
The Virginia force in May was dispersed by Gov. Dinwiddie (slightly different
from what Lord Loudoun directed) as follows: Fort Loudoun, 100; Maidstone,
70; Edward's, 25; Pearsall's, 45; neighborhood of Butter Milk Fort, 70; Dicker-
son's Fort, 70; Vause's Fort, 70—total 450.

33. Dinwiddie to Washington, April 5 and April 7, 1757. At a Council of War held at Fort Cumberland, April 16, 1757, Washington to Stephen, April 17, 1757, *A-WP*, 4:128–30, 136–38; Hillman, *Executive Journals*, 6: April 4, 1757, 38.

34. Washington to Stephen, April 17, 1757, *A-WP*, 4:138, 196n. Washington left Fort Cumberland on April 17 for Fort Loudoun, where he made his headquarters until he took leave at the end of the year (Lowdermilk, *Cumberland*, 226).

35. Washington to Dinwiddie, Sept. 17, 1757, *A-WP*, 4:408, 197–98n.

36. Washington to Dinwiddie, May 24, June 10, July 11, 1757, Memoranda [Fort Loudoun], June 8, 1757, ibid., 163, 194, 297, 190.

37. Washington to Speaker John Robinson, May 30, 1757, ibid., 174.

38. Dinwiddie to Washington, June 1, June 24, 1757, ibid., 175, 255.

39. Washington to Robert McKenzie, July 29, 1757, ibid., 352.

40. Dinwiddie to Washington, May 23, 1757, ibid., 157–58, 159n.; Dinwiddie to Stephen, May 26, 1757, to Benjamin Stead, May 26, 1757, Brock, *Records of Dinwiddie*, 2:634–35.

41. Dinwiddie to Washington, June 1, 1757, *A-WP*, 4:175–76.

42. Washington to Dinwiddie, May 24, 1757, ibid., 163.

43. Court of Inquiry, Fort Loudoun, June 9, 1757, Washington to Dinwiddie, June 12, 1757, ibid., 207–8, 204, 130n., 345n.

44. Ibid., 177n.; Bouquet to Amherst, May 25, 1757, Public Record Office, WO 34/40, 59, micro. VSL.

45. Bouquet to Amherst, June 23, 1757, Public Record Office, WO 34/40, micro. VSL; Bouquet to Gov. Henry Ellis, June 23, 1757, to Dinwiddie, Oct. 18, 1757, Stevens and Kent, *Bouquet Papers*, mimeographed, nos. 21631, 21632; Dinwiddie to Stephen, Nov. 24, 1757, Brock, *Records of Dinwiddie*, 2:718; Bouquet to Ellis, Aug. 26, Aug. 29, 1757, to Loudoun, Oct. 16, Oct. 21, 1757, to Dinwiddie, Oct. 18, 1757, *HBP*, 1:177, 178–79, 213, 223–34, 220; John R. Alden, *John Stuart and the Southern Colonial Frontier, 1754–75* (Ann Arbor, Mich., 1944), 58–59, 91; Alfred P. James, *George Mercer of the Ohio Company* (Pittsburgh, 1963), 22–23.

46. Dinwiddie to Stephen, July 22, 1757, Brock, *Records of Dinwiddie*, 2:674–75.

47. Bouquet to Amherst, Dec. 10, 1757, Public Record Office, WO 34/40, micro. VSL.

48. George Mercer to Washington, Aug. 17, 1757, Stephen to Washington, Aug. 20, 1757, *A-WP*, 4:370–74, 375–76; Don Higginbotham, *George Washington and the American Military Tradition* (Athens, Ga., 1985), 32.

49. Dinwiddie to Bouquet, Sept. 24, 1757, Brock, *Records of Dinwiddie*, 2:703; Bouquet to Gov. Henry Ellis, Nov. 12, 1757, in James, *George Mercer of the Ohio Company*, 23.

50. George Mercer to Washington, Nov. 2, 1757, *A-WP*, 5:40–41.

51. Stephen to Washington, April 22, 1758, Washington to St. Clair, April 27, 1758, ibid., 136, 148; *Maryland Gazette*, April 27, 1758; Maj. John Tulleken to Amherst, Jan. 29, 1758, Public Record Office, WO 34/40, micro. VSL; John Blair to St. Clair, April 15, 1758, John Forbes Papers, University of Virginia Library.

52. Stanislaus M. Hamilton, ed., *Letters to Washington and Accompanying Papers* (5 vols., Boston, 1898–1902), 2:316n.; Richard Corbin to James Buchanan, April 26, 1758, Richard Corbin Letter Book, transcript, VHS.

53. St. Clair to Bouquet, May 27, 1758, *HBP,* 2:374–75; St. Clair to Bouquet, May 28, May 31, 1758, British Museum Add. MSS no. 21639, Virginia Colonial Records program, VSL; Stephen to Bouquet, June 6, 1758, William Trent to Bouquet, June 5, June 7, 1758, Stevens and Kent, *Bouquet Papers,* mimeographed, nos. 21643, 21655; Orders for Lt. Col. Adam Stephen, May 24, 1758, *F-WW,* 2:203–4; Hugh Cleland, ed., *George Washington in the Ohio Valley* (Pittsburgh, 1955), 164. By May 28, 950 troops had been raised for the 1st Regiment; 900 for the 2d.

CHAPTER FOUR

1. John W. Huston, "Fort Pitt, 1758–72" (Ph.D. diss., University of Pittsburgh, 1957), 39; Nellie Norkus, "Virginia's Role in the Capture of Fort Duquesne, 1758," *WPHM* 45 (1962): 300–302, 307; Charles M. Stotz, "Defense in the Wilderness," ibid., 41 (1958): 94; Douglas E. Leach, *Arms for Empire: A Military History of the British Colonies in North America, 1607–1763* (New York, 1973), 419.
2. Stephen to Washington, June 25, 1758, WP-LC.
3. Stephen to Bouquet, June 7, 1758, Stevens and Kent, *Bouquet Papers,* mimeographed, no. 21643.
4. Adam Hoops to Bouquet, June 9, 1758, Stevens and Kent, *Bouquet Papers,* mimeographed, no. 21643; Alfred P. James, "Decision at the Forks," *WPHM* 41 (1958): 45–48.
5. Niles Anderson, "The General Chooses a Road: The Forbes Campaign of 1758 to Capture Fort Duquesne," *WPHM* 42 (1959): 129. At Raystown, in mid-June, Stephen had six Virginia companies with him: Washington's, Stephen's, Andrew Lewis's, Robert Stewart's, Thomas Bullitt's, and Walter Stewart's—total 535 rank and file, 19 officers, and 35 noncommissioned officers (Stephen to Washington, June 13, 1758, Hamilton, *Letters to Washington,* 2:357).
6. Frederick County Order Book, no. 8, July 6, 1785, 7, VSL, Adam Stephen plaintiff against John Harrow defendant, In Case of Assumpsit; Freeman, *Washington,* 2:317–20; Clark, *Colonial Soldiers,* 513–19.
7. Estimate of Distance to Fort Duquesne, [ca. July 1758], and Bouquet to Forbes, Aug. 8, 1758, *HBP,* 2:279, 336; Stephen to Washington, Aug. 2, 1758, Bouquet to Washington, Aug. 10, 1758, Hamilton, *Letters to Washington,* 3:8, 24–25; William A. Hunter, ed., "Thomas Barton and the Forbes Expedition," *PMHB* 95 (1971): 447n. A return of the "Virginia Detachment" under Stephen at Raystown showed 615 men (Hamilton, *Letters to Washington,* 3:7).
8. A Report of Captain Wood . . . , [July 1758], and Bouquet to Forbes, July 21, 1758, *HBP,* 2:237n., 243, 252; Stephen to Bouquet, Aug. 8, 1758, Stevens and Kent, *Bouquet Papers,* mimeographed, no. 21643.
9. Stephen to Bouquet, Aug. 8, 1758, *HBP,* 2:341–42.
10. Maj. George Armstrong to Bouquet, Aug. 8, 1758, Stephen to Bouquet, Aug. 13, Aug. 15, 1758, ibid., 340, 363, 370, 236n.
11. Stephen to Bouquet, Aug. 10, 1758, ibid., 349.
12. Stephen to Bouquet, [ca. Aug. 12, 1758], ibid., 361.
13. Stephen to Bouquet, Aug. 18, 1758, ibid., 386.

14. Bouquet to Forbes, Aug. 20, 1758, ibid., 395–96.
15. Colby Chew: Report on Road, [ca. Aug. 21, 1758], ibid., 401; Norkus, "Virginia's Role . . . Fort Duquesne," 302–3.
16. Stephen to Bouquet, Aug. 26, 1758, *HBP*, 2:430–33.
17. James Burd to Bouquet, Aug. 28, 1758, ibid., 438.
18. St. Clair to Bouquet, Aug. 27, 1758, ibid., 434–35.
19. Bouquet to St. Clair, Aug. 28, 1758, ibid., 435–36.
20. James Burd to Bouquet, Aug. 30, 1758, Stevens and Kent, *Bouquet Papers*, mimeographed, no. 21643.
21. William Ramsay to Washington, Sept. 3, 1758, Hamilton, *Letters to Washington*, 3:81–82.
22. Stephen to Washington, Sept. 9, 1758, ibid., 88.
23. Forbes to Pitt, Sept. 6, 1758, Alfred P. James, ed., *Writings of General John Forbes* (Menasha, Wis., 1938), 205.
24. Forbes to Bouquet, Sept. 23, 1758, ibid., 221; Stephen to Washington, Sept. 9, 1758, Hamilton, *Letters to Washington*, 3:88.
25. Stephen to Washington, Sept. 14, 1756, Hamilton, *Letters to Washington*, 3:98; Hunter, "Thomas Barton and the Forbes Expedition," 473. For a reference by Gen. Arthur St. Clair (no relation to Sir John) concerning the Stephen–St. Clair controversy as a precedent defining the limitations of a staff officer's command, see George D. Albert and Thomas L. Montgomery, eds., *Report of the Commission to Locate the Site of the Frontier Forts of Pennsylvania* (Harrisburg, 1916) 2:272–73.
26. Stephen to Col. James Wood, April [Aug.?] 30, 1758, owned by Mr. and Mrs. G. Roderick Cheeseman, and copied in Guy L. Keesecker typescripts of Adam Stephen correspondence, Martinsburg Public Library.
27. James Burd to Bouquet, Sept. 6, 1758, *HBP*, 2:418–19.
28. Stephen to Washington, Sept. 13, 1758, Hamilton, *Letters to Washington*, 3:96.
29. An Account of Major Grant's Defeat near Fort Duquesne, Annapolis, Oct. 5, 1758, *Pennsylvania Archives*, 2d ser. (19 vols., Philadelphia and Harrisburg, 1874–90), 6:429–30; Bouquet to Forbes, Sept. 17, 1758, *HBP*, 2:519–20; C. Hale Sipe, *The Indian Wars of Pennsylvania* (Harrisburg, 1929), 395–96; C. Hale Sipe, *Fort Ligonier and Its Times* (Harrisburg, 1932), 43–48; Freeman, *Washington*, 2:339–47.
30. Stephen to Bouquet, Sept. 15, 1758 (two letters of same date), Bouquet to Forbes, Sept. 17, 1758, *HBP*, 2:511–12, 517–20.
31. Norkus, "Virginia's Role . . . Fort Duquesne," 305; Clark, *Colonial Soldiers*, 530.
32. Norkus, "Virginia's Role . . . Fort Duquesne," 305–6.
33. Stephen to Washington, Sept. 9, 1758, Hamilton, *Letters to Washington*, 3:88.
34. Forbes to Bouquet, Sept. 23, 1758, *HBP*, 2:536; Freeman, *Washington*, 2:333–34.
35. Extract of a letter from Raystown, Oct. 16, 1758, *Pennsylvania Gazette*, Oct. 26, 1758; Extract of a letter from [Joseph Shippen?], Oct. 12, 1758, *HBP*, 2:566–67; Freeman, *Washington*, 2:351–52; James, "Decision at the Forks," 50–51.
36. Knollenberg, *Washington: The Virginia Period*, 68; Archer B. Hulbert, *The Old Glade (Forbes's) Road* (Cleveland, 1903), 156; Bliss Isely, *The Horsemen of the Shenandoah: A Biographical Account of the Early Days of George Washington* (Milwaukee, 1962), 175. On Oct. 21 troops of the Virginia Regiment numbered

461 at Fort Ligonier: Washington's, Stephen's, Lewis's, and Bullitt's companies. On the march to Fort Duquesne there were 10 Virginia companies (A Return, Nov. 18, 1758, Clark, *Colonial Soldiers*, 539, and A Daily Return . . . , Oct. 21, 1758, Thomas Balch, ed., *Letters and Papers Relating Chiefly to the Provincial History of Pennsylvania* [Philadelphia, 1855], 146).

37. Montgomery, *Report . . . Frontier Forts*, 2:204–5; Anderson, "The General Chooses a Road," 391–92. On Oct. 30 Stephen was president of a court-martial at Loyalhanna (Clark, *Colonial Soldiers*, 537).

38. Extract of a letter from Pittsburgh, Nov. 26, 1758, *Pennsylvania Gazette*, Dec. 14, 1758; Forbes to Pitt, Nov. 27, 1758, James, *Writings of Forbes*, 267–69; J. P. McLean, *An Historical Account of the Settlements of Scotch Highlanders in America* (1900; rept. Baltimore, 1978), 268; Anderson, "The General Chooses a Road," 392–97; Huston, "Fort Pitt," 58–59; Hulbert, *Old Glade (Forbes's) Road*, 157–58; James, "Decision at the Forks," 52–53. Fort Ligonier was named for John Ligonier, Baron Ligonier of Enniskillen, head of the British army (Sipe, *Fort Ligonier*, 43).

39. Forbes to Abercromby, Nov. 26, 1758, James, *Writings of Forbes*, 221.

40. Stephen to Bouquet, Dec. 2, 1758, *HBP*, 2:618; Stephen to Bouquet, Dec. 16, Dec. 18, 1758, Stevens and Kent, *Bouquet Papers*, mimeographed, no. 21643; Sipe, *Indian Wars of Pennsylvania*, 402–3.

41. Robert Stewart to Washington, Dec. 29, 1758, Hamilton, *Letters to Washington*, 3:142; Marion Tinling, ed., *The Correspondence of the Three William Byrds of Westover, Virginia, 1684–1776* (2 vols., Charlottesville, 1977), 2:670n.

42. Edward Hubbard to Bouquet, March 9, 1759, *HBP*, 3:182.

43. *JHB* (1758–61), March 17, March 20, 1759, 97, 102; Freeman, *Washington*, 3:10.

44. Stanwix, to Amherst, March 25, 1759, Public Record Office, WO 34/35, micro. VSL; Hillman, *Executive Journals*, 6: April 3, 1759, 677; Stephen to Bouquet, May 2, May 27, 1759, *HBP*, 3:265–66, 329; letter from Byrd (concerning March 22, 1759), Governor and Council [Minute] and Bouquet "Outline," April 13, 1759, Tinling, ed., *Correspondence of Byrds*, 2:671, 673; Nicholas B. Wainwright, *George Croghan: Wilderness Diplomat* (Chapel Hill, N.C., 1959), 160–61.

45. Stephen to Bouquet, May 3, 1759, *HBP*, 3:266.

46. Stephen to Bouquet, May 17, 1759, ibid., 292; Stephen to Gen. John Stanwix, May 17, May 25, 1759, Stevens and Kent, *Bouquet Papers*, mimeographed, no. 21644, pt. 1; Stotz, "Defense in the Wilderness," 97.

47. Stephen to Bouquet, May 27, 1759, *HBP*, 3:328–29.

48. Bouquet to Stephen, May 26, 1759, Stanwix: Orders for the Communication, May 31, 1759, Bouquet to Mercer, June 1, 1759, ibid., 328, 349, 358.

49. Croghan to Bouquet, July 11, 1759, Mercer to Bouquet, July 11, 1759, ibid., 398–99; Stephen to Stanwix, July 7, 1759, Gratz Collection, HSP; Sipe, *Fort Ligonier*, 129–35; Samuel Niles, "The Wars of New England with the French and Indians in the Several Parts of the Country," *Collections of the Massachusetts Historical Society*, 4th ser., 5 (1861): July 6 1759, 515.

50. Stephen to Richard Henry Lee, Aug. 26, 1759, Lee Family Papers, micro. ed., VSL.

CHAPTER FIVE

1. Stephen to Stanwix, [ca. July 25, 1759], *HBP*, 3:454; Hunter, *Forts*, 163–66.
2. Stephen to Richard Henry Lee, Aug. 26, 1759, Lee Family Papers, micro. ed., VSL.
3. Stanwix to Bouquet, Sept. 2, 1759, Bouquet to Stephen. Sept. 11, 1759, Armstrong to Bouquet, Sept. 14, Sept. 18, 1759, Bouquet to Stanwix, Sept. 16, 1759, Horatio Gates to Bouquet, Sept. 24, 1759, *HBP*, 4:26, 73–74, 94, 120, 109, 138.
4. Armstrong to Bouquet, Oct. 29, 1759, ibid., 277.
5. Armstrong to Bouquet, Sept. 14, 1759, Stephen to Bouquet, Sept. 16, 1759, ibid., 94, 114.
6. Armstrong to Bouquet, Sept. 23, 1759, ibid., 136.
7. Fauquier to Stephen, Oct. 24, 1759, George Reese, ed., *The Official Papers of Francis Fauquier, Lieutenant Governor of Virginia* (3 vols., Charlottesville, 1980–83), 1:256; Morton, *Colonial Virginia*, 2:714.
8. Stotz, "Defense in the Wilderness," 110–13.
9. Anthony F. C. Wallace, *King of the Delawares: Teedyuscung, 1700–1763* (Philadelphia, 1949), 231–32, 235.
10. Stephen to Fauquier, Oct. 29, 1759, Reese, *Papers of Fauquier*, 1:258; [John Mercer] to Fauquier, [ca. July–Oct. 1759], Lois Mulkearn, ed., *George Mercer Papers* (Pittsburgh, 1954), 93–94.
11. [John Mercer] to Fauquier, [ca. July–Oct. 1759], Mulkearn, *George Mercer Papers*, 612; Freeman, *Washington*, 3:38–39.
12. Stephen to Richard Henry Lee, Feb. 24, 1760, Lee Family Papers, micro. ed., VSL.
13. George Mercer to Washington, Feb. 17, 1760, Hamilton, *Letters to Washington*, 3:174–75.
14. Donald Jackson and Dorothy Twohig, eds., *The Diaries of George Washington* (5 vols., Charlottesville, 1976–79), 1:245n.; Freeman, *Washington*, 3:38–39.
15. Robert Stewart to Washington, April 14, 1760, Hamilton, *Letters to Washington*, 3:179.
16. Stephen's petition to Fauquier, n.d. [ca. 1760], ASP-LC. Stephen was a plaintiff in a suit against William Williams, which was put in abatement (Frederick County Order Book, no. 9, Aug. 7, 1760, 126, VSL).
17. Stephen to Richard Henry Lee, Sept. 1, 1760, Lee Family Papers, micro. ed., VSL.
18. Monckton to Bouquet, Nov. 13, 1760, *HBP*, 5:106; Hening, *Statutes*, 7: May 1760, 357–58.
19. Robert Stewart to Washington, June 3, 1760, Hamilton, *Letters to Washington*, 3:184; Reese, *Papers of Fauquier*, 1:374n.
20. Fauquier to Monckton, June 12, 1760, Reese, *Papers of Fauquier*, 1:374.
21. Thomas Caton to Stephen, Aug. 28, 1760, ASP-LC; Monckton to Amherst, July 30, 1760, Public Record Office, WO 34/35, micro. VSL; Richard Mather to Bouquet, Aug. 23, 1760, *HBP*, 4:699–700; William Byrd to [Monckton], June 29, 1760, Tinling, *Correspondence of Byrds*, 2:694.
22. Stephen to [George] Gordon, May 20, 1760, ASP-LC.

23. Monckton to Bouquet, Oct. 30, *HBP*, 4:89 and n. (concerning Fauquier to Monckton, Oct. 17, 1760).
24. Monckton to Bouquet, Nov. 13, 1760, Bouquet to Robert Stewart, Nov. 28, 1760, Bouquet to Monckton, Nov. 29, 1760, Jan. 14, 1761, ibid., 106, 131, 134, 246; Hillman, *Executive Journals*, 6: Oct. 30, 1760, 174.
25. Fauquier to Byrd, Feb. 16, 1761, Tinling, *Correspondence of Byrds*, 2:712; Stephen to Bouquet, April 1, 1761, *HBP*, 5:387.
26. Stephen to Bouquet, Feb. 21, April 1, May 12, 1761, Bouquet to Stephen, April 12, 1761, *HBP*, 5:304–5, 386–87, 476, 402–3. For Stephen's problem with a neighbor whose cattle trampled on Stephen's crops on farmland that Stephen had bought in 1760, see Stephen to ——, March 14, 1761, Stephen Papers, Maryland Historical Society. In fall 1761 three of Stephen's servants (two of them convict indentures) absconded; see James Livingston to Bouquet, Sept. 2, 1761, *HBP*, 5:729.
27. Washington to Capt. Van Swearingen, May 15, 1761, *F-WW*, 2:358; Jackson and Twohig, *Diaries of Washington*, 1:289n.; Freeman, *Washington*, 3:55.
28. Robert Stewart to Washington, Feb. 13, 1761, Hamilton, *Letters to Washington*, 3:201–2.
29. Robert Stewart to Washington, March 12, 1761, ibid., 204.
30. Washington to Capt. Van Swearingen, May 15, 1761, *F-WW*, 2:359.
31. *JHB*, March 1, 1761, quoted in Garland R. Quarles, *George Washington and Winchester, Virginia, 1748–1758, Winchester-Frederick County Historical Society Papers* 8 (1974): 43.
32. Poll taken at the election of burgesses, Frederick County, May 18, 1761, Clark, *Colonial Soldiers*, 546–56.
33. Hamilton, *Letters to Washington*, 3:217n.; Martha W. McCartney, "History of Fort Chiswell, Wythe County, Virginia," typescript, 1976, 12, VSL; F. B. Kegley, *Kegley's Virginia Frontier: The Beginning of the Southwest, the Roanoke in Colonial Days, 1740–83* (Roanoke, Va., 1938), 266.
34. Governor and Council Minute, June 20, 1761, Tinling, *Correspondence of Byrds*, 2:731.
35. Governor and Council Minute, June 23, 1761, Fauquier to Byrd, July 1, 1761, Byrd to [Amherst], July 1, 1761, ibid., 736, 739, 742; Stephen to Bouquet, May 26, 1761, *HBP*, 5:509; Hillman, *Executive Journals*, 6: June 10, 1761 (concerning letter from Stephen), 194–95. As Byrd reported on the stationing of Virginia troops, June 6: Staunton, 355; Fort Fauquier, 54; Fort Lewis, 54; Fort Chiswell, 145; western quarter, 29; Blackwater, 75; Winchester, 15; furlough, 23—688 fit for duty, the rest sick or deserted (Kegley, *Virginia Frontier*, 62).
36. Adam Hoops to Bouquet, July 20, 1761, *HBP*, 5:641; Robert Stewart to Washington, July 7, 1761, Hamilton, *Letters to Washington*, 3:218–19.
37. Stephen to Amherst, Oct. 5, 1761, Public Record Office, WO 34/37, micro. VSL; Byrd to Amherst, Aug. 1, Sept. 7, 1761, Tinling, *Correspondence of Byrds*, 2:748, 754; Stephen to Fauquier, Sept. 7, 1761, Reese, *Papers of Fauquier*, 2:569; Hillman, *Executive Journals*, 6: Oct. 17, 1761, 197; Kegley, *Virginia Frontier*, 63–65, 69. As of Oct. 9, 1761, the Virginia regiment had 740 men in the field: 540 at Great Island; 87, Fort Attakullakulla; 90, Fort Chiswell; 13, Fort Fauquier; and 10, Fort Lewis.

38. Stephen to Fauquier, Sept. 7, 1761 [copy], Public Record Office, WO 34/37, micro. VSL; David Corkran, *The Cherokee Frontier: Conflict and Survival, 1740–62* (Norman, Okla., 1962), 249–63.

39. Stephen to Charles Lee, June 4, 1789, Gratz Collection, HSP; Stephen to Amherst, Oct. 5, 1761, Public Record Office, WO 34/37, micro. VSL; Hillman, *Executive Journals*, 6: Oct. 26, 1761, 199.

40. Stephen to Amherst, Oct. 24, 1761, Public Record Office, WO 34/37, micro. VSL.

41. Col. Stephens Speech to the King & Governor Warriors . . . , Nov. 20, 1761, ibid., 34/40; Stephen to Charles Lee, June 4, 1789, Gratz Collection, HSP; Fauquier to Amherst, Jan. 8, 1762, to Board of Trade, April 16, 1762, Reese, *Papers of Fauquier*, 2:652, 719; *JHB* (1761–65), Nov. 9, 1761, 18; Hillman, *Executive Journals*, 6: Dec. 10, 1761, 678; Samuel C. Williams, ed., *Lieut. Henry Timberlake's Memoirs, 1756–65* (1765; Johnson City, Tenn., 1927), 38–39; Alden, *John Stuart*, 132; Corkran, *Cherokee Frontier*, 264–66.

42. Mary B. and F. B. Kegley, *Early Adventures on the Western Waters* (2 vols., Orange, Va., 1980), 1:64; Corkran, *Cherokee Frontier*, 266–67. The Carolina treaty with the Cherokees is printed in Reese, *Papers of Fauquier*, 2:685–88.

43. Hillman, *Executive Journals*, 6: April 21, 1762, 213; Henry T. Malone, *Cherokees of the Old South* (Athens, Ga., 1956), 4; Alden, *John Stuart*, 132–33. At the end of Nov. 1761, the troops at Great Island: Virginia, 744; North Carolina, 408 (including 52 Tuscaroras)—total, 1,152 (A General Return of the Troops Commanded by Col. Adam Stephen, Nov. 28, 1761, Reese, *Papers of Fauquier*, 2:654.)

44. Fauquier to Stephen, Jan. 25, 1762, Stephen to Fauquier, Jan. 30, 1762, Reese, *Papers of Fauquier*, 2:668, 670; *JHB* (1761–65), Jan. 2, 1762, 33.

45. Fauquier to Stephen, Jan. 25, 1762, Reese, *Papers of Fauquier*, 2:668.

46. Kegley and Kegley, *Adventures*, 1:64.

47. Stephen to Charles Lee, June 4, 1789, Gratz Collection, HSP; "Virginia Council Journals," *VMHB* 32 (1924): 397.

48. Fauquier to Board of Trade, Feb. 24, 1762, Reese, *Papers of Fauquier*, 2:692; Alden, *John Stuart*, 134–36; Malone, *Cherokees*, 8, 202n.; Mark M. Boatner, *Encyclopedia of the American Revolution* (New York, 1966), 944, 1068–69.

49. Amherst to Stephen, March 2, June 5, 1762, Public Record Office, WO 34/38, micro. VSL.

50. Fauquier to Stephen, [Feb. 2, 1762], Reese, *Papers of Fauquier*, 2:671.

51. Hening, *Statutes*, Jan. 1762, 7:492–93; Hillman, *Executive Journals*, 6: March 11, 1762, 209 (Stephen was at Fort Lewis, Jan. 30, 1762, as Council noted a letter from him of that date); Angus McDonald to Bouquet, April 1, 1762, Stevens and Kent, *Bouquet Papers*, mimeographed, no. 21648, pt. 1.

52. Fauquier to Amherst, April 7, 1762, Reese, *Papers of Fauquier*, 2:709.

53. Washington to John Augustine Washington, May 14, 1755, *A-WP*, 4:278.

54. Amherst to Fauquier, Nov. 6, 1763, Reese, *Papers of Fauquier*, 2:1042 and n.; Adam Hoops to Stephen, April 12, 1762, ASP-LC.

55. Robert Stewart to Washington, Feb. 26, 1762, Hamilton, *Letters to Washington*, 3:234.

56. Recruiting Orders to Capt. Fleming, n.d. [1762], William Fleming Papers, Washington and Lee University Library.

57. Amherst to Stephen, June 5, 1762, Public Record Office, WO 34/40, micro. VSL; Stephen to Bouquet, May 21, June 29, 1762, Stevens and Kent, *Bouquet Papers*, mimeographed, no. 21648, pt. 1; Amherst to Fauquier, July 8, 1762, Reese, *Papers of Fauquier*, 2:767–68. Actually 177 men departed.
58. Amherst to Stephen, July 8, 1762, Public Record Office, WO 34/93, micro. VSL.
59. Stephen to Amherst, July 9, 1762, ibid., 34/91.
60. Stephen to Amherst, Aug. 6 (includes "A General Return of the Virginia Regiment commanded by Colo. Adam Stephen"), Aug. 12, 1762, ibid.
61. Hillman, *Executive Journals*, 6: Dec. 7, 1762, 242; Titus, "Soldiers When They Choose," 240. In Oct. 1762 Gov. Fauquier confirmed to Stephen authority to hold courts-martial and to "put in Execution all the Powers and Authorities mentioned in the Act of Assembly against Mutiny and Desertion, by punishing all Offenders" (Fauquier to Stephen, Oct. 3, 1762, ASP-LC).
62. *JHB* (1761–65), Dec. 22, 1762, 162–63. With the disbandment, Stephen received £207.18.2. in pay (Alexander Boyd to Stephen, Dec. 31, 1762, Receipt, BR Box [4], Huntington Library).
63. Virginia State Land Office, Northern Neck Grants, book K, July 3, 1762, and book M, Feb. 5, 1763, VSL.
64. Memorial of George Washington and Others, enclosed in Fauquier to Board of Trade, July 10, 1762, Reese, *Papers of Fauquier*, 2:774–75.
65. Petition of Sundry Inhabitants of Great Britain, Virginia, and Maryland, Dec. 1768, PCC; Jackson and Twohig, *Diaries of Washington*, 2:311n.; Louis W. Potts, *Arthur Lee: A Virtuous Revolutionary* (Baton Rouge, La., 1981), 57; Kenneth P. Bailey, *The Ohio Company of Virginia and the Westward Movement, 1748–92* (Glendale, Calif., 1939), 229–30; Freeman, *Washington*, 3:96n., 245–46. The articles of the Mississippi Company are printed in Archer B. Hulbert, ed., "Washington's 'Tour of the Ohio' and Articles of the Mississippi Company," *Ohio Archaeological and Historical Quarterly* 17 (1908): 436–38.

CHAPTER SIX

1. See Howard H. Peckham, *Pontiac and the Indian Uprising* (1947; rept. Chicago, 1961), 212–17; Cyrus Cort, *Col. Henry Bouquet and his Campaigns* (Lancaster, Pa., 1883), 22; Niles Anderson, "Bushy Run: Decisive Battle in the Wilderness: Pennsylvania and the Indian Rebellion of 1763," *WPHM* 46 (1963): 214–15.
2. Amherst to Fauquier, June 30, 1763, Reese, *Papers of Fauquier*, 2:983; Hillman, *Executive Journals*, 6: Aug. 1, 1763, 267; Allan W. Eckert, *The Conquerors: A Narrative* (Boston, 1970), 444; Rice, *Allegheny Frontier*, 58.
3. William Greene to Stephen, July 28, 1763, ASP-LC.
4. Washington to Robert Stewart, Aug. 13, 1763, *F-WW*, 2:403.
5. Ourry to Amherst, Aug. 17, 1763, Public Record Office, WO 34/95, micro. VSL; James Livingston to Bouquet, June 27, June 29, 1763, Stevens and Kent, *Bouquet Papers*, mimeographed, no. 21649, pt. 1; Nellie Norkus, "Francis Fauquier, Lieutenant-Governor of Virginia, 1758–1768" (Ph.D. diss., University of Pittsburgh, 1954), 296–97.

6. Amherst to Bouquet, Aug. 25, 1763, to Stephen, Aug. 25, 1763, Public Record Office, WO 34/41, 34/97, micro. VSL.

7. J. Clarence Webster, ed., *The Journal of Jeffery Amherst, 1758–1763* (Toronto, 1931), 316–19; Sewell E. Slick, *William Trent and the West* (Harrisburg, Pa., 1947), 123–24; Charles A. Hanna, *The Wilderness Trail* (2 vols., New York, 1911), 2:377; Peckham, *Pontiac,* 212–13.

8. Ourry to Bouquet, Aug. 27, 1763, and "Memorandum of Agreement," Stevens and Kent, *Bouquet Papers,* mimeographed, nos. 21642, 21649, pt. 2.

9. Ourry to Amherst, Sept. 6, Sept. 11, 1763, Public Record Office, WO 34/95, micro. VSL.

10. Fauquier to Stephen, Sept. 4, 1763, ASP-LC.

11. Hillman, *Executive Journals,* 6: Sept. 15, 1763, 269–70, concerning letters from Stephen and Andrew Lewis.

12. Joseph Martin to——, Sept. 23, 1763, Fort Young (Augusta County), VSL; Extract of letter . . . , Oct, 28, 1763, Draper Collection: Kings Mountain, 15DD4, State Historical Society of Wisconsin; Kegley, *Virginia Frontier,* 285–86.

13. E.g., Extract of a letter from Col. Adam Stephen to Henry Lee, Aug. 30, 1763, from *New York Gazette,* Oct. 3, 1763, in Parkman Collection, Massachusetts Historical Society.

14. Amherst to Fauquier, Aug. 29, 1763, to Stephen, Aug. 31, 1763, Public Record Office, WO 34/37, 34/41, micro. VSL; Hanna, *Wilderness Trail,* 2:383. Hanna thinks it was Stephen who originally proposed an expedition against the Ohio Indians.

15. Stephen to Bouquet, Sept. 15, 1763, Stevens and Kent, *Bouquet Papers,* mimeographed, no. 21649, pt. 1.

16. Bouquet to Stephen, Sept. 30, 1763, ibid., pt. 2.

17. Bouquet to Amherst, Sept. 30, 1763, quoted in Norkus, "Fauquier," 302.

18. Ibid., 302–3; Stephen to Bouquet, Oct. 10, Nov. 7, 1763, Stevens and Kent, *Bouquet Papers,* mimeographed, no. 21649.

19. Ourry to Amherst, Oct. 8, 1763, Stephen to Amherst, Oct. 12, 1763, Amherst to Maj. Allan Campbell, Oct. 27, 1763, Public Record Office, WO 34/95, 34/97, micro. VSL; Stephen to Bouquet, Oct. 10, 1763, Stevens and Kent, *Bouquet Papers,* mimeographed, no. 21649, pt. 2.

20. Amherst to Stephen, Oct. 27, 1763, Public Record Office, WO 34/97, micro. VSL; Stephen to Bouquet, Nov. 7, 1763, Stevens and Kent, *Bouquet Papers,* mimeographed, no. 21649, pt. 2; Hanna, *Wilderness Trail,* 383.

21. Bouquet to Stephen, May 5, 1763, Stephen to Bouquet, Nov. 7, 1763, Stevens and Kent, *Bouquet Papers,* mimeographed, nos. 21650, pt. 1, 21649, pt. 2; Norkus, "Fauquier," 299.

22. Stephen to Bouquet, April 16, 1764, Stevens and Kent, *Bouquet Papers,* mimeographed, no. 21650, pt. 1.

23. Bouquet to Stephen, May 5, 1764, ibid.

24. Fauquier to Bouquet, April 19, 1764, ibid.

25. James Livingston to Bouquet, June 5, 1764, ibid.

26. Ibid.

27. Bouquet to Stephen, July 5, 1764, ibid., pt. 2.

28. Thomas Rutherford to Bouquet, Aug. 2, 1764, ibid.

29. John Field to Bouquet, July 28, 1764, ibid.
30. Rutherford to Bouquet, Aug. 2, 1764, ibid.
31. [Stephen to the Militia], [Aug. 8, 1764], ibid.
32. Depositions: Capt. Jacquett Morgan, Lt. James Chew, Sgt. Jacob Pricket, Richard Hogland, ibid.
33. Fauquier to Bouquet, Aug. 17, 1764, ibid.
34. Stephen to Bouquet, Aug. 23, 1764, ibid.
35. Fauquier to Bouquet, Sept. 5, Sept. 13, 1764, ibid.
36. Bouquet to Gage, Aug. 10, 1764, Gage to Bouquet, Aug. 18, Aug. 25, 1764, ibid., nos. 21637, 21638.
37. Gage to Halifax, Nov. 9, Dec. 13, 1764, Clarence E. Carter, ed., *The Correspondence of General Thomas Gage with the Secretaries of State, 1763–1775* (2 vols., New Haven, 1931–33), 1:43, 45–46; Cort, *Bouquet*, 61–62; Peckham, *Pontiac*, 255, 262–63; Reese, *Papers of Fauquier*, 3:1233n.
38. Hillman, *Executive Journals*, 6: Nov. 6, 1764, 27n.; Reese, *Papers of Fauquier*, 3:1196n.; Katherine B. Greene, *Winchester, Virginia and Its Beginnings, 1743–1814* (Strasburg, Va., 1926), 186. Stephen asked Capt. James Wood to appear at the Virginia Council with all the orders received while Wood was in the service.
39. Thomas Barnsley to Bouquet, Nov. 11, 1761, Thomas Rutherford to Thomas Barnsley, Nov. 14, 1764, Stevens and Kent, *Bouquet Papers*, mimeographed, no. 21651; *JHB* (1761–65), Nov. 5, 1764.
40. Fauquier to Bouquet, Dec. 15, 1764, Stevens and Kent, *Bouquet Papers*, mimeographed, no. 21651; *JHB* (1761–65), Nov. 5, Dec. 15, 1764, 25, 298. The House of Burgesses voted to pay the expenses for witnesses giving depositions at Winchester and elsewhere—22 persons; paid 4,823 pounds of tobacco (*JHB* [1761–65], May 15, 1765, and [1766–69], March 17, 1767, 84). Rutherford was allowed £41 for his expenses (H. R. McIlwaine, ed., *Legislative Journals of the Council of Virginia* [3 vols, Richmond, 1918–19], 3: Dec. 9, 1766, 1334).
41. Rutherford to Bouquet, Jan. 5, 1765, Stevens and Kent, *Bouquet Papers*, mimeographed, no. 21651.
42. Mary V. Mish, "General Adam Stephen and His Home," typescript, Feb. 17, 1979, General Adam Stephen Memorial Association; Lyman L. Chalkley, ed., *Chronicles of the Scotch-Irish Settlement in Virginia: Extracted from the Original Court Records of Augusta County, 1745–1800* (3 vols., 1912; rept. Baltimore, 1965), 3:409, 420.
43. Virginia State Land Office, Northern Neck Grants, book M, June 8, 1765, 389, and book P, Feb. 7, 1771, 8, VSL; Brown, *Virginia Baron*, 158.
44. Land Office Warrants, French and Indian War, March 20, 1781, Warrants nos. 732–37, VSL; Peter Hog to Washington, Dec. 11, 1773, Hamilton, *Letters to Washington*, 3:279; Toner, *Journal of Washington*, Appendix: French and Indian War Lands, 208–9; Roy Cook, *Washington's Western Lands* (Strasburg, Va., 1930), 37 and passim; Henderson, "Thomas Walker," 106–9; Kegley and Kegley, *Adventures*, 1:72; Chalkley, *Chronicles*, 2:49, 54, 251; Freeman, *Washington*, 2:215, 238–39, 299–301, 333.
45. "Merchants and Mills—from the Letterbooks of Robert Carter of Nominy, Westmoreland County [ca. 1770–71]," *WMQ*, 1st. ser., 11 (1903): 246; Thomas M. Preisser, "Eighteenth-Century Alexandria, Virginia, before the Revolu-

tion, 1749–76" (Ph.D. diss., College of William and Mary, 1977), 129–33; Robert D. Mitchell, *Commercialism and Frontier: Perspectives on the Early Shenandoah Valley* (Charlottesville, Va., 1977), 173, 200; Gaspare J. Saladino, "The Maryland and Virginia Wheat Trade from Its Beginnings to the American Revolution" (M.A. thesis, University of Wisconsin, 1960), 17–19, 34.

46. E.g., Stephen to Moses Strecker, Aug. 10, 1764, C. D. B. Dandridge MSS, Duke University Library.

47. Stephen to Hugh Mercer, Jan. 31, Aug. 10, 1765, and Stephen's accounts with Hugh Mercer, ca. 1761–66, University of Pittsburgh Library; Blanton, *Medicine in Virginia in the Eighteenth Century*, 222. See Miles S. Malone, "Falmouth and the Shenandoah Trade before the Revolution," *American Historical Review* 40 (1935): 693–703, for development of trade between Frederick County and Falmouth.

48. Arrest Warrant—"To the Sheriff of Frederick County," May 6, 1767, *Stewart v. Stephen*, May 6, 1767, Gen. Court S/Edmund Pendleton, and Memorandum, Sept. 28, 1767, S/John Greenfield, Miscellaneous Adam Stephen Papers, University of Pittsburgh Library.

49. Stephen to William David Brown, July 23, 176[9?], ibid.

50. Brown, *Virginia Baron*, 159, 170, 179.

51. Ibid., 162–63, 228n.; Jackson and Twohig, *Diaries of Washington*, vols. 1, 3; Stan Cohen, *Historic Springs of the Virginias: A Pictorial History* (Charleston, W.Va., 1981), 132–33; Freeman, *Washington*, 3:186–87.

52. Jackson and Twohig, *Diaries of Washington*, 2: Aug. 28, 1769, 177.

53. Ibid., Oct. 6 and 15, 1770, 286, 290, 28on.

54. *Pennsylvania Gazette*, May 19, 1768. On Alexander Stephen, see also Adam Stephen to Washington, Dec. 23, 1755, *A-WP*, 2:226–27, 228n.

55. Frederick County Will Book, no. 3, Aug. 3, 1768, 452–53, VSL; Alexander White to ——, June 17, 1768, ASP-LC.

56. Everard K. Meade, *Frederick Parish, Virginia, 1744–80* (Winchester, 1947), 55; Van Metre, "Adam Stephen—The Man," 16.

57. Frederick County Order Book, no. 15, Feb. 5, 1771, 5, and nos. 14 and 15, passim, VSL; William J. Barnhart, "Old Norborne Parish," *Magazine of the Jefferson County Historical Society* 45 (Dec. 1979): 13–19; Bushong, *Jefferson County* 39; Lorraine Minghini and Thomas E. Van Metre, *History of Trinity Episcopal Church and Norborne Parish, Martinsburg, Berkeley County, West Virginia, 1771–1956* (n.p., 1956), 46, 50; Mignon Larche, *Pioneers of the Bullskin: The Stephenson Story* (Eureka Springs, Ark., 1960), 77.

58. H. R. McIlwaine, comp., "Justices of the Peace of Colonial Virginia, 1757–75," *Bulletin of the VSL* 15, nos. 2, 3 (April, July 1921): 80, 82, 92, 95, 114, 118–19; Charles S. Sydnor, *American Revolutionaries in the Making* (New York, 1965; orig. pub. 1952 as *Gentlemen Freeholders*), 78–79.

59. John W. Wayland, ed., *Hopewell Friends History, 1734–1934, Frederick County, Virginia, Records* (Strasburg, Va., 1936), Jan. 4, 1789. Various documents signed by Stephen as justice of the peace are in the Ohio Company Papers, University of Pittsburgh Library.

60. *JHB* (1766–69), Dec. 15, 1766, 71.

61. James Graham, *The Life of General Daniel Morgan* (New York, 1856), 42–43.

62. *JHB* (1766–69), March 23, 1767, Nov. 23, 1769, 91, 286; Freeman H. Hart, *The Valley of Virginia in the American Revolution* (Chapel Hill, N.C., 1942), 15.

63. Hillman, *Executive Journals*, 6: Aug. 8, 1769, 326–27; Stephen to Lord Botetourt, July 29, 1769, Botetourt to Earl of Hillsborough, Aug. 5, 1769, Dianne J. McGaan, ed., "The Official Letters of Norborne Berkeley, Baron de Botetourt, Governor of Virginia, 1768–70" (M.A. thesis, College of William and Mary, 1971), 326–27.

64. Extracts of letters from Stephen to Botetourt, Sept. 14, Sept. 27, 1769, Botetourt to Stephen, Sept. 27, Oct. 19, 1769, and the Speech of a Noted Indian, Aug. 10, 1769, McGann, "Official Letters of Botetourt," 148–53.

65. Hillman, *Executive Journals*, 6: Oct. 3, 1769, 327–28.

66. Extract of a letter from Botetourt to Stephen, Oct. 19, 1769, and Proclamation of Lord Botetourt, McGaan, "Official Letters of Botetourt," 153–55.

67. Hillman, *Executive Journals*, 6: Oct. 31, 1769, concerning letter from Stephen, Oct. 22, 1769.

CHAPTER SEVEN

1. Ann Henshaw Gardiner Papers: Legal Papers, 1772, Duke University Library; Berkeley County Order Book, (1772–73), pt. 1 and 2, May 19, 1772, CJCLS; Hillman, *Executive Journals*, 6: April 16, 1772, 457; J. E. Norris, *History of the Lower Shenandoah Valley Counties of Frederick, Berkeley, Jefferson, and Clarke* (1890; rept. Berryville, Va., 1972), 222–24; Martha W. Hiden, *How Justice Grew—Virginia Counties: An Abstract of Their Formation* (Williamsburg, 1957), 30, 34–37; Mabel H. and Ann H. Gardiner, *Chronicles of Old Berkeley: A Narrative History of a Virginia County from Its Beginnings to 1926* (Durham, N.C., 1938), 16. Signing Stephen's bond as sheriff were Stephen, George Cunningham, Archibald Shearer, George Stogdon, George Briscoe, Daniel Morgan, and Henry Newkirk. The Berkeley County population in 1775 was 10,000 whites and 2,000 slaves; according to the 1790 census, it was 19,713 (Miles S. Malone, "The Distribution of Population on the Virginia Frontier in 1775," vol. 1, "The Lower Shenandoah Valley" [Ph.D. diss., Princeton University, 1935], 67).

2. Hite to Pinkney, *Virginia Gazette* (Pinkney), July 6, 1775; Hugh F. Rankin, *Criminal Trial Proceedings in the General Court of Colonial Virginia* (Charlottesville, 1965), 59–60; Sydnor, *American Revolutionaries*, 69, 78; John A. Washington, "Samuel Washington," *Magazine of the Jefferson County Historical Society* 36 (1970): 20.

3. William Couper, *History of the Shenandoah Valley* (2 vols., New York, 1952), 2:1093; "Historic Buildings along the Tuscarora Creek," *Berkeley Journal* 4 (1975): 15; Gardiner and Gardiner, *Chronicles of Old Berkeley*, 20; Norris, *Lower Shenandoah Valley*, 229–31.

4. Berkeley County Minute Book, (1772–78), Nov. 19, 1772, Jan. 19, 1773, 41, 66, and Berkeley County Order Book, (1772–73), Nov. 19, 1772, 140, CJCLS; "Plotted by . . . Robert Cockburn," Feb. 24, 1775, from Berkeley County Records, in Gardiner and Gardiner, *Chronicles of Old Berkeley*, 22–23; William T. Doherty, *Berkeley County, U.S.A.: A Bicentennial History of a Virginia and West Virginia County, 1772–1972* (Parsons, W.Va., 1972), 28; Willis F. Evans, *History of Berkeley County, West Virginia* (Martinsburg, 1928), 62.

5. Mish, "General Adam Stephen and His Home," 1; Mary V. Mish, "General

Adam Stephen, Founder of Martinsburg, West Virginia," *West Virginia History* 22 (1961): 69; F. B. Voegele, "Washington's Chairs and Adam Stephen," *Autograph Collectors' Journal* 4 (1952): 29.

6. Max W. Grove, *Reconstructed Census, 1774–1810: Berkeley County, Virginia* (Colesville, Md., 1970), 13; Rent Roll of Berkeley County for 1774 . . . 1781, in Danske Dandridge, *Historic Shepherdstown* (Charlottesville, Va., 1910), 71–73; Kegley and Kegley, *Adventures*, 71. Stephen had 5,381 acres; Charles Lee, 2,081; Samuel Washington, 4,469; Horatio Gates, 659; Robert Stephen, 325.

7. Commission [for court of oyer and terminer], April 14, 1773, Berkeley County MSS, VHS; Rankin, *Criminal Trial Proceedings*, 45–46; Rhys Isaac, *The Transformation of Virginia, 1740–90* (Chapel Hill, N.C., 1982), 92.

8. Dandridge, *Shepherdstown*, 74.

9. Berkeley County Order Book, (1772–73), Aug. 18, 1772, 32, CJCLS.

10. Berkeley County Deed Book, (1774–76), April 16, 1761, proved at court March 17, 1774, 10, CJCLS; Jacob Hite to Stephen, 1771, ASP-LC; Mildred B. Whitmire, "A Man and His Land: The Story of Jacob and Francis Madison Hite and the Cherokees," *Magazine of the Jefferson County Historical Society* 44 (1978): 37–38.

11. Hillman, *Executive Journals*, 6: April 14, 1773, 522; Bushong, *Jefferson County*, 23.

12. Berkeley County Minute Book, (1772–78), May 7, 1774, 187–88, CJCLS; Jacob Hite to Gates, May 2, 1774 (from Emmet Collection, NYPL) and Gates to Benjamin Waller, March 12, 1775, Gates Papers, NYHS micro. ed.; Depositions of Alexander Drumgold, April 16, 1774, and David Gilkey, April 14, 1774, James Mercer to Stephen, April 19, May 17, 1774, [item,] April 30, 1774, S/M. Morgan, Petition to Dunmore, May 1774, [General Court?] order to Sheriff of Berkeley County (concerning *Hunter* v. *Hite*), May 20, 1774, ASP-LC; Hart, *Valley*, 56–58.

13. Stephen to Gates, Nov. 24, 1772, Gates Papers, NYHS micro. ed.

14. Stephen to Gates, Dec. 20, 1772, ibid.

15. Berkeley County Deed Book, (1772), March 16, 1773, CJCLS; Allen K. McIntosh, "Traveller's Rest," *Magazine of the Jefferson County Historical Society* 37 (1971): 13–14. For discussion of Gates's arrival and settling in America, see Paul D. Nelson, *General Horatio Gates* (Baton Rouge, La., 1976), 29–35, and Samuel W. Patterson, *Horatio Gates: Defender of American Liberties* (New York, 1941), 38–39. See also "General Horatio Gates House," *Magazine of the Jefferson County Historical Society* 30 (1964): 36–37.

16. "General Charles Lee House," *Magazine of the Jefferson County Historical Society* 30 (1964), 38–39; Samuel W. Patterson, *Knight Errant of Liberty: The Triumph and Tragedy of General Charles Lee* (New York, 1958), 27–28; John R. Alden, *General Charles Lee: Traitor or Patriot?* (Baton Rouge, La., 1951), 69, 296, 321n.; Whitmire, "A Man and His Land," 40–41; Boatner, *Encyclopedia*, 605.

17. Rice, *Allegheny Frontier*, 80–84. See Samuel Kercheval, *A History of the Valley of Virginia* (Strasburg, 1925), 111–13, for the various atrocities against the Indians.

18. Stephen to Gates, Aug. 20, 1774, Frederic R. Kirkland, ed., *Letters on the American Revolution in the Library of "Karolfred"* (2 vols., Philadelphia, 1941, and New York, 1952), 2:11; Nelson, *Gates*, 35–36.

19. Stephen to Gates, Aug. 24, 1774 (from Emmet Collection, NYPL), NYHS micro. ed.
20. Gates to Stephen, Aug. 26, 1774, ibid.
21. Stephen to Richard Henry Lee, Aug. 27, 1774, Richard H. Lee, ed., *Memoir of the Life of Richard Henry Lee and His Correspondence* (2 vols., Philadelphia, 1825), 2:207.
22. Nicholas B. Wainwright, ed., "Turmoil at Pittsburgh: Diary of Augustine Prevost, 1774," *PMHB* 85 (1961), 133, 137–39; Irene B. Brand, "Dunmore's War," *West Virginia History* 40 (1979): 37–38; William C. Pendleton, *History of Tazewell County and Southwest Virginia, 1748–1920* (Richmond, 1920), 307; Virgil A. Lewis, *History of the Battle of Point Pleasant* (Charleston, W.Va., 1909), 22–23; Thomas C. Miller and Hu Maxwell, *West Virginia and Its People* (3 vols., New York, 1913), 1:102.
23. William Fleming to Stephen, Oct. 8, 1774, Reuben G. Thwaites and Louise P. Kellogg, eds., *Documentary History of Dunmore's War, 1774* (Madison, Wis., 1905), 236; Miller and Maxwell, *West Virginia*, 1:106; Rice, *Allegheny Frontier*, 84–85.
24. E. O. Randall, "The Dunmore War," *Ohio Archaeological and Historical Society Publications* 11 (1903): 179; James A. James, *The Life of George Rogers Clark* (Chicago, 1928), 19.
25. *Virginia Gazette* (Pinkney), Oct. 13, 1774; Pendleton, *Tazewell County*, 316–17; Rice, *Allegheny Frontier*, 87; Lewis, *Point Pleasant*, 61.
26. William Fleming, Orderly Book, Oct. 8, 1774, Thwaites and Kellogg, eds., *Documentary History of Dunmore's War*, 340 and n.
27. Resolutions of Dunmore's Soldiers at Fort Gower, Nov. 5, 1774, Appendix B, Randall, "The Dunmore War," 196–97; also printed in Edward G. Williams, *Fort Pitt and the Revolution on the Western Frontier* (Pittsburgh, 1978), 38–39.
28. Stephen to Richard Henry Lee, Aug. 27, 1774, Lee, *Memoir of Richard Henry Lee*, 2:207–8, and also in Lee Family Papers, micro. ed., VSL.
29. Saladino, "The Maryland and Virginia Wheat Trade," 150–51; Continental Association, Oct. 20, 1774, in Jack P. Greene, ed., *Colonies to Nation, 1763–89: A Documentary History of the American Revolution* (New York, 1975), 245–50.
30. *RV*, 3:59n.; Charles R. Lingley, *The Transition in Virginia from Colony to Commonwealth* (New York, 1910), 97; Dandridge, *Shepherdstown*, 80.
31. Stephen to Richard Henry Lee, Feb. 1, 1775, Lee Family Papers micro. ed., VSL.
32. *Virginia Gazette* (Purdie and Dixon), Nov. 3, 1774; Cora Bacon-Foster, "Early Chapters in the Development of the Potomac Route to the West," *Records of the Columbia Historical Society* 15 (1912): 116–23; Hart, *Valley*, 154–56; Freeman, *Washington*, 3:290–92.
33. Stephen to Richard Henry Lee, Dec. 27, 1774, Lee Family Papers, micro. ed., VSL.
34. Stephen to Richard Henry Lee, Feb. 1, 1775, ibid.
35. Stephen to Richard Henry Lee, Feb. 17, 1774, Peter Force, ed., *American Archives* (ser. 4, 6 vols., and ser. 5, 3 vols., Washington, D.C., 1837–53), ser. 4, 1:1244.

CHAPTER EIGHT

1. For the record of the 2d Virginia convention, see *RV*, 2:334–38.
2. James Parker to Charles Steuart, April 6, 1775, Charles Steuart Papers, National Library of Scotland, micro. VSL; Terrance Mahan, "Virginia's Reaction to British Policy, 1763–76" (Ph.D. diss., University of Wisconsin, 1960), 295.
3. Don Higginbotham, *Daniel Morgan: Revolutionary Rifleman* (Chapel Hill, N.C., 1961), 20; Robert D. Meade, *Patrick Henry: Practical Revolutionary* (2 vols., Philadelphia, 1957, 1969), 2:44–53.
4. Dunmore's Proclamation, May 6, 1775, in Hillman, *Executive Journals*, 6: 665–66.
5. *JHB* (1773–76), June 14, 1775, 230; *Virginia Gazette* (Purdie), June 23, 1775.
6. Stephen to William Fleming, May 31, 1775, Emmet Collection, NYPL.
7. John R. Sellers, "The Virginia Continental Line, 1775–80" (Ph.D. diss., Tulane University, 1968), 6–8; Dandridge, *Shepherdstown*, 77–82; Barnhart, "Old Norborne Parish," 30; Freeman, *Washington*, 3:523n.
8. E.g., Berkeley County Deed Book, (1774–76), pertaining to sale of lots, July 4, 1774, Feb. 24, May 17, May 25, June 1, Aug. 15, Nov. 21, 1775, CJCLS.
9. *RV*, 3:59n.; Sydnor, *American Revolutionaries*, 21.
10. Advertisement of Requests and an Order, April 24, 1775, *RV:* 3:59n.
11. "Protest against a Scheme Alleged to Have been Laid in Berkeley County," June 7, 1775, *RV*, 3:191–93, also in "Virginia Legislative Papers," *VMHB* 13 (1906): 412–15.
12. Convention, June 14, 1775, *RV*, 3:202; Proceedings of the Berkeley County Committee, June 1775, "Virginia Legislative Papers," *VMHB* 13 (1906): 415.
13. Jacob Hite to Mr. [John] Pinkney, *Virginia Gazette* (Pinkney), July 6, 1775.
14. Stephen to John Dixon and William Hunter, ibid. (Dixon and Hunter), Sept. 30, 1775; Whitmire, "A Man and His Land," 42–43.
15. *RV*, 3:July 27, 1775, 350–55.
16. Ibid., 3:357n., 4:104n., 409n., 5:28n. Rutherford also succeeded Stephen as chairman of the Berkeley County committee.
17. Ibid., 3:July 19, 1775, 319, 324n.; Hening, *Statutes*, 9:9–35.
18. Benjamin Rush to John Adams, Feb. 12, 1812, Lyman H. Butterfield, ed., *Letters of Benjamin Rush* (2 vols., Princeton, N.J., 1951), 2:1120.
19. Thomas Walker, Andrew Lewis, Adam Stephen, and James Wood to Thomas Jefferson, Sept. 13, 1775, *JP*, 1:244–45; Rice, *Allegheny Frontier*, 90–91; Hanna, *Wilderness Trail*, 2:77–78; Williams, *Fort Pitt and the Revolution*, 66.
20. Hanna, *Wilderness Trail*, 2:80; Lewis, *Point Pleasant*, 64–65.
21. *The Journal of Nicholas Cresswell, 1774–77* (New York, 1924), Sept. 17, Sept. 24, Oct. 10, 1775, 75, 114–15, 124.
22. "Report of Indian Commissioners Including a Talk to Young Brothers, Chiefs, and Warriors on the Way," Sept. 12, 1775, *RV*, 4:98, 104n., also 3:328n. The complete proceedings of the Treaty of Fort Pitt are found in the "Diary of Thomas Walker," Sept. 10–Oct. 21, 1775, Reuben G. Thwaites and Louise P. Kellogg, eds., *The Revolution on the Upper Ohio, 1775–77* (1908; rept. Port Washington, N.Y., 1970), 25–127.
23. *Journal of Cresswell*, Oct. 10, 1775, 116–19; Williams, *Fort Pitt and the Revolution*, 58–59; Lewis, *Point Pleasant*, 65; "Diary of Walker," in Thwaites

and Kellogg, *Revolution on the Upper Ohio*, 89n., 91n.; Allan W. Eckert, *The Frontiersmen: A Narrative* (Boston, 1967), 19–20, 373. The Half-King of the Wyandots is not to be confused with the Senecan chief of the same name who aided Washington in 1753–54.

24. Virginia Indian Commissioners to Edmund Pendleton, n.d., *RV*, 4:250; "Diary of Walker," in Thwaites and Kellogg, *Revolution on the Upper Ohio*, 29–30, 92.

25. Stephen to Richard Henry Lee, Sept. 23, 1775, Lee, ed., *Memoir of Richard Henry Lee*, 2:211, also in Lee Family Papers, micro. ed., VSL.

26. Richard Henry Lee to Washington, Oct. 22, 1775, James C. Ballagh, ed., *The Letters of Richard Henry Lee* (2 vols., New York, 1911, 1914), 1:153.

27. Miller and Maxwell, *West Virginia*, 1:119.

28. "Diary of Walker," in Thwaites and Kellogg, *Revolution on the Upper Ohio*, 84.

29. E.g., see ibid., 85–86.

30. "At a Conference held with the Different Nations of Indians," Oct. 19, 1775, *RV*, 4:241; Williams, *Fort Pitt and the Revolution*, 59–60.

31. *Virginia Gazette* (Dixon and Hunter), Nov. 18, 1775; Miller and Maxwell, *West Virginia*, 1:119.

32. *Virginia Gazette* (Pinkney), Jan. 6, Jan. 13, 1776; Force, ed., *American Archives*, ser. 4, 4:119–20; *RV*, 5: Convention, Jan. 12, 1776, 390; Sellers, "Virginia Continental Line," 50–58.

33. *RV*, 6: Convention, Feb. 19, 1776, 113–14; Edmund Pendleton to Charles Scott, Feb. 18, 1776, David J. Mays, ed., *The Letters and Papers of Edmund Pendleton, 1734–1803* (2 vols., Charlottesville, 1967), 1:152; Stephen to Richard Henry Lee, Feb. 4, 1776, Lee Family Papers, micro. ed., VSL.

34. *JCC*, 4: Feb. 13, 1776, 132.

CHAPTER NINE

1. Brent Tarter, ed., "The Orderly Book of the Second Virginia Regiment, Sept. 27–April 15, 1776," *VMHB* 85 (1977): April 5, 1776, 331; Orderly Book [4th Regiment], May 13–Sept. 20, 1776, Peter Force Collection, LC; Charles Lee to Edmund Pendleton, June 1, June 29, 1776, *RV*, 7:327, 660–61, also 248n.; Alden, *Lee*, 119.

2. Charles Lee to John Pate, April 21, 1776, *RV*, 6:431; Orderly Book [4th Regiment], May 24, June 9, June 15, Aug. 25, 1776, Peter Force Collection, LC; "Orderly Book of the Company of Captain George Stubblefield, 1776," *Collections of the VHS*, n.s., 6 (1887): May 5, May 24, 1776, 168, 175; Sellers, "Virginia Continental Line," 122.

3. Alf J. Mapp, Jr., "The 'Pirate' Peer: Lord Dunmore's Operation in the Chesapeake Bay," in Ernest M. Eller, ed., *Chesapeake Bay in the American Revolution* (Centreville, Md., 1981), 64, 90–91; Sellers, "Virginia Continental Line," 118–21, 126.

4. Stephen to Edmund Pendleton, May 25, 1776, D. R. Anderson, ed., "The Letters of Col. William Woodford, Col. Robert Howe, and Gen. Charles Lee to Edmund Pendleton," *Richmond College Historical Papers* 1 (Richmond, 1915): 161–63.

5. Stephen to Dudley Digges, May 27, 1776, Huntington Library.

6. Gen. Andrew Lewis to Charles Lee, June 12, 1776, *The Lee Papers, NYHS Collections* (vols. 4–7, New York, 1871–74), 5:63.
7. Washington to Stephen, July 20, 1776, *F-WW,* 5:312–13.
8. John Page to Charles Lee, July 7, July 12, VSL; Stephen to Charles Lee, July 13, 1776, Harvard University Library; David Griffith to Leven Powell, July 8, 1776, "Correspondence of Leven Powell," *John P. Branch Historical Papers of Randolph-Macon College* 1 (1901): 42; *Virginia Gazette* (Purdie), July 12, 1776; Mrs. Catesby W. Stewart, *The Life of Brigadier General William Woodford of the American Revolution* (2 vols., Richmond, 1973), 688–91; Hart, *Valley,* 91; Sellers, "Virginia Continental Line," 131–32. See letters and accounts pertaining to the encounter at Gwynn's Island, Force, *American Archives,* ser. 5, 1:150–52.
9. "Narrative of Captain Andrew Snape Hamond," William J. Morgan et al., eds., *Naval Documents of the American Revolution* (9 vols. to date, Washington, D.C., 1964—), 6: Aug. 6, 1776, 174; Adele Hast, *Loyalism in Revolutionary Virginia: The Norfolk Area and the Eastern Shore* (Ann Arbor, Mich., 1982), 65.
10. Stephen to Charles Lee, July 13, 1776, Harvard University Library, a slightly different copy from the published version in *Lee Papers, NYHS Collections,* 5:136–39.
11. John Page to the North Carolina Council of Safety, July 26, 1776, H. R. McIlwaine, ed., *Official Letters of the Governors of the State of Virginia* (3 vols., Richmond, 1926–29), 1:16–17.
12. Stephen to Jefferson, July 29, 1776, *JP,* 1:480–82.
13. Journal of the Virginia Navy Board, Aug. 12, Oct. 19, 1776, Morgan et al., *Naval Documents,* 6:199, 1334.
14. John Page to Charles Lee, Aug. 13, 1776, Andrew Lewis to Charles Lee, Aug. 13, 1776, *Lee Papers, NYHS Collections,* 5:216.
15. A. S. Hamond to Hans Stanley, Sept. 24, 1776, Naval Papers of Sir Andrew Snape Hamond, micro. ed., University of Virginia Library; "Narrative of Hamond," Aug. 6, 1776, Morgan et al., *Naval Documents,* 6:174.
16. "Narrative of Hamond," Aug. 6, Aug. 13, 1776, Morgan et al., *Naval Documents,* 6:173–74; Hast, *Loyalism in Revolutionary Virginia,* 65.
17. Richard Henry Lee to Jefferson, Nov. 3, 1776, *JP,* 1:590.
18. *JCC,* 5: Sept. 3, Sept. 4, 1776, 733–34.
19. *Virginia Gazette* (Dixon and Hunter), Sept. 27, 1776.
20. Ibid., Oct. 11, 1776.
21. Andrew Lewis to John Hancock, Sept. 10, 1776, PCC.
22. Anthony Noble to Stephen, Nov. 14, 1776, ASP-LC.
23. Noble to Stephen, April 12, 1777, ibid.
24. Noble to Stephen, June 17, 1777, ibid.
25. Noble to Stephen, Oct. 21, 1777, ibid.
26. Ibid.
27. Noble to Stephen, April 12, June 17, Oct. 21, 1777, ibid.
28. Journal of Council, Sept. 25, 1776, McIlwaine, *Official Letters,* 1:46.
29. Richard Henry Lee to James Maxwell, Dec. 1, 1776, Paul H. Smith, ed., *Letters of Delegates to Congress, 1774–89* (9 vols., Washington, D.C., 1976–82), 5:562.
30. Navy Board Letter Book, Sept. 11, 1776, Morgan et al., *Naval Documents,* 6:784.

31. Maryland Council of Safety, Oct. 6, 1776, Force, *American Archives*, ser. 5, 2:639.
32. Charles Lee to John Hancock, Oct. 10, 1776, quoted in Sellers, "Virginia Continental Line," 180.
33. Ibid., 180–81; *JCC*, 6: Nov. 16, 1776, 957; Stephen to Francis L. Lee of the . . . Board of War, Oct. 17, 1776, to President of Congress, Nov. 16, 1776, PCC; Stephen to the Board of War, Nov. 8, 1776, Mercer to the Board of War, Nov. 8, 1776, Force, *American Archives*, ser. 5, 3:600; Board of War to Washington, Oct. 24, 1776, Smith, ed., *Letters of Delegates*, 5:375; Washington to Greene, Nov. 8, Nov. 9, 1776, Green to Washington, Nov. 9, 1776, Richard K. Showman, ed., *The Papers of General Nathanael Greene* (4 vols. to date, Chapel Hill, N.C., 1976—), 1:343, 345, 343–44n.
34. Clement Biddle to President of Congress, Nov. 17, 1776, PCC; Sellers, "Virginia Continental Line," 1968, 183–84.
35. *Journal of Cresswell*, Oct. 10, 1776, 163–64. Stephen's brigade had 600 fit for duty at the end of Nov. See army returns in Force, *American Archives*, ser. 5, 3:822, 1035–36.
36. *JCC*, 6: Nov. 1, Nov. 6, 1776, 916–17, 929.
37. Stephen to Livingston, Nov. 22, 1776, Gratz Collection, HSP; Livingston to John Hancock, Dec. 7, 1776, PCC, also in Carl E. Prince and Dennis P. Ryan, eds., *The Papers of William Livingston* (3 vols., Trenton, 1979–86), 1:192, 192n., 213n.; Carl E. Prince, *William Livingston: New Jersey's First Governor* (Trenton, 1975), 16; William Dwyer, *The Day Is Ours! Nov. 1776–Jan. 1777: An Inside View of the Battles of Trenton and Princeton* (New York, 1983), 38.
38. Jared C. Lobdell, ed., "The Revolutionary Journal of Sergeant Thomas McCarty," *Proceedings of the New Jersey Historical Society* 82 (1964): 38–39; Sellers, "Virginia Continental Line," 184–85.
39. Joseph P. Tustin, trans. and ed., *Diary of the American War: A Hessian Journal* (New Haven, 1979), 27–32; Washington to President of Congress, Dec. 13, 1776, F-WW, 6:364; Sellers, "Virginia Continental Line," 186; Ann H. Hutton, *Portrait of Patriotism: "Washington Crossing the Delaware"* (Philadelphia, 1959), 88–89; Richard Hanser, *The Glorious Hour of Lt. Monroe* (New York, 1976), 104.
40. Earl S. Miers, *Crossroads of Freedom: The American Revolution and the Rise of a New Nation* (New Brunswick, N.J., 1971), 28, 41.
41. Stephen to Jefferson, Dec. [20], 1776, *JP*, 1:659–60; Theodore Thayer, *Nathanael Greene: Strategist of the American Revolution* (New York, 1960), 113, 115, 117–18.
42. Benjamin Rush to Richard Henry Lee, Dec. 21, 1776, Butterfield, *Letters of Rush*, 1:121–22.
43. "Return of the Forces . . . under . . . Washington," Dec. 22, 1776, Charles H. Lessler, ed., *The Sinews of Independence: Monthly Strength Reports of the Continental Army* (Chicago, 1976), 43, and also, with some variation, in Force, *American Archives*, ser. 5, 3:1401–2; David Hawke, *Paine* (New York, 1974), 61; Leonard Lundin, *Cockpit of the Revolution: The War for Independence in New Jersey* (1940; rept. New York, 1972), 191; William S. Stryker, *The Battles of Trenton and Princeton* (Boston, 1898), 85.
44. Alfred H. Bill, *The Campaign of Princeton, 1776–77* (Princeton, N.J., 1948), 14–15; Hutton, *Portrait of Patriotism*, 83, 91–92.

45. Plan of General Stephen, Force, *American Archives*, ser. 5, 3:1314–15; Washington to President of Congress, Dec. 20, *F-WW*, 6:406.
46. David Griffith to Leven Powell, Dec. 27, 1776, "Correspondence of Leven Powell," *John P. Branch Historical Papers* 1 (1901): 46; Richard M. Ketcham, *The Winter Soldiers* (Garden City, N.Y., 1973), 292; Stryker, *Trenton and Princeton*, 84; Hanser, *Lt. Monroe*, 124.
47. Hutton, *Portrait of Patriotism*, 98–99; Samuel S. Smith, *The Battle of Trenton* (Monmouth Beach, N.J., 1965), 19–20; William H. Smith, ed., *The St. Clair Papers* (2 vols., Cincinnati, 1882), 1:31; Ketcham, *Winter Soldiers*, 295; *F-WW*, 6:438–39n.
48. Stephen to Jonathan Seaman, Jan. 5, 1777, ASP-LC; Excerpt from Robert Beale's "Memoirs," Dec. 25, 1776–Jan. 3, 1777, in Dennis P. Ryan, ed., *A Salute to Courage: The American Revolution as Seen through Wartime Writings of Officers of the Continental Army and Navy* (New York, 1979), 55; "Colonel Rall at Trenton, from the Diary of Captain Andreas Wiederhold," *PMHB* 22 (1898): 464–65; E. L. Anderson, *Soldier and Pioneer: A Biographical Sketch of Lt.-Col. Richard C. Anderson* (New York, 1879), 18–20; Lundin, *Cockpit of the Revolution*, 195; Rodney Atwood, *The Hessians: Mercenaries from Hessen-Kassel in the American Revolution* (Cambridge, Eng., 1980), 92; Lyon G. Tyler, ed., "The Old Virginia Line in the Middle States during the American Revolution," *Tyler's Quarterly* 12 (1931): 7. The traditional story, inaccurate though long accepted by historians, was that Richard Clough Anderson led the search party. This version is based solely on the narrative of Anderson's grandson (E. L. Anderson) long after the fact. Stephen, in his letter to Jonathan Seaman, identified Wallis (Walls) as the leader of the search party. Douglas S. Freeman erred in saying that the name was Wall and not to be found in Francis B. Heitman, *Historical Register of Officers of the Continental Army during the War of the Revolution* (1914; rept. Baltimore, 1973). A more careful check would have yielded the name of Capt. George Wallis (Walls). Freeman speculated incorrectly that the person involved was either Lt. Adam Wallace of the 7th Virginia Regiment or Capt. Gustavus Wallace of the 3d. Freeman also was mistaken in saying that these regiments belonged to Stephen's brigade; rather, they were in Sterling's brigade (see Freeman, *Washington*, 4:312–13, 313n.).
49. Smith, *Trenton*, 20; Ketcham, *Winter Soldiers*, 304, 311; Bill, *Campaign of Princeton*, 45, 52, 56; Stryker, *Trenton and Princeton*, 161–65, 194–95; Robert O. Slagle, "The Von Lossberg Regiment: A Chronicle of Hessian Participation in the American Revolution" (Ph.D. diss., American University, 1965), 96–98.
50. Stephen to Jonathan Seaman, Jan. 5, 1777, ASP-LC.
51. Richard Henry Lee to Stephen, Jan. 5, 1777, Smith, *Letters of Delegates*, 6:36.

CHAPTER TEN

1. Washington to Heath, Dec. 28, 1776, *F-WW*, 6:448; Tustin, *Diary of the American War*, 45–48; Sellers, "Virginia Continental Line," 198–200; Samuel S. Smith, *The Battle of Princeton* (Monmouth Beach, N.J., 1967), 8–9, 13–15;

Freeman, *Washington,* 4:332, 336–39; James Wilkinson, *Memoirs of My Own Times* (3 vols., Philadelphia, 1816), 1:136–38.

2. *Virginia Gazette* (Dixon and Hunter), Jan. 24, 1777; letter from [Benjamin Rush] . . . , *Maryland Journal,* Jan. 7, 1777, in Stryker, *Trenton and Princeton,* 466; Christopher Ward, *The War of the Revolution* (2 vols., New York, 1952), 1:308–9.

3. "John Howland's Journal," in C. C. Haven, *Thirty Days in New Jersey* (Trenton, 1867), 50–51; Smith, *Princeton,* 18; Stryker, *Trenton and Princeton,* 270–76; William B. Reed, ed., *Life and Correspondence of Joseph Reed* (2 vols., Philadelphia, 1847), 288–89.

4. George F. Scheer and Hugh F. Rankin, *Rebels and Redcoats* (Cleveland, 1957), 216–17; Stryker, *Trenton and Princeton,* 438–39: Smith, *Princeton,* 25–27.

5. Henry Knox to Mrs. Knox, Jan. 7, 1777, Knox Papers, Massachusetts Historical Society.

6. Washington to Joseph Reed, Jan. 12, 1777, *F-WW,* 6:501; Stryker, *Trenton and Princeton,* 303, 441–42.

7. Washington to Stephen, Jan. 13, 1777, and General Orders, Jan. 13, 1777, *F-WW,* 7:5–6; Melvin J. Weig, *Morristown National Historical Park, New Jersey: A Military Capital of the American Revolution* (Washington, D.C., 1957), 9; Sellers, "Virginia Continental Line," 212; Lobdell, "Journal of McCarty," Jan. 11–13, 1777, 42–43.

8. Washington to Israel Putnam, Feb. 3, 1777, *F-WW,* 7:97; Weig, *Morristown Historical National Park,* 9.

9. Richard Parker to Weedon, Jan. 24, 1777, Correspondence of George Weedon, American Philosophical Society; Washington to President of Congress, Jan. 26, 1777, *F-WW,* 7:66; "Diary of Lieutenant James McMichael of the Pennsylvania Line, 1776–78," *PMHB* 16 (1892): 142.

10. Washington to President of Congress, Feb. 5, 1777, *F-WW,* 7:105; Extract of a Letter from an Officer of Distinction [presumably Stephen], Chatham, Feb. 3, 1777, in *Pennsylvania Gazette,* March 5, 1777, in William S. Stryker, ed., *Documents Relating to the Revolutionary History of the State of New Jersey. Extracts from American Newspapers. New Jersey Archives,* 2d ser. (5 vols., Trenton, 1901–7), 1:306; Extract of a Letter . . . , Feb. 10, 1777, *Virginia Gazette* (Purdie), March 14, 1777; [item], *Almon's Remembrancer,* in Ambrose E. Vanderpoel, *History of Chatham, New Jersey* (Chatham, 1959), 163; Tyler, "Old Virginia Line in the Middle States," 199; William S. Powell, ed., "A Connecticut Soldier: Elisha Bostwick's Memoirs," *WMQ,* 3d ser., 6 (1946): 105–6; Jared C. Lobdell, "Two Forgotten Battles in the Revolutionary War," *New Jersey History* 85 (1967): 226–28; Harry M. Lydenberg, ed., *Archibald Robertson: His Diaries and Sketches in America, 1762–80* (New York, 1930), Feb. 1, 1777, 123; Howard H. Peckham, *The Toll of Independence: Engagements & Battle Casualties of the American Revolution* (Chicago, 1974), 30.

11. Copy of a letter of Stephen to Sir William Erskine, Feb. 4, 1777, PCC; an edited copy is printed in Stryker, *Documents . . . New Jersey, New Jersey Archives,* 2d ser., 1:364–66.

12. Washington to President of Congress, Feb. 5, 1777, to Samuel Chase, Feb. 5, 1777, *F-WW,* 7:103, 108–9.

13. William Erskine to Stephen, Feb. 10, 1777, PCC; an edited version is in Stryker, *Documents . . . New Jersey, New Jersey Archives*, 2d ser., 1 : 366–67.
14. Washington to Gov. William Livingston, Feb. 14, Feb. 17, 1777, *F-WW*, 7 : 152, 155; Livingston to Washington, Feb. 22, 1777, Prince and Ryan, *Papers of Livingston*, 1 : 251.
15. E.g., Robert Forsythe to Dixon and Hunter, Feb. 14, 1777, *Virginia Gazette* (Dixon and Hunter), March 7, 1777.
16. Stephen to Washington, April 20, 1777, WP-LC; Washington to Stephen, April 20, 1777, *F-WW*, 7 : 443.
17. *JCC*, 7: Feb. 19, 1777, 133. The major generals outranking Stephen were Charles Lee, Philip Schuyler, Israel Putnam, Horatio Gates, William Heath, Joseph Spencer, John Sullivan, and Nathanael Greene. See a List of General Officers in the Army of the United States, May 6, 1777, WP-LC, and Heitman, *Historical Register*, 8. Of course, Mifflin, Lincoln, Stirling, and St. Clair also were ninth in ranking behind Washington.
18. Patrick Henry to Richard Henry Lee, Jan. 9, 1777, McIlwaine, *Official Letters*, 1 : 91.
19. Thomas Burke's Notes on Debates, Smith, *Letters of Delegates*, 6 : 263–64.
20. Benjamin Rush to Robert Morris, Feb. 22, 1777, Edmund C. Burnett, ed., *Letters of Members of the Continental Congress* (8 vols., Washington, D.C., 1921–36), 2 : 271; John C. Matthews, "Richard Henry Lee and the American Revolution" (Ph.D. diss., University of Virginia, 1939), 209–10.
21. Washington to Andrew Lewis, March 3, 1777, *F-WW*, 7 : 234; Smith, *Papers of St. Clair*, 1: Feb. 19, 1777, 44, 44n. Arnold's commission was redated Feb. 17, 1777, thus giving him rank over Stephen and the other generals promoted on Feb. 19.
22. Stephen to [Richard Henry Lee?], March 10, 1777, Gratz Collection, HSP. The internal evidence in the letter, e.g., reference to Francis Lee, suggests that it was written to Richard Henry Lee.
23. Stephen to Messrs. Bradfords, March 10, 1777, in *Pennsylvania Journal*, March 26, 1777, in Vanderpoel, *Chatham*, 186–87.
24. Stephen to Angus McDonald, March 15, 1777, ASP-LC, also printed in Vanderpoel, *Chatham*, 187; *A-WP* 1 : 153n. See William N. McDonald, "The McDonald Who Turned Washington Down," *West Virginia History* 37 (1977): 315–17.
25. William Woodford to Weedon, March 14, 1777, Allyn K. Ford Collection, Minnesota Historical Society; *The Kemble Papers* (2 vols., *NYHS Collections*, vols. 16–17, New York, 1884–85), 16: Feb. 21, 1777, 110; Robert Forsythe to Dixon and Hunter, Feb. 15, 1777, and Capt. Bauman to Gen. Knox, March 20, 1777, Vanderpoel, *Chatham*, 86, 170; Hubert G. Schmidt, ed., *Lesser Crossroads: Edited from the Story of an Old Farm* (New Brunswick, N.J., 1948), 230.
26. Stephen to General—[Woodford or Weedon], March 15, 1777, Massachusetts Papers, Massachusetts Historical Society.
27. *Virginia Gazette* (Purdie), May 2, 1777, supplement; Stephen to Richard Henry Lee, April 22, 1777, Lee Family Papers, micro. ed., VSL; Richard Henry Lee to Governor of Virginia, April 22, 1777, Ballagh, *Letters of Richard Henry Lee*, 1 : 283; Washington to President of Congress, April 18, 1777, *F-WW*, 7 : 434;

Mann Page to Weedon, April 22, 1777, Smith, *Letters of Delegates*, 6:634.
28. Col. William Harcourt to his father, March 17, 1777, Edward W. Harcourt, ed., *The Harcourt Papers* (14 vols., Oxford, Eng., 1880–1905?), 11:208; Robert F. Seybolt, ed., "A Contemporary Account of General Howe's Military Operations in 1777," *Proceedings of the American Antiquarian Society*, n.s., 40 (193): 71; *The Kemble Papers, NYHS Collections*, 16:111; Boatner, *Encyclopedia*, 634.
29. Lundin, *Cockpit of the Revolution*, 222–25.
30. Stephen to Washington, April 14, April 26, WP-LC.
31. Washington to Stephen, April 26, 1777, *F-WW*, 7:473.
32. General Orders, April 7, 1777, ibid., 365.
33. Stephen to Stirling, Jan. 8, 1777, Executive Committee of Congress to Washington, Jan. 9, 1777, PCC; Executive Committee of Congress to John Hancock, Jan. 10, 1777, Smith, *Letters of Delegates*, 6:79.
34. John Bakeless, *Turncoats, Traitors, and Heroes* (Philadelphia, 1959), 170–73.
35. William Maxwell to Stephen, April 10, 1777, ASP-LC.
36. Stephen to Washington, April 14, 1777, WP-LC.
37. Greene to Benjamin Lincoln, April 19, 1777, Showman, *Greene Papers*, 2:57; *F-WW*, 7:438n.
38. Stephen to Washington, April 23, 1777 (two letters), PCC; *F-WW* 7:462n.
39. Washington to John Hancock, April 23, 1777, PCC.
40. Patrick Henry to Stephen, March 31, 1777, McIlwaine, *Official Letters*, 1:133.
41. Stephen to Richard Henry Lee, April 22, 1777, Vanderpoel, *Chatham*, 190–91, also Lee Family Papers, micro. ed., VSL.
42. Proceedings of Council of General Officers, May 2, 1777, Showman, *Greene Papers*, 2:63, 64n.
43. Stephen to Richard Henry Lee, May 11, 1777, Lee Family Papers, micro. ed., VSL; Extract of a Letter from Ash Swamp, May 20, 1777, in *Pennsylvania Evening Post*, May 24, 1777, Letter of May 11, 1777, in *Pennsylvania Journal*, May 21, 1777, in Stryker, *Documents . . . New Jersey, New Jersey Archives*, 2d ser., 1:383–85; Extract of a Letter from the Jersies, May 19, 1777, in *Pennsylvania Gazette*, May 28, 1777, in Vanderpoel, *Chatham*, 199; *Virginia Gazette* (Purdie), May 23, 1777, and (Dixon and Hunter), June 6, 1777.
44. Lydenberg, *Archibald Robertson . . . Diaries*, 131.
45. Samuel S. Smith, ed., and Ernst Kipping, trans., *At General Howe's Side, 1776–78: Diary of General William Howe's Aide de Camp, Captain Friedrich Von Muenchhausen* (Monmouth Beach, N.J., 1974), May 12, 1777, 12.
46. Bernhard A. Uhlendorf, ed., *Revolution in America: Confidential Letters and Journals, 1776–84, of Adjutant General Major Baurmeister of the Hessian Forces* (New Brunswick, N.J., 1957), May 10, 1777, 86–87.
47. *New York Gazette and Weekly Mercury*, May 19, 1777, in Stryker, *Documents . . . New Jersey, New Jersey Archives*, 2d ser., 1:377–78.
48. Stephen to Washington, May 12, 1777, Vanderpoel, *Chatham*, 193–94.
49. Washington to Stephen, May 12, 1777, ibid.; also in *F-WW*, 8:53.
50. Stephen to Washington, May 14, 1777, Vanderpoel, *Chatham*, 194–95.
51. Peckham, *Toll*, 34. Here the British casualties are listed as 70; American—7 killed, 15 wounded, 5 captured.
52. Stephen to Washington, May 15, 1777, WP-LC.

53. Stephen to Washington, May, 17, 1777, ibid.
54. Tench Tilghman to Stephen, May 17, 1777, ibid.; Sellers, "Virginia Continental Line," 236.
55. Washington to Stephen, May 17, 1777, *F-WW*, 8:80–81.
56. Washington to Stephen, May 19, 1777, ibid., 86–87.
57. Stephen to Washington, May 24, 1777, Vanderpoel, *Chatham*, 198–99.
58. Washington to Stephen, May 24, 1777, *F-WW*, 8:119–20.
59. General Orders, May 20, 1777, ibid., 99–100.
60. Stephen to Sullivan, June 1, 1777, John Sullivan Papers, Massachusetts Historical Society.
61. Stephen to Sullivan, June 4, 1777, ibid.
62. Henry Knox to Henry Jackson, June 21, 1777, Knox Papers, Massachusetts Historical Society; General Orders, July 22, 1777, Washington to President of Congress, July 27, July 30, 1777, to Stephen, July 24, July 26, 1777, *F-WW*, 8:446–47, 487–88, 502, 462, 481; Showman, *Greene Papers*, 2:128n.; Worthington C. Ford, ed., *Defenses of Philadelphia in 1777* (1897; rept. New York, 1971), June 12, 1777, 2–5, 41–42; John W. Jordan, ed., "Orderly Book of the Pennsylvania State Regiment of Foot, May 10 to Aug. 16, 1777," *PMHB* 22 (1898): 203–10, 306, 475; Seybolt, "A Contemporary Account . . . ," 73–74; Tustin, *Diary of the American War*, 64–69; Schmidt, *Lesser Crossroads*, 240–41, 258–59; Sellers, "Virginia Continental Line," 241–45; John Chilton to his brother, Aug. 1, 1777, Tyler, "Old Virginia Line . . . ," 130–31; T. E. Davis, *The Battle of Bound Brook* (Bound Brook, N.J., 1895), 15. A Council of General Officers met, Aug. 6, 1777, at Stephen's quarters at the home of Rev. William Smith (first provost of the College of Philadelphia) near the Schuylkill Falls (Jordan, "Orderly Book," 309–10; *F-WW*, 9:27).
63. Capt. John Chilton to his brother, Aug. 1, 1777, Tyler, "Old Virginia Line . . . ," 131.
64. Samuel Adams to Richard Henry Lee, July 22, 1777, James Lovell to Richard Henry Lee, July 22, 1777, Smith, *Letters of Delegates*, 7:360, 363.

CHAPTER ELEVEN

1. William Carson to William Paca, Aug. 29, 1777, Maryland State Papers, Maryland Hall of Records; General Orders, Aug. 24, Aug. 27, 1777, *F-WW*, 9:129, 140; Edward H. Tatum, Jr., ed., *The American Journal of Ambrose Serle, Secretary to Lord Howe, 1776–78* (San Marino, Calif., 1940), Aug. 22–25, 1777, 245; John R. Reed, *Campaign to Valley Forge, July 1, 1777–Dec. 19, 1777* (Philadelphia, 1965), 74–75, 79–83; William J. Buck, "Washington's Encampment on the Neshaminy," *PMHB* 1 (1877): 283–84.
2. "Diary of John Chilton," in Tyler, "Old Virginia Line . . . ," 289; "Diary of Joseph Clark," *Proceedings of the New Jersey Historical Society* 7 (1853–55): 97; Stephen to Richard Henry Lee, Sept. 5, 1777, Lee Family Papers, micro. ed., VSL; General Orders, Sept. 4, 1777, *F-WW*, 9:179; Peckham, *Toll*, 40.
3. "Diary of Clark," *Proceedings of the New Jersey Historical Society* 7 (1853–55): 28; "Diary of Chilton," Tyler, "Old Virginia Line . . . ," 289; S. Sydney Bradford, ed., "A British Officer's Revolutionary War Journal, 1776–78," *Maryland*

Historical Magazine 56 (1961): 168–69; Ward, *War of the Revolution*, 1:342; Curt Johnson, *Battles of the American Revolution* (New York, 1984), 64.

4. Weedon to [John Page], Sept. 11, 1777, Weedon-Page Correspondence, Chicago Historical Society; Knox to President of the Council of Massachusetts, Sept. 13, 1777, Knox Papers, Massachusetts Historical Society; "Before and after the Battle of Brandywine: Extracts from the Journal of Sergeant Thomas Sullivan of H. M. Forty-Ninth Regiment of Foot," *PMHB* 31 (1907): Sept. 11, 1777, 415–16; Lydenberg, *Archibald Robertson . . . Diaries*, Sept. 11–13, 1777, 146; Showman, *Greene Papers*, 2:160–61; Sellers, "Virginia Continental Line," 253–56; Samuel S. Smith, *The Battle of Brandywine* (Monmouth Beach, N.J., 1976), 16–19; Reed, *Joseph Reed*, 1:306–11; Tyler, "Old Virginia Line . . . ," *Tyler's Quarterly* 25–28; Ward, *War of the Revolution*, 1:349–51; Reed, *Campaign to Valley Forge*, 127–34; Glenn Tucker, *Mad Anthony Wayne and the New Nation* (Harrisburg, Pa., 1973), 76–77; Charles P. Whittemore, *A General of the Revolution: John Sullivan of New Hampshire* (New York, 1961), 61–63.

5. Showman, *Greene Papers*, 2:161.

6. Tustin, *Diary of the American War*, Sept. 11, 1777, 87.

7. As reprinted in *Almon's Remembrancer*, in Tyler, "Old Virginia Line . . . ," 200–201.

8. Sullivan to . . . Powars & Willis, Printers in Boston, ibid., 201–3; Sullivan to John Hancock, Sept. 27, 1777, to Gen. Alexander McDougall, Jan. 27, 1781, Otis G. Hammond, ed., *Letters and Papers of Major-General John Sullivan* (3 vols., vols. 13–15 of the *Collections of the New Hampshire Historical Society*), 1:460–68, 3:271–75; Thomas C. Amory, *The Military Services and Public Life of Major-General John Sullivan of the American Revolutionary Army* (Boston, 1868), 53, 55.

9. Whittemore, *Sullivan*, 64–67, 75, 226–27.

10. Charles Carroll to Washington, Sept. 27, 1777, Smith, *Letters of Delegates*, 8:22.

11. Stephen to Sullivan, Sept. 20, 1777, Hammond, *Papers of Sullivan*, 3:455–56. Stephen was referring to François-Marie de Broglie, but it was Charles-L. A. Forquet, duc de Belle-Isle, not Broglie, who commanded the French troops during the retreat from Prague, 1742–43.

12. Henry Knox to Mrs. Knox, Sept. 24, 1777, Knox Papers, Massachusetts Historical Society; "Pickering's Journal," Sept. 12–16, 1777, in Octavius Pickering and Charles W. Upham, *The Life of Timothy Pickering* (2 vols., Boston, 1867, 1873), 1:58–161; Henry Pleasants, Jr., *The Battle of the Clouds* (Philadelphia, 1965), 11–13; Benson J. Lossing, *The Pictorial Field-Book of the Revolution* (2 vols., 1851; rept. Freeport, N.Y., 1969), 2:385–86; Reed, *Campaign to Valley Forge*, 151–56.

13. "Pickering's Journal," Pickering and Upham, *Life of Pickering*, 1: Sept. 12–16, 1777, 161; Council of War, Sept. 23, Sept. 28, 1777, Ford, *Defenses of Philadelphia*, 49–54; Wayne K. Bodle and Jacqueline Thibaut, *Valley Forge Historical Research Report* (2 vols., Valley Forge, Pa., 1980), 1:17–21; Peckham, *Toll*, 41; Johnson, *Battles*, 65.

14. Stephen to Washington, Oct. 9, 1777, WP-LC; John W. Jackson, *With the British Army in Philadelphia* (San Rafael, Calif., 1979), 29–32; General Orders, Oct. 3, 1777, F-WW, 9:307; Showman, *Greene Papers*, 2:174; Whittemore, *Sullivan*, 70–71; Tyler, "Old Virginia Line . . . ," 28–29; Alfred C. Lambdin,

"Battle of Germantown," *PMHB* 1 (1877): 383–84; Pickering and Upham, *Pickering*, 1:166–67; Uhlendorf, Revolution in America, Oct. 4, 1777, 119.

15. Weedon to John Page, Oct. 4, 1777, Weedon-Page Correspondence, Chicago Historical Society; Gen. McDougall's Account of the Battle of Germantown, Bancroft Transcripts, NYPL; "Pickering's Journal," Pickering and Upham, *Pickering*, 1:168; Jackson, *British in Philadelphia*, 43–44; Tucker, *Anthony Wayne*, 95–97; Paul D. Nelson, *The Life of William Alexander, Lord Stirling* (University, Ala., 1987); Ward, *War of the Revolution*, 1:365.

16. Walter Stewart to Gates, Oct. 12, 1777, "Unpublished Papers Relating to the Battle of Germantown," *PMHB* 1 (1877): 400; "Col. John Eager Howard's Account of the Battle of Germantown," Maryland Historical Magazine 4 (1909): 319–20; Sullivan to Mesech Weare, Oct. 25, 1777, Hammond, *Papers of Sullivan*, 1:542–47; Tucker, *Anthony Wayne*, 98–103; John B. Trussell, *Birthplace of an Army: A Study of the Valley Forge Encampment* (Harrisburg, 1976), 10; Danske Dandridge, *George Michael Bedinger: A Kentucky Pioneer* (Charlottesville, 1909), 33; Joseph P. Mitchell, *Decisive Battles of the American Revolution* (New York, 1962), 120–21; Tyler, "Old Virginia Line . . . ," 29–31; Showman, *Greene Papers*, 2:175; Freeman, *Washington*, 4:512–13; Johnson, *Battles*, 68–69. A pensioner, Thomas Blackwell, in a recollection after many years, also said that Stephen "ordered prematurely and improperly a retreat" (John F. Dorman, comp., *Virginia Pension Applications* [37 vols., Washington, D.C., 1958–82], 7:35).

17. Anthony Wayne to Mrs. Wayne, Oct. 6, 1777, Anthony Wayne Papers, HSP.

18. Wayne to Washington, Oct. 4, 1777, ibid.

19. Report of Court of Enquiry, Nov. 1, 1777, Showman, *Greene Papers*, 2:189.

20. Washington to President of Congress, Oct. 5, 1777, *F-WW*, 9:310; Peckham, *Toll*, 42.

21. Showman, *Greene Papers*, 2:178–79, 188.

22. General Greene's Orders, Oct. 7, 1777, ibid., 171.

23. Dr. James Wallace to Michael Wallace, Oct. 12, 1777, Tyler, "Old Virginia Line . . . ," 134.

24. Stephen to Washington, Oct. 9, 1777, WP-LC.

25. General Orders, Oct. 10, 11, 12, 15, 16, 23, 26, 30, Nov. 1, 1777, *F-WW*, 9:347, 352–53, 361, 379, 379–80, 421, 438, 470, 491.

26. John Sullivan, William Maxwell, and Anthony Wayne to Washington, Nov. 23, 1777, WP-LC.

27. George Washington Parke Custis, *Recollections and Private Memoirs of Washington* (Philadelphia, 1859), 196.

28. Charles Carroll of Carrollton to Charles Carroll, Sr., Oct. 12, 1777, Smith, *Letters of Delegates*, 8:113.

29. Henry Laurens to John Wells, Oct. 20, 1777, ibid., 151.

30. S. Weir Mitchell, ed., "Historical Notes of Dr. Benjamin Rush, 1777," *PMHB* 27 (1903): 147.

31. Butterfield, *Letters of Rush*, 1:140–45, 145–146n.; Schmidt, *Lesser Crossroads*, 387.

32. Lafayette to Washington, Oct. 12, 1777, Stanley J. Idzerda et. al., eds., *Lafayette in the Age of the American Revolution: Selected Letters and Papers, 1776–90* (5 vols. to date, Ithaca, N.Y., 1977—), 1:123.

33. Ibid., 101n.
34. General Orders, Oct. 18, 1777, *F-WW*, 9:390–91; *Valley Forge Orderly Book of General George Weedon of the Continental Army under the Command of General George Washington in the Campaign of 1777–78* (1911, rept. New York, 1971), Oct. 17, 1777, 94.
35. Hugh McDonald, "A Teen Ager in the Revolution," pt. 2: "From Brandywine to Valley Forge," *American History Illustrated* 1, no. 3 (June 1966): 41.
36. General Orders, Oct. 5, 1777, *F-WW*, 9:436; Report of a Court of Enquiry, Nov. 1, 1777, Showman, *Greene Papers*, 2:189.
37. Report of a Court of Enquiry, Nov. 1, 1777, Showman, *Greene Papers*, 2: 188–89.
38. At a Council of War . . . , Oct. 29, 1777, Ford, *Defenses of Philadelphia*, 207–11.
39. General Orders, Nov. 2, 1777, *F-WW*, 9:493; *Valley Forge Orderly Book of Weedon*, Nov. 1–2, 115–16; Pickering and Upham, *Pickering*, 1:180; Reed, *Campaign to Valley Forge*, 363.

CHAPTER TWELVE

1. John Laurens to Henry Laurens, Jan. 3, 1778, William G. Simms, ed., *The Army Correspondence of Colonel John Laurens in the Years 1777–78* (1867; rept. New York, 1969), 102–3. For the Muhlenberg anecdote, see Henry A. Muhlenberg, *The Life of Major-General Peter Muhlenberg of the Revolutionary Army* (Philadelphia, 1849), 113–14.
2. Stephen to Henry Laurence [Laurens], Dec. 6, 1777, PCC; *Valley Forge Orderly Book of Weedon*, Oct. 24, 1777, 101; Boatner, *Encyclopedia*, 534, 752–53.
3. John Sullivan to John Adams, Feb. 14, 1777, Robert J. Taylor et al., eds., *Papers of John Adams*, ser. 3 (6 vols. to date, Cambridge, Mass., 1977–), 5:86.
4. General Orders, Nov. 2, 1777, *F-WW*, 9:493.
5. Stephen to Henry Laurence [Laurens], Dec. 6, 1777, PCC; Robert H. Berlin, "The Administration of Military Justice in the Continental Army during the American Revolution, 1775–83" (Ph.D. diss., University of California, Santa Barbara, 1976), 187, 226; *Valley Forge Orderly Book of Weedon*, 135.
6. Stephen to Henry Laurence [Laurens], Dec. 6, 1777, PCC; Woodford to Washington, Oct. 16, 1777, WP-LC; Stephen to Richard Henry Lee, Nov. 25, 1777, Lee Family Papers, micro. ed., VSL; Washington to President of Congress, Oct. 7, 1777, to Woodford, Oct. 6, 1777, *F-WW*, 9:322, 319. Woodford did not serve as a brigadier general of the day from Sept. 9 to Oct. 23, 1777 (*Valley Forge Orderly Book of Weedon*, 42–100). For Woodford's feeling toward Stephen, see Edmund Pendleton to Woodford, Oct. 25, Nov. 29, 1777, Mays, *Letters of Pendleton*, 1:231, 239.
7. General Orders, Nov. 29, 1777, *F-WW*, 10:89.
8. General Orders, Oct. 26, 1777, ibid., 9:438–39. For an evaluation of Stephen's court-martial, see Robert Lisle, "The Court-Martial of Adam Stephen, Major-General, Continental Army," *Madison College Studies and Research* (March 1972): 35–43.
9. Berlin, "Administration of Military Justice," 190.
10. Stephen to Henry Laurence [Laurens], Dec. 6, 1777, PCC.

11. *JCC*, 9: Dec. 8, 1777, 1008. Stephen probably was not aware at the time of the mutual admiration between Laurens and Lafayette, Stephen's successor. Lafayette was also becoming fast friends with Laurens's son, John. Henry Laurens had met Lafayette when he arrived in Philadelphia and possibly before at Charleston, S.C. Laurens, on his way from Philadelphia to the convening of Congress at Lancaster in September 1777, took the wounded Lafayette in his own carriage from Bristol to the hospital at Bethlehem (David D. Wallace, *The Life of Henry Laurens, with a Sketch of the Life of Lieutenant-Colonel John Laurens* [1915; rept. New York, 1967], 231, 472).

12. For the Lee court-martial, see the *Lee Papers, NYHS Collections*, 6 (1873); Alden, *Lee*, chap. 15; Harry M. Ward, *Charles Scott and the "Spirit of '76"* (Charlottesville, Va., 1988) chap. 3.

13. Stephen to Richard Henry Lee, Nov. 25, 1777, Lee Family Papers, micro. ed., VSL.

14. At a Council of War, Nov. 8, 1777, Ford, *Defenses of Philadelphia*, 101.

15. President of Congress [Laurens] to John Adams, Dec. 3, 1777, James Lovell to John Adams, Dec. 11, 1777, Taylor et al., *Papers of John Adams*, ser. 3, 5:344–45, 374; Greene to Washington, Nov. 26, 1777, Showman, *Greene Papers*, 2:218–19.

16. Washington to President of Congress, Nov. 26–27, *F-WW*, 9:109–10.

17. General Orders, Dec. 4, 1777, ibid., 138; *JCC*, 9: Dec. 1, 1777, 983; President of Congress to Washington, Dec. 1, 1777, Idzerda, *Lafayette . . . American Revolution*, 1:165.

18. Elbridge Gerry to Joseph Trumbull, Nov. 27, 1777, James Lovell to Joseph Trumbull, Nov. 28, 1777, Smith, *Letters of Delegates*, 8:327, 339.

19. Lovell to Gates, Nov. 27, 1777, ibid., 329.

20. Lafayette's "Memoir of 1776," in Idzerda, *Lafayette . . . American Revolution*, 1:100.

21. Gen. Alexander McDougall to Greene, Feb. 14, 1778, Showman, *Greene Papers*, 2:284.

22. Dorman, *Virginia Revolutionary Pension Applications*, 3:52.

23. McDonald, "A Teen Ager in the Revolution," 42.

24. Dandridge, *Bedinger*, 33–34.

25. Edmund Pendleton to Woodford, Nov. 29, 1777, Mays, *Letters of Pendleton*, 1:239.

26. Patrick Henry to Washington, Dec. 9, 1777, William W. Henry, *Patrick Henry: Life, Correspondence and Speeches* (3 vols., New York, 1891), 3:130–31.

27. Washington to Patrick Henry, Dec. 27, 1777, *F-WW*, 9:208. Stephen's plan was enclosed in Washington's letter to President of Congress, Dec. 20, 1777, PCC.

28. Bernhard Knollenberg, *Washington and the Revolution* (New York, 1940), 190–94, including quotes.

29. James T. Flexner, *Doctors on Horseback: Pioneers of American Medicine* (New York, 1937), including quote.

30. Stephen to Jonathan Seaman, Nov. 7, 1777, C. D. B. Dandridge MSS, Duke University Library.

31. *The Key* (Frederick, Md.), Feb. 3, 1793, quoted in Alden, *Lee*, 353n.

32. Stephen to Robert Carter Nicholas, Dec. 15, 1777, Gratz Collection, HSP.

33. Stephen to Wayne, Aug. 10, 1779, Anthony Wayne Papers, HSP.
34. Stephen to Gates, Feb. 4, Feb. 7, May 28, June 11, 1780, Gates Papers, NYHS micro. ed.
35. Stephen to William Fleming, April 1, 1780, Etting Collection: Generals of the American Revolution, HSP.

CHAPTER THIRTEEN

1. Thomas Gilpin, ed., *Exiles in Virginia, with Observations on the Conduct of the Society of Friends during the Revolutionary War . . . 1777–78* (Philadelphia, 1848), 212–14; Wayland, *Hopewell Friends History*, 127–28; Elizabeth G. Vining, *The Virginia Exiles* (Philadelphia, 1955), 248–65; Theodore Thayer, *Israel Pemberton: King of the Quakers* (Philadelphia, 1943), 219–31.
2. Stephen to [James Pemberton], Aug. 14, 1779, Etting Collection: Generals of the American Revolution, HSP.
3. Berkeley County Deed Books, (1778–80), (1782–85), and (1786–87), CJCLS; Centennial Address, C. J. Faulkner Papers–Berkeley County Centennial Celebration, VHS; Mabel H. Gardiner, "History of Martinsburg and Vicinity, 1778–1926" (M.A. thesis, West Virginia University, 1930), 17; Berkeley County Historical Society, *Historic Martinsburg Guide* (Martinsburg, n.d.); Norris, *Lower Shenandoah Valley*, 232.
4. Berkeley County Petitions, May 4, 1777, VSL.
5. Hening, *Statutes*, 9: Oct. 1778, 569–71; Norris, *Lower Shenandoah Valley*, 242–45; St. Clair quote, Freeman, *Washington*, 4:513n.
6. Norris, *Lower Shenandoah Valley*, 243; Minghini and Van Metre, *Trinity Episcopal Church*, 49; Brown, *Virginia Baron*, 170.
7. Gardiner and Gardiner, *Chronicles of Old Berkeley*, 35.
8. Gardiner, "History of Martinsburg," 56.
9. Mish, "Home of General Stephen," two versions, March 17, 1969, and Feb. 17, 1979, General Adam Stephen Memorial Association.
10. *Journals of the House of Delegates* (1776–90, Richmond, 1827–28), 1780: May session—June 6, 22 and Oct. session—Nov. 3; 1781: Oct. session—Oct. 1, Nov. 24, 28, Dec. 1, 4, 14, 19, 24; 1782: Oct. session—Oct. 28, Nov. 4, 16, 18; 1783: May session—May 26, June 7 and Oct. session—Oct. 23, Nov. 17, Dec. 3, 10; 1784: passim; Cynthia M. Leonard, comp., *The General Assembly of Virginia, 30 July 1619–11 January 1778: A Bicentennial Register of Members* (Richmond, 1978), 137, 141, 145, 153, 156, 160; Hugh B. Grigsby, *The History of the Virginia Federal Convention of 1788, Collections of the VHS*, n.s. (vols. 9 and 10, 1890–91; rept. New York, 1969), 10:72–119.
11. Mish, "Stephen," 74.
12. Stephen to Gates, May 20, June 11, June 17, Gates Papers, NYHS micro. ed.
13. Gates to Stephen, July 25, 1784, ibid.
14. Chastellux, *Travels in North America*, 1:265.
15. Patterson, *Lee*, 252, 276, including quote; Nelson, *Gates*, 277; Alden, *Lee*, 294.
16. Robert L. Skidmore, "A Social History of the Eastern Panhandle Counties of West Virginia to 1810" (M.A. thesis, West Virginia University, 1953), 68–74; Doherty, *Berkeley County, U.S.A.*, 37; Elmer T. Clark et al., eds., *The Journal*

and Letters of Francis Asbury (3 vols., Nashville, 1958), 1: May–June 1781, July 1782, and June 1783, 404–5, 429, 443.

17. Advertisement, *New York Packet*, Jan. 1, 1784, in *Lee Papers, NYHS Collections*, 7:38.

18. Norris, *Lower Shenandoah Valley*, 232.

19. Don. C. Wood, "Major General Adam Stephen's Daughter, Ann, Her Family and the Hunters," typescript, 1973, General Adam Stephen Memorial Association. For Stephen's family and descendants, Dandridge and Hunter lines, see Kennedy, *Seldens*, 22–31, 134–37, 423–39. For a young Quaker girl's impressions of Stephen's son-in-law, see "Journal of Miss Sally Wister," *PMHB* 9 (1885): 477–78.

20. Patrick Henry to Stephen, June 10, 1779, "Notes and Queries," *VMHB* 9 (1903): 216–17.

21. Berkeley County Deed Book (1782–85), Nov. 11, concerning deed of May 6, 1780, CJCLS; Wood, "Stephen's Daughter . . . ," General Adam Stephen Memorial Association.

22. For a touching letter of condolence from Patrick Henry's wife, see Dorothea [Mrs. Patrick] Henry to Ann Stephen Dandridge, Kennedy, *Seldens*, 27–28.

23. Of the children of Adam Stephen Dandridge (Stephen's grandson), three may be noted: Adam Stephen Dandridge (1814–90); Alexander Spotswood Dandridge (1819–89); and Mary Evelina Dandridge, who married Robert M. T. Hunter, U.S. congressman and senator, Confederate senator and secretary of state, and afterwards, treasurer of Virginia (Kennedy, *Seldens*, 29–30).

24. *Baltimore Journal*, May 1, 1787, quoted, ibid., 135–36.

25. Ibid., 136; Wood, "Stephen's Daughter," General Adam Stephen Memorial Association. The children of Ann Stephen and Moses Hunter were Ann Evelina, Moses T., and David. Ann Evelina married, in 1806, Judge Henry St. George Tucker, congressman and Virginia senator. Moses T. married Mary Snickers. David was killed in military action during the War of 1812.

26. General Return of the Commissioners of the Land Tax in Berkeley County, 1783, Berkeley County Land Book, (1782–94), and Berkeley County Deed Book, (1778–82), Aug. 20, 1782 (concerning sale of Stephen's property on Buffalo Creek for £1,000), CJCLS; Berkeley County Land Tax Book, micro. VSL. The 2,500 acres were assessed at £1,145.11.7.

27. Stephen's Will, June 1791, proved Sept. 6, 1791, Kennedy, *Seldens*, 433–34; Bounty Warrant to Adam Stephen, June 21, 1780, S/Thomas Jefferson, VHS.

28. E.g., Articles of Agreement between Adam Stephen . . . and George Wright, Sept. 14, 1785, ASP-LC. Regarding wide-scale tenancy in the Valley, see Willard F. Bliss, "The Rise of Tenancy in Virginia," *VMHB* 58 (1950): 428–31.

29. Grove, *Reconstructed Census*, 36; Mitchell, *Commercialism . . . Shenandoah Valley*, 103n.

30. Jefferson to Stephen, June 19, 1785, to Joseph Jones, June 19, 1785, John Polson to Jefferson, [ca. July 20, 1788], *JP*, 8:236–38, 13:388–89; John Polson to Stephen, Feb 17, 1790, ASP-LC.

31. James Adam to Stephen, Nov. 2, 1788, Daniel and Isacc McPherson to Stephen, March 16, ——, Dec. 28, 1789, Feb. 25, May 25, 1790, Hartshorn and Donaldson to Stephen, Feb. 23, April 26, 1791, Richard Hooe to Stephen, June 3, 1785, July 5, 1786, ASP-LC; Adam Stephen Account with Hooe and

Harrison, 1783, and with Isaac McPherson, Dec. 1790, and lease S/David Harris, Oct. 6, 1795, Bedinger-Dandridge Family Papers, Duke University Library; Willard F. Bliss, "The Tuckahoe in the Valley" (Ph.D. diss., Princeton University, 1946), 193, 197; Hart, *Valley,* 149–50; Mitchell, *Commercialism . . . Shenandoah Valley,* 172–76, 200, 215; Preisser, "Eighteenth-century Alexandria," 154; Skidmore, "Social History . . . Panhandle," 47; Fairfax Harrison, *Landmarks of Old Prince William: A Study of Origins in Northern Virginia* (Berryville, 1964), 409.

32. Mitchell, *Commercialism . . . Shenandoah Valley,* 222n.

33. Hooe and Harrison to Stephen, n.d., ASP-LC.

34. Harrison Clark, "Northern Virginia Agriculture in 1791," *Magazine of the Jefferson County Historical Society* 35 (1969): 32; Bliss, "Tuckahoe in the Valley," 68; Hart, *Valley,* 149–50; Mitchell, *Commercialism . . . Shenandoah Valley,* 186, 208.

35. James Adam to Stephen, Nov. 2, 1782, ASP-LC; Clark, "Northern Virginia Agriculture in 1791," *Magazine of the Jefferson County Historical Society* 35 (1969): 33; Leland D. Baldwin, *Whiskey Rebels* (Pittsburgh, 1939; rept. 1967), 68–69.

36. Bacon-Foster, "Early Chapter . . . Potomac Route," 29, 136, 143–44, 149–50; Harold E. Cox, "Federalism and Anti-Federalism in Virginia—1787: A Study of Political and Economic Motivations" (Ph.D. diss., University of Virginia, 1958), 136, 143; Ella M. Turner, *James Rumsey: Pioneer in Steam Navigation* (Scottdale, Pa., 1930), 64–65, 73, 81–91.

37. Stephen to Isaac Shelby, Aug. 6, 1787, Draper Collection, Kings Mountain Papers, 16DD26a, State Historical Society of Wisconsin.

38. Stephen to James Madison, Nov. 25, 1787, Robert A. Rutland and Charles F. Hobson eds., *The Papers of James Madison* 10 (Chicago, 1977): 271–72.

39. William Grayson to Zachariah Johnston, Nov. 3, 1787, Zachariah Johnston Papers, photostats, VSL.

40. Stephen to Madison, Nov. 25, 1787, Rutland and Hobson, *Papers of Madison,* 10:272.

41. Cox, "Federalism and Anti-Federalism," 113, 161–63; Myra Rich, "The Experimental Years: Virginia, 1781–89" (Ph.D. diss., Yale University, 1966), 261, 276.

42. *Pennsylvania Journal and Weekly Advertiser,* Oct. 31, 1787 (concerning Sept. 28, 1787).

43. Thomas W. White, comp., *Journal of the Convention of Virginia Held in the City of Richmond [June 1788]* (Richmond, 1827), 5.

44. Stephen to Gates, Dec. 19, 1787, Gates Papers, NYHS micro. ed.

CHAPTER FOURTEEN

1. Virginia Convention Election Certificates of Delegates, May 20, 1788, Virginia Convention of 1788, VSL; Daniel and Isaac McPherson to Stephen, April 16, 1788, ASP-LC. The *Virginia Independent Chronicle* (Richmond), March 26, 1788, stated that Gates and Stephen had been elected delegates. Ap-

parently, however, Gates did not seek to be a candidate, and he probably was not elected; but if so, he refused to serve. See Hart, *Valley*, 176.

2. F. Vernon Aler, *History of Martinsburg and Berkeley County, West Virginia* (Hagertown, Md., 1888), 194–97.

3. Albert J. Beveridge, *The Life of John Marshall* (4 vols., Boston, 1916–19), 1:476.

4. Hening, *Statutes*, 2:340–44.

5. Robert E. Thomas, "The Virginia Convention of 1788: A Criticism of Beard's *An Economic Interpretation of the Constitution*," *Journal of Southern History* 19 (1953): 67.

6. Roy B. Cook, "Western Virginia's Contribution to the Adoption of the Federal Constitution," *West Virginia History* 13 (1951): 96–105; Leonard Baker, *John Marshall: A Life in Law* (New York, 1974), 121; Hart, *Valley*, passim.

7. Madison to Jefferson, April 22, 1788, *JP*, 13:98.

8. Patrick Henry to John Lamb, June 9, 1788, William Grayson to John Lamb, June 19, 1788, quoted in Henry, *Henry*, 2:342–44.

9. For the record of the Virginia Convention I have relied on Jonathan Elliot, ed., *The Debates in the Several State Conventions on the Adoption of the Constitution* (5 vols., 1888; rept. New York, 1965), vol. 3. This volume is a reproduction of David Robertson's record, which was published in two editions, with an occasional word change. Henry, *Henry*, vols. 2 and 3, gives thorough coverage of Patrick Henry, with reproduction of his speeches, Grigsby, *The History of the Virginia Federal Convention of 1788*, depicts the convention manily through the eyes of the participants, with lengthy biographical background of the key leaders. White, *Journal of the Convention of Virginia*, simply indicates actions of the convention but has no record of the debates.

10. Elliot, *Debates*, 3:642–44.

11. Quoted in Henry, *Henry*, 2:346–47.

12. Elliot, *Debates*, 3:642–44.

13. Ibid., 59–60, 178, 378–79, 390, 400, 440–41; Charles Royster, *Light-Horse Harry Lee and the Legacy of the American Revolution* (New York, 1981), 96. For discussion of militarism in the debates over ratification of the Constitution, see Richard H. Kohn, *Eagle and Sword: The Federalists and the Creation of the Military Establishment in America, 1783–1802* (New York, 1975), chap. 5.

14. Grigsby, *The History of the Virginia Federal Convention of 1788*, 9:336.

15. Stephen to Robert Lawson, 1789, Lawson MSS, Duke University Library.

16. Stephen to Madison, Sept. 12, 1789, quoted in *JP*, 19:13, 12n.

17. Ibid., 20n.; Freeman, *Washington*, 231. For full discussion of the capital site controversy, see *JP*, 19:3–58.

18. Winfred E. A. Bernhard, *Fischer Ames: Federalist and Statesman, 1758–1808* (Chapel Hill, N.C., 1965), 70, 79, 113, 117, 152; Ainsworth R. Spofford, *The Founding of Washington City* (Baltimore, 1881), 22–35.

19. Hening, *Statutes*, 13:43–44 (passed Dec. 3, 1789).

20. Alexander White to Stephen, March 24, 1789, ASP-LC.

21. Stephen to Madison, March 3, April 25, 1790, Charles F. Hobson and Robert A. Rutland, eds., *The Papers of James Madison* 13 (Charlottesville, Va., 1981): 83, 176–77.

22. Stephen to Madison, March 3, 1790, ibid., 13:82–83.

23. Stephen to Madison, April 25, 1790, ibid, 176–77.
24. Stephen to Gates, May 23, 1790, Gates Papers, NYHS micro. ed.
25. Berkeley County Deed Book, (1788–91), CJCLS, lots: Stephen to Charles McKewan, £30, and to William Maxwell, Sept. 21, 1790; to Robert Wilcox, £50, July 27, 1791 (recorded 11 days after Stephen's death); Berkeley County Land Book, (1782–91), Proprietors Names, CJCLS.
26. Hartshorn and Donaldson to Stephen, April 26, 1791, ASP-LC.
27. E.g., an old case involving John Syme and George Fleming versus Stephen as defendant (Bedinger-Dandridge Family Papers, Legal Papers, May 22, 1790, Berkeley County Court, Duke University Library; bill of complaint, Elizabeth Syme, Dec. 21, 1786, VHS); note from John Morrow relating to £3.17.10 debt (Nov. 1790–June 1791) (Bedinger-Dandridge Family Papers, Duke University Library); Stephen's suit in action of debt (Ohio Company Papers, University of Pittsburgh Library).
28. The sermon is in ASP-LC, apparently in handwriting other than Stephen's (possibly that of his brother Robert). It is undated but placed chronologically near the end of the collection. The preacher or church is not identified.
29. *Virginia Herald and Fredericksburg Advertiser*, Aug. 4, 1791; *Virginia Gazette and General Advertiser* (Richmond), Aug. 10, 1791.
30. *New-York Magazine: or Literary Repository*, Aug. 1, 1791, 488.
31. John Mark to Gates, Aug. 20, 1791, Gates Papers, NYHS micro. ed.
32. Philip P. Dandridge to Lyman Draper, Sept. 8, 1848, Draper Collection, ZZ39, vol. 8, State Historical Society of Wisconsin; Couper, *Shenandoah Valley*, 2:1074, 1096; Evans, *Berkeley County*, 227; Gardiner and Gardiner, *Chronicles of Old Berkeley*, 208–9.
33. Berkeley County Court, Last Will of Adam Stephen and Estate Settlement, 1791 and 1811, Huntington Library. Stephen's will and probate are published various places, including: Wood, "The General Adam Stephen House," 32–39, and Kennedy, *Seldens*, 431–39. Phoebe Seaman in 1792 was listed as owning 300 acres in Berkeley County (Berkeley County Land Book [1782–94], CJCLS). She also inherited a 720-acre plantation on Opequon Creek in Berkeley County from her brother, Jonathan Seaman (Berkeley County Land Grants, [1772–1861], CJCLS).

Bibliography of Unpublished Materials

Many of the manuscripts were available on microfilm and other photo-duplication and through interlibrary loan and individual order. Except for microfilm editions, which sometimes include material from various collections, the manuscript listing cites the actual depositories.

MANUSCRIPTS

American Philosophical Society, Philadelphia
  Correspondence of George Weedon
  Sol Feinstone Collection
Berkeley County Courthouse, Martinsburg, W.Va.
  Adam Stephen file: Letters to Francis Silver from University of Edinburgh Library and Scots Ancestry Research Society, Edinburgh; miscellaneous items
Chicago Historical Society
  Weedon-Page Correspondence
Church of Jesus Christ of Latter-day Saints Archives, Genealogical Department, microfilm collection of courthouse records, Salt Lake City
  Berkeley County Records:
    Minute Books
    Order Books
    Deed Books
    Land Books
    Land Entry Books
    Land Grants: (1772–1836) and (1777–1861)
Duke University Library, Durham, N.C.
  Bedinger-Dandridge Family Papers

Lawson MSS
B. Muse MSS
C. D. B. Dandridge MSS
Undated Biographical Sketch of Stephen, Thomas E. Buchanan Papers
Ann Henshaw Gardiner Papers, Legal Papers, 1772
Harvard University Library, Cambridge, Mass.
    Adam Stephen to Charles Lee, July 13, 1776
Henry E. Huntington Library, San Marino, Calif.
    Adam Stephen to Dudley Digges, May 27, 1762
    Berkeley County Court, Last Will of Adam Stephen and Estate Settle-
      ment, 1791 and 1811
    Lars Anderson to William Marshall Anderson, Feb. 21, 1758
    Information of William Johnson, Oct. 16, 1756
    Adam Stephen to William Denny, April 27, 1757
    Monthly Return of Detachment . . . South Carolina, Dec. 24, 1757
    Receipt, Dec. 31, 1762
Historical Society of Pennsylvania, Philadelphia
    Gratz Collection
    Shippen Papers
    Anthony Wayne Papers
    Etting Collection: Generals of the American Revolution
    Penn Papers: Indian Affairs
    Society Collection
Library of Congress, Washington, D.C.
    Adam Stephen Papers
    Peter Force Collection
    Orderly Book (Stephen, 4th Regiment), May 13–Sept. 20, 1776
    Obadiah Johnson Papers
    Miscellaneous Collection: Adam Stephen to Angus McDonald, March
      15, 1777
    George Washington Papers
Martinsburg, West Virginia, Public Library
    Guy L. Keesecker Typescripts of Adam Stephen Correspondence
Maryland Hall of Records, Annapolis
    Maryland State Papers: William Carson to William Paca, Aug. 29, 1777
Maryland Historical Society, Baltimore
    Stephen Papers
Massachusetts Historical Society, Boston
    Parkman Collection
    Jefferson Papers
    Henry Knox Papers
    Massachusetts Papers
    John Sullivan Papers

Minnesota Historical Society, Minneapolis
   Allyn K. Ford Collection
Morristown National Historical Park, Morristown, N.J.
   Lloyd W. Smith Collection
National Archives, Washington, D.C.
   Papers of the Continental Congress
New-York Historical Society, New York City
   Horatio Gates Papers, microfilm edition
New York Public Library, New York City
   Horatio Gates Papers
   Emmet Collection
   Bancroft Transcripts
State Historical Society of Wisconsin, Madison
   Draper Collection: Kings Mountain (Shelby) Papers DD
                    Virginia Papers ZZ
University of Pittsburgh (Darlington Memorial) Library
   Adam Stephen Accounts with Hugh Mercer
   Miscellaneous Adam Stephen Papers
   Ohio Company Papers
University of Virginia Library, Charlottesville
   John Forbes Papers, including Sir John St. Clair Letter Book
   Naval Papers of Sir Andrew Snape Hamond, microfilm edition
Virginia Historical Society, Richmond
   Richard Corbin Letter Book, transcript
   Peter Halkett Receipt, May 30, 1755
   Egerton MSS, British Museum, microfilm
   Alexander White to James Wood, Nov. 14, 1763
   Will of Alexander Stephen, Principal Probate Registry (Great Britain),
      typescript
   Charles James Faulkner Papers–Berkeley County Centennial
      Celebration
Berkeley County MSS: Commission, April 14, 1773
   Bill of Complaint, Elizabeth Syme, Dec. 21, 1786
   Bounty Warrant to Adam Stephen, June 21, 1780, Signed/Thomas
      Jefferson
Virginia State Library and Archives, Richmond
   Frederick County Order Books
   Frederick County Will Books
   Photostats: Patrick Henry to John Lamb, June 9, 1786, and David
      Griffith to ——, June 16, 1776
   Lee Family Papers, microfilm edition
   Virginia Colonial Records Program
   Public Record Office (Great Britain), War Office MSS, microfilm

Berkeley County Petitions
Land Office Warrants, French and Indian War
Virginia State Land Office, Northern Neck Grants, Books H, K, and M
John Page to Charles Lee, July 7, July 12, Aug. 13, 1776
Berkeley County Land Tax Book, microfilm
Joseph Martin to ——, Sept. 23, 1763
Charles Steuart Papers (National Library of Scotland), microfilm
Virginia Convention of 1788, includes Journal, Attendance Book, and
    Election Certificates
Zachariah Johnston Papers, photostats
Washington and Lee University Library, Lexington, Va.
William Fleming Papers

UNPUBLISHED STUDIES

Aldridge, Frederick S. "Organization and Administration of the Militia
    System of Colonial Virginia." Ph.D. diss., American University, 1964.
Berlin, Robert H. "The Administration of Military Justice in the Conti-
    nental Army during the American Revolution, 1775–83." Ph.D. diss.,
    University of California, 1976.
Bliss, Willard F. "The Tuckahoe in the Valley." Ph.D. diss., Princeton
    University, 1946.
Caley, Percy B. "Dunmore: Colonial Governor of New York and Vir-
    ginia." Ph.D. diss., University of Pittsburgh, 1939.
Cocke, Lelia S. "William Fleming: A Man of Colonial Affairs, 1755–74."
    M.A. thesis, University of Virginia, 1941.
Cox, Harold E. "Federalism and Anti-Federalism in Virginia—1787: A
    Study of Political and Economic Motivations." Ph.D. diss., University
    of Virginia, 1958.
Gardiner, Mabel H. "History of Martinsburg and Vicinity, 1778–1926."
    M.A. thesis, West Virginia University, 1930.
Huston, John W. "Fort Pitt 1758–72." Ph.D. diss., University of Pitts-
    burgh, 1957.
McCartney, Martha W. "History of Fort Chiswell, Wythe County, Vir-
    ginia." Typescript, 1976, VSL.
McGaan, Dianne J., ed. "The Official Letters of Norborne Berkeley,
    Baron de Botetourt, Governor of Virginia, 1768–70." M.A. thesis,
    College of William and Mary, 1971.
Mahan, Terrance. "Virginia's Reaction to British Policy, 1763–76." Ph.D.
    diss., University of Wisconsin, 1960.
Malone, Miles S. "The Distribution of Population on the Virginia Fron-
    tier in 1775." Vol. 1: "The Lower Shenandoah Valley." Ph.D. diss.,
    Princeton University, 1935.

Matthews, John C. "Richard Henry Lee and the American Revolution." Ph.D. diss., University of Virginia, 1939.

Mish, Mary V. "Home of General Stephen," March 17, 1969, and "General Adam Stephen and His Home," Feb. 17, 1979. Typescripts. General Adam Stephen Memorial Association, Martinsburg, W.Va.

Mitchell, Robert D. "The Upper Shenandoah Valley of Virginia during the Eighteenth Century: A Study in Historical Geography." Ph.D., diss., University of Wisconsin, 1969.

Norkus, Nellie. "Francis Fauquier, Lieutenant-Governor of Virginia, 1758–68." Ph.D. diss., University of Pittsburgh, 1954.

Parker, King L. "Anglo-American Wilderness Campaigning, 1754–64: Logistical and Tactical Planning." Ph.D. diss., Columbia University, 1970.

Preisser, Thomas M. "Eighteenth-Century Alexandria, Virginia, before the Revolution, 1749–76." Ph.D. diss., College of William and Mary, 1977.

Rich, Myra. "The Experimental Years: Virginia, 1781–89." Ph.D. diss., Yale University, 1966.

Saladino, Gaspare J. "The Maryland and Virginia Wheat Trade from Its Beginnings to the American Revolution." M.A. thesis, University of Wisconsin, 1960.

Schick, James B. "The Antifederalist Ideology in Virginia, 1787–88." Ph.D. diss., Indiana University, 1971.

Sellers, John R. "The Virginia Continental Line, 1776–80." Ph.D. diss., Tulane University, 1968.

Skidmore, Robert L. "A Social History of the Eastern Panhandle Counties of West Virginia to 1810." M.A. thesis, West Virginia University, 1953.

Slagle, Robert O. "The Von Lossing Regiment: A Chronicle of Hessian Participation in the American Revolution." Ph.D. diss., American University, 1965.

Titus, James R. W. "Soldiers When They Chose to Be So: Virginians at War, 1754–63." Ph.D. diss., Rutgers University, 1983.

Wood, Don C. "Major General Adam Stephen's Daughter, Ann, Her Family, and the Hunters." Typescript. General Adam Stephen Memorial Association, 1973.

Young, Chester R. "The Effects of the French and Indian War on Civilian Life in the Frontier Counties of Virginia, 1754–63." Ph.D. diss., Vanderbilt University, 1969.

Index